CHRISTIAN ETHICS AND CONTEMPORARY MORAL PROBLEMS

D0199753

This book addresses such key ethical issues as euthanasia, the environment, biotechnology, abortion, the family, sexual ethics and the distribution of scarce resources for health care. Michael Banner argues that the task of Christian ethics is to understand the world and human kind in the light of the credal affirmations of the Christian faith, and to explicate this understanding in its significance for human action through a critical engagement with the concerns, claims and problems of other ethics. His book illustrates both the distinctiveness of Christian convictions in relation to the above issues, and also the critical dialogue with practices based on other convictions which this sense of distinctiveness motivates but does not prevent. The book's importance lies in its attempt to show the crucial difference which Christian belief makes to an understanding of these issues, whilst at the same time demonstrating some of the weaknesses and confusions of certain popular approaches to them.

MICHAEL BANNER is the F. D. Maurice Professor of Moral and Social Theology in the Department of Theology and Religious Studies at King's College, London. He is the author of *The Justification of Science and the Rationality of Christian Belief* (1990) and has published a number of articles in academic journals. Professor Banner is a priest in the Church of England and is a member of the Royal Commission on Environmental Pollution. From 1993 to 1995 he chaired the Government Committee of Enquiry on the Ethics of Emerging Technologies in the Breeding of Farm Animals. Since 1998 he has been Chairman of the Home Office's Animal Procedures Committee.

CHRISTIAN ETHICS AND CONTEMPORARY MORAL PROBLEMS

MICHAEL BANNER

King's College, University of London

CAMBRIDGE
UNIVERSITY PRESS

CAMBRIDGE UNIVERSITY PRESS
Cambridge, New York, Melbourne, Madrid, Cape Town, Singapore, São Paulo

Cambridge University Press
The Edinburgh Building, Cambridge CB2 2RU, UK

Published in the United States of America by Cambridge University Press, New York

www.cambridge.org
Information on this title: www.cambridge.org/9780521623827

First published 1999
Reprinted 2003

A catalogue record for this publication is available from the British Library

Library of Congress Cataloguing in Publication data
Banner, Michael C.
Christian ethics and contemporary moral problems / Michael Banner.
p.   cm.
Includes bibliogaphical references and index.
ISBN 0 521 62382 0 (hardback). – ISBN 0 521 62554 8 (paperback)
1. Christian ethics – Anglican authors.
2. Ethical problems.   I. Title.
BJ1251.B28   1999
241′.043 – dc21   99–10371   CIP

ISBN-13 978-0-521-62382-7 hardback
ISBN-10 0-521-62382-0 hardback

ISBN-13 978-0-521-62554-8 paperback
ISBN-10 0-521-62554-8 paperback

Transferred to digital printing 2006

To the memory of and in gratitude for
PBH
1929–1995

'I thank my God in all remembrance of you, always in every prayer of mine for you all making my prayer with joy, thankful for your fellowship in the gospel from the first day until now.'

(Philippians 1: 3–5)

Contents

Preface

In *After Virtue*, Alasdair MacIntyre tells the story of the companions of Captain Cook who, despite their best efforts, were
quite unable to make sense of the morals of the people of
Polynesia, which in certain matters were unexpectedly severe:
men and women were forbidden to eat together, for example,
because this was taboo, though sexual relations between them
were quite unregulated. Their attempts to understand the
natives' claims that such and such was taboo produced no
insight – they could fathom no rationale for the surprising
proscriptions and the equally surprising permissions, and they
could only judge the system of taboo unintelligible. Anthropol-
ogists in our day have concluded that, by the time of Cook, the
cultural background in virtue of which the taboo rules had
originally been understood and made sense had been quite
forgotten, so that what remained seemed to Europeans and, on
reflection, to Polynesians too, arbitrary prohibitions. So it was
that under the questioning which the outsiders provoked, the
whole system, plainly bereft of intelligibility, crumbled in the
space of a generation.[1]

For MacIntyre, the story serves as a parable of our present
circumstances. As a result of the pressures of the diverse
intellectual forces we name the Enlightenment, we have been
led to forget the deep accounts of the human good which could
render our moral beliefs intelligible. In this state of collective
amnesia, our moral discourse amounts to no more than fragments of a once coherent conversation, and increasingly ceases
to have the character of conversation at all – thus, for
MacIntyre, the assertion and counter-assertion of the advocates

[1] A. MacIntyre, *After Virtue: A Study in Moral Theory*, 2nd edn (London, 1985), 111–12.

and opponents of various rights typifies the shrill insistence which is bound to replace genuine discussion and argument in a culture which has forgotten the frameworks in which such discussion and argument is possible.

A good parable illustrates the essence of our situation or circumstances with a certain power and economy – and this the tale of Cook's companions surely does. And if, when we lay this parable against the reality it is meant to characterise – namely, the contemporary practice of moral discourse and debate – we find ourselves in need of a story with a somewhat finer mesh than it provides, this is not to reject the parable, but rather to elaborate it. In broad terms, MacIntyre's parable serves us well enough – reflective moralists, like Cook's comrades, will often find themselves looking on with blank incomprehension as the natives declare this and that taboo, whilst untroubled by actions we might have expected to be subjects at least of some concern (one thinks, for example, of fiery indignation regarding the use, without a women's consent, of the 'products of conception', from those who entertain no scruples about abortion). But there are interesting additional features which render the scene some-what more complex and intricate. For certain of those who are nonchalantly using the ancient taboo system whilst not obvi-ously able to offer an account of its foundations, grounds or rationale, are so thoroughly unaware of the system's historic roots, that they proclaim themselves its inventors! (Here one might think of the touching *naïveté* involved in the supposition that it is our century which has discovered human rights.) And then there are some who sense something of the difficulties with the taboo system, and placate their consciences by rejecting, in tones of shock and indignation, a part of it, while making use of another part. (Those who claim that economics is a science which dispenses with 'subjective' ethics provide a textbook example.) Additionally – to add an element which may or may not have been there in the original case – supposed guardians of at least certain elements of the taboo system, who should be able, as a matter of fact, to expound and explicate it, prove unable or unwilling to do so and indeed become some of its sternest (though least interesting) critics. (Certain self-professed

practitioners of Christian ethics, especially those who pride
themselves on 'beginning where people are', come to mind.)

If the reader doubts that things are quite as bleak as this
extended parable suggests, I can only suppose that he or she has
thus far been spared that important rite of intellectual passage,
becoming a reviewer of books. Of course, there are other
experiences which might bring one to one's senses as regards
the state of contemporary moral discourse, but amongst those
on offer book reviewing has the virtue (for those who dive
rather than edge into bodies of cold water) of accomplishing the
immersion with a certain rapidity. For, if one is to review
honestly, and not simply for the sake of enlarging one's circle of
friends, one has to face rather directly a question as to the
merits of the book in hand. And repeated confrontation with
this question persuades one, so I have found at least, of the
general applicability of the parable, even if, thankfully, there are
exceptions.

Mindful of Jeremiah, 6: 20b, it seems best not to dredge the
past for the evidence which would serve to vindicate claims as
to the utility of MacIntyre's story. (I shall, however, allow myself
to refer the reader to a particular volume which, being a
collection of essays, has the merit of displaying under one roof,
so to speak, the rich variety of intellectual confusion, unintelligibility and inadequacy which, taken as a whole, is known as
'bioethics'.[2]) It is altogether more decent to move on and ask:
what, in these circumstances, is the task of the moralist, and in
particular the task of the Christian moralist?

It will be apparent to those who read the first chapter in this
volume that, of the various uses to which an inaugural lecture
can be put, I elected to issue a manifesto, and one on the very
subject just mentioned. It contains a simple thesis: that the task
of Christian ethics is to understand the world and humankind
in the light of the knowledge of God revealed in Jesus Christ,
witnessed to by the Scriptures, and proclaimed in the Creeds,
and that Christian ethics may and must explicate this under-

---

[2] The book in question is *The Ethical Dimensions of the Biological Sciences*, ed. R. Bulger,
E. Heitman and S. Reiser (Cambridge, 1993); for my discussion, see *Minerva*, 34
(1996), 199–204.

standing in its significance for human action through a critical engagement with the concerns, claims and problems of other ethics. The chapter attempts to explain this thesis, and in particular to argue against the widespread fallacy which has it that Christian ethics which conceives of itself in the terms of the first half of the thesis, is prevented from taking up the tasks mentioned in the second half; that is, that Christian ethics which is aware of its particularity is unable to be a participant in contemporary debate.

Subsequent chapters, written on a variety of topics and for a variety of audiences, serve to illustrate both the distinctiveness of Christian convictions in relation to such issues as euthanasia, abortion, the family and so on, and also the critical dialogue with practices based on other convictions or none, which this sense of distinctiveness motivates but does not prevent. They also serve to illustrate what the first chapter refers to as the range of argumentative strategies and objectives which fully Christian ethics will employ. The final goal of Christian ethics must be to understand and represent human life in any and every sphere as it is determined by the action of God to which Christian faith bears witness. But this understanding, plainly, and to put it rather weakly, is not easily won. In the first place there is the matter of that in the light of which human life and action is to be comprehended; it is enough to note on this point perhaps, that, however long Barth had lived, the *Church Dogmatics* could only have been abandoned, but never finished. On the other side, however, the exact character of, say, the particular practices in question may be difficult to determine, perhaps because of their complexity or because the existing accounts of them are so pervasive, including within the Christian tradition itself, that even those who sense something of their inadequacy must struggle to escape from them. For whatever reason, Christian ethics may lack that understanding of the form of authentic human action to which it aspires, or have at best only glimmerings of it, and where this is so, and in the meantime, may intervene in contemporary debate with something less at its disposal than the comprehensive and fully adequate viewpoint which it hopes to be granted. (But then, it consoles itself with the thought that blowing up bridges behind enemy lines, even if it is neither the final work of an army of liberation nor necessarily of assistance to it, may at least serve to prevent the army of occupation oppressing the inhabitants as effectively as it otherwise would, and may also flush out collaborators who falsely claim to work for the liberation.) Readers will form for themselves a view of the modesty of the achievements of the chapters which follow, but will grasp straightaway, I hope, that in relation to a number of the topics treated in the chapters which follow – such as the environment and biotechnology – I have been only too aware of lacking an understanding of the subject which would permit something more than what might be deemed theologically inspired resistance.

What is the task of the Christian moralist, I asked a few paragraphs back, in the light of the circumstances depicted in the parable? As a matter of fact, the task of the Christian moralist is always and ever the same, and what changes are only the conditions in which this task is to be accomplished. These chapters display the very particular circumstances in which they were written, and not only the particular circumstances of the broad intellectual landscape pictured by MacIntyre, but also the local features of debates which have arisen at particular times and particular places within this landscape. But, if the contemporary Christian moralist properly recognises that he or she labours alongside others such as Augustine and Benedict and Vitoria (if only as an under-labourer), particularity of time and place should not, I hope, present a bar to understanding, let alone to disagreement.

Acknowledgements

Some of the chapters appeared in earlier versions as follows, and I am grateful to those who have given permission for them to be used here: chapter 2: *Scottish Journal of Theology*, 51 (1998), 22–60; chapter 4: *The Dependent Elderly: Autonomy, Justice and the Quality of Care*, ed. L. Gormally (Cambridge, 1992), 158–80; chapter 6: *Animal Biotechnology and Ethics*, ed. A. Holland and A. Johnson (London, 1997), 225–39; chapter 7: *Studies in Christian Ethics*, 9 (1996), 1–22; chapter 8: *Theology*, 96 (1993), 276–89.

The assistance of particular people with particular chapters is acknowledged at the appropriate point. There are some, however, who provided assistance more generally, and I am glad to be able record my thanks to them.

Some of the chapters were written while I was a Fellow of Peterhouse, Cambridge, and the Fellows' Secretary at that time, Mrs Hazel Dunn, cheerfully and efficiently helped with their production. At King's College, London, Mrs Lavinia Harvey has undertaken similar tasks with the same good grace and skills, and has in addition tried to ensure that I do not undertake too many obligations, and, furthermore, that I have meet those that I have. I am therefore not the only person indebted to her. It goes without saying, perhaps, that to both Peterhouse and King's College London I am grateful for making such assistance available, and also for periods of sabbatical leave which enabled the completion of various chapters. The value of such leave would be much less if one could not count on excellent library facilities, and I have had the advantage of making use of the University Library in Cambridge, where the members of staff are unfailingly helpful.

A book reveals many of its author's other dues through its footnotes, but not all those dues, and not always in a way which distinguishes between lesser and greater ones. Amongst the latter I should mention those to Basil Mitchell, my former research supervisor, and to Stanley Hauerwas and Oliver O'Donovan. Basil Mitchell's work is marked by the virtues of fairness, clarity, patience and rigour in the construction of an argument, and I hope that my admiration for him and his work exercises some discipline over my own. Formally speaking, I have been a pupil of neither Stanley Hauerwas nor Oliver O'Donovan; indeed, I have met Stanley Hauerwas on only a couple of occasions. I have been a pupil of both informally, however, and recall that it was a combination of reading *The Peaceable Kingdom* and attending some of the first lectures Oliver O'Donovan gave on his return to Oxford, which caused me to entertain the thought, radical in its context, that there really might be something distinctive about Christian ethics. If others have now joined Stanley Hauerwas in protesting at the 'Babylonish captivity' of the Church, it is right to recognise that at times he sounded a somewhat lone voice, albeit a voice of great vigour, imagination, insight and wit, the latter being the cause of the greatest offence to his rather humourless critics. Since my first encounter with Oliver O'Donovan, I have come to rely on his judgment, guidance and friendship, as well as on his magisterial contributions to the subject.

King's College, London, in general, and the Department to which I belong, in particular, is animated by an admirable spirit of commitment to and co-operation in the pursuit of research. I count myself especially fortunate in those immediate colleagues within the Department of Theology and Religious Studies with whom I share common interests and concerns, namely Colin Gunton, Paul Helm, Brian Horne, Alan Torrance and Francis Watson, and value immensely the opportunities which I have to learn from them. I should also mention Ben Quash, once one of my students and now Dean of Peterhouse, Cambridge, who, though he is not a colleague in this sense, fulfils such a role, for which I am grateful, as for his friendship.

CHAPTER I

Turning the world upside down – and some other tasks for dogmatic Christian ethics

I

When Barth once likened the entrance of Christianity into human life to that of the Commendatore in his beloved Mozart's *Don Giovanni*, it is plain what motivated the comparison.[1] What Barth wanted to stress with this imagery was a theme which lay close to his heart from the beginning of his revolutionary commentary *The Epistle to the Romans* to the final pages of the last volume of the monumental *Church Dogmatics*; it is that the Word of God, Jesus Christ, comes upon history, as it is humanly conceived, as an abrupt and unanticipated word, giving to this history an ending which could not be anticipated or expected, humanly speaking. No inference or induction, be it grounded in philosophy or psychology, in the natural sciences or in historical knowledge, could lead us to anticipate this conclusion to the story of human life. If it is anticipated, it is anticipated only prophetically – which is to say, that it is anticipated as 'unanticipatable' – as by the prophet Isaiah when

---

[1] When a version of this chapter was given as an inaugural lecture at King's College, London, I was able to take the opportunity to acknowledge an intellectual debt to Professor Basil Mitchell who supervised my doctoral studies and since then has provided unstinting support and encouragement. It is characteristic of his intellectual generosity and integrity that he should continue this support even when his erstwhile pupil has since taken a path somewhat different from the one he has himself mapped out and followed. It is also characteristic of him that he should have taken the trouble to offer a patient critique of this chapter, to which I shall hope to reply with the care it deserves in the further elaboration and defence of this chapter's thesis I shall hope, on another occasion, to provide. I am also grateful to Colin Gunton, Alan Torrance and Francis Watson for comments on an earlier draft and to an audience in the Faculty of Religious Studies at McGill University for questions and discussion.

he declares: 'Thus saith the Lord . . . Remember ye not the former things, neither consider the things of old. Behold, I will do a new thing.' (Isaiah 43: 16 and 18–19 and see 65: 17f.)

It was the newness of this new thing which Barth was seeking to represent when he likened the entrance of Christ into history to the entrance of the Commendatore, and yet it was a far from happy comparison; indeed we might put it more strongly and say that it was a singularly unhappy one, since the Commendatore, with his icy grip, drags the sinful and unrepentant Don Giovanni down to the flames of hell. But God's decisive intervention, his doing a new thing, is not the intervention of an icy hand. 'And he that sat upon the throne' according to John the Divine, 'said, Behold, I make all things new' (Revelation 22: 5). The new thing which God intends and accomplishes is not to be understood, that is to say, without qualification, as a sweeping away of the old, but as its renewal and re-creation. Specifically, God's new deed is not finally directed at human condemnation, but at human liberation, and in the very particular sense that God's action seeks to evoke and evince a newness in the life and action of those who are its object. God does a new thing that humankind may do a new thing. So it is that in the Book of Acts, those who are the first and privileged objects of God's original action, of his doing of a 'new thing', those Christians whose lives have been shaped by the gift of the Spirit at Pentecost, are themselves the doers of new things – a fact which is not concealed even from the rabble who denounce the Christians as 'these that have turned the world upside down', who 'do contrary to the decrees of Caesar, saying that there is another king, one Jesus' (Acts 17: 6–7).

Though Barth's comparison of Christianity with the entrance of the Commendatore is thus in certain respects somewhat unfortunate, we can hardly suppose that we should set ourselves to teach Barth wisdom on this point. For, in spite of the false note struck on this occasion, Barth's pre-eminence as the most significant of modern moral theologians (and we should give an extremely generous construal to that word 'modern') lies in the very fact that he sought to understand ethics as determined by the relationship between divine and human action of which we

have been speaking.[2] There is, so Barth claimed, a form of life –
a turning 'the world upside down' – which corresponds to, and
is established by, the action of God. This correspondence of
divine and human action is neatly expressed in a formula which
was consistently to govern his thought on these matters: 'Dogmatics itself is ethics; and ethics is also dogmatics.'[3] With this
slogan, with the insistence that dogmatics is ethics and ethics
dogmatics, Barth asserts at one and the same time the essentially ethical significance of the subject matter of dogmatics, and
the essentially dogmatic character of the presuppositions of a
genuine ethics; he asserts, that is to say, that an account of the
action of God is an account of an action to which certain
human action properly and necessarily corresponds and by
which it is evinced; and, conversely, that an account of good
human action properly and necessarily makes reference to the
action of God by which it is both evoked and warranted.

According to this way of thinking, the task of Christian ethics
lies in the description of human action called forth by the reality
of the action of God to which dogmatics bears witness. In
understanding itself thus, Christian ethics takes on a form which
can be differentiated from that accorded to it in a number of
alternative accounts. In section two of this chapter, we follow
Barth in making this differentiation. In section three we shall
attempt to illustrate the form of dogmatic ethics, as we may term
it, not by reference to its theory, but by reference to its practice
in relation to a quite specific area of debate. And then in the
fourth and fifth sections we shall face and reply to certain
objections which may be put to dogmatic ethics, and which can
be indicated sufficiently for the moment by wondering what

[2] The centrality of ethics in Barth's understanding of Christian doctrine is rightly
stressed in two recent and significant treatments of Barth's thought: John Webster's
Barth's Ethics of Reconciliation (Cambridge, 1995) and Bruce McCormack's *Karl Barth's
Critically Realistic Dialectical Theology* (Oxford, 1995), especially 274–80. According to
Webster, for example, 'the *Church Dogmatics* is a work of moral theology as well as a
systematics' (1); more particularly, Barth maintains that 'a Christianly successful
moral ontology must be a depiction of the world of human action as it is enclosed and
governed by the creative, redemptive, and sanctifying work of God in Christ, present
in the power of the Holy Spirit' (2).
[3] K. Barth, *Church Dogmatics*, I: 2, trans. G. Thomson and H. Knight (Edinburgh, 1956),
793.

account we might give of the tasks of dogmatic ethics, and whether that account will make reference to any tasks other than the one which the critic accusingly reckons to be its sole form of engagement with the world: preaching.

II

Section 36 of the *Church Dogmatics*, 'Ethics as a Task of the Doctrine of God', is the *locus classicus* for Barth's understanding of the nature of Christian ethics (at least on its interpretative side[4]) – or, as the critic would doubtless prefer to say, borrowing Macaulay's description of Castle Howard, 'The most perfect specimen of the most vicious style'.

Barth's account begins from the assertion that it is only in the concept of 'covenant that the concept of God can itself find completion'.[5] Why? Because 'God is not known and is not knowable except in Jesus Christ.'[6] Hence 'The Christian doctrine of God cannot have "only" God for its content, but since its object is *this* God it must also have man, to the extent that in Jesus Christ man is made a partner in the covenant decreed and founded by God.'[7]

This covenant or partnership has, however, for the human partner, two aspects, both the election of humankind and its claiming; or, in this order, grace and law.[8] As Barth puts it:

---

[4] I mean to avert to the contrast indicated by Webster when he notes that 'the relation to itself which the Word of God establishes for its human recipient is not simply noetic, a matter of interpretation, but ethical, a matter of action' (*Barth's Ethics of Reconciliation*, 33), and to note that I mean to deal here chiefly with the noetic aspect of the relationship.

[5] K. Barth, *Church Dogmatics*, II: 2, trans. G. Bromiley et al. (Edinburgh, 1957), 509.

[6] Ibid.

[7] Ibid. As Webster puts it, 'Because – and only because – it is an exposition of the statement "God is", the *Church Dogmatics* is also all along the line an anthropology. For the form of God's aseity, the chosen path of the divine being, is specified in the history of Jesus Christ; God's freedom is freedom for fellowship' (3). As he puts it again, Barth's work is governed by the 'inherent twofoldness of the reality with which Christian theology is concerned' (32). The presence of this theme at the heart of the *Church Dogmatics* gives the lie to the notion that Barth's lecture of 1956, 'The Humanity of God', somehow represents a radical shift in his thinking.

[8] In Webster's words, 'On Barth's reading, election is a teleological act on the part of God, having as its end the life-act of the creature whom God elects into covenant with himself'; *Barth's Ethics of Reconciliation*, 49.

The concept of the covenant between God and man concluded in Jesus Christ is not exhausted in the doctrine of the divine election of grace. The election itself and as such demands that it be understood as God's command directed to man; as the sanctification or claiming which comes to elected man from the electing God in the fact that when God turns to Him and gives Himself to him He becomes his Commander.[9]

In other words, 'The truth of the evangelical indicative means that the full stop with which it concludes becomes an exclamation mark. It becomes itself an imperative.'[10] Hence – recalling one side of the slogan we have already cited – 'The doctrine of God must be expressly defined and developed and interpreted as that which it also is at every point, that is to say, *ethics*.'[11] To use another formula, 'The one Word of God which is the revelation and work of His grace is also Law';[12] more specifically, 'The summons of the divine predecision, the sanctification which comes on man from all eternity and therefore once and for all in the election of Jesus Christ, is that in all its human questionableness and frailty the life of the elect should becomes its image and repetition and attestation and acknowledgement.'[13]

If, however, Christian ethics understands itself in this highly particular way, how is it to understand its relationship to, and indeed the very existence of, a general definition or conception of ethics? Writing around the time of the publication of volume II: I of the *Church Dogmatics* Bonhoeffer gave the following answer to such a question:

The knowledge of good and evil seems to be the aim of all ethical reflection. The first task of Christian ethics is to invalidate this knowledge. In launching this attack on the underlying assumption of all other ethics, Christian ethics stands so completely alone that it becomes questionable whether there is any purpose in speaking of Christian ethics at all. But if one does so notwithstanding, that can only mean that Christian ethics claims to discuss the origin of the whole problem of ethics, and thus professes to be a critique of all ethics simply as ethics.[14]

[9] Barth, *Church Dogmatics*, II: 2, 512.   [10] Ibid.
[11] Barth, *Church Dogmatics*, II: 2, 513.
[12] Barth, *Church Dogmatics*, II: 2, 511.
[13] Barth, *Church Dogmatics*, II: 2, 512.
[14] D. Bonhoeffer, *Ethics*, ed. E. Bethge, trans. N. H. Smith (London, 1955), 3.

Barth's answer has the same contours. The existence of a general conception of ethics confirms, says Barth, the 'truth of the grace of God which as it is addressed to man puts the question of the good with such priority over all others that man cannot evade it and no other question can completely hide or replace it'.[15] And yet as that general conception invites humankind to attempt to answer that question for themselves, 'the general conception of ethics coincides exactly with the conception of sin'.[16] Theological ethics issues no such invitation: 'If dogmatics, if the doctrine of God, is ethics, this means necessarily and decisively that it is the attestation of that *divine* ethics, the attestation of the good of the command issued to Jesus Christ and fulfilled by Him.'[17] Hence, dogmatic ethics can relate to the general conception of ethics only in a way which, 'From the point of view of the general history of ethics',

means an annexation of the kind that took place on the entry of the children of Israel into Palestine. Other peoples had for a long time maintained that they had a very old, if not the oldest, right of domicile in this country. But, according to Josh. 9: 27, they could now at best exist only as hewers of wood and drawers of water. On no account had the Israelites to adopt or take part in their cultus or culture.[18]

Why must it relate thus? Just because:

Ethics in the sense of that general conception is something entirely different from what alone the Christian doctrine of God can be as a doctrine of God's command. Whatever form the relationship between the two may take, there can be no question either of a positive recognition of Christian ethics by that conception or of an attachment of Christian ethics to it. Christian ethics cannot be its continuation, development and enrichment. It is not one disputant in debate with others. It is the final word of the original chairman – only discussed, of course, in Christian ethics – which puts an end to the discussion and involves necessarily a choice and separation.[19]

Thus when Christian moralists 'enter the field of ethical reflection and interpretation they must not be surprised at the contradiction of the so-called (but only so-called) original inhabitants of this land. They cannot regard them as an authority

---

[15] Barth, *Church Dogmatics*, II: 2, 518.   [16] Ibid.   [17] Ibid.
[18] Barth, *Church Dogmatics*, II: 2, 518–19.
[19] Barth, *Church Dogmatics*, II: 2, 519.

before which they have to exculpate themselves, and to whose arrangements they must in some way conform. The temptation to behave as if they were required or even permitted to do this is one which must be recognised for what it is and avoided.'[20]

What ought to be resisted and avoided is, however, embraced, says Barth, in two common Christian approaches to the question of the relationship between Christian ethics and general ethics. The one approach attempts a synthesis of the two spheres through apologetics, the other opposes a synthesis by seeking to establish a diastasis. Both are to be rejected.

Apologetics is here understood as 'the attempt to establish and justify the theologico-ethical inquiry within the framework and on the foundation of the presuppositions and methods of non-theological, of general human thinking and language'.[21] Now, 'The only possible meaning of this apologetic is a sincere conviction that theological ethics must be measured against a general ethics.' To this Barth responds:

[W]hat can be legitimated in this way, what can be indicated as included in the content of a general ethical enquiry and reply, is certainly not the distinctively theological enquiry and reply in which we have to do with the grace of God in the issuing and fulfilling of His command. The ethical bent of the religious self-consciousness, a 'value attitude' and the like, may be justified in this way, but not the attestation of the commandment of God as the form of his grace. This theme is automatically lost when apology succeeds. For the man who – as a philosopher, perhaps, or even as a politician – thinks that he knows a general principle which is actually superior to the origin and aim of theologico-ethical enquiry and reply, and who in the matter of the doctrine of God thinks that he can actually step forward as judge in the question of truth, a theological ethic with its Whence? and

---

[20] Barth, *Church Dogmatics*, II: 2, 520.
[21] Ibid. I have here amended the English translation which renders 'allgemein menschlichen Denkens' as 'wholly human thinking'; 'general' or 'prevailing' is the proper reading and some pages later (534) 'general human thought' is given as the translation of the same German expression. This amendment is important since the expression 'wholly human thinking' creates a difficulty on two fronts. In the first place, though Barth will maintain that Thomism is finally apologetic, he would not describe its conception of ethics as of ethics as being based on 'wholly human thinking'. In the second place, the claim that theological ethics can often be 'comprehensive' in relation to general ethics makes sense only if general ethics itself is not 'wholly human', but, even if unwittingly, witnesses to the reality of God. The translators have made Barth's position somewhat more stark than it really is.

Whither? will necessarily be an objectionable undertaking, which he will regard either as insignificant or even perhaps as dangerous. And theological ethics on its part will cease to be what it is, if it dares to free itself from this offensiveness, if it dares to submit to a general principle, to let itself be measured by it and adjusted to it.[22]

This refusal of apologetics does not imply for Barth – and this will be important later on – a refusal to engage with general ethics. Whilst theological ethics must maintain that 'the command of God is not founded on any other command, and cannot therefore be derived from any other, or measured by any other, or have its validity tested by any other',[23] it can and must, 'Without detriment to its loyalty to its own task, indeed, in its very loyalty to it in this aspect too . . . establish a continuous relationship of its thinking and speaking with the human ethical problem as a whole.'[24] Why? Because it knows that 'finally and properly its own Whence? and Whither? are not alien to any philosophic moralist . . . but regards and addresses him unswervingly on the basis that grace, and there-fore the command of God, affects him too'.[25] Just because this is so, it can even be said that theological ethics 'will be absolutely open to all that it can learn from general human ethical enquiry and reply', even while it declines to 'set up general ethics as a judge' over itself.[26]

The temptation to regard general ethics as an authority before which theological ethicists 'have to exculpate themselves, and to whose arrangements they must in some way conform' is acceded to not only in the attempt at an apologetics which would dissolve theological ethics, but also in 'the attempt . . . to show that, whatever may be the interconnexion between them, there is a twofold ethical inquiry, . . . a "theological" and a "philosophical", which touch and limit but do not abolish each other'[27] – a strategy motivated perhaps by a realisation of the redundancy which theological ethics has wished on itself by apologetics. Thus it might be reckoned that theological ethics has a special and particular source, subject, presupposition or

[22] Barth, *Church Dogmatics*, II: 2, 521–2.   [23] Ibid.
[24] Barth, *Church Dogmatics*, II: 2, 524.
[25] Ibid.   [26] Ibid.   [27] Ibid.

content which gives it a task in addition to, but not at odds with, philosophical ethics. This is not synthesis then, as attempted by apologetics, but diastasis, the 'friendly demarcation' of two spheres; but 'it is no less suspect' than the former.[28] 'What we have to ask in relation to this view is whether theology can seriously contemplate two things', a sphere determined by revelation, grace and so on, and another by reason, experience, and the like.[29] Or, 'to put the question differently':

> Is God's revelation revelation of the truth, or is it only the source of certain religious ideas and obligations, alongside which there are very different ones in other spheres? Outside and alongside the kingdom of Jesus Christ are there other respectable kingdoms? Can and should theology of all things be content to speak, not with universal validity, but only esoterically? Is it, or is it not, serious in its alleged knowledge of a Whence? and Whither? of all ethical enquiry and reply which are superior to all reason, experience and self-determination? If it is serious about this, how can it, even if only for a moment, take seriously and accept the validity of an ethics which necessarily lacks or even disavows this knowledge? How can it liberate this ethics, as it were, by entering into an armistice with it? How can it imagine that it can secure its own right to exist in this way? Does it really believe in its own theme if it concedes that the other ethics has its own source and subject in reason, experience and self-determination? – as if all this did not lie from the very outset in its own sphere, the sphere of theological ethics; as if it could be right to accept all these quantities as self-evident, to concede autonomy to man's knowledge of good and evil; as if Jesus Christ had not died and risen again; as if we could salute the grace of God, as it were, and then go our own way; as if it were the task of theology positively to encourage and invite people to do this by the establishment of this diastasis.[30]

Theological ethics cannot tolerate the establishment of such diastasis and, for this very reason, far from detaching itself from other ethics, it takes up 'the legitimate problems and concerns and motives and assertions of every other ethics . . . after testing them in the light of its own superior principles'.[31] Hence, 'its attitude to every other ethics is not negative but comprehensive' in so far as such ethics is aware of, or attests to,

[28] Barth, *Church Dogmatics*, II: 2, 525.
[29] Barth, *Church Dogmatics*, II: 2, 526.   [30] Ibid.
[31] Barth, *Church Dogmatics*, II: 2, 527.

explicitly or implicitly, 'its origin and basis in God's command'; it is exclusive only as 'it [i.e., other ethics] tries to deny or obscure its derivation from God's command'.[32]

On the one side, therefore, it absorbs it into itself, and on the other it opposes it . . . Either way, it necessarily accepts full responsibility for handling the whole problem of ethics – and not merely of an esoteric ethics which appeals to special sources and proceeds according to a special method, but of ethics generally and as such.[33]

The 'Roman Catholic view of the matter' can be treated, at least initially, as a 'third possible way of defining the relationship between theological ethics and other ethics' and as one which seems to avoid the pitfalls of these others: 'we certainly cannot accuse it directly of either surrender of theology to the authority and judgment of principles alien to it, or escaping into the narrow confines of a special theological task'.[34] Indeed, in its understanding of the co-ordination of moral theology and moral philosophy, it seems properly to relate the two disciplines – the two are certainly not the same, but neither can they be separated nor proceed in essentially opposed directions:

Does it not maintain that the knowledge of God must necessarily be one and the same ultimate presupposition not only of theological but of all ethics? Is it not shown that theological ethics – deriving like every other ethics from this ultimate knowledge, but drawing incomparably much more illumination from it – cannot possibly allow this other ethics to put and answer the question of truth, as though it were an exercise set and corrected by it? Could it not give us the necessary irenic and polemic – the claiming and acknowledging of other ethics in respect of the remnants of that presupposition still to be found in them, and the rejection of all other ethics in so far as they do not know or indeed deny this presupposition? At a first glance we may even be tempted to regard this solution as ideal.[35]

And yet on reflection it cannot be so regarded, for 'within this framework the command of the grace of God as the content

---

[32] Ibid. For Barth's understanding of the comprehensiveness of Christian ethics, see his treatment of the doctrine of creation, and in particular the discussion of anthropology, *Church Dogmatics*, III, 2, trans. H. Knight et al. (Edinburgh, 1960), esp. section 44.

[33] Barth, *Church Dogmatics*, II: 2, 527–8.

[34] Barth, *Church Dogmatics*, II: 2, 528.

[35] Barth, *Church Dogmatics*, II: 2, 529.

of theological ethics cannot have the status which properly belongs to it':

For this Roman Catholic co-ordination of moral philosophy and moral theology is based on the basic view of the harmony which is achieved in the concept of being between nature and super-nature, reason and revelation, man and God. And it is quite impossible to see how in this basic view grace can really emerge as grace and the command as command.[36]

Grace cannot emerge as grace because 'grace which has from the start to share its power with a force of nature is no longer grace';[37] and the command cannot emerge as a command because 'if obligation is grounded in being, this undoubtedly means that it is not grounded in itself, but ontically subordinated to another, and noetically to be derived from this other. It is imperative only in virtue of that which is over it; and it becomes imperative for us only in virtue of its derivation from it'.[38] But this is not how it is with the God with whom Christian dogmatics is concerned.

[W]hat has that metaphysics of being to do with the God who is the basis and Lord of the Church? If this God is He who in Jesus Christ became man, revealing Himself and reconciling the world with Himself, it follows that the relationship between Him and man consists in the event in which God accepted man out of pure, free compassion, in which He drew him to Himself out of pure kindness, but first and last in the eternal decree of the covenant of grace, in God's eternal predestination. It is not with the theory of the relationship between creaturely and creative being, but with the theory of this divine praxis, with the consideration and conception of this divine act, of its eternal decree and its temporal execution, that theology and therefore theological ethics, must deal.[39]

It turns out, then, that the avoidance of pitfalls of the 'apologetic and differentiating movements of the theological ethics of Neo-Protestantism' is more apparent than real. The 'gross blunders of apologetics and isolationism' are not evident 'only because they are in some sense committed in principle,

[36] Barth, *Church Dogmatics*, II: 2, 530.
[37] Barth, *Church Dogmatics*, II: 2, 531.
[38] Barth, *Church Dogmatics*, II: 2, 532.
[39] Barth, *Church Dogmatics*, II: 2, 531.

and therefore do not need to be committed in particular'.[40]
That is to say, Roman Catholicism is:

the wisest of all mediating systems because it is apologetic from the
very outset in its understanding of grace and revelation and God, i.e.,
because it is an establishment and justification of the Christian
position before the forum of general human thought, and accomplishes the fatal assimilation of the Christian to the human. But it is
also the wisest because, without any inner conflict, it works with that
division of roles, and in this way safeguards its task as theological
ethics, although obviously rendering it innocuous.[41]

Hence, though Roman Catholicism does classically what in
neo-Protestantism is only 'epigonous' (i.e., a less distinguished
imitation of an earlier and more illustrious practice), the former
is no more satisfactory than the latter.[42]

Theological ethics must, then, maintain the distinctiveness
which belongs to it in virtue of its having its source in 'a
knowledge of the God who elects man'.[43] It must, that is to say,
be an ethics which understands its task as 'a task of the doctrine

---

[40] Barth, *Church Dogmatics*, II: 2, 534.   [41] Ibid.

[42] Barth's treatment of Roman Catholic ethics, here meaning the ethics of Thomism,
plainly depends on wider theological questions and its adequacy can hardly be
settled within the ambit of this chapter – this point must be stressed. It can be said,
however, that study of a recent attempt to restate and defend the main lines of a
Thomist ethics shows only too well the relevance of the critique. S. Pinckaer's *Sources
of Christian Ethics*, trans. from the 3rd edn by M. Noble (Edinburgh, 1995), seeks to
save Thomas from what is reckoned to be the misinterpretation of the casuists, for
whom his treatise on the natural law is central. According to Pinckaers, however,
Thomas's treatment of the natural law must be read only in the context of his
treatment of human happiness as finding its end in God, and of the virtues as shaped
by this end and as nourished by grace. Read thus, we find that the leading category
in Thomas's moral theology is not the category of obligation, but the category of
freedom; Thomas, that is to say, preaches a Gospel of the liberation of the human
subject through the action of God. But, even when Thomas is construed as avoiding
the blatant 'blunders' of apologetics and diastasis, to use Barth's terms, the question
which Barth poses is highly pertinent: are not these blunders evident below the
surface? When we find that theological ethics is treated as a deepening of human
wisdom, on the basis of an anthropology and doctrine of God which permits such co-
ordination, what is this but the classic assimilation and division of Roman Catholic
ethics? And the matter of the plausibility of this co-ordination is sharply brought to
our attention by the claim that 'the natural inclination to marriage is universal' (447);
for what does this suggest but a readiness to ignore the particularities not only of
theology but also of the wisdom it is held to augment, and to do so on the basis of
some a priori and barely acknowledged account of the compatibility of moral
theology and moral philosophy?

[43] Barth, *Church Dogmatics*, II: 2, 535.

of God', and thereby as determined by the fact that ' "what is good" has been "said" to man (Micah, 6: 8)'.[44] Thus determined, 'the ethical problem of Church dogmatics can consist only in the question whether and to what extent human action is a glorification of the grace of Jesus Christ . . . It asks about the action of the man who is actually placed in the light of grace.'[45]

'The act of the God who in grace has elected man for the covenant with Himself' and who thereby claims the actions of humankind, can, however, be characterised in the 'shortest possible form' as an act of creation, reconciliation and redemption.[46] Hence, the one command of God by which humans are claimed can itself be understood in threefold form as 'the command of God the Creator, the command of God the Reconciler and the command of God the Redeemer'.[47] Thus it belongs to theological ethics to 'explain and recapitulate in their ethical content' the 'fundamental concepts of dogmatics'.[48] In the completion of this task lies the chief concern of a dogmatic ethics.

III

Where Christian ethics understands itself as dogmatic ethics – that is, as providing an account of human action as it corresponds to the reality of the action of God – it necessarily understands itself in such a way as to differentiate itself from a number of other accounts of ethics, even when those are given from the Christian side. In the previous section we followed Barth in his attempt to make this theoretical differentiation. Now, however, we shall seek to understand this differentiation not from the side of theory, but from the side of practice.

We could, of course, attempt once more to follow the path taken by Barth, and certainly the early lectures published as *Ethics*, volume III: 4 of the *Church Dogmatics* (a consideration of our being as God's creatures) and the fragment of IV: 4 which

---

[44] Barth, *Church Dogmatics*, II: 2, 537.
[45] Barth, *Church Dogmatics*, II: 2, 540.
[46] Barth, *Church Dogmatics*, II: 2, 549.   [47] Ibid.   [48] Ibid.

appears as *The Christian Life* (the unfinished development of the theme of human being as the being of pardoned sinners), provide richly suggestive treatments of what Barth terms 'special ethics'.[49] It seems better, however, to follow a different route at this point for a number of reasons. In the first place, for all its undoubted richness, Barth's uncompleted treatment of special ethics requires that we must, to some extent, engage in a task of sympathetic reconstruction before attempting either appropriation or critique.[50] More importantly it may more effectively serve our purpose to characterise the practice of dogmatic ethics, at least to begin with, by offering not a eulogy on a position with which it shares common ground, but by offering a modest critique of one with which it may be confused but from which it in actual fact differs. Having made this distinction we may then turn to two specific examples of the practice which we mean to commend.

Amongst contemporary positions in the field of Christian ethics there are, to be sure, a good number from which dogmatic ethics will be distinguished with an ease (though not without attention to the details of the matter) which reassures us that there is little risk of confusion. Plainly, it should be distinguished from the intellectually highly vigorous critiques and developments of Thomism associated with Grisez and Finnis on the one hand, and with MacIntyre on the other.[51] (This is not to say that there is nothing to be learnt from these projects, pursued as they are with philosophical rigour and, in the first case, theological seriousness, but only that in their

[49] K. Barth, *Ethics*, ed. D. Braun, trans. G. Bromiley (Edinburgh, 1981) and *The Christian Life*, trans. G. Bromiley (Edinburgh, 1981).

[50] N. Biggar's study *The Hastening that Waits: Karl Barth's Ethics* (Oxford, 1993), provides a careful and critical delineation of the form which Barth's ethics might be supposed to have taken had the *Church Dogmatics* been completed.

[51] For the first see especially G. Grisez's important study *The Way of the Lord Jesus* – of which three volumes have thus far appeared, *Christian Moral Principles* (Chicago, 1983), *Living a Christian Moral Life* (Quincy, IL, 1993), and *Difficult Moral Questions* (Quincy, IL, 1997) – and J. Finnis, *Natural Law and Natural Rights* (Oxford, 1980) and *Moral Absolutes: Tradition, Revision, and Truth* (Washington, 1991). For MacIntyre's developing position, see *After Virtue: A Study in Moral Theory*, 2nd edn (London, 1985), *Whose Justice? Which Rationality?* (London, 1988), *Three Rival Versions of Moral Enquiry* (London, 1990), and 'Moral Relativism, Truth and Justification' in *Moral Truth and Moral Tradition*, ed. L. Gormally (Dublin, 1994), 6–24.

broad lines these projects do not understand themselves, and cannot be understood, as exercises in dogmatic ethics as we have delineated it.) Furthermore, dogmatic ethics can be distinguished from the intellectually far from vigorous body of broadly neo-Protestant writing which doubtless reckons itself a contribution to the work of Christian ethics though without having anything but the vaguest idea of what it might be to make such a contribution. If it betrays even a hint of anything approaching methodological self-consciousness, it is unlikely to rise far above the maxim chosen by a certain theologian to sum up the theme of a chapter on ethics: 'The sense of God's presence, which is the crown of the religious life, reaches over into the sphere of ethics and glorifies it.'[52] (Surveying this body of material, we can hardly fail to note that the contemporary Christian moralist, afflicted by a certain methodological whimsicality, often resembles the extremely genial and well-liked Prince Oblonsky of *Anna Karenina*, whose 'tendencies and opinions' says Tolstoi, 'were not his by deliberate choice: they came of themselves, just as he did not choose the fashion of his hats and coats, but wore those of the current style'. But the survey will also have to note an added layer of pathos, or better, bathos – for when the self-professed Christian ethicist who has learnt his ethics from the world returns to the world from writing his most recent book or paper on some aspect of Christian ethics, he finds to his great satisfaction that he can congratulate himself and his colleagues on the quite remarkable influence they have exerted over contemporary life and thought, quite oblivious to the fact that the world's agreement with him is in reality founded on his agreement with the world. How else should we explain finding one such – hence the male pronoun in the last sentence – describing Christian ethics as having been 'remarkably successful' over the last twenty years?)

It is easy enough to distinguish the practice of dogmatic ethics from the practice of those who quite consciously, or rather unselfconsciously, are set on a different path. But it must also be distinguished, and with some care, from an approach –

[52] J. Macquarrie, *Principles of Christian Theology*, revised edn (London, 1977), 503, quoting W. Adams Brown, *Christian Theology in Outline*.

that of Stanley Hauerwas – with which it shares many concerns while doubting the adequacy of its practice. To be precise, we must ask of Hauerwas whether or not he is sufficiently dogmatic – an enquiry on which Hauerwas may be able to smile in so far as it represents questioning from a position which is ready to learn from the major themes of his work and which, with him, finds little of merit (as we shall see in the next section) in the complaints of the majority of his critics!

A recent collection of Hauerwas's papers, which may be taken as representative of Hauerwas's position, has a title which hints at something of the commonality between his concerns and those of dogmatic ethics: *Dispatches from the Front: Theological Engagements with the Secular.*[53] Hauerwas, that is to say, characteristically and consistently seeks a theological engagement with the secular; that is, he seeks an unapologetic portrayal of the 'world envisioned in Christian discourse',[54] with all the difference between this world and the secular world in relation to issues of war, medical practice, the treatment of the mentally handicapped and so on. But, as this theme of difference and distinctiveness is developed, through Hauerwas's characteristic and important reflections on narrative, the Church and the virtues, a question begins to take form as to whether the 'world envisioned in Christian discourse' is properly conceived and thus the difference truly displayed.

Take to begin with an essay entitled 'Creation as Apocalyptic'. Here Hauerwas insists that 'the nonapocalyptic vision of reality that dominates American public life tempts American Christians, like other Americans, to accept, with despair and relief, the inevitability and thus the goodness of things as they are'.[55] Thus it is no surprise to find Hauerwas warning that 'appeals to creation too often amount to legitimating strategies for the principalities and powers that determine our lives'[56] – since forgetfulness of apocalyptic is also forgetfulness of the Fall,

---

[53] S. Hauerwas, *Dispatches from the Front: Theological Engagements with the Secular* (Durham, NC, 1994).

[54] Hauerwas, *Dispatches from the Front*, 7.

[55] Hauerwas, *Dispatches from the Front*, 114.

[56] Hauerwas, *Dispatches from the Front*, 111.

a nonapocalyptic vision is likely to lead to appeals to creation which do indeed 'often amount to legitimating strategies' by which Christians simply come to terms with what is the case; strategies, that is to say, which take from our lips the prayer 'hallowed be thy name', by which we ask that God would bring to an end the twilight of good and evil in which we presently live. Notoriously, the Lutheran handling of the notion of the orders of creation (particularly in the work of Gogarten, for example) is held to be susceptible to just such a charge, and even in Bonhoeffer's self-conscious re-interpretation of this notion in his treatment of 'mandates', Barth wonders whether there is not a 'suggestion of north German patriarchalism'.[57] Examples could be multiplied (and readily gleaned, for example, from the teachings of Augustine's Pelagian opponents in relation to matters of human sexuality, as we shall presently see), but this is hardly to the point. To say that appeals to creation '*too often*' amount to legitimating strategies surely suggests that there is no necessity here. Can there not be, we must ask, a corrected account of creation; i.e., one which does not crassly identify what is the case with God's will for the world? Is it not on the basis of just such a possibility that Augustine, to mention that example again, endeavours to treat of human sexuality, and Barth, more broadly, of anthropology? And, if that possibility does not lie open to us, if we cannot with them envision the world which lies behind the Fall, are we not destined to find ourselves incapable of anything other than, on the one hand, a polemical protest at what is, and, on the other, a somewhat inarticulate hope for what shall be?

In an essay entitled, 'Killing Compassion', Hauerwas seems explicitly to rule out such a possibility – or at least, not to take it seriously – with his rather quick criticisms of Oliver O'Donovan's *Resurrection and Moral Order.* 'O'Donovan', he claims:

> seeks an account of natural law which is not governed by the eschatological witness of Christ's resurrection. We cannot write about *Resurrection and Moral Order* because any order that we know as Christians is resurrection. I am not denying that we are creatures of a good creator; I am simply suggesting that as Christians we know

[57] Barth, *Church Dogmatics*, III: 4, 22.

nothing about what we mean by creation separate from the new order we find through the concrete practices of baptism and Eucharist, correlative as they are to Christ's resurrection.[58]

Hauerwas's point here is difficult to fathom. O'Donovan is said to be looking for 'an account of natural law which is not governed by the eschatological witness of Christ's resurrection.' But, as Hauerwas knows very well, O'Donovan is committed to a thoroughly Christian and Christological epistemology, and thus takes the resurrection to be the key to our knowledge of the created order – hence the title of his book. Far from being ungoverned by the eschatological witness of Christ's resurrection, then, knowledge of creation is knowledge of a beginning which is found only in knowledge of the end. So, for example, we find O'Donovan saying that:

the creation was given to us with its own goal and purpose, so that the outcome of the world's story cannot be a cyclical return to the beginnings, but must fulfil that purpose in the freeing of creation from its 'futility' . . . Thus there is an important place in Christian thought for the idea of 'history', using the term as it is widely used in philosophy and theology to mean, not mere events on the one hand, nor their narration in an intelligible story on the other, but their inherent significance and direction which makes them intelligible and narratable. The Christian understanding of this idea is, of course, only to be reached through a Christian understanding of the end towards which events are directed, that is, through eschatology.[59]

Since O'Donovan understands creation from its purpose, and understands that purpose from what is disclosed in the life, death and resurrection of Jesus Christ, he is not guilty of separating creation from eschatology, as Hauerwas charges, but seeks to allow the latter to interpret the former. In this, of course, he conforms to the practice of, to take one of the examples already mentioned, Karl Barth in his working out of a doctrine of creation in general, and of humankind in particular. In that latter case, Barth proposes, as is well known, to understand anthropology from Christology, thus turning the nineteenth century's attempt to found Christology on anthropology

[58] Hauerwas, *Dispatches from the Front*, 175.
[59] O. M. T. O'Donovan, *Resurrection and Moral Order* (Leicester, 1986), 55.

on its head. But to mention the example of Barth's anthropology and the attempt to understand the creation as itself inherently eschatologically ordered is to bring to the fore, perhaps more clearly, a point already made, namely that there is no reason to suppose that appeals to creation should be identified with strategies for legitimating the twilight world of good and evil against which Hauerwas properly protests; in Barth's hands, for example, an eschatologically conditioned doctrine of creation provides the very grounds on which he seeks to challenge Nietzsche's anthropology of the *übermensch*, of the 'I am' without and against the other, an anthropology which, as Barth sees it, expresses the *telos* of the modern conception of humanity.[60]

Hauerwas's charge against O'Donovan, and his blanket suspicion of appeals to the created order, are both misplaced; there is, however, a charge which relates to his own work which he needs to address. If O'Donovan is said to seek 'an account of natural law which is not governed by the eschatological witness of Christ's resurrection', might we not counter-charge that Hauerwas seems to seek an account of the eschaton which is not governed by the belief in creation which he avows? Might we not even be tempted to say of Hauerwas what has been said of Moltmann: that here God is present to the world solely as future, and thus in such a way that that presence cannot be understood as an expression of his faithfulness?[61] Is this not an instance, in a phrase of von Balthasar's, of 'an Omega that has no Alpha'. Or to put it another way – ought we not to remind ourselves that it is Augustine's willingness to attempt the discernment of the goodness of the created order (an order which is, after all, not overlooked in salvation, but is its object) which gives proof of the distance he places between his Christian present and his Manichee past? Can we not ask, that is to say, whether a fuller account of Christian life and witness than Hauerwas has thus far given, and one more dogmatically

---

[60] K. Barth, *Church Dogmatics*, III: 2, section 45, esp. 231 42.

[61] See, e.g., D. Schuurman, *Creation, Eschaton, and Ethics: The Ethical Significance of the Creation Eschaton Relation in the Thought of Emil Brunner and Jürgen Moltmann* (New York, 1991).

determined than his thought seems to be, would make reference not only to moments of protest and expectation, but also to moments of joy, celebration and acceptance?

It is important to stress that the point which we are making is not one which is found amidst the many criticisms of Hauerwas which Gustafson scatters with a certain abandon when he contends that 'Nature is . . . of no ethical significance as a source of direction in Hauerwas's ethics. Hauerwas becomes a twentieth-century version of Marcion.'[62] Gustafson demands that an understanding of nature should serve to govern theology; we demand of Hauerwas that theology should serve to govern our understanding of nature. The general complaint we make against Hauerwas is, in other words, that his ethics is insufficiently dogmatic.[63]

Having attempted to distinguish dogmatic ethics from a practice which does not fully conform to its sense of what is required, but with which it may be confused, we must now venture to give a better example of its practice. It will be

---

[62] J. Gustafson, 'A Response to Critics', *Journal of Religious Ethics*, 13 (1985), 191.

[63] We might note that this is criticism which is relevant to the work of certain members of what we might term the 'school of Hauerwas'; V. Guroian's *Ethics After Christendom: Toward an Ecclesial Christian Ethic* (Grand Rapids, 1994), provides an example. When Guroian tells us that 'liturgy is a primary context and source for Christian ethics' (7), we can hardly fail to wonder whether the properly dogmatic basis of ethics is here maintained. To say that liturgy is a primary context for Christian ethics is one thing; after all, the indefinite article qualifies the claim somewhat, and what remains is, given Guroian's explication, surely acceptable: the liturgy serves to frame, interpret and articulate the Christian understanding of God's salvific action so that in the liturgy we discern the character of the action called forth from us by that original action. But what can it mean to say that liturgy is a 'source for Christian ethics', or for that matter to speak of 'liturgical theology'? Certainly, as we have said, liturgy in general, and the lectionary in particular, presents an interpretation of the story of salvation and thus of the human action appropriate as a response to it; but this does not make liturgy a source of Christian ethic in any interesting sense. Indeed, most of the time Guroian is careful to avoid any such claim; thus he concludes his essay 'The Bible in Orthodox Ethics' by saying that it has attempted to show 'that the Orthodox tradition possesses a rich treasury of liturgies and rites in which the biblical world with its images is powerfully narrated, enacted, and embodied communally' (80). Plainly the liturgy cannot be the source of what it narrates, enacts and embodies. Its role in relation to this source is heuristic, and only confusion about the nature of 'an ecclesial Christian ethic' can result unless this point is maintained with a certain definiteness and clarity. Guroian then, needs to focus on what lies behind – and what lies behind is the biblical world to which dogmatics is responsible, and by which our liturgies, whether Orthodox, Anglican, Roman Catholic, or whatever, must ultimately be judged.

recalled that the essence of this practice is that it attempts to conceive of human action as corresponding to the action of God. And we shall now illustrate somethings of what this might mean for sexual ethics.

Augustine's treatment of sexual ethics can be regarded as paradigmatic just because it is an attempt, as Paul Ramsey has importantly argued, to understand the meaning and place of human sexuality, in faithfulness to the biblical witness, within the history of creation, reconciliation and redemption.[61] It is thus, so we would claim, an example of dogmatic ethics; that is, an envisioning of the world in the light of what is the case in Jesus Christ – and whether or not we are content with the details of his thought, the logic of his position is exemplary from a dogmatic perspective.

In dealing with this issue, Augustine had, in effect, three sets of opponents who, though they must be answered separately, could not be answered without an awareness of the need for the answer to one set to be consistent with the answer given to another. The first two sets of opponents Augustine identifies as Manichees and Pelagians. The third group of opponents are not so easily categorised and do not obviously belong to a particular philosophical or theological school; if we were to label them pejoratively on Augustine's behalf we might call them Sadducees, a label which we will explain shortly. Each set of opponents can be understood as denying aspects of reality as understood from the dogmatic centre – the reality of creation, the reality of reconciliation and the reality of redemption – and Augustine's teaching in relation to sexual ethics can be presented as falling under these heads.

First, against any disparagement of it, he insists on marriage's goodness following especially Matthew 19: 4–6 and an increasingly literal reading of Genesis. This reading of Genesis led him to the view that sexual union between man and woman is natural to them as presupposed in their creation in sexual differentiation; he thus rejected not only the views of the Manichees who denied, as he claimed, 'that God is both the

[61] P. Ramsey, 'Human Sexuality within the History of Redemption', *Journal of Religious Ethics*, 16 (1988), 56–88.

creator of man, and the uniter in marriage of husband and wife',[65] but also the views of those such as Gregory of Nyssa who taught that sexual union belonged after the Fall, being made possible by a divine dispensation intended to moderate the bitterness of humankind's punishment by death.[66] As Augustine insisted in the *City of God*, 'It is certain that at the beginning male and female were constituted just as two human beings of different sex are now, in our observation and knowledge', and furthermore that even 'if there had been no sin, marriage would have been worthy of the happiness of paradise, and would have given birth to children to be loved'.[67] This notion that 'marriage would have been worthy of the happiness of paradise' (that is, the grounding of a defence of it in an unambiguous account of marriage and sexual union as belonging to the original, created goodness of humanity), gave Augustine, as against pagan and Christian defenders of marriage, not only an altogether more secure basis for that defence, but also the motive to think out a richer account of the goods of marriage. Thus, against Clement of Alexandria, for example, who had answered an extreme asceticism by praising marriage, in terms almost wholly borrowed from classical sources, as pre-eminently a means for providing future generations,[68] Augustine finds the chief goods of marriage not only in progeny, but also in fidelity and, following Ephesians 5: 32, in the sacrament or sign of indissolubility, whereby marriage is a figure of the union between Christ and the Church.[69]

If human sexuality and marriage belong to the created order, it is not to be supposed with Pelagianism, however, that they lie

---

[65] Augustine, *De Nuptiis et Concupiscentia* (*On Marriage and Concupiscence*), PL 44, 413–74, trans. P. Holmes and R. Wallis, *Nicene and Post-Nicene Fathers*, 1st series, vol. v (Edinburgh, 1991), ii, 9.

[66] Gregory of Nyssa, *De Hominis Opificio* (*On the Making of Man*), PG 44, 123–256, trans. W. Moore and H. Wilson, *Nicene and Post-Nicene Fathers*, 2nd series, vol. v (Edinburgh, 1994).

[67] Augustine, *De Civitate Dei* (*City of God*), PL 41, 13–804, trans. H. Bettenson (London, 1972), xiv, 23.

[68] See, e.g., Clement of Alexandria, *Stromata*, PG 8, 685–1382, trans. W. Wilson, *Ante-Nicene Fathers*, ed. A. Roberts and J. Donaldson, vol. ii (Edinburgh, 1977), ii, 23 and iii, passim.

[69] Augustine, *De Bono Conjugali* (*On the Good of Marriage*), PL 40, 373–96, trans. C. T. Wilcox in *Augustine: Treatises on Marriage and Other Subjects* (New York, 1955).

outside the shadow of the Fall. This is the second main element in Augustine's teaching, refined in particular in his controversy with Julian of Eclanum. The handling of this theme required considerably subtlety if Augustine was to find a way between Manichaean disparagement of marriage on the one hand, and Pelagian insistence on its essential innocence on the other; between, as he puts it, 'the detestable censure' of human nature by the Manichees and the 'cruel praise' of the Pelagians.[70] In his own praise of marriage, and more especially his defence of the piety of the Old Testament patriarchs against the slurs of the Manichees in *De Bono Conjugali*, for example, Augustine had, at the least, been incautious in certain formulations of his position, and as he attempted to map out a middle path he had cause to provide some of these formulations with a gloss.[71] The route he took was as follows: although marital intercourse for the sake of procreation is not itself sinful (unlike intercourse for other reasons which is sinful, though 'venially' or pardonably so) even reasonable marital intercourse is touched by the 'malady' of concupiscence, which is to say that division of the self against the self, or flesh against the spirit, which is expressed in a disorderly sexual desire, and is since the Fall 'both a consequence and a cause of sin'.[72] Prior to the Fall, Augustine maintains, Adam and Eve would have engaged in sexual intercourse at the bidding of their wills alone, untouched by the disorderly lust which now animates and afflicts even marital union – and at some length in Book xiv of the *City of God* Augustine seeks to persuade us of the possibility of such a wholly rational control of the sexual organs and the sexual act. It is the movement of disorderly lust, not subject to the will, which explains the shame invariably associated with even the

---

[70] Augustine, *De Nuptiis et Concupiscentia*, ii, 3.

[71] See, e.g., *De Bono Conjugali*, 18: '[W]hat food is to the health of man, intercourse is to the health of the race, and both are not without carnal pleasure [delectatione carnali], which, however, when modified, and put to its natural use with a controlling temperance, cannot be a passion [libido, i.e., lust]', and *Retractiones*, 2.22: 'This was said since the good and proper use of passion is not a passion. Just as it is wicked to use good things wrongly, it is good to use wicked things rightly. I argued more carefully about these things on another occasion, especially against the new Pelagian heretics.' (Cited by Wilcox, in his translation of *De Bono Conjugali*.)

[72] G. Bonner, *St Augustine of Hippo, Life and Controversies*, revised edn, (Norwich, 1986), 375.

most honourable uses of marriage, so Augustine teaches; in this shame we implicitly recognise human sexuality as a force for unreason, distracting us from our pursuit of the *summum bonum*. None of this, however, Augustine insists, is to detract from his defence of marriage against the Manichees.[73] Concupiscence is not caused by marriage, but rather, where intercourse is for the sake of progeny, marriage directs it to a good use; and even where marital intercourse is for the sake of concupiscence, marriage has in its favour that it pardons such excess.[74]

Though marriage is a good, virginity and continence are to be preferred; this is the third main element in Augustine's teaching, owing much to Paul. Plainly, in maintaining this thesis the insistence on the goodness of marriage can easily be endangered and both Tertullian (quite consciously in *De Exhortatione Castitatis*) and Jerome (in effect, if not in declared intention) were so vigorous in their espousal of celibacy as to forget that, as Augustine has it, virginity is simply the 'better of two good things'. In *Adversus Jovinianum*, Jerome had attacked the views of a monk who had maintained that the salvation of the married and of the celibate, is, so to speak, indistinguishable.[75] But, in arguing that celibacy is a higher state than marriage and thus deserves a higher reward, Jerome had seemed to question the goodness of marriage; his letters of self-justification,[76] defending himself against such a charge, only made matters worse – he speculates that in Genesis' account of the second day of creation we do not read that 'it was good' because there is 'something not good in the number two, separating us as it does from unity, and prefiguring the marriage tie. Just as in the account of Noah's ark all the animals that enter by twos are

---

[73] See Augustine, *De Nuptiis et Concupiscentia*, i, 35: 'In respect . . . to this concupiscence of the flesh, we have striven . . . to distinguish it accurately from the goods of marriage. This we have done on account of our modern heretics, who cavil whenever conscupiscence is censured, as if it involved a censure of marriage . . . [and whose] object is to praise conscupiscence as a natural good.'

[74] Augustine, *De Nuptiis et Concupiscentia*, i, 14.

[75] Jerome, *Adversus Jovinianum (Against Jovinianus)*, PL 23, 221–352, trans. W. H. Freemantle, *Nicene and Post-Nicene Fathers*, 2nd series, vol. VI, ed. P. Schaff and H. Wace (Edinburgh, 1989).

[76] Jerome, *Letters, Nicene and Post-Nicene Fathers*, vol. VI, letters xlviii–l.

unclean';[77] furthermore, he remarks, 'I should like every one to take a wife who, because he gets frightened in the night, cannot manage to sleep alone.'[78]

Augustine's defence of the superiority of virginity and continence does not rest on any such scorn for marriage, but on an eschatological perspective which in no way impugns the created goodness of sexual union.[79] Celibacy is preferred to marriage as witnessing that though marriage is good, it is a good which will be surpassed. Hence we may label his opponents on this matter Sadducees, since practically, if not theoretically, they deny the resurrection of the dead to which celibacy bears witness, not as a denial of the good of community, but as an expression of the hope that the good of community will be realised in a radical non-particularity which transcends the possibilities of purely human community. As such, celibacy is integral to the witness of the Church which, without this sign, so easily slips into a settled worldliness which places its hope for community in the ties of marriage and blood.

For all the brilliance with which he maintained his position against Manichees, Pelagians and over enthusiastic defenders of celibacy, Augustine's treatment of sexuality bequeathed various problems to the tradition. Like the elements of his treatment, these can be thought of as threefold, and as concerning (i) the adequacy of his specification of the goods of marriage and the relationship between them; (ii) the propriety of an anthropology which located the fallenness of human sexuality in the overpowering of the will by passion; and (iii) the satisfactoriness of his particular valuation of virginity and continence.[80] Nothing said thus far means to deny the need to examine Augustine's legacy in the light of these concerns. But such an examination is not presently to the point; here we mean simply to hold up Augustine's systematic treatment of human sexuality as paradigmatic for dogmatic ethics, concerned as such ethics must be, to maintain that this sphere of human life, as any other, is truly understood and rightly ordered only as it is understood and

[77] Jerome, *Letters*, xlviii.   [78] Jerome, *Letters*, l.
[79] For the details of Augustine's argument, see 301–7 below.
[80] On the second and third of these issues, see 297–307 below.

ordered in the light of a knowledge of God as creator, reconciler and redeemer. And such an understanding and ordering will produce a sexual ethics free from the Manicheeism (the denial of the goodness of creation), the Pelagianism (the praise of concupiscence) and the Sadducean tendencies (the rejection of the teleological ordering of the goods of earthly life), which Augustine would find as prevalent amongst his modern detractors as amongst his contemporary opponents.

Though I have chosen to illustrate the particularity of Christian ethics through an account of the dogmatic form of sexual ethics, other examples could have served the purpose quite as well or better. We might have asked, for example, what it would mean for contemporary medical practice in relation to the dying to be governed by a fully Christian anthropology.[81] Or, to pose another question, what would it be for economics to take seriously the fact, proclaimed in that same anthropology, that the human good consists in being 'conjubilant', to use a splendid word from a hymn of Bernard of Cluny? These questions, and any number of others, provide the agenda for dogmatic ethics, devoted as it is to conceiving human action as determined by the action of God.

IV

In the preceding sections an account has been given of the theory and form of dogmatic ethics, an attempt has been made to distinguish its practice from that of other conceptions of Christian ethics, and an illustration of that practice has been provided through a brief engagement with a particular issue. But now we must face an objection to the conception of Christian ethics here elaborated, which is all the more difficult to deal with, though no less real, for being somewhat inchoate. The sort of objection I have in mind sometimes comes in gentle tones of enquiry and sometimes in less gentle tones of outrage and indignation. Either way, what lies behind the questioning is a sense that what I have been calling dogmatic ethics is

---

[81] See 'Christian Anthropology at the Beginning and End of Life', below.

inappropriate to our present circumstances. Of course, it may be said, dogmatic ethics will be appropriate to debates internal to the Church's life – suppose, for example, that a Church has to decide whether it will make use of pension funds which may invest in firms implicated in some way in the arms trade. In such a debate the giving of reasons for and against a particular course of action may, quite naturally and properly, be a giving of Christian reasons. But such a mode of discourse and reasoning can make no contact, it may be said, with public discussions; dogmatic ethics, that is to say, is ill-equipped to maintain a Christian voice in the arena of debate and discussion in which that voice has sought, and continues to seek, to make itself heard. Is not preaching and confession the characteristic mode of address of a dogmatic ethics, and is not preaching and confession peculiarly inept as a form of public discourse? Indeed, is it not the case that a dogmatic ethics must eschew public discourse and with it a genuine and responsible engage-ment with the world? Do we not have here, that is to say, an invitation to the sectarianism of the ghetto and a turn away from a larger sphere of life and action? Or, to put the point in terms of our title, if dogmatic Christian ethics claims as its chief task turning the world upside down (that is, describing the new world and new form of life which corresponds to the action of God in Jesus Christ) can it have any other task at all?

The familiarity of this objection comes, of course, from its being just the sort of objection which is made to the work of Hauerwas, and, though we have attempted to distinguish the form of dogmatic ethics from Hauerwas's work, in relation to this objection that distinction is not obviously relevant.[82] That is to say, though we give different accounts of the particularity of Christian life and thought, we are both concerned to give an account of that particularity and it is this very concern for particularity which motivates the objection. Hauerwas is some-

---

[82] For some critics of Hauerwas, see subsequent discussion. Similar objections are made to the work of Lindbeck. For details and discussion see W. C. Placher, 'Revisionist and Postliberal Theologies and the Public Character of Theology', *The Thomist*, 49 (1985), 392–417, and G. E. Michalson, 'The Response to Lindbeck', *Modern Theology*, 4 (1988), 107–21.

what wearied by this sort of complaint – 'such labeling is the refuge of mediocre minds and lazy intelligence'[83] – and not without some justification, since it typically declines to proceed in a way which makes discussion easy; that is, it does not identify a premise in the defence of the particularity of Christian ethics as unacceptable, nor does it challenge as invalid an inference made in the reasoning based on those premises. Rather it tends to satisfy itself with vague expressions of discontent, floating rather free of any fundamental issues. Thus it strikes a curious pose – as one might in complaining of a theory of gravity not that it is wrong, but that it will make flying more difficult! It hardly adds to its lustre by seeking to 'psychologise' the concern for particularity, as when Hauerwas's critics portray him as moved by an understandable temptation to preserve the identity of the church in the face of contemporary anxieties as to its specific role and mission. One might limit oneself to noting that this game can be played in reverse – then the advocate of particularity explains that he or she understands only too well the temptation to minimise or ignore particularity for the sake of social and intellectual esteem and out of fear of an accusation of intellectual parochialism. But, since the game proceeds just as well from this end as from the other, it is better not played at all.

What substance, however, can we give to the charge of sectarianism? We shall seek to understand and reply to it in three steps. In the first place, we will note that the making of this charge often trades on a certain ambiguity between descriptive and evaluative senses of sectarianism. In the second place, we will consider what the advocates of a 'public theology' demand by way of a proof of non-sectarianism. And then, in the third place, we shall ask whether there is any reason to think that a Christian ethics which refused these demands need be withdrawn or isolated in any interesting sense, and shall conclude this section by saying that the charges are not made out. (Whether this is to show that the position defended is not sectarian, or that it is, but that it does not matter, is of no great

---

[83] S. Hauerwas, 'Will the Real Sectarian Stand Up?', *Theology Today*, 44 (1987), 94.

consequence; it is simply to note that here description and evaluation are two tasks and that the second is not adequately accomplished by the critics.) In the next section, we shall put to one side the slightly defensive tone which we might be thought to adopt in dealing with these critics, and argue not simply that dogmatic ethics can speak to the world but that, as against its critics, it can speak to the world with a moral and intellectual seriousness which they most plainly cannot.

In Troeltsch's much cited characterisation of a sect it is:

a voluntary society, composed of strict and definite Christian believers bound to each other by the fact that all have experienced 'the new birth'. These 'believers' live apart from the world, are limited to small groups, emphasise the law instead of grace, and in varying degrees within their own circle set up the Christian order, based on love; all this is done in preparation for and expectation of the coming of the Kingdom of God.[84]

It will be obvious that there is nothing sacrosanct about this characterisation. Troeltsch's identification and description of the sect as a form of organisation of believers to be distinguished from the church-type is what Bryan Wilson terms a 'stereotype' or 'ideal type'[85] and thus an 'extended hypothesis and prox-imate definition' which can thus be modified and refined as the empirical evidence suggests.[86] But nothing turns theologically, so to say, on whether or not the honing of the definition places one within or outside the category. If the criteria are reduced so that 'cognitive dissonance' with the host society is sufficient for one to qualify as 'sectarian', then so be it – if one wakes up to find oneself a sectarian, it is not (like waking to find oneself Arian) a cause for groaning. And, if one happens to be alarmed, or if someone supposes that a person so labelled ought to be alarmed, all that is going on is that a sociological description is mistakenly reckoned to be, of itself, an important theological evaluation.

[84] E. Troeltsch, *The Social Teaching of the Christian Churches*, trans. O. Wyon (London, 1931), vol. II, 993.

[85] B. Wilson, *Social Dimensions of Sectarianism* (Oxford, 1990), 2–3; see also *Religious Sects* (London, 1970), ch. 2.

[86] B. Wilson, 'Sects' in *Dictionary of Ethics, Theology and Society*, ed. P. B. Clarke and A. Linzey (London, 1996).

That one is descriptively a sectarian in terms of a sociological category is of no account, as such. Suppose, however, that there is no intention to achieve a condemnation of one's opponents simply by a sleight of hand of labelling, what might be judged objectionable in those who are reckoned to be sectarian? We can arrive at an answer to this question by addressing it in a slightly different form: what is it that the advocates and defenders of the importance of a 'public theology' demand by way of a proof of non-sectarianism? For all the deep differences between them, the four critics we shall look at – Tracy, Gustafson, McCormick and Thiemann – each demand essentially the same thing of an ethics which could be deemed public and non-sectarian: belief in the possibility, and commitment to the practice, of versions of what in Barth's terms is an apologetic ethic (that is, to give his definition again, an ethic which attempts to justify itself 'within the framework and on the foundation of the presuppositions and methods of non-theological, of general thinking and language'[87]). Unless one makes this commitment, one is, so it seems, to be deemed sectarian.

According to Tracy in *The Analogical Imagination*, theology is inherently public because it addresses the questions which 'are fundamental for any authentically human existence' and thus the questions of 'any fellow human being'.[88] It answers these questions by reference to a 'religious reality' witnessed to by 'the symbols of explicitly religious traditions', which are in turn to be understood as further expressions of the 'religious dimension to the everyday disclosed in limit-situations and limit-questions'.[89] And the publicness of its questions and answers is not, so to say, contingent – 'God as understood as by the Jewish, Christian or Muslim believer is either universal in actuality or sheer delusion . . . Any authentic speech on the reality of God which is really private or particularist is unworthy of that reality. . . If this faith in God is serious, then any discourse about it must be universal and public.'[90] Indeed, 'except for

[87] Barth, *Church Dogmatics*, II: 2, 520. See footnote 21.
[88] D. Tracy, *The Analogical Imagination* (New York, 1981), 4.
[89] Tracy, *The Analogical Imagination*, 11.
[90] Tracy, *The Analogical Imagination*, 51–2.

versions of Christian theology that are explicitly or implicitly sectarian . . . the universalist thrust of Christian self-understanding demands a real affirmation of the world and thereby a real coming to terms with the publics of society and academy'.[91] But what exactly does this 'affirmation' and 'real coming to terms' – this publicness – require of the theologian? '[T]he word "public" here refers to the articulation of fundamental questions and answers which any attentive, intelligent, reasonable and responsible person can understand and judge in keeping with fully public criteria for argument.'[92] Nor does this demand pose any problem; what is required in theory is possible in practice: 'In the western tradition of ethical philosophy, for example, one finds authentically public ways to discuss policy issues. Whether those ways be based upon teleological, deontological, axiological or responsibility models for ethical reasoning, or upon some "mixed theory", there seems little doubt that all ethical arguments are in principle open to all intelligent, reasonable and responsible persons.'[93]

According to Gustafson 'Hauerwas's is an intellectual and moral sectarianism of the most extreme sort'[94] which has the effect of 'isolating Christianity from taking seriously the wider world of science and culture and limits the participation of Christians in the ambiguities of moral and social life in the patterns of interdependence in the world'.[95] But 'faithful witness to Jesus is not a sufficient theological and moral basis for addressing the moral and social problems of the twentieth century. The theologian addressing many issues – nuclear, social justice, ecology, and so forth – must do so as an outcome of a theology that develops God's relation to all aspects of life in the world, and develops those relations in terms which are not exclusively Christian in sectarian form.'[96] A model for this theology is provided, says Gustafson, by Aquinas: 'It seems to

---

[91] Tracy, *The Analogical Imagination*, 50.
[92] Tracy, *The Analogical Imagination*, 63.
[93] Tracy, *The Analogical Imagination*, 9.
[94] Gustafson, 'Response to Critics', 196.
[95] J. Gustafson, 'The Sectarian Temptation: Reflections on Theology, Church, and the University', *Proceedings of the Catholic Theological Society*, 40 (1985), 84.
[96] Gustafson, 'The Sectarian Temptation', 93.

me that what Thomas Aquinas did was similar to what I have done, namely to use a contemporary understanding of the relations of things to each other in nature, society, and culture as indications of how God is related to and is ordering the world and thus the ground of morality.'[97] For Hauerwas, however, 'nature is . . . of no ethical significance as a source of direction in [his] ethics' – a sentence of rather uncertain meaning, but which, given the wider context of Gustafson's thought, seems to complain of Hauerwas that he eschews an apologetic ethics which makes reference to nature as a common arbiter of morality.[98]

McCormick's complaints tread a similar path. Hauerwas is accused of a 'counterproductive sectarianism' as a result of which 'what goes for moral theology will increasingly become . . . sectarian exhortation' and 'inherently isolationist'.[99] 'What it seems . . . Hauerwas is actually doing is denying the relevance, perhaps even the existence, for the Christian, of what has been badly called for centuries the natural moral law.'[100] And again, Hauerwas's methodology, so we are told, 'is deeply antithetical to the natural law method of Catholic moral theology. It does not pretend to be based on a universally valid stand applicable to all persons irrespective of their story. In this sense it may be called sectarian.'[101]

---

[97] Gustafson, 'Response to Critics', 189.

[98] For doubts about the moral perception of nature on which Gustafson's own theory depends, see S. Toulmin, 'Nature and Nature's God', *Journal of Religious Ethics*, 13 (1985), 37–52.

[99] R. McCormick, *Notes on Moral Theology: 1981 Through 1984* (Lanham, MD, 1984), 27 and 23–4.

[100] McCormick, *Notes on Moral Theology*, 26.

[101] McCormick, *Notes on Moral Theology*, 125. It is interesting to observe that McCormick is content to offer arguments of no great weight against Hauerwas. McCormick contends, for example, that the existence of knowledge of the natural law 'is admitted, so many exegetes argue, in Romans, where the fault of non-believers is said to be precisely suppressing such knowledge . . . If Hauerwas exalts Christian warrants so much that he denies the existence of such knowledge . . . it must be said that he has diminished the very Christian story to which he appeals, for part of that story is that basic moral knowledge and correlative justifications are not exclusive to this community' (24). If this is thought to be a serious point one might have expected McCormick to rely on something more solid than the authority of certain unnamed 'exegetes'; certainly there is a discussion to be had about the relevant passages in Romans, but the implicit supposition that they constitute a knock-down argument against Hauerwas is hardly sustainable. One can be no more charitable towards the

Thiemann is an interesting case because he is at once sympathetic to important elements in Hauerwas's position while at the same time more than slightly troubled by the consequences which Hauerwas's position seems to have for the possibility of what Thiemann refers to as 'public theology'. On the face of it, Thiemann should hardly be listed with those who think that public theology must be founded on a belief in the natural law. Indeed, in his *Constructing a Public Theology: The Church in a Pluralistic Culture*, he is distinctly sympathetic to the case for the theological particularity of ethics and to the possibility of such an ethics having a public voice.[102] Thus he 'seeks to show that a theology shaped by the biblical narratives

observation that Hauerwas's methodology commits him to thinking that Christian moral claims are 'limited in application to a particular historical community as if it were wrong to abort Catholic babies but perfectly all right to do so with Muslim, Protestant or Jewish babies' (127). Here McCormick simply misses the point that the universality of the Christian story, and thus the universality of the demands it makes on human action, are logically quite distinct from the universality of knowledge of that story and its demands; thus, while denying the universality of knowledge of the Gospel, we may still say with Bonhoeffer (*Ethics*, 322) that 'the whole law and the whole Gospel belong equally to all men'. Nor does McCormick do much to advance his case with his comment on Yoder's scepticism concerning the availability of a shared public language for moral debate he claims that Yoder observes 'the use of justice language commonly available to all "hardly helped" debates about abortion funding, multinational corporations, and arms limitation'. There are many reasons', replies McCormick, 'other than justice language for this "hardly helped": for instance ingrained interests and ideology, the complexity of the matter, differing metaethical suppositions, etc.' (128). This is all as may be, but the plausibility of a theory is hardly enhanced when the failure to observe what the theory predicts is quite as prevalent as it surely is in the case of the natural law theory McCormick supports as O'Donovan observes 'the *epistemological* programme for an ethic that is "natural", in the sense that its contents are simply known to all, has to face dauntingly high barriers' (*Resurrection and Moral Order*, 19). Appeals to 'ideal observers' are certainly possible as a way of overcoming these barriers, even when these appeals are made by the Vatican against Roman Catholic laity and theologians (as on such matters as contraception); but the frequency of such appeals is in danger of giving the game away that for this theory the compatibility between Christian moral truth and natural moral knowledge is most definitely asserted a priori and on the basis of some rather sketchy theology, so far as we can tell from McCormick (or Gustafson or Tracy).

[102] R. F. Thiemann, *Constructing a Public Theology: The Church in a Pluralistic Culture* (Louisville, 1991). Indeed, he maintains that in his book *Revelation and Theology: The Gospel as Narrated Promise* (Notre Dame, IN, 1985) he had argued 'that Christian theology ought to be both "nonfoundational" and "descriptive", eschewing general explanatory schemes and seeking to provide a "justification of Christian belief [that] is specific to the Christian faith, community and tradition"'; he is thus a critic of Tracy (23).

and grounded in the practices of the Christian community can provide resources to enable people of faith to regain a public voice in our pluralistic culture'.[103] Furthermore, he is, so he reckons, an admirer of Barth, and claims we can 'receive both instruction and support for our task' from his theology.[104]

Inspite of these declared sympathies, however, Thiemann is uneasy:

theologies that seek to preserve the characteristic language and patterns of Christian narrative and practice too often fail to engage the public realm in an effective and responsible fashion. Either they eschew public discourse altogether in order to preserve what they see as the uniqueness of Christian life, or they enter the public fray with single-minded ferocity, heedless of the pluralistic traditions of our democratic polity.[105]

Who does he have in mind and what exactly is the sin of which they are guilty? Hauerwas and Lindbeck are, it seems, the culprits since he mentions the need to distinguish his position from theirs.[106] But the nature of their sin is more difficult to determine. Suppose for the moment that the charge against Hauerwas is warranted (even though it is not) – suppose, that is to say, that Hauerwas really does eschew 'public discourse altogether in order to preserve . . . the uniqueness of Christian life' or enters 'the public fray with single-minded ferocity, heedless of the pluralistic traditions of our democratic polity', or both. As such, this tells us nothing of interest – the fact that Hauerwas does not do the one thing or does the other, or both, may, for all we know, be a matter of temperament rather than of deep theory. But Thiemann thinks it is a matter of theory, not simply of temperament; those strategies of the type to which he objects 'assume that our differences are so profound that we cannot work together for some common human good. All have abandoned the hope that we can forge a political community in which genuine disagreement and genuine conviction can coexist.'[107] Against such positions he 'argue[s] . . . that one of

103 Thiemann, *Constructing a Public Theology*, 19.
104 Thiemann, *Constructing a Public Theology*, 92.
105 Thiemann, *Constructing a Public Theology*, 19.
106 Thiemann, *Constructing a Public Theology*, 12.
107 Thiemann, *Constructing a Public Theology*, 119.

the most important political tasks for the contemporary Christian community is to be a community of hope in a culture that is increasingly cynical about our common human future'.[108]

Now no one would deny that the Christian community should exhibit the virtue of hope, but its being appropriately hopeful is not a matter of its hoping for anything we care to name. To be specific, is a hope that we can 'work together for some common human good' or that we have a 'common human future' an appropriate hope to have, theologically speaking? It does not obviously look to be so, nor does Thiemann really argue that it is a theological hope. But if the hope is not grounded theologically, where is it grounded? Should we not suspect that Thiemann's faith in the possibility of this 'common human future' reveals, in spite of his debts to MacIntyre (or perhaps because of these debts), a faith that there is some account of the human good which can be agreed upon apart from any religious convictions, and thus form the basis for political life? And what is this but a faith in the possibility of something like a natural law argument, even if one relatively modest in its ambitions? (We are reminded of Alvin Plantinga's observation that 'we are all peeping Thomists'.) Thus Thiemann's implied criticism of Hauerwas and Lindbeck is one with which we are already very familiar – only an apologetic Christian ethic allows the Christian moralist to engage 'the public realm in an effective and responsible fashion'.

To Tracy, Gustafson, McCormick and Thiemann, then, we may pose the same question. Is there any reason to think that a Christian ethics, fully aware of its own particularity, and possessed of no a priori faith in the possibility of finding a realm of autonomous values with which it can make common cause, need be withdrawn or isolated from public discussion? Does dogmatic ethics deprive Christianity of a public voice? Must one somehow abandon the viewpoint of a dogmatic ethics if one is to take a part in public discussion?

It is tempting to observe quite simply that these objections betray, amongst other things, a distinct and rather severe failure

---

[108] Thiemann, *Constructing a Public Theology*, 25.

of imagination, which ought to be dispelled by the truism that even non-democrats vote in elections. (Indeed, remembering the slogan heard in Balliol JCR at the times of student elections – 'Vote early, vote often' – one might add that far from being prevented from taking a part in public life, non-democrats can take a fuller part than many others.) Or again, supposing the failure of imagination to be rather too severe to be dealt with thus, perhaps one could point out that the dialectical strategies of Socrates, Kierkegaard and Wittgenstein, to name but three, can hardly be accounted for by those who suppose that all argument is essentially aimed at the justification of belief on some common ground. But, if these gentle ways of making the point are insufficiently explicit, one might add a number of comments.

The complaint that we are entertaining fails to note the rich range of argumentative strategies and objectives which are open even to those who doubt the general possibility of achieving consensus concerning the truth, apart, that is, from reliance on theological presuppositions. That is to say, that if dogmatic ethics does not rule out that sometimes the only words it can appropriately address to a particular situation are those declared by Hosea – 'Ephraim has joined himself to idols, leave him alone' (4: 17) – there is no reason to suppose that this will be its only mode of address (nor even that where it does so speak that this does not itself constitute a mode of address specifically directed at the reform of the situation). On other occasions it may enter public debate with different words on its lips, set on accomplishing one or more of a range of tasks. It may seek to test the claims of those who pretend that their own ethical positions are well grounded; it may choose to examine not the alleged grounds but the consistency of these positions; it may think it worth exploring the wider presuppositions and implications of certain moral claims so as to draw those who support them to other conclusions which they have not yet embraced; or it may explore those same presuppositions and implications with a view to exposing those which might render the previous position dubious to some who have hitherto supported it; sometimes it may enter the field to assert what it knows to be good and right in the hope that 'the wisdom and patience of God, and the inconsequence of men', as Barth puts it,[109] may yet find it supporters amongst those who may, strictly speaking, have no fully adequate reason for supporting it. Far from being disabled from engaging with the public realm, dogmatic ethics may do all these things and more.

One example of the variety of types of engagement possible for dogmatic ethics must suffice. A theologian who is concerned to maintain the tradition of Christian teaching in relation to abortion may profitably compare the work of philosophers in addressing questions associated on the one hand with the beginning of human life, and on the other hand with the environment. In the case of abortion and the like, a good number of secular philosophers have developed an account of what it is to be morally considerable in terms of the possession of an interest, and, in turn, an account of the possession of an interest which denies that the foetus does or could possess an interest in life. Thus, to cite a particular instance of this argument, according to Michael Tooley, what 'makes an individual a person – that is, that makes the destruction of something intrinsically wrong . . . – is the property of being an enduring subject of non-momentary interests'.[110] Now since Tooley holds that the possession of such interests in turn requires the possession of certain rational capacities, and since he deems the potential to exercise those capacities in the future irrelevant to the present status of a human being, not only the unborn but also the newborn (and others too) are reckoned not to be wronged by their destruction.

Down the corridor, so to say, secular philosophers with a concern for the environment have been explicating and defending some rather more generous accounts of what it is to have an interest and thus, in this way of seeing things, of what it is to be morally considerable. To use the terminology of this area of debate, anthropocentrism (the view that only humans

---

[109] Barth, *Church Dogmatics*, II: 2, 542.
[110] M. Tooley, *Abortion and Infanticide* (Oxford, 1983), 303.

are morally considerable),[111] has given way to zoocentrism (the view that animals are such too),[112] which has been attacked by biocentrism (according respect to living things),[113] which has itself been criticised by ecocentrism (which judges living systems morally considerable).[114] And, typically, the move from one to other has involved an argument which maintains that the basis of moral regard for humans in actual fact provides the grounds for the extension of that regard to other, wider classes of being; so, for example, Taylor has maintained that zoocentrism is mistaken in regarding sentience as a necessary condition for possessing an interest, and that the capacity to flourish possessed by lower animals and plants is itself sufficient.

My point here is not to comment on these various debates but to note that even the theologian who doubts the ability of an apologetic strategy to maintain traditional teaching on the subject of abortion in the face of contemporary dissent, may yet have some helpful work to do in encouraging one body of philosophers to take note of the fact that there is another body who regards as quite evidently stipulative the accounts of interest which the former favour in providing a rationale for current practice in relation to abortion.[115] At the very least the theologian may perform a useful role in reminding those who are inclined to take the first group of philosophers seriously that the second group stands in the way.

Of course, these remarks are by no means intended to amount to a typology of the varieties of public discourse in which dogmatic ethics may engage, but they ought to be enough to indicate something of the range of strategies it may employ without in any way qualifying its refusal of apologetics. Sectarian or not, dogmatic ethics is by no means unable to raise its voice in the public arena, not only in sharp condemnation of

111 E.g., J. Passmore, *Man's Responsibility for Nature: Ecological Problems and the Western Tradition* (New York, 1974) and, more briefly, 'Attitudes to Nature' in *Nature and Conduct*, ed. R. S. Peters (New York, 1975), 251–64.

112 E.g., T. Regan, *The Case for Animal Rights* (Berkeley, 1983).

113 E.g., P. W. Taylor, *Respect for Nature: A Theory of Environmental Ethics* (Princeton, 1986).

114 E.g., L. Johnson, *A Morally Deep World* (Cambridge, 1991).

115 For a careful critique of Tooley see R. Hursthouse, *Beginning Lives* (Oxford, 1987), esp. 107–17.

certain secular practices, but also in other modes too. In all cases, it does so on the basis of its own distinctive premise (namely, the premise of faith in the life, death and resurrection of Jesus Christ), a distinctiveness it can only betray when it allows its contribution to be determined apart from this ground. Far from making dialogue impossible we might even say that such an understanding of our engagement with the public realm is a precondition of it, since where one partner in a conversation allows his or her contribution to be decisively shaped by the need to avoid disagreement, what results is not dialogue at all but the absurd (and finally rather patronising) attempt to echo in advance the views of the other. Christianity should not submit to such policing, let alone subject itself to such policing – where it does, we find that it speaks with a voice not at all its own: typically in our day, the voice of a bourgeois liberalism which, for example, celebrates the availability of abortion and euthanasia as an expansion of the realm of choice or the practice of cohabitation as 'on the way to marriage'. Declining this policing, self-imposed or otherwise, Christian ethics may quite genuinely take part in a dialogue of the sort which a supposedly pluralist society ought, so one would have thought, to welcome – a dialogue between those who differ, aimed at the negotiation of a public policy which those who differ may none the less, to some extent, support.

Our account of the nature and character of dogmatic ethics should not, however, end on this rather defensive note, with our parrying of the charge that dogmatic ethics is, in the usual and derogatory sense, sectarian because cut off from contemporary debate and discussion. Instead, let us note that in an earlier usage the word 'sect' was capable of meaning something rather different from that which it does now: thus where the *Romaunt of the Rose* observes 'ne were ther generacioun Our sectis strene to save' (4589), it refers to nothing less than the human race. Understanding 'sect' and thus 'sectarian' in that earlier and universal sense, let us now claim that dogmatic ethics is truly sectarian – that is, that it can and does speak to the world with a universality which an apologetic ethics of the kind favoured by Tracy, McCormick, Gustafson and Thiemann cannot. To be specific, the dogmatic ethics we have outlined, far from being isolationist, tribal, cut off or whatever, can alone engage the modern world fully and confidently.

But which world is this? We have been treating the objection we have entertained against dogmatic ethics as if the 'world' from which dogmatic ethics is said to be cut off is not itself in need of some specification. But the moment we attend to this matter we shall see that dogmatic ethics does indeed inhabit the world, supposing the world is that of Feuerbach, Nietzsche, Marx, Darwin, Freud and Foucault, the world of the 'genealogists', to use MacIntyre's label for them, the world which has shaped irrevocably the modern mind and is thus the world not only of these, but also of Tolstoi, Dostoevsky, Camus, Manet and Conrad. It is this world, so we shall claim, which dogmatic ethics can inhabit and address, an altogether larger world than the world of the apologists which is still, we might say, the world of Archdeacon Paley and moral sentiments, the world not of Tolstoi, Dostoevsky and the like, but really the rather smaller world of John Betjeman and Barbara Pym.

v

In the patio littered with straw, a practicante, one of Dr Monygham's native assistants, sat on the ground with his back against the rim of the fountain fingering a guitar discreetly, while two girls of the lower class, standing before him, shuffled their feet a little and waved their arms, humming a popular dance tune. Most of the wounded during the two days of rioting had been taken away by their friends and relations, but several figures could be seen sitting up balancing their bandaged heads in time to the music. Charles Gould dismounted. A sleepy mozo coming out of the bakery door took hold of the horse's bridle; the practicante endeavoured to conceal his guitar hastily; the girls, unabashed, stepped back smiling; and Charles Gould, on his way to the staircase, glanced into a dark corner of the patio at another group, a mortally wounded Cargador with a women kneeling by his side; she mumbled prayers rapidly, trying at the same time to force a piece of orange between the stiffening lips of the dying man.[116]

This quietly observed moment stands at the very centre of

---

[116] J. Conrad, *Nostromo*, ed. C. Watts (London, 1995), 264–5.

Conrad's unfolding in *Nostromo* of the story of the Gould concession, the great silver mine which dominates the town of Sulaco
as much as does the mountain in which it is found. And it is
right that this juxtaposition of the shuffling feet and the
mumbled prayers should stand at the centre; for it is this
juxtaposition of a shadowy joy with a sorrow tinged with hope
which provides a simple and striking human witness to the
'irreconcilable antagonisms' of which, according to Conrad,
human life, and with it the world, are made up.[117]
These 'irreconcilable antagonisms' fatally subvert the
reading of existence favoured by Captain Mitchell, who was
'utterly in the dark, and imagining himself in the thick of
things'.[118] For Mitchell, 'Almost every event out of the usual
daily course "marked an epoch" . . . or else was "history";
unless with his pomposity struggling with a discomfited droop
of his rubicund, rather handsome face, set off by snow white
close hair and short whiskers, he would mutter – "Ah, that!
That, sir, was a mistake."'[119] Supplementing these two categories ('history' and 'mistake') Mitchell has at his disposal a
third: '"Sir," he used to say afterwards, "that was no mistake. It
was a fatality. A misfortune, pure and simple, sir."'[120] Such a
reading of existence, which seems to place some events on the
side of history or of progress, some against, and treats others as
mere contingencies with which history or its opponents must
deal, will not, however, suffice for the story of which Mitchell is
himself a part.[121] So it is that years later the 'privileged
passengers', calling in at Sulaco and finding Mitchell their host
and guide in the town, would, at the end of the long day, 'listen
like a tired child to a fairy tale'.[122] For Mitchell's story is

---

[117] Conrad, Letter to New York Times, cited by K. Carradine in introduction to
Nostromo (Oxford, 1984), viii.
[118] Conrad, *Nostromo*, 86.   [119] Ibid.
[120] Conrad, *Nostromo*, 99.
[121] According to R. Roussel, *The Metaphysics of Darkness* (Baltimore, 1971), 'The process
by which Gould's idealistic visions of rational justice are born in reaction to the
moral darkness of Costaguana and then are, in turn, transformed into only another
manifestation of this darkness is symbolic not only of the law which ordains his
personal fate but of the law which has determined the whole history of his country'
(128).
[122] Conrad, *Nostromo*, 353.

nothing but a fairy tale; there is no history to be discerned in the events which have turned one way and then another, only to end where they have begun. The idealistic political schemes which have been hatched and seemingly accomplished are, at one and the same time, history, mistakes and fatalities, so that the great sceptic Decoud's comment on such schemes – 'ploughing the sea'[123] – is the only judgment which the story will bear.

The opacity of human existence with its 'irreconcilable antagonisms' is an opacity which spreads itself necessarily over the moral world. Decoud, who sees that history is not history in Mitchell's sense, who as he sails into the darkness of the vast gulf which separates Sulaco from the sea finds that no intelligence could overcome its 'impenetrable obscurity',[124] finally 'lost all belief in the reality of his action past and to come'.[125] And this is right – for the two great actors of the story, Nostromo himself and Charles Gould, themselves become the servants of the silver of the mine which they seek to control and use, but which subverts their actions. In the darkness of the Gulf, there can be no clear-sighted knowledge of the good and the right; what is left is a human uncertainty which at one and the same time shuffles its feet in a rather desultory dance or moves its lips in a prayer which can only be mumbled.

The point we are making allusively can be briefly elaborated by reference to the recent work of the most subtle of apologists, Alasdair MacIntyre. MacIntyre's attempt to develop an account of moral reasoning and justification as highly tradition-specific, whilst at the same time offering an account of how traditions may lay claim to, and indeed contest alternative claims to, rational justification, represents a position for which what I have termed dogmatic ethics will have a certain sympathy – it promises, after all, to protect to a considerable extent, the particularity of moral vision and practice which we attribute to the Christian tradition. Looked at from the other side, however, the confidence that the superior rationality of the Christian position can (or must?) be universally displayed, seems to

[123] Conrad, *Nostromo*, 140.
[124] Conrad, *Nostromo*, 207.   [125] Conrad, *Nostoromo*, 361.

represent a continuing affinity with the aspirations of the so-called 'enlightenment project' of which MacIntyre has been such a stern and penetrating critic. This continuing affinity is expressed in particular in MacIntyre's presentation of the resolution of the dispute between moral realism and moral relativism as one which depends crucially on the willingness of advocates of a realist viewpoint to maintain, inter alia, that any moral traditional they support is capable of exhibiting its argumentative superiority to its rivals. In MacIntyre's words

> if the scheme and mode of justification to which they at present appeal to support the conclusions which constitute their own account of the moral life were to turn out to be, as a result of further enquiry, incapable of providing the resources for exhibiting its argumentative superiority to such a rival, then it must be capable of being replaced by some scheme and mode of justification which does possess the resources *both* for providing adequate rational support for their account and for exhibiting its rational superiority to any scheme and mode of justification which supports conclusions incompatible with central theses of that account. For otherwise no claim to truth could be sustained.[126]

The possibility that is overlooked is the one which is central to the work of Barth and Bonhoeffer alike; that is, to put it in MacIntyre's terms, that the 'genealogists' need not be overcome by the demonstration of the existence of an epistemological space in which rational ethics can make its way, but that needing no such space in which to speak, the Church may maintain its knowledge of good and evil as given in and with knowledge of God, and thus, as itself gracious revelation. MacIntyre, on the other hand, along with any others who seek to establish ethics apologetically, must repudiate to a greater or lesser extent the world as it is construed and presented by the genealogists. Contrary to the claims of the latter, there must be some secure bridgehead from which knowledge of good and evil can advance – it might be, for example, from a knowledge of what properly belongs to human nature. Dogmatic ethics, however, claims no such bridgehead and hence does not

---

[126] MacIntyre, 'Moral Relativism, Truth and Justification', 12.

require a repudiation of the genealogists in so far as their understanding of the world, in which claims to knowledge of the truly human are irredeemably insecure, is understood as precisely what it is – an account of the limits of a human understanding of the world. Humanly speaking the world is properly known as it is here represented. But dogmatic ethics does not know the world humanly speaking; the ground which the genealogists have taken away is not the ground on which it stands. It does not need to live in a world where there is a knowledge of the good and the right on which it can build, or to which it can appeal.

Who, we might wonder, are the sectarians now, understanding 'sectarian' in the sense in which it was used *against* dogmatic ethics? Is it not those who must look on the genealogists' portrayals of the modern predicament and judge them somewhat exaggerated? Are not the sectarians those who, to be blunt, endeavour to inhabit the eighteenth century rather than the twentieth? If so, the dogmatic ethicist can not only repudiate the label 'sectarian' in the narrow sense, but can quite properly claim the label in its different and wider sense, since the world which dogmatic ethics addresses is not some idealised world which is, in actual fact, unknown to its inhabitants, but the very world they inhabit in all its questionableness and ambiguity. Of course, this is not to lay the grounds for another form of apologetics. There is no place within this world from which Christianity can speak; but because Christianity cannot speak from within this world, it does not follow that Christianity cannot speak to it.

As witness on this point let us note the unwitting testimony of Nietzsche: for did not Nietzsche himself implicitly and perversely pay tribute to Christianity of this sort – Christianity which speaks from its unfounded givenness and not from some supposed point of contact – in maintaining his virulent attack against it into his last works? He did not bother himself with exposing or parading the philosophical and historical weaknesses of various forms of Christian apologetics – 'God is dead' – and such engagements were beneath one who thought of himself (in *Ecce Homo*) as 'a destiny, breaking the history of humanity into two parts'.[127] 'Why is it' then, Barth asks, 'that he must finally act in this matter as if there were no other foe upon earth, and no more urgent task than to vanquish it?'[128] Is it not because he knew that in a world which had destroyed the ground on which some had sought to found their faith, presenting it as a reasonable philosophy or as a probable historical conjecture, Christianity still deserved the energies he devoted to attacking it just because it might speak authentically and forcefully as a rejection of worldly wisdom and as the proclamation of a wisdom from elsewhere?

VI

'Reason, moral fanaticism, conscience, duty, free responsibility and silent virtues, these', writes Bonhoeffer, 'are the achievements and attitudes of a noble humanity'.

It is the best of men who go under in this way, with all that they can do or be. Here is the immortal figure of Don Quixote, the knight of the doleful countenance, who takes a barber's dish for a helmet and a miserable hack for a charger and who rides into endless battles for the love of a lady who does not exist. That is how it looks when an old world ventures to take up arms against a new one and when a world of the past hazards an attack against the superior forces of the common-place and mean . . . It is a mean-spirited man who can read of what befell Don Quixote and not be stirred to sympathy. Yet our business now is to replace our rusty swords with sharp ones.[129]

What are these sharp swords, which can serve us better than the various strategies which, though based on 'the achievements and attitudes of a noble humanity', are finally ineffectual? Simplicity and wisdom says Bonhoeffer – the first consists in fixing 'one's eye solely on the simple truth of God at a time when all concepts are being confused, distorted and turned upside down'. And 'simplicity becomes wisdom', since 'the wise man is the one who sees reality as it is, and who sees into the depths of things. That is why only that man is wise who sees

---

[127] F. Nietzsche, *Ecce Homo*, trans. R. J. Hollingdale (Harmondsworth, 1992), 103.
[128] Barth, *Church Dogmatics*, III: 2, 239.
[129] Bonhoeffer, *Ethics*, 49 50.

reality in God.'[130] But this, of course, is for Bonhoeffer, to see reality in Jesus Christ: 'It is in Jesus Christ that God's relation to the world is defined. We know of no relation of God to the world other than through Jesus Christ.'[131] And because we know of no other such relation we can, says Bonhoeffer, only refuse the 'view that the Church can speak to the world on the basis of some particular rational or natural-law knowledge which she shares with the world, that is to say, with an occasional temporary disregard for the Gospel.'[132]

So it is, according to Bonhoeffer, the business of Christian ethics to dispense with its rusty swords and to prefer to them the sharper sword placed in its hands by the Word of God which, enabling it to see reality in Jesus Christ, enables it to know that reality aright. But let us complete the circle and return from where we began by stressing that if the Christian ethicist takes up this sword it is a sword which, like the action of God, serves our liberation. It is a sword, that is to say, which cuts the ropes of all those myths and ideologies to which the world is subject and which bind and constrain its inhabitants and prevent that truly human action which it is the purpose of God's action in Christ to evoke and evince. If sometimes, then, the Christian ethicist must say 'No', and say it with a certain resoluteness and determination, he or she knows just as well that this is not the first and proper word of Christian ethics, and that if it is said at all, it is only said for the sake of that proper word, which proclaims in each and every sphere of human life the liberation of that sphere by the liberating action of God in Christ. Thus Christian ethics may and must take as its proper theme not a negative but a wholly positive and evangelical one; its motto is provided by words of Paul in his Second Letter to the Cor-inthians: 'As surely as God is faithful our word to you is not "Yes" and "No". For the Son of God, Jesus Christ, who was preached among you . . . was not "Yes" and "No", but in him it has always been "Yes" ' (2 Corinthians, 1: 18–19).

---

[130] Bonhoeffer, *Ethics*, 50.   [131] Bonhoeffer, *Ethics*, 321.   [132] Ibid.

CHAPTER 2

Christian anthropology at the beginning and end of life[1]

I

If theological ethics speaks about man, it does not have in view man as he understands himself but man as he knows that he is understood, as he finds himself addressed by the Word of God that has come to him.[2]

Christian medical ethics, in so far as it is *Christian* medical ethics, speaks on the basis of the distinctive knowledge of humankind which is given by the Word of God. It thus does not and cannot make common cause with 'bioethics', or 'biomedical ethics', as these are usually practised, for as thus practised they do not view humankind in the light of this knowledge.[3]

---

[1] I am grateful to Ben Quash, Germain Grisez, Basil Mitchell, Michael Bourke, Alasdair McFadyen and my King's colleagues Doug Farrow, Colin Gunton, Brian Horne, Alan Torrance and Francis Watson, for their critical comments on an earlier draft of this chapter, which was given at a meeting of the Society for the Study of Theology. It will be obvious that what follows could be intended only as an outline of an argument which, to be fully satisfactory, would need a much more lengthy exposition than it can receive here. There is, however, I hope, some merit in the attempt to offer a map of a theological treatment of the questions with which it deals, even if the details of the case must await further statement.

[2] K. Barth, *Ethics*, ed. D. Braun, trans. G. Bromiley (Edinburgh, 1981), 461. Although this statement comes from one of Barth's relatively early works (that is, from lectures given in Münster in 1928 9) it is consistent with the anthropology which he developed some twenty years later in *Church Dogmatics*, III: 2, trans. H. Knight et al. (Edinburgh, 1960), from the insight that 'anthropology should be based on Christology and not the reverse' (46). Thus, 'in our exposition of the doctrine of man we must always look in the first instance at the nature of man as it confronts us in the person of Jesus and only secondarily asking and answering from this place of light at the nature of man as that of every man and all other men' (ibid.).

[3] Indeed, what is increasingly characteristic of bioethics is a pretence to viewing humankind from no-where, so to say; the cost of the pretence is, naturally enough, that bioethics is often rather obviously incomplete and arbitrary, being the application

47

Christian medical ethics is, rather, obliged to begin from its own starting place, taking up its constructive task from its unique and distinctive presupposition, namely the Gospel of Jesus Christ. For it is in the light of this Gospel of the Word spoken to humankind, that humankind gains a true self-understanding.

The subject of medical ethics can be thought of, we might say, as the beginning, being and ending of human life in so far as this beginning, being and ending properly become the concern of medicine and, in turn, pose ethical questions. On the basis of what has already been said, however, it will be clear that our very identification of these questions, as well as our answering of them, must be determined by the understanding of humankind gained from our knowledge of the Word of God. Thus it is appropriate to approach the concerns of this chapter by reflecting on a text which speaks of the decisive being of this Word, a being which is itself without beginning and ending: 'Fear not, I am the first and the last, and the living one.'[4] On the basis of the anthropology implicit in this text, we shall learn how we are to question contemporary medical practice at the beginning and end of life.[5]

II

The 'I am' who is the first and the last and the living one, is identified in the Book of Revelation with Jesus Christ, 'who is

---

to a variety of problems of values which, lacking a place in a coherent, cogent and compelling anthropology or metaphysics, amount to little more than barely comprehensible prohibitions and permissions: I have made out this charge in some further detail in a review article discussing *The Ethical Dimensions of the Biological Sciences* (Cambridge, 1993), ed. R. Bulger, E. Heitman and S. Reiser; see 'The Taboos of Bioethics', *Minerva*, 34 (1996), 199–204.

[4] Revelation, 1: 17. Biblical quotations in this chapter will be from the Revised Standard Version.

[5] The scope of this chapter would expand beyond manageable bounds if, as well as trying to illustrate the questions which Christian ethics poses to medical practice at the beginning and ending of human life, an attempt were made to illustrate the questions to be posed as regards the being of human of life. Something of what is required on this point, specifically in relation to gamete donation, is suggested in a chapter which is, however, chiefly concerned with other issues: ' "Who are my Mother and my Brothers?": Marx, Bonhoeffer and Benedict and the Redemption of the Family'.

and was and is to come'.[6] As the one who is, and was and is to come, he is the living one in a radically unqualified sense. Any other 'I am' is, so to say, a 'tensed proposition', to use Prior's term.[7] That is, if 'I am' is true of me, it is true now; but just as there was a time when it was not true, so there will come a time when it will not be true. It is a proposition which having become true, will cease to be true – or perhaps better, is true only during a specified time. But the proposition 'I am' affirmed of or by Jesus Christ is untensed. The stories of resurrection and ascension tell us that there is no time when this 'I am' will become an 'I was' – since on the third day he rose again and is now seated at the right hand of God. The story of the nativity interpreted in John's Gospel, tells that there is no time when his 'I am' was really an unspoken, or rather unspeakable, 'I shall be' – since the Word was, in the beginning, with God. This 'I am', Jesus Christ, simply is: there is no time in which he is not, for there is no time which is before Jesus Christ, and there is no time which is after Jesus Christ. This 'I am' is, was and will be – 'the living one'.

But we must say more even than this: not simply that the 'I am', Jesus Christ, is, was and will be; not simply that this 'I am', unlike any other 'I am', is eternally present and thus, without qualification, the living one. For, so our text tells us, he is not *at* the beginning and the end, but *is* the beginning and the end, 'the first and the last', 'the alpha and the omega'. It is not enough then, to affirm that there is no time which is before Jesus Christ and no time which is after Jesus Christ; it is not enough to say that there is no time in which he is not. Saying this we may seem to claim only that all time contains Jesus Christ, when what we must say rather is that Jesus Christ contains all time. That is, we must now affirm that there is no time which is not – we need a possessive – *Christian* time. For he

---

[6] Revelation, 1: 8; see the argument of Richard Bauckham's two recent treatments of the book of Revelation: *The Theology of the Book of Revelation* (Cambridge, 1993), esp. ch. 3, and *The Climax of Prophecy: Studies on the Book of Revelation* (Edinburgh, 1993), esp. ch. 4. In my reading of Revelation I have been greatly assisted by these studies. It will also be clear that I have taken up many points from Barth's reflections on 'Jesus, Lord of Time' in *Church Dogmatics*, III: 2, 437–511.

[7] See A. Prior, *Past, Present and Future* (Oxford, 1967).

is not present at the beginning, but is the beginning; he is not present at the end, but is the end. He is not from the first to the last, but is 'the first and the last', the one from whom and in whom is the beginning, and in whom and to whom is the end.

But our text says yet more – something which tells us that this affirmation is not the affirmation of esoteric knowledge concerning the true Lord of time. For it reads not simply 'I am the first and the last, and the living one' but *'Fear not*, I am the first and the last and the living one.' That is to say, it crucially connects the affirmation that Jesus Christ is Lord of time with the first word of the proclamation of the Gospel, 'fear not' – the word spoken at the becoming flesh of the 'I am', to shepherds, to Mary and to Joseph.[8]

Why is this connection made? How is it that the affirmation that Jesus Christ is the Lord of time, from and in whom is the beginning, and to and in whom is the end, is the basis for the great 'fear not!' of the Gospel? How and why does the text make this connection? The New Testament answers by saying that the revelation in the becoming flesh of the 'I am', is a revelation of the mystery that in him and through him God intends to be gracious to his creation. It is a revelation of the fact that God wills not to be against us, though we are against him, but wills to overcome this enmity by his offering of himself in Jesus Christ, through whom he intends the reconciliation and election of humankind and the manifestation of his glorious mercy. But this revelation in Jesus Christ is not a revelation of a moment in God's being – of, as it were, an impulse suddenly formed which might just as well be suddenly recanted. To confess that what was made flesh was this Word – which was in the beginning with God and was God, and is the beginning and the end, the first and the last and the living one – is to confess that within and without time, 'in human history, and beyond all history, human or otherwise, there is no other or higher law than that of the divine mercy, now revealed, established and applied in the oblation of the Lamb of God'.[9] Thus, just

---

[8] Luke, 2: 10 and 1: 30; Matthew 1: 20.
[9] Barth, *Church Dogmatics*, III: 2, 484.

because 'the future to which we look forward from the present of the man Jesus is, like this present itself, and the past which lies behind it, His time, the time of the man Jesus',[10] we are addressed by this 'fear not'.

All human action ordered in the light of what is the case is action which stands under this Gospel. If it does not understand this Gospel, if it does not hear and live by this 'fear not', it can only be action which arises from the confusions, illusions and mythologies which pass for truth in a world which lives in untruth, and is shaped, in particular, by the fear that both the past and the future are an abyss, a blank and threatening mystery, out of which the present must be snatched or against which it must be protected.

The practice of medicine, no more and no less than any other sphere of human action, is asked whether it orders itself in virtue of what is the case. It too must submit to the judgment of this reality, allowing its practice to be governed by the truth of the Gospel, if it is to be truthful medical practice. It too must answer the question as to whether its conduct arises from, is compatible with, and a fitting response to, the understanding of humankind declared in and by the history of Jesus Christ. Does it act at the beginning and ending, and in the being of human life, as towards those whose beginning, being and ending stands under the gracious being without beginning and ending of Jesus Christ? Does it act as towards those who are addressed by the decisive 'fear not' of the Gospel? Our contention will be that in various of its practices, some routine and some less routine, it does not so act – to take the two examples to be discussed, that in relation both to the unborn who are aborted or experimented upon, and to the dying who are killed, overtreated or neglected, it denies the reality that Jesus Christ is the first and the last. In both cases, so we shall argue, the decisive word of liberation and judgment comes from the Gospel with its declaration 'fear not!'

---

[10] Barth, *Church Dogmatics*, III: 2, 493.

III

Our first question is this: does medical practice believe that the past is the past of Jesus Christ?[11] It will be alleged that where it does not, it will tend either to its own abolition or to its own aggrandisement, either withdrawing from the service of the body, or wanting to manipulate and shape it, regarding the body as a proper object of human creativity and design. In either case, whether in repudiation of human life, or in its thorough-going manipulation, medicine would come to express a hatred of the body which is unknown to orthodox Christian thought and its associated forms of life and practice. As an example of Christian orthodoxy, we shall take the teaching of Augustine, arguing that his affirmation of the goodness of bodily life presupposes an anthropology shaped by the truth that the past is, like the present, a sphere of God's grace in Jesus Christ. We shall further argue that medicine's complicity in the destruction of the unborn is to be understood as presupposing an anthropology of a quite different sort, an anthropology which involves a repudiation of the good of the body, and thus expresses itself in hatred of it.[12]

The New Testament bears witness to the fact that the past is the past of Jesus Christ in the hope which it proclaims: a hope for the redemption *of* creation, not a hope for redemption *from* creation.[13] Christian hope for the liberation of the material

[11] It may be worth stressing that this formulation of the question is not meant to suggest that we might interrogate medicine on the basis of three distinct and discrete questions. There is really only one threefold question, for it is not as if medicine which reckoned with the past as a time of grace, but not with the present and the future, or which reckoned with the present as a time of grace in ignorance of the grace of yesterday and tomorrow, or which looked for the grace of the future, and knew nothing of its past or present reality, could be anything but seriously distorted. All medical practice must be interrogated in the light of the threefold affirmation and promise found in the text.

[12] Throughout the chapter I have found it convenient to speak of medicine as an acting subject. This is not intended to deny the following points; first, that it is not medicine, but doctors who do this or that; second, that many individual doctors act in ways which are opposed to the way of action I attribute to 'medicine'. In any case, this chapter is not concerned chiefly with attributing motives and intentions but with examining the underlying logic of actions which may be performed under a variety of rationales.

[13] O. M. T. O'Donovan, *Resurrection and Moral Order* (Leicester, 1986), 14ff.

world, not from it, is represented in two notable aspects of the Gospel narratives. In the first place, the coming of the kingdom of God which Jesus announces, begins to take form here and now through miracles which address the subjection of the creation to that which menaces and threatens it: thus, 'Go and tell John what you have seen and heard; the blind receive their sight, the lame walk, lepers are cleansed, and the deaf hear, the dead are raised up, the poor have good news preached to them.'[11] Secondly, for the Gospels, the resurrection of Jesus is manifestly the resurrection of his body – the empty tomb and the various post-resurrection meals bear witness to this truth, and so, quite unambiguously, do Jesus' wounds: thus, 'put out your hand, and place it in my side'.[15]

The New Testament knows no opposition between salvation and creation, and proclaims in Christ salvation of, not from, the material world, just because the living one is also the first. He is the one in whom 'all things were created, in heaven and on earth, visible and invisible, whether thrones or dominions or principalities or authorities – all things were created through him and for him.'[16] The grace of God shown in salvation is thus a continuation of the grace shown in creation, or better perhaps, its renewal – Christ does not come as the last to redeem us from a world for which he was not the first, but comes to restore and reconcile this world to its creator.

Such an understanding of salvation has implications for an understanding of the body, implications which led Christianity to distinguish itself in theory and in practice, though not without a certain difficulty and equivocation, from Platonism and Neoplatonism. The difficulty and equivocation has something to do with the fact that Platonic and Neoplatonic thought is more subtle than a simple and unexplicated charge of dualism supposes, so that the contrast between philosophy and Christianity can only be drawn with care.[17] Plotinus, for example, is

---

[11] Luke, 7: 22.   [15] John, 20: 27.   [16] Colossians, 1: 16.

[17] Thus, when R. Bultmann finds a negativity in Paul's 'treatment of the marriage question' in I Corinthians 7: 1–7 which is reckoned to be deeply influenced by 'the Hellenistic dualistic depreciation of the body', we may suspect that there has been a certain carelessness in the reading of the Greeks as in the reading of Paul – see

as scathing about gnostic dualism in regard to matter as many a Christian writer, and, according to Rist, 'there is no evidence that Plotinus thinks that the creation and the existence of the world is evil *per se*'.[18] What Plotinus does maintain, however, is that 'there will be no weakness in a soul which is wholly apart from matter'; from which 'It inevitably follows that there will only be weakness where there is matter, and thus entry into matter is the fall of the soul and its weakness.'[19]

Now, although this is, plainly, no simple dualism, it does make assumptions about matter which are incompatible with Christian teaching,[20] and further more creates an ethos, so to say, regarding matter and the body quite distinct from a Christian one. According to A. H. Armstrong, Plotinus' attitude to the body 'is one of austere detached tolerance'.[21] In the thought of his pupil Porphyry, however, this detached tolerance seems to have been transformed into a somewhat more critical distancing; 'he popularised the emotional impact of such ideas [i.e., the Platonic and Neoplatonic ideas derived in particular from the *Phaedo*] with his slogan "all body must be escaped"'.[22] The body, it was often said, was the dungeon of the soul.

Significantly, early Christian thought, whilst not unaffected by pagan attitudes to the body, maintained a distinctive stance over against them. In his important work *The Body and Society*, a study of the theme of sexual renunciation (and hence of understandings of the significance and meaning of the body) from the time of the New Testament until the time of St Augustine, Peter Brown notes the subtle inflections which Christians imposed on ways of life which were not, as such, without pagan parallels. Thus, the practice of the Desert Fathers, who looked back to Anthony of Egypt as their forebear, is associated with a rigour,

R. Bultmann, *Theology of the New Testament*, vol. 1, trans. K. Grobel (London, 1952), 202.

[18] J. M. Rist, *Plotinus: The Road to Reality* (Cambridge, 1967), 129. See further, J. M. Rist, 'Plotinus on Matter and Evil', *Phronesis*, 6 (1961), 154–66.

[19] Rist, *Plotinus*, 128, citing *Ennead* 1.8.14.

[20] See footnote 32 below.

[21] A. H. Armstrong, 'Plotinus' in *The Cambridge History of Later Greek and Early Medieval Philosophy*, ed. Armstrong, 229 (Cambridge, 1967), cited by P. Brown, *The Body and Society: Men, Women and Sexual Renunciation in Early Christianity* (London, 1989), 179.

[22] J. M. Rist, *Augustine* (Cambridge, 1994), 93.

privation and, as we say, mortification which might be compared with the discipline which Plotinus took for granted as appropriate for a soul mastering a body. But there is a difference, and one which we shall miss if we take the ascetics' notion of mortifying the body too literally. For 'the ascetics', says Brown, 'imposed severe restraints on their bodies because they were convinced that they could sweep the body into a desperate venture'.[23] The discipline of the ascetic life was, that is to say, intended for the sake of the body, not to spite it, for there is here 'a sense of the shared momentum of body and soul'.[24] So although in the desert tradition:

> vigilant attention to the body enjoyed an almost oppressive prominence . . . to describe ascetic thought as 'dualist' and as motivated by hatred of the body, is to miss its most novel and its most poignant aspect. Seldom, in ancient thought, had the body been seen as more deeply implicated in the transformation of the soul; and never was it made to bear so heavy a burden. For the Desert Fathers, the body was not an irrelevant part of the human person, that could, as it were, be 'put into brackets'. It could not enjoy the distant tolerance that Plotinus and many pagan sages were prepared to accord it, as a transient and accidental adjunct to the self. It was, rather, grippingly present to the monk: he was to speak of it as 'this body, that God has afforded me, as a field to cultivate, where I might work and become rich'.[25]

The ascetics, so it might be suggested, regard the body not simply as good, but perhaps as 'good for'. However that may be, no such suspicion should attach itself to Augustine's teaching in which he rejected not only Plotinus' 'distant tolerance of

---

[23] Brown, *Body and Society*, 222.   [24] Brown, *Body and Society*, 235.
[25] Brown, *Body and Society*, 235–6. We might also observe that in the later development of the ascetic tradition, the same perspective is maintained. In his study *John Cassian*, 2nd edn (Cambridge, 1968), Owen Chadwick notes that 'The use of Platonic language by the monks led extreme critics to accuse them of adopting a non-Christian doctrine of an evil body. The mortifications of the body, it was sometimes alleged, were intended to strip the good soul of its evil clothing. A father of the desert explained his self-maceration thus: "My body kills me, I kill it." Whatever justification this theory of dualism might have among simpletons or fanatics, the myth of Evagrius [i.e., the Origenist account of the relationship of body and soul taught by Evagrius, Cassian's teacher] shows that it was not a charge which could be lodged against the Origenists. For in that myth the body was created to save the soul. The body is good. The natural world is good. "We are taught" said Abba Poemen in the Apophthegmata, "to kill not the body, but the passions"' (92).

the body', but also the sharper repudiation of it by Plotinus'
pupil Porphyry: in Porphyry there is a certain emphasis on the
conviction that the body could not share in salvation. Of
course, in Augustine's attitude to this last matter, and in his
general attitudes to the body, a development occurs as he moves
away from his early Platonism.[26] But, by the time of the *City of
God*, he is undoubtedly an advocate of the goodness of the body,
and of its destiny in resurrection.[27] 'Why. . . are [these philoso-
phers]' asks Augustine, having Porphyry especially in view, 'so
unwilling to believe that by God's will and power earthly bodies
can be made immortal, and souls can live in those bodies
everlastingly and in felicity, not separated from them by any
death, nor weighed down by their burden?'[28] The question is,
of course, rhetorical – Augustine rehearses and answers the
various difficulties which seem to 'these philosophers' to stand
in the way of belief in the resurrection of the body, judging none
of them decisive.[29] Thus reason does not stand opposed to what
'the Christian faith declares', 'that at the resurrection the saints
will inhabit the actual bodies in which they suffered the hardships of this life on earth; yet these bodies will be such that no
trace of corruption or frustration will affect their flesh, nor will
any sorrow or mischance interfere with their felicity'.[30] Furthermore, the 'actual bodies' to be borne in the resurrection will,
significantly, be the bodies of both men and women. 'Some
people suppose', says Augustine, 'that women will not keep
their sex at the resurrection'. He holds, however, that 'the more
sensible opinion' is 'that there will be both sexes in the resurrection'; for, 'while all defects will be removed from those bodies,
their essential nature will be preserved. Now a woman's sex is
not a defect; it is natural'[31] – a point for which he had argued,

---

26 See Rist, *Augustine*, esp. ch. 4, and M. R. Miles, *Augustine on the Body* (Ann Arbor, MI,
    1979), *passim*. And contrast *City of God* with his *Confessions*.
27 See also *Sermons*, 30, 4: 'What I want is for it to be healed as a whole, for I am one
    whole. I do not want my flesh to be removed from me for ever, as if it were something
    alien to me, but that it be healed, a whole with me.' (Cited in Rist, *Augustine*, 92.)
28 Augustine, *De Civitate Dei* (*City of God*), PL 41, 13–804, trans. by H. Bettenson (London,
    1972), xiii, 17.
29 See *City of God*, xiii, 16–24 and xxii, 4, 11–21 and 24–9.
30 *City of God*, xiii, 19.
31 *City of God*, xxii, 17.

in effect, in Book xiv, with its argument that sexual differentiation (and hence sexual union) were found in Eden.[32]

The unity of Augustine's thought about the human body in its past and future is a consequence, so it can be maintained, of his knowing both its past and future from a knowledge of its being taken up in the reconciliation achieved in the Word made flesh – it is from this centre that it is affirmed that the salvation for which Christians look is one in which 'the gifts of nature, that is the gifts bestowed on our nature by the creator of all natures, will be not only good but also everlasting; and this applies not only to the spirit, which is healed by wisdom, but also to the body which will be renewed by resurrection'.[33] The renewal is plainly of something good which has come from the hands of the creator, and even now, between the times, it is not inappropriate for the body to share in the paeon of praise to the creation found in the *City of God*, xxii, 24. '[E]ven here [i.e., in the body] what evidence we find of the goodness of God, of the providence of the mighty creator' – including, argues Augustine, the 'rational loveliness' of the internal organs, as well as the body's purely aesthetic additions: 'for example, the nipples on a man's chest, and the beard on his face'!

[32] Augustine is opposing arguments of the kind advanced by Gregory of Nyssa in *De Hominis Opificio* (*On the Making of Man*), PG 44, 123–256, trans. W. Moore and H. Wilson, *Nicene and Post-Nicene Fathers*, 2nd series, vol. v (Edinburgh, 1994). Gregory argues, on the basis of an interpretation of Genesis 1: 27, that our creation is, so to say, 'twofold', in the image of God, but then, as male and female, as sharing in an animal nature – 'for something like this the passage darkly conveys by its arrangement when it first says "God created man, in the image of God created He him", and then, adding to what has been said, "male and female created He them" – a thing which is alien from our conception of God' (xvi, 8). And creation is twofold 'that the multitude of human souls might not be cut short by its fall from that mode by which the angels were increased and multiplied [i.e., non-sexually] – for this reason, I say, He formed for our nature that contrivance for increase which befits those who had fallen into sin, implanting in mankind instead of an angelic majesty of nature, that animal and irrational mode by which they now succeed one another' (xvii, 4). It is worth observing that even here, with a thinker much closer to Platonism than the later Augustine, there is a significant divergence from the assumptions of Neoplatonism. For Gregory, as Brown says (*The Body and Society*, 300), 'formulations from Plato and Plotinus dropped easily from his pen . . . But they had changed their meaning. For the soul to find itself in the body in its present, fallen state was a sad and perilous situation for Gregory; but it was no longer the principal cause of the present anomaly of the human condition' – as, of course, Plotinus held.

[33] Augustine, *City of God*, xix, 10.

Augustine's affirmation of the goodness of bodily life as belonging to our creation, and his conviction of the part it will have in the resurrection – his affirmation, that is to say, that the body is a temple, and not a prison, to avert again to the contrast with the more extreme Platonists[34] – is an expression of an anthropology which presupposes that the past and the future, like the present, are spheres of God's grace. And this anthropology determines not only certain what we might term theoretical commitments, but also a range of teaching in relation to various practices and forms of life: amongst other things, his magisterial attempt to understand human sexuality within the history of creation, reconciliation and redemption;[35] his understanding of asceticism;[36] his insistence on the goodness of progeny and his repudiation (along with the rest of the Fathers) of abortion and infanticide;[37] and, perhaps most strikingly of all,

---

[34] Rist, *Augustine*, 102.

[35] For an important treatment of Augustine's account of human sexuality, see Paul Ramsey's discussion, 'Human Sexuality within the History of Redemption', *Journal of Religious Ethics*, 16 (1988), 56–88. I have tried to display the strength of the overall conception which determines Augustine's teaching, albeit within short articles, in 'Sexuelle (Ethique)', in *Dictionnaire de Théologie*, ed. Jean-Yves Lacoste (Paris, 1998) and in 'Sexualität' in *Theologische Realenzyklopädie* (Berlin, forthcoming). In relation to the alleged pessimism of Augustine's treatment, it must suffice here to record a comment of Peter Brown's (*The Body and Society*, 425): 'The fatal flaw of concupiscence would not have seemed so tragic to Augustine, if he had not been ever more deeply convinced that human beings had been created to embrace the material world. The body was a problem to him precisely because it was to be loved and cherished.' (The refusal of most contemporary popular books on sexual ethics to engage with anything but a second-hand parody of Augustine's thought in particular, or of Patristic thought in general, reveals plainly enough the underlying conceit of an age which none the less manages to pride itself on its tolerance. Whatever else might be said about these books, they do at least make a contribution, however unintentionally, to the theatre of the absurd, for how else should we regard the sight of these modern-day midgets swiping at the ankles of giants?)

[36] See, e.g., *De Doctrina Christiana* (*On Christian Doctrine*), PL 34, 15–122, trans. J. F. Shaw, in *Nicene and Post-Nicene Fathers*, 1st series, vol. II (Edinburgh, 1993), i, 24: 'And as to the fact that they seem in some sort to scourge their bodies by abstinence and toil, those who do this in the right spirit do it not that they may get rid of their body, but that they may have it in subjection and ready for every needful work.' These are to be contrasted with those 'who do this in a perverse spirit', and 'make war upon their own body as if it were a natural enemy'.

[37] On abortion in Augustine and the Fathers, see J. T. Noonan, 'An Almost Absolute Value in History', in *The Morality of Abortion: Legal and Historical Perspectives*, ed. Noonan (Cambridge, MA, 1970), 1–59.

his attitudes towards the 'care to be had for the dead',[38] which came to be regarded as providing an authoritative defence of the practice of the veneration of relics.

Augustine argues in Book i of the *City of God* that the dead suffer no deprivation through lack of an honourable burial. However:

This does not mean that the bodies of the departed are to be scorned and cast away, particularly not the bodies of the righteous and the faithful, of which the Spirit has made holy use as instruments for good works of every kind. For if such things as a father's clothes, and his ring, are dear to their children in proportion to their affection for their parents, then the actual bodies are certainly not to be treated with contempt, since we wear them in a much closer and more intimate way than any clothing. A man's body is no mere adornment, or external convenience; it belongs to his very nature as a man.[39]

Aquinas was not wrong, then, in citing this passage in the *Summa Theologiae* in the *responsio* to the question 'should any form of veneration be paid the relics of the saints?'[40] Although Augustine's remarks could not be taken to warrant the later abuses of relics, of which Aquinas is well aware (with his distinction between honouring and worshipping) and against which the Council of Trent would pronounce, it is evident that Augustine's respect for the body lays the ground for a regard for relics. 'A man's body is no mere adornment or external convenience', but 'belongs to his very nature as a man'; so it is that

---

[38] The translation of the title of the short treatise *De Cura Pro Mortuis*, which includes book i, 13 of the *City of God*.

[39] Augustine, *City of God*, i, 13.

[40] Thomas Aquinas, *Summa Theologiae*, 3a, 25, 6; in vol. 50 of the Blackfriars edition, trans. C. E. O'Neill (London, 1965). It is noticeable, however, that in his explication of the authoritative text, Aquinas sounds more like Origen than Augustine. Thus he claims that 'We do not venerate a lifeless body for what it is in itself, but by reason of the soul which was once united to it and which now enjoys God'. Compare Origen, *Contra Celsum*, trans. H. Chadwick (Cambridge, 1980), v, 24, where Origen remarks that a verse of Heraclitus cited by Celsus ('corpses ought to be thrown away as worse than dung') 'causes us not the least difficulty'. 'Yet someone might say even of this that while dung should be thrown away, yet human corpses should not be thrown away, out of respect for the soul that has dwelt within, and especially if it is a soul of a good character. For according to good customs they are thought worthy of burial with all the honour possible appropriate to their character so that, as far as possible, we may not insult the soul that has dwelt within by casting out the body when the soul has gone out of it, as we do with the bodies of beasts.'

the physical remains of the saints can come to be thought of as deserving a respect due to temples of the Holy Spirit, awaiting their resurrection.[41]

If we find here, and in other matters, Augustine's veneration of the body arising from an anthropology determined by the fact that Jesus Christ is the first and the last, in the practice of modern medicine, so I shall argue, we find an implicit refusal of such an anthropology. If the goodness of human life includes the goodness of bodily life and if this body is itself to be caught up in the redemption for which the Christian hopes, then medicine is permitted, vindicated and honoured. It is hereby commanded and summoned to serve the good of the body, which genuinely is a human good, belonging to our past, present and future. We find, however, that medicine refuses this calling either by withdrawing altogether from the service of the body, or by converting service into manipulation. If we were to discuss the latter, we might do so in relation, for example, to certain uses of genetic engineering which are plainly eugenic or perfective, or might follow O'Donovan in his insightful critique of trans-sexual surgery.[42] Here, however, we shall be concerned with the former manifestation of the refusal of this calling, and in particular with the repudiation of the goodness of human life expressed in the current practice of abortion.

The charge that by its complicity with the practice of abortion medicine is involved in a repudiation of the goodness of human life, could, of course, be rebutted if two things were to be shown: both that the foetus is not to be regarded as sharing in human life, and in addition that medical practice is actually based on a belief that the foetus does not share in human life. The addition is important – even if some argument can be

---

[41] A careful treatment of the history and theology of relics is provided by P. Séjourné, 'Reliques', *Dictionnaire de Théologie Catholique*, 13 (Paris, 1936), 2312–76. In addition see F. Chiovaro, 'Relics' in *New Catholic Encyclopedia* (New York, 1967) – which is not, however, to be relied upon for its knowledge of Calvin! It is surprising that the recent *Catechism of the Catholic Church* (English trans., London, 1994) provides so little by way of theological interpretation of a practice which it seems inclined to treat as a form of popular piety, and thus perhaps as lacking a profound theological rationale and therefore simply to be tolerated; see para 1674.

[42] O. M. T. O'Donovan, 'Transsexualism and Christian Marriage', *Journal of Religious Ethics*, 11 (1983), 135–62.

offered for the contention that the foetus is not to be regarded as sharing in human life, if medical practice is not founded on any such argument or belief, but is in fact quite indifferent to the question, it can hardly claim mere thoughtlessness as a defence to the charge. When, however, we look for an argument which might support the basic contention about the foetus and has, in addition, been important to medical practice, we shall be struck by the fact (as was J. T. Noonan more than twenty-five years ago) that there is in public discussion a distinct 'indifference to fundamental questions'[43] of this sort.

The Warnock Report provides compelling evidence of such indifference, even though in its 'Foreword' it claims to 'have attempted in what follows to argue in favour of those positions which we have adopted, and to give due weight to the counter-arguments where they exist'.[44] We must notice, to begin with, that crucial to *The Warnock Report's* central recommendation permitting non-therapeutic research on embryos up to fourteen days (subsequently enshrined in the Human Fertilisation and Embryology Act, 1990), is the presupposition that, prior to fourteen days at least, the embryo is not an appropriate subject of the moral concern otherwise normally shown to human life: such an embryo, whatever status it may be said to have, does not deserve absolute protection from non-therapeutic experimentation which foresees and intends its death.[45] The crucial nature of this presupposition arises from the fact that the *Report* does not espouse (and indeed, explicitly rejects[46]) a consequentialist position, a position which would free it from the need for making any such assumption. That is to say, since a consequentialist holds that actions are good or right, bad or wrong, in virtue, and solely in virtue, of their consequences, and, further, that the morally best action in any situation is just that one

[43] Noonan, ed., *The Morality of Abortion*, 'Introduction', xviii.

[44] *Report of the Committee of Inquiry into Human Fertilisation and Embryology, The Warnock Report* (London, 1984), paragraph 2. (Subsequent references will be to paragraph numbers.)

[45] According to *The Warnock Report* the early embryo does have a certain status — it is because of this that research, even if permissible, 'must be subject to stringent controls and monitoring' (11.18).

[46] *The Warnock Report*, 4.

which will maximise good consequences, questions as to the status of the embryo pre- or post-fourteen days cannot be decisive in determining its proper treatment – even were the early embryo reckoned to be morally indistinguishable from a later one, both early and late embryos could find their good or interest outweighed in the calculus of consequences by which the consequentialist resolves ethical questions. *The Warnock Report*, however, plainly rejects such an approach in holding that after fourteen days the embryo is to be accorded an absolute respect (supposing, that is, that it is *in vitro* not *in utero*); it is not to be used as the object of research no matter how advantageous this research promises to be.

But if this presupposition – that the embryo prior to fourteen days is not an appropriate recipient of the moral respect usually shown to human subjects – is crucial to *Warnock* and to the legislation which is based upon it, is it, to come back to our main point, in any way defended? The *Report* tells us that at around fourteen days in the development of an embryo, scientists are able to observe the appearance of the so-called 'primitive streak', which 'appears as a heaping-up of cells at one end of the embryonic disc'.[47] It is also noted that this is the latest stage at which the embryo can divide to form twins. But there is no argument to show that either the formation of the primitive streak or the end of the possibility of twinning, is of any moral relevance to the question of the status of the embryo. It is simply asserted, prior to laying down the fourteen day rule, that 'the formation of the primitive streak' can be said to be 'one reference point in the development of the human individual' and that it 'marks the beginning of the individual development of the embryo'.[48] Whether or not this claim is true, is this a moral reference point? Perhaps the remark about the 'beginning of the individual development of the embryo' is to be taken as an assertion that only at fourteen days is there an individual who could be the subject of a moral respect; perhaps the claim is that what we observe when we observe the emergence of the primitive streak is the emergence of this individual. Perhaps this

[47] *The Warnock Report*, 11.5.   [48] *The Warnock Report*, 11.22.

is the relevance of the observation about twinning – does it suggest that we can only know we have an individual when we can be sure we do not have two? Maybe, but *The Warnock Report* does not make these assertions – there is no explicit argument to convince us that this observation of the formation of the primitive streak is of *moral* significance, that here there is an important divide, on the one side of which lies an appropriate subject of non-therapeutic experimentation, on the other side of which lies a subject worthy of protection. The *Report*, we might say, gives us a ruling, not a judgment, an assertion, not an argument.[49]

Naturally, unless it is to rely on consequentialist moves, a defence of abortion must itself presuppose a solution to the 'fundamental questions' (though not the answer which the advocates of the fourteen-day divide presuppose) – and plainly the practice of abortion in both the UK and the USA, for example, makes no sense in consequentialist terms.[50] Conse-

---

[49] This is not to say that no argument whatsoever could be made for the significance of the fourteen-day divide, and N. M. Ford's *When Did I Begin? Conception of the Human Individual in History, Philosophy and Science* (Cambridge, 1988) is a defence of the proposition that the human individual is to be thought of as coming into existence at approximately two weeks after conception. I believe that his argument is flawed for the sort of the reasons set out in the following papers: G. Grisez 'When Do People Begin', in *Abortion: A New Generation of Catholic Responses*, ed. S. J. Heaney (Braintree, MA, 1992), 3 27; A. Fisher, 'Individuogenesis and a Recent Book by Fr. Norman Ford', *Anthropotes*, 8 (1991), 199 244 and '"When did I begin?" Revisited', *Linacre Quarterly*, 58 (1991), 59 68; and N. Tonti-Filippini, 'A Critical Note', *Linacre Quarterly*, 56 (1989), 36 50. Specifically, both Ford's biology, and the inferences he draws from the possibility of twinning and the formation of chimæras, are alike suspect. My point here, however, is not that no even prima-facie plausible case can be made for the distinction on which *The Warnock Report's* central recommendation depends it is simply that *The Warnock Report* shows no interest in making such a case. It was noticeable that the advocates of experimentation on embryos in the debate surrounding the implementation of *The Warnock Report* showed, for the most part, a similar lack of interest, and seemed satisfied simply to employ the terms 'pre-embryo' and 'conceptus' to label the early embyro, as if thereby marking an important difference of some moral consequence. The use of these terms, however, no matter the air of scientific authority which they suggest, does not establish but merely asserts such a difference.

[50] In Britain, the *Abortion Act* of 1967 allows legal termination of pregnancy prior to the 28th week in order to avoid injury to the 'physical or mental health' of the mother or 'any existing child of her family', or where 'there is a substantial risk that if the child were born it would suffer such physical or mental abnormalities as to be seriously handicapped'. This is now amended by the Human Fertilisation and Embryology Act, 1990, which substituted 24 weeks for 28, but excluded the severely handicapped

quentialism, after all, would allow both more and less: more, since it would see no reason for according absolute respect, and hence legal protection, to the foetus at twenty-four weeks (whether or not handicapped) or, for that matter, even after birth; less, since a consistent consequentialist would want to consider in each case whether the mother's unwillingness to carry her child to term represents a cost which outweighs potential benefits, including the benefit of life to the child, to the family who might adopt him or her, and so on – certainly it could not be ruled out in advance that the calculation would go in favour of the unborn child.

Here again, however, if present practice requires a solution to 'fundamental questions' it is not obvious that there has been a real concern to address those questions.[51] It is noticeable, for example, that one of the most important slogans in the abortion

from this restriction, so that they may now be aborted up to term. The judgment of the Supreme Court of the United states in *Roe v. Wade* in 1973 is seemingly more radical in holding the prohibition of abortion prior to viability unconstitutional, thereby denying the foetus the prima-facie protection which the English law seems to enshrine. However, the interpretation of the 1967 Act by medical practitioners as permitting abortion on demand suggests that there is little difference in practice between the two countries.

[51] An example of a failure to realise even what is needed in a treatment of this subject is found in the article 'Abortion' in the *New Dictionary of Christian Ethics and Pastoral Theology*, ed. D. J. Atkinson and D. H. Field (Leicester, 1995), written by D. Cook. Perhaps it will not surprise us unduly that an article even in a publication with a broadly evangelical provenance should be unconstrained by Christian principles, but the manner in which the article likewise turns its back on the most basic principles of rational discussion ought to cause us greater surprise. The author plainly does not understand the doctrine of double effect and hence Roman Catholic teaching on the subject; the question of the legality of abortion is quite absurdly discussed without reference to any particular jurisdiction; various ideas relating to the issue of when the embryo becomes worthy of protection are listed without any critical comment, even when some of those ideas are so highly questionable as to verge on the absurd. ('Medical practitioners favour viability', so we are told, 'as the point when a clear patient becomes the responsibility of the doctor'; but should not the moralist pose the pointed question whether then, in private practice, the opening of a bank account is the key moment as being 'the point when a clear patient' hoves into view?) The evasion of rational engagement with the issues does not, however, inhibit the author from solemn pronouncements on his theme: thus we are warned that 'Christians . . . do not have the right to inflict their morality on society' – which can only cause us to be grateful that our Christian forebears who campaigned for the abolition of slavery were not weighed down by the fatuous pieties of modern liberalism. (The warmth in this complaint lies in the fact, which a *Dictionary of Christian Ethics and **Pastoral** Theology* ought to know very well, that the Christian ethicist should take up a question such as abortion seriously, or not at all.)

debate – 'a woman's right to choose' – is, at least on the surface, no more than an assertion by a particular group of a claim to be entitled to act in this matter as they alone determine; it is as if, that is to say, a case against slavery were met with the assertion of 'a slave-owner's right to choose'. The underlying question is simply refused by the slogan, which declines to recognise that what is needed is an argument on the fundamental point as to whether or not the foetus is the sort of thing whose death can be licitly chosen by anyone.

Of course, those who assert 'a woman's right to choose' may be appealing, behind that assertion, to an anthropology which warrants the view that to choose the death of a foetus is not, to use our terms, a repudiation of human life (in which case, we might mention in passing, the appeal to the interests of women in the matter is largely superfluous). What sort of anthropology might that be? The answer is: any anthropology which thinks of human life as being worthy of respect only on the basis of its possession of certain specified attributes or properties which foetuses lack. Thus, to cite one example, according to Michael Tooley, what 'makes an individual a person – that is, that makes the destruction of something intrinsically wrong . . . – is the property of being an enduring subject of non-momentary inter-ests'.[52] Now since Tooley holds that the possession of such interests in turn requires the possession of certain rational capacities, and since he deems the potential to exercise those capacities in the future as irrelevant to the present status of a human being, not only the unborn but also the newborn (and others too) are reckoned not to be wronged by their destruction.

Anthropologies of the same general type as Tooley's are numerous – implicit in all such anthropologies is the claim that human bodily life is not, as such, worthy of respect. There are, that is to say, countless proposals for viewing humanity as, as it were, an achievement, such that to be a human being worthy of protection and respect, certain qualifications, so to say, are necessary. Tooley specifies 'the property of being an enduring subject of non-momentary interests'; Joseph Fletcher lists

[52] M. Tooley, *Abortion and Infanticide* (Oxford 1983), 303.

possession of 'freedom, self-determination, rationality, the ability to choose either means or ends, and knowledge of . . . circumstances';[53] a BMA report, discussing handicapped newborns, speaks of 'the capacity to love and be loved';[54] some point to viability; others to being wanted. We could make a very long list of anthropologies of this sort, each embodying a slightly different presupposition about the human.

All of them, we might note, bear at least a family resemblance to the anthropology of Aristotle's *Politics*, Books I and III, which was to play such a large part in 'the question of the Indians' as it was known, in sixteenth century Spain. According to Aristotle, just as 'some men are by nature free', others are 'slaves, and . . . for these latter slavery is both expedient and right'.[55] These natural slaves participate 'in reason enough to apprehend, but not to have, reason'; that is, they can receive, but not give commands.[56] For those considering the rights and wrongs of the Spanish conquest of the Americas, the question whether the Indians were slaves by nature was a matter of some importance: the Thomist Vitoria holds that they cannot be so considered, the great humanist Aristotelian Sepúlveda that they can.[57]

One of the participants in the famous formal debate at Valladolid framed in these terms, was Las Casas, who on a previous occasion is reported as having been driven to exclaim in some vexation that 'Aristotle is a Gentile burning in hell, whose doctrine we do not need to follow except in so far as it conforms with Christian truth.'[58] Anthropologies of the same

[53] J. Fletcher, *Morals and Medicine* (Boston, 1954), cited in G. Grisez's important study *Abortion: the Myths, the Realities and the Arguments* (New York, 1970), 280.

[54] *Report of the Working Party to Review the British Medical Association's Guidance on Euthanasia* (London, 1988), paragraph 132.

[55] Aristotle, *The Politics*, trans. B. Jowett (Oxford, 1905), II, v.   [56] Ibid.

[57] See, Francisco de Vitoria, *De Indis*, q1, conclusion, in *Political Writings*, ed. and trans. A. Pagden and J. Lawrance (Cambridge, 1991). For Sepúlveda and the general background to the debate see A. Pagden, *The Fall of Natural Man: The American Indian and the Origins of Comparative Ethnology*, 2nd edn (Cambridge, 1986). A readable, but not entirely reliable, introduction is L. Hanke's *Aristotle and the American Indians* (Chicago, 1959); it fails, in particular, to understand the way in which Thomism is reponsible for the use to which Aristotle was put.

[58] Cited in Hanke, *Aristotle and the American Indians*, 16. See also *The Defence of the Most Reverend Lord, Don Fray Bartolomé de Las Casas, of the Order of Preachers, Late Bishop of Chiapa, Against the Persecutors and Slanderers of the Peoples of the New World Discovered Across the Seas*, ed. and trans. S. Poole (DeKalb, IL, 1974).

type as Aristotle's may be met with the same underlying claim – that they constitute a departure from the proper basis for Christian reflection.

Prior to making this point, we might, of course, insist on the utter arbitrariness of each of these anthropologies – the choosing of a particular attribute or set of attributes as a qualification for respect and regard is just that, a choice, and is not obviously compelled by anything other than a determination to arrive at an already desired solution to certain practical problems; so we might say of Tooley's stipulations about which lives are or are not wronged by their destruction.[59] And arbitrariness leads to circularity – for how else is one to commend an arbitrary stipulation except by noting that it reaches the conclusion which it is claimed to warrant?[60] But with or without those points, which properly need fuller statement, we surely do well to recall the Christian truth against which these anthropologies should be measured.

How in the light of this truth will we assess anthropologies implicit in which is the claim that human bodily life is not, as such, worthy of respect, but that some further attribute or accomplishment is necessary for such life to be deserving of protection? The conviction that Jesus Christ is the first is the conviction that the grace of God shown in Jesus Christ is shown in creation. It is in virtue of this conviction, so I have argued, that Augustine commends all those practices which honour and cherish the body (of the self, the other, the unborn, and of the dead) rather than repudiate it. These practices value the body as itself a gift from the hand of the creator, and not as a thing of indifference, as it were, of which truly valuable human life simply makes use.

[59] So we might say, in addition, of the stipulation that it is present possession of this attribute or attributes (not simply potential to possess them in the future) which counts. After all, it would be odd to maintain that the sterilisation of a boy at the age of ten does him no wrong simply because he presently possesses only the potential to reproduce in the future.

[60] See, on this point, the patient critique of Tooley in R. Hursthouse, *Beginning Lives* (Oxford, 1987), esp. 107–17. 'Tooley's conclusion (C1), "Foetuses and babies do not have a right to life" was based on the premise (P2) "Only persons have a right to life" and the supposed definitional truth (D1) "Foetuses and babies are not persons." But now it has emerged that (P2) and (D1) simply assume the truth of (C1)' (117).

In so far as defences of abortion rely on anthropologies which claim that bodily life is not as such, worthy of respect, they rely on anthropologies inconsistent with a Christian understanding of creation. And in so far as medicine is led into practices which presuppose such anthropologies, or is even simply indifferent to the question as to whether such anthropologies exist or are warranted, it shows a disregard for the good of the body and learns to express hatred towards it. In the Gospel, and perhaps only in the Gospel, we find sure grounds for the repudiation of these alternative anthropologies with their competing and arbitrary distinctions and hence for the assertion of the fundamental equality of human beings.[61] Thus may practices of hatred give way to practices of veneration.[62]

IV

Just as the practice of abortion is at the least prima facie inconsistent with the anthropology presupposed in Christianity's various practices of respect and reverence for the body, so the practice of euthanasia, I shall now argue, is inconsistent with an anthropology of the kind presupposed in a Christian conception of martyrdom. The practice of martyrdom within the Christian tradition properly expresses a respect for life but not for death – it does so on the basis of a knowledge of the alpha and the omega, the beginning and the end. The practice of euthanasia, arising apart from this knowledge, expresses

[61] I have put 'perhaps' in this sentence, since I have not found room to argue fully for the stronger thesis. When we find, however, philosophers such as James Rachels declaring that 'the idea of human dignity turns out . . . to be the moral effluvium of a discredited metaphysics', it is clear that grounds exist, even from the side of secular philosophy, for making a case for the removal of the 'perhaps'. For Rachels, see: *Created from Animals: The Moral Implications of Darwinism* (Oxford, 1990), 5. Nietzsche might also be brought forward as a witness, with his clear sense of the distinctiveness of Christianity. See his insistence that on a scientific view of humankind, the idea of human dignity is not *gegeben* (i.e., given) but *aufgegeben* (i.e., abandoned); *The Anti-Christ*, trans. R. J. Hollingdale (Harmondsworth, 1968).

[62] It ought to be clear that nothing said here is taken to provide a defence of an exceptionless moral norm which would always and ever preclude abortion. Whether such a norm could be defended is not settled in this chapter which is concerned more to establish the presumption in its favour which a properly Christian anthropology warrants.

more regard for death than for life and, with other aspects of the treatment of the dying, is determined by a doubtfulness about life's beginning and, above all, a fear of its end. Our claim will be that it is only where this fear is silenced that we can escape from the confusions of a medical practice which is tempted to aggressive maintenance of life in intensive-care units, neglect in its departments of geriatrics, and euthanasia in its oncology wards.

Specifically we now ask of the practice of euthanasia, as of any other human practice, whether or not it is appropriate to the life of those who should live by the fact that the future is the time of Jesus Christ in redemption, in which our calling to be children and heirs of his Father will be fully manifest.[63] Here,

---

[63] For the sake of simplicity I deal only with voluntary euthanasia. The treatment of involuntary or non-voluntary euthanasia would require a somewhat extended analysis, which would draw attention to the usual reliance of the case for involuntary or non-voluntary euthanasia on 'anthropologies of qualification' of the sort we have already referred to in the discussion of abortion — see, for example, D. W. Brock, *Life and Death: Philosophical Essays in Biomedical Ethics* (Cambridge, 1993): killing certain patients is permissible where those patients fail 'to have the properties of personhood necessary and sufficient for possessing the right not to be killed.' (102) (Any anxieties such a proposal is likely to raise are hardly quelled by the assurance that 'Moderately demented patients, *in the absence of democratically based public decisions to the contrary*, have roughly the same claims to care as nondemented patients' (16) — emphasis added. Pope John Paul II's warning in *Centesimus Annus*, English trans. (London, 1991), para. 46, that 'a democracy without values easily turns into open or thinly disguised totalitarianism' is surely apposite.)

We might note just how difficult it is, however, to maintain the voluntary/involuntary distinction both in theory and practice. As regards the problems in maintaining the distinction in theory, see the extremely lucid 'Submission to the Select Committee of the House of Lords on Medical Ethics from the Linacre Centre for Health Care Ethics', reprinted in *Euthanasia, Clinical Practice and the Law*, ed. L. Gormally (London, 1994), 111–65. The relevant argument is as follows (131–2) since a doctor could not regard a request for euthanasia as sufficient to warrant killing a patient (the request may arise from a faulty grasp of the prognosis, relievable depression, or whatever), he or she will only accede to this request on the basis of a judgment that the patient really does no longer have a worthwhile life. Now, since the doctor is responsible for this judgment, not the patient, the justification of the killing is the same as the justification of involuntary or non-voluntary euthanasia that the patient no longer has a worthwhile life.

On the difficulty in maintaining the distinction in practice, see J. Keown, 'Some Reflections on Euthanasia in the Netherlands' in *Euthanasia, Clinical Practice and the Law*, ed. Gormally, 193–218. Keown argues that 'the significance of the Dutch euthanasia experience for law, medicine and social policy in other countries is considerable, not least in respect of the support it lends to the "slippery slope" argument' (216) — i.e., the slope from voluntary to involuntary euthanasia. He cites the conclusion to C. Gomez's study, *Regulating Death: Euthanasia and the Case of the*

then, we return to the significance of the promise contained in the command of Jesus Christ, 'fear not: I am the first, the last and the living one', to consider what it says to us, and asks of us, in this particular context.

This command affirms in the first place that this living one not only is and was, but will be. But it does more than that – for the living one is determined to be not alone, but to be the first of many brothers and sisters, the first fruits from the dead. If the future is the time of Jesus Christ, it is, that is to say, a time into which we are summoned. Thus amidst the contradictions of our present time, we are told, as Barth puts it, that:

[I]n his Word, in Jesus Christ, [God] does not stand among us as the living among the dead but as the ζωοποιῶν [the quickener, John 5: 21], the life giver among the dead, giving life as by his Word he gives us a share in himself, in his own superiority to death, and thereby giving us eternal life . . . What is promised, the inheritance, is that God is not only in himself the A and O, the first and the last, but that there is for us a last as well as a first, that our temporal life does not begin with God and end with death, but ends also with God, and thus has eternity for all its temporality.[64]

This promised consummation, no less than the facts of creation and reconciliation, does not leave our present untouched. We are to live in the light of a revolutionary horizon, as those 'awaiting our blessed hope, the appearing of the glory of our great God and Saviour Jesus Christ'.[65]

[T]he kingdom which has already come in Jesus, which now hastens towards the revelation of its splendour, and which bounds the final age and therewith this peace, is not a rigid border with no practical actuality, a beyond which for all its majesty is, like the *Ding an sich* or transcendence of the philosophers, once and for all confined to its

---

Netherlands (New York, 1991): 'on the core issues of the controversy – how to control the practice, how to keep it from being used on those who do not want it, how to provide for public accountability – the Dutch response has been, to date, inadequate'. See further, J. Keown 'Euthanasia in the Netherlands: Sliding Down the Slippery Slope?' in *Euthanasia Examined: Ethical, Clinical and Legal Perspectives*, ed. J. Keown (Cambridge, 1995), 261–96. And on the problems with the theoretical distinction, see further, in the same volume, L. Gormally, 'Walton, Davies, Boyd and the Legalization of Euthanasia', 113–40.

[64] Barth, *Ethics*, 468–9.   [65] Titus, 2: 13.

place and limits and therefore without concrete and practical effects in the here and now.[66]

This kingdom then, so we should say, is the measure of our conduct and our living in this present. For:

We are children of God. Our citizenship is in heaven, in the Jerusalem that is above. This is no less true than that we must die. It replaces that truth. Where we see death coming, the Lord comes, the kingdom of God, that which is perfect. We are responsible to this future of ours. Whether our conduct can stand when measured by the standard that we are God's children and on the way to this goal is the ethical question from this final standpoint. It is required of us that we should walk and act as those who have the promise, who are heirs of God and joint heirs with Christ. We are asked whether we are true to our calling, not now our creaturely calling alone, nor our calling to be members of the people of God, but, as the point of these callings, our heavenly and eternal calling.[67]

And what might it be to be true, in this present, to this calling? The question which is put is:

whether and how far my conduct, my conduct at this moment, is a forward step, i.e., a step toward the future which is promised me by God's Word, the future of the Lord and his Lordship over all people and things . . . Ultimately we may simply say that we are asked whether we have a hope, not just any hope, but fundamentally and radically *the* hope, i.e., the orientation of what we are and do to what we are to become according to the Word of God, in keeping with his will, and in his strength.[68]

We are asked whether we are servants of this revolution or not, whether we seek our future 'wholly and utterly in God and expect it from God', whether we '*breathe* in the atmosphere of the redemption hidden in the future'.[69]

And we are asked this question in relation to the end of our lives – not only here of course, but here too. We are asked, that is to say, whether we 'breathe in the atmosphere of redemption' with our last breath, or rather, not just with our last breath but with all those breaths which we take in our dying. For the early Church this question was often posed as a question about the

---

[66] K. Barth, *Church Dogmatics*, III: 4, trans. A. T. Mackay et al. (Edinburgh, 1961), 263.
[67] Barth, *Ethics*, 469 70.
[68] Barth, *Ethics*, 486 7.   [69] Barth, *Ethics*, 490.

Christian's readiness for martyrdom, and required an understanding not only of such readiness, but also of the relationship
between a willingness to accept martyrdom and the belief in the
goodness of bodily life to which we have already referred. And
as the practice of martyrdom is defined and understood in the
elucidation of this relationship, so it can be regarded as an
embodiment of a practice of dying consistent with a Christian
anthropology.

In the course of his discussion and rejection of suicide in
Book i of the *City of God*,[70] Augustine imagines the following
objection to his teaching: 'But . . . in time of persecution there
were holy women who escaped those who threatened their
chastity by throwing themselves into rivers for the stream to
whirl them away to death: and after such a death they were
venerated as martyrs in the Catholic Church, and crowds
thronged their tombs.'[71] Augustine is cautious: 'I would not
presume to make a hasty judgment on their case.' It may be
that these 'martyrs' acted out of obedience to a direct divine
command: 'this is what we are bound to believe in Samson's
case'.[72] But supposing that they did not act out of obedience,
his criticisms of suicide apply even here: suicide is self murder
and wrong, and is warranted neither to prevent another's sin,
nor to prevent oneself from falling into sin or evil. Indeed, as
well as being objectively in error morally speaking, the suicide
may also act subjectively out of questionable motives. Some
speak of 'greatness of spirit' in relation to suicide, but, insists
Augustine, 'greatness of spirit is not the right term to apply to
one who has killed himself because he lacked the strength to
endure hardships, or another's wrong doing'. Thus of two
Roman heroes, he prefers Regulus to Cato: Cato, in defeat,
took his own life because, says Augustine, 'he grudged the
praise that Caesar would win by sparing' him; Regulus, on the
other hand, 'chose to let his life be ended by any kind of torture,
rather than to die by his own hand'.[73]

Augustine's discussion of suicide involves, then, albeit almost
incidentally, the distinguishing of suicide from martyrdom –

[70] Augustine, *City of God*, i, 17–27.   [71] Augustine, *City of God*, i, 26.
[72] Ibid.   [73] Augustine, *City of God*, i, 23 and 24.

suicide is death wrongly sought (except in those exceptional cases where God commands it, when it thereby ceases to be suicide); martyrdom is death rightly suffered. Such a distinction was already presupposed in the thought of other of the Fathers, some of them writing in different contexts, at times when the correct understanding of martyrdom (rather than the correct attitude to suicide) motivated the discussion. Thus we find Clement of Alexandria implicitly enunciating a similar distinction between the two in his discussion of martyrdom in Book iv of the *Stromata*.[74]

Like Augustine, Clement turns to Matthew 10: 23: 'When they persecute you in one town, flee to the next.' In his appeal to the text, Augustine argues that since the Lord 'could have advised them [i.e., the apostles] to take their own lives to avoid falling into the hands of their persecutors' but did not, 'it is clear that this course is not allowed to those who worship the one true God, whatever examples may be put forward by "the Gentiles who have no knowledge of him" '.[75] Clement uses the text in a different but related way: to argue that there is a courting of martyrdom which makes the martyr an accomplice in his own death.

When, again, He says, 'When they persecute you in this city, flee ye to the other', He does not advise flight, as if persecution were an evil thing; nor does He enjoin them by flight to avoid death, as if in dread of it, but wishes us neither to be authors nor abettors of any evil to any one, either to ourselves or the persecutor and murderer. For He, in a way, bids us take care of ourselves. But he who disobeys is rash and foolhardy. If he who kills a man of God sins against God, he also who presents himself before the judgment-seat becomes guilty of his death. And such is also the case with him who does not avoid persecution, but out of daring presents himself for capture. Such a one, as far as in him lies, becomes an accomplice in the crime of the persecutor. And if he also uses provocation, he is wholly guilty, challenging the wild beast. And similarly, if he afford any cause for conflict or punishment,

---

[71] Clement of Alexandria, *Stromata*, trans. W. Wilson, *Ante-Nicene Fathers*, ed. A. Roberts and J. Donaldson, vol. ii (Edinburgh, 1977), 299–567. For a treatment of the history and theology of martyrdom up to AD 361, see W. H. C. Frend, *Martyrdom and Persecution in the Early Church: A Study of a Conflict from the Maccabees to the Donatists* (Oxford, 1965).

[75] Augustine, *City of God*, i, 22, quoting I Thessalonians 4: 5.

or retribution or enmity, he gives occasion for persecution. Wherefore, then, we are enjoined not to cling to anything that belongs to this life; but 'to him that takes our cloak to give our coat', not only that we may continue destitute of inordinate affection, but that we may not by retaliating make our persecutors savage against ourselves, and stir them up to blaspheme the name.[76]

Earlier in his discussion he had anticipated the criticism of 'some of the heretics' who, far from seeking or commending martyrdom, maintain that 'the man is a self-murderer and a suicide who makes confession by death'. Clement will allow that those who have 'rushed on death' – 'who are in haste to give themselves up, the poor wretches, dying through hatred to the Creator' – 'banish themselves without being martyrs, even though they are punished publicly'.[77] There are, none the less, occasions when martyrdom may be required of us, even if 'to make a defence of our faith [i.e., by martyrdom] is not universally necessary'.[78]

In treating critically both an enthusiasm for, and a refusal of, martyrdom, Clement develops an understanding of it which bespeaks a particular attitude to death.[79] Too ready a relinquishing of life, amounting to a seeking of death, is

---

[76] Clement, *Stromata*, iv, 11. It is likely that the soldier whose actions provide the occasion for Tertullian's *De Corona* had been accused by fellow Christians of acting in an unnecessarily provocative way – Tertullian's treatise constitutes a defence of him against such a charge. Tertullian, of course, provides a sharp contrast with his near contemporary Clement's careful approach in delineating the proper readiness for martyrdom. Note, for example, that in *De Fuga*, Tertullian rules out an interpretation of Matthew 10: 23 of the sort favoured not only by Clement and Augustine but also indeed in his own earlier treatise *Ad Uxorem* (at 1, 3) – now he argues that Jesus' command is given only to the Apostles and to their times and circumstances. He even maintains that it is wrong to ransom prospective martyrs with money when they have already been ransomed by Christ's blood. But in addition his praise of martyrdom, to Clement's ears at least, would have come too close to encouraging Christians to be accomplices in their own deaths. Besides *De Corona*, *De Fuga* and *Ad Uxorem*, see *Ad Martyras*, *Scopiace* and *Apologeticum*, trans. S. Thelwall in *The Ante-Nicene Fathers*, vols. III and IV, ed. A. Roberts and J. Donaldson (Edinburgh, 1976).

[77] Clement, *Stromata*, iv, 4.

[78] Clement, *Stromata*, iv, 9.

[79] It would be interesting to trace the place this attitude would have in subsequent Christian thinking about martyrdom down to, and beyond, the Reformation when we find Cranmer taking a line close to Clement's in a letter to Peter Martyr of 1555. See J. Ridley, *Thomas Cranmer* (Oxford, 1962), 369.

incompatible with faith in the creator whose gift of life may be yielded in case of necessity, but not cast aside with an alacrity which renders one an accomplice to one's own murder. Too studied a refusal of martyrdom betrays 'an impious and cowardly love of life',[80] and is incompatible with faith in the redeemer, who, as Augustine puts it (in arguing that 'a decent funeral and proper burial . . . are a consolation to the living rather than a help to the departed'), promises Christians 'that their bodies and all their limbs will be restored and renewed, in an instant, not only from the earth, but also from the remotest hiding-places in the other elements into which their dead bodies passed in disintegration'.[81]

If the practice of martyrdom, thus elucidated, can be regarded as embodying a practice of dying consistent with a Christian anthropology – a dying which is filled with hope and not fear, but which is suffered rather than sought – how shall we assess many of the dyings accomplished under the rule of contemporary medicine, or under the rule of medicine as some would like it to be? Does medicine, that is to say, allow for or encourage a dying in which we may be said, with our last breaths, 'to breathe in the atmosphere of redemption'? Or is its practice comprehensible only as founded on an anthropology which knows nothing of such a future? We shall allege that euthanasia is a practice in which medicine turns its back not only on the created goodness of human life, but also on the goodness of its redeemed future; we shall further allege that this practice commends itself to its modern advocates principally as a more rational (and existentially satisfying) response to the hopelessness of the human predicament than the practices of

---

[80] Clement, *Stromata*, iv. 4. It is, of course, characteristic of Clement that he should be arguing for a, so to say, *via media* in relation to martyrdom, and particularly against those whose enthusiastic renunciation of life might be taken as expressing a doubt as to its goodness. The same concern is found in his critique of sexual asceticism in Book iii of the *Stromata*, as in his best-known treatise, on the proper use of wealth, *Who is the Rich Man That Shall be Saved?*, also in *The Ante-Nicene Fathers*, vol. ii.

[81] Augustine, *City of God*, i, 12. It is presumably a belief of this kind which explained how veneration of the bodies of the saints came to be thought compatible with the dismemberment of their corpses, a practice which became commonplace by the sixth century in spite of the prohibition found in the Theodosian Code.

neglect and overtreatment which express this same sense of hopelessness chiefly through a denial of the reality of death.[82]

A practice of neglect of the dying need not arise from any ill-will on the part of a doctor, and may, in the first instance, begin from the simple and sober recognition that nothing more can be done for the patient. Of course, this conclusion is not strictly true – 'there is nothing more we can do' usually means that there is nothing more to be done in fending off death. Perhaps much can be done in other ways – but at least some of the things which can be done may require from patient and doctor a mutual confession that the goal of seeking a cure no longer makes sense. This confession, however, may be one which both decline to make. For the patient it would mean confronting his or her mortality; for the doctor it means confronting the limit of medical art and skill, the defeat of its technological prowess and thus in the recognition of this defeat, his or her own mortality prefigured in this dying patient. From this confession and recognition both doctor and patient may turn, engaging in a knowing deceit in which each reassures the other by their offer and acceptance of equivocations, ambiguities or lies that 'everything possible is being done' or even – to take the game to a higher level – that 'everything will be all right'. By means of such evasions both are enabled to turn away from what they cannot face, driven by fear to a silence demanded by a denial of reality. Thus the patient will die in neglect – denied not only the possibility of dying in the truth, but also the possibility that the doctor, as May might say, will be true to his or her patient in their dying.

The denial and unreality which breeds neglect may also lead (to turn now to a seemingly opposed movement) to overtreatment. Here again – perhaps this time in the intensive care

---

[82] It will be obvious to those who know his writings that, in what follows as regards medicine's handling of death, I owe a very great debt to W. F. May's analysis of medical practice, and in particular to *The Physician's Covenant: Images of the Healer in Medical Ethics* (Philadelphia, 1983). For a bibliography and discussion of May's work see G. Meilaender's 'Corrected Vision for Medical Ethics' in *Theological Voices in Medical Ethics*, ed. A. Verhey and S. Lammers (Grand Rapids, 1993). See also Philippe Ariès, *The Hour of Our Death*, trans. H. Weaver (Harmondsworth, 1983) – significantly his discussion of modern behaviour in relation to death is headed 'Death Denied'.

ward, or more desperately in the neonatology unit – the imminence and certainty of death is refused on one or both sides of the encounter between patient and doctor, or between doctor and parent. In this mode, 'we are doing everything we can' is no empty formula to conceal doing nothing, but becomes a dreadful threat. The patient is intubated, resuscitated, subjected to more and heavier doses of chemo- or radiotherapy, undergoes yet another transplant or whatever, in spite of the fact that doing everything means doing all sorts of things which should not be done, things which can serve for this patient no recognisable palliative or therapeutic goal. Certainly it may advance medical technique, and it may give the patient some more time, against the loss of which this futile battle is being fought. But the time which is gained is time which had better been given up and would indeed have willingly been given up had there been no conspiracy between patient or parent and doctor, or even by the doctor against the patient, in a denial of the reality of unavoidable death. It is this denial which leads to that aggressive maintenance of life, resistance to the very end, and striving against the inevitable which, pursuing victory in the face of certain defeat, merely adds to the woes of the patient.

The advocates of voluntary euthanasia know that the approach to death which they recommend – that is, the killing of a patient, whether by act or omission, on that patient's request – has the advantage over neglect and overtreatment in this respect at least: that it does not avoid or ignore or deny the fact of death. Indeed, it is rather scornful, and to some extent rightly, of the deceptions which underlie both neglect and overtreatment, priding itself on its steady and rational approach to a topic elsewhere concealed by embarrassed silence, equivocation or ambiguity. And much of the sympathy which there undoubtedly is for the practice of euthanasia arises, quite reasonably, not only from the contempt which the other practices invite, but also from the prospects which they offer. Death by neglect is, after all, no more attractive a proposition than death despite overtreatment. Against these two euthanasia steps forward as the 'reasonable' and 'caring' answer. Using their medical skills in the service of the patient, so advocates of euthanasia will say, doctors should assist the patient in ending a life which has reached its conclusion in a way which will be painless, planned and dignified. This, it is said, is the proper, humanitarian response to the dilemma presented by the limits of medicine, and the proper contribution of medicine at the point where a patient's life has become, for the patient, simply a burden.

As should be obvious, however, this case for euthanasia relies on a false dilemma: as if the choice which is presented to us is exhaustively one between a 'good death' as the advocate of euthanasia understands it, and the bad death of neglect or overtreatment so vividly portrayed in the cases which are the stuff of the propaganda for euthanasia. What is excluded is the alternative 'good death' which is aimed at in the hospice – a death which is as free from pain as possible, and thus as open as possible to the care and love which both the one who is dying and those who are soon to be bereaved owe one another.

If, however, the case for euthanasia often rests on a false dilemma, there is no doubt that a case can be made for euthanasia without such a move. For, even when it has been conceded by the advocate of euthanasia that medicine can indeed offer a better alternative than either the over-treatment or neglect in the light of which death is understandably entertained as being preferable, it may still be the case, so they would maintain, that this better alternative seems to the patient in actual fact no better, and perhaps worse, than the killing which they advocate. Doubtless there are patients whose desire for euthanasia arises from a fear that they will either be over treated or overlooked; but are there not cases where the rationale for euthanasia consists in the fact that even the best palliative care offers a life which is perceived to be worse than death?

There are a number of moves which might be made against this argument. In the first place it might be pointed out that even if the case for voluntary euthanasia avoids some of the difficulties as regards the assessments of patients which the cases for involuntary or non-voluntary euthanasia must surmount, reliance on self-assessment is hardly without its problems. In the context of the discussion of another issue than euthanasia, May tells the story recounted by André Malraux in *Man's Hope* of the prisoners of the Fascists in the Spanish Civil War who would not only obediently dig their own graves, but would arrange themselves carefully in front of them 'so that their bodies would fall conveniently into place after their executioners had shot them'.[83] No observer, one takes it, would think it wise to infer a degree of consent to what was about to occur from the undoubted fact of the prisoners' ready co-operation. Similarly one might say, even self-assessments and requests for euthanasia should be treated with a degree of caution – and even if we were to judge them to be genuine, we might wonder about the nature of a society in which such requests do genuinely arise. After all, to take just one example, the conviction that euthanasia is a good which will allow one to escape from a degrading existence of dependence on others is a judgment more likely to arise in a society which is in the grip of an ideology of self-reliance, than in a society where the giving and receiving of care is reckoned to be constitutive of genuinely social life – such as the society governed by the maxim 'Before all things, and above all things care must be taken of the sick, so that they may be served in very deed as Christ himself.'[84]

In the second place, this argument for euthanasia might be resisted by one who points out that even where we have put to one side doubts as regards the patient's self assessment, the case for euthanasia does not follow without more argument. Of course, the judgment that a particular person believes him or herself to have such a burdensome life that death is preferable, may be reckoned by some to provide a warrant for killing patients, but, if it is so taken, what is ignored is the gap between the judgment and the justification of the deed. The case for euthanasia, that is to say, cannot rely simply on the fact that in some circumstances some patients wish to be killed; this may be necessary for the justification of the case for voluntary euthanasia, but it can hardly be sufficient. What is needed is an

[83] W. F. May, *The Patient's Ordeal* (Bloomington, IN, 1991), 119.
[84] *The Rule of St Benedict*, trans. J. McCann (London, 1976), chapter 36.

argument to show not just that patients want to be killed, but that it is permissible for doctors to kill them.

The advocate of euthanasia is likely to reply that to decline to take the step from an acknowledgement of the patient's predicament to action intended to end it, is both irrational and inhumane. Irrational because, so it will be said, if we are prepared to concede, as the Christian tradition has always maintained, that in certain circumstances not all measures should be taken to preserve life, is it not 'mere casuistry' to decline to take measures to bring about the death which the patient sees as the best outcome – after all, both courses of action (non-treatment and euthanasia) have the same outcomes. And not only irrational, but inhumane too, since to decline to take steps to kill a patient may destine a patient to a fate which is judged by that patient to be worse than death.

It is, of course, an empirical question whether there are any, or many, patients whose illnesses taking their natural course, unimpeded by any counter-measures, are such that acceptable levels of palliation are unachievable. But for the moment let us allow that there may be such patients. If we would concede, as we are pressed to concede, that killing patients and declining to pursue all steps to preserve life are morally speaking equivalents, we could deal with these cases by adding euthanasia to the medical repertoire. If however, we hold that to permit intentional killing of the innocent (whether by act or omission) would be to cross a line which preserves the moral integrity of medicine (both in the sense of stopping it doing bad things and also stopping it from becoming an incoherent practice) we will resist this pressure, maintaining instead that whilst it may be right in some circumstances not to do everything to lengthen a dying patient's life, we should never intend to kill.[85]

---

[85] The Linacre Centre's 'Submission to the Select Committee of the House of Lords on Medical Ethics' states the point neatly: 'It can be morally acceptable to withhold or withdraw treatment precisely because it is reasonably judged inefficacious (futile) or excessively burdensome, even if one foresees that in consequence death will occur earlier than it might otherwise have done. One's *reason* for withholding treatment is not a judgment about the desirability of putting an end to the patient's life, but a judgment about the desirability of putting an end to *treatment*, either because it is inefficacious or because it is imposing excessive burdens on the patient' (144).

These are some of the issues which arise for discussion where the advocate of euthanasia is met on his or her own ground. There are reasons, however, for thinking that the case for euthanasia is not to be met only on these grounds. In spite of the fact that the case for euthanasia is often presented as expressing a rational and modern attitude to death which overcomes the temptations to neglect and overtreatment to which we have referred, there is every reason to view it as a practice as much in the grip of a fear of death as those from which it claims to distinguish itself. And if we understand the case for euthanasia in these terms, we shall understand that the case needs to be answered not solely in the terms it offers by way of its own self-understanding, but, in addition and indeed more appropriately, on the sure ground of the proclamation of the hope in God's good future given in Jesus Christ.

The practice of euthanasia, whilst it must be distinguished from the practices of neglect and overtreatment in certain respects, shares with these practices the fact that it is enthralled by death. For if it disdains the avoidance of the reality of death, still it is to be understood, like the avoidance, as a practice which is itself determined by the fear of this reality. This, in effect, is the basis for Camus' contention that 'even if one does not believe in God, suicide is not legitimate'.[86] 'Suicide' he says, 'is acceptance at its extreme'.[87] Man sees 'his future, his unique and dreadful future – he sees it and he rushes towards it. In its way, suicide settles the absurd. It engulfs the absurd in the same death.'[88] But this 'engulfing of the absurd' is to be rejected. 'There is no fate that cannot be surmounted by scorn';[89] thus 'One must imagine Sisyphus happy.'[90] What is surely the case, however, contrary to Camus' argument, is that euthanasia appeals to many of its advocates just because it seems an expression of scorn not acceptance. Death cannot be defeated, it must defeat us. But, in the face of such a fate, the illusions which are involved in its avoidance, only add to the defeat the

[86] A. Camus, *The Myth of Sisyphus*, trans. J. O'Brien (Harmondsworth, 1975), 7.
[87] Camus, *The Myth of Sisyphus*, 54.   [88] Ibid.
[89] Camus, *The Myth of Sisyphus*, 109.
[90] Camus, *The Myth of Sisyphus*, 111.

ignominy of cowardice. If fate cannot be avoided or resisted it may at least be defied by being chosen; if death cannot be beaten, it may at least be 'engineered'[91] and managed in an act of human defiance and dominion; if my much vaunted 'right to life' is about to expire, I can at least claim a 'right to die' in one last gasp of assertion; if we cannot hide from death, we can at least go out to meet it in an act of noble challenge, robbing it of its victory over us by scornfully giving up our lives before they can be taken from us.

Suicide and euthanasia's scorn of death, as much as the defiant revolt and refusal of death which Camus prefers, have, however, a distinctly paradoxical character. There are, we might say, many ways to live under and in relation to a tyranny which cannot be shaken off, and amongst these, defiance is by no means unworthy of a certain respect. But whether in ignoble illusion, or whether in a more noble and clear-sighted defiance, even one aimed at scorning death, life is determined by the tyranny and the fear it inspires. Of course, cowardice is one thing, and courage is another – but courage is only courage because we acknowledge the propriety of fear. Both the courageous and the cowardly travel round this one sun, albeit in different orbits.

The Gospel, however, addresses us with an imperious 'fear not!' We are to defy death certainly, but not simply with a scorn which robs the victor of some pleasure in his victory. Our defiance is not a defiance which aims to 'surmount our fate' by a moment of human assertion, but a defiance which celebrates our ultimate release from this fate in the fact that: 'Beyond the antithesis of being and nonbeing, beyond all dialectic, it is true in Jesus Christ that God is our Father and we are his children.'[92] Our action, that is to say, is called to be not first of all an act of courage, but of confession, a confession of the hope we have in the future as the time of the grace of God shown in Jesus Christ. It is not a scornful defiance of the fact that we have no future except the absurd, but a joyous proclamation of the good future into which we are summoned.

[91] May, *The Physician's Covenant*, 84.   [92] Barth, *Ethics*, 467.

To what practice should this hope give rise? We have maintained that martyrdom, as elucidated within the Christian tradition, can be regarded as embodying a practice of dying consistent with a Christian anthropology – a dying which is filled with hope and not fear, and which is suffered rather than sought. And in relation not to martyrs, but to these others who, like them, are called to 'breathe in the atmosphere of redemption' with all those breaths they are to take in their dying, we may commend a related practice. Plainly it will need to surround the subject of death with none of that ambiguity and silence in which even those who face death cannot and must not admit the inevitable, subjecting themselves to either neglect or vain and painful overtreatment to maintain an illusion. Nor will it be a practice which is determined by the need to save face as it confronts its impotence and imminent defeat, by scornfully giving up the life it is about to lose. Freed of the fear which determines these responses and actions – seeing the gods of this world as no more than hollow idols, to whom the knee need not be bowed – it may be a practice in which the dying can quite simply and honestly accept, and the living offer, care. Such care will involve sensitive and skilled palliative treatment, whether in the hospice or elsewhere – treatment which can only begin when there is a mutual and open recognition of the fact that the goal of cure or of extending life has ceased to be appropriate. On the basis of this recognition there can be a clearsighted refusal of those heroic measures which will simply prolong, to no obvious point or purpose, the patient's dying. But this refusal does not leave the patient simply to endure neglect – liberated from the illusions and denials which tempt the patient and doctor into the practices of neglect or overtreatment, medicine may find a better role, through its compassion (its suffering with), in sustaining the patient in being a patient – one who witnesses to a trust in God's providence, which extends to and beyond death, by living to and through it, and who, in so doing, both displays and instills the virtues of 'humility and courage and hope'.[93]

---

[93] To name the virtues which, as May puts it (*The Physician's Covenant*, 84), the community's 'aged and dependent, its sick and dying' may display to it – but which

v

In the midst of his discussion of abortion, having contended that 'a definite No must be the presupposition of all further discussion', Barth comments that 'the question arises, however, how this No is to be established and stated if it is to be a truly effective No'.[94] His answer, which applies equally to the No which he takes to be the presupposition of all further discussion of euthanasia, is that the 'Church knows and has the Word of the free mercy of God which also ascribes and grants freedom to man. It could and can tell and show humanity which is tormented by life because it thinks it must live it, that it may do so.'[95] Thus the Protestant Church:

neither could nor can range itself with the Roman Catholic Church and its hard preaching of the Law. It must proclaim its own message in this matter, namely the Gospel. In so doing, however, it must not underbid the severity of the Roman Catholic No. It must overbid its abstract and negative: 'Thou shalt not', by the force of its positive: 'Thou mayest', in which, of course, the corresponding: 'Thou mayest not', is included, the No having the force not merely of the word of man but of the Word of God.[96]

Whatever the justice of such a charge against the teaching of the Roman Church of the 1930s, it is clear that a Pope who can declare that 'Jesus is the only Gospel: we have nothing further to say or any other witness to bear', is not insensitive to the concerns which lie behind Barth's complaint.[97] Indeed, in his important encyclical letter, *Evangelium Vitae*, from which this declaration is taken, we find John Paul II engaged in an attempt to display the teaching of the Church on the fundamental questions of life and death as Gospel: that is, to show that any 'must' is first of all and really a 'may', that any No is first of all and really a Yes. Thus his engagement with the problems of medical practice begins from the affirmation that 'the joy which

they will learn to display, of course, only in so far as the Church reappropriates, with some caution, the tradition of reflection to which, for example, Jeremy Taylor's *Holy Dying* is a contribution.
[94] Barth, *Church Dogmatics*, III: 4, 417.
[95] Barth, *Church Dogmatics*, III: 4, 418.   [96] Ibid.
[97] John Paul II, *Evangelium Vitae*, English trans. (London, 1995), para. 80.

accompanies the Birth of the Messiah is . . . the foundation and fulfilment of joy at every child born into the world'.[98]

My purpose in this chapter has not been to offer an exhaustive analysis of the entire field, nor even to offer an exhaustive analysis of the particular topics and issues on which I have commented. My purpose has been the altogether more limited one of illustrating something of the implications for Christian medical ethics of its taking up its constructive task, confidently and unapologetically, from its own distinctive presupposition, namely the Gospel of Jesus Christ which tells of the one who is 'the foundation and fulfilment' of joy in human life. Taking up its task from this point, it would learn to speak that decisive 'fear not' which would liberate medical practice from all those strategies by which it vainly seeks to secure human life and to ensure its meaning and value – it might be by the eradication or manipulation of unborn life, by the moulding of human life in genetic engineering, by the killing of the terminally ill or elderly. Proclaiming that human life has been secured and rendered meaningful and valuable by its place in the story of creation, reconciliation and redemption, it addresses contemporary medical practice in a wholly evangelical voice – announcing to it humankind's release from all those fears for the past, present and future which determine so much of medicine's practice and conduct.

[98] John Paul II, *Evangelium Vitae*, para. 1. I have discussed this encyclical at greater length in 'Catholics and Anglicans and Contemporary Bioethics: Divided or United?' in *Issues for a Catholic Bioethic*, ed. L. Gormally, forthcoming..

CHAPTER 3

The practice of abortion: a critique[1]

I INTRODUCTORY

Destruction of the embryo in the mother's womb is a violation of the right to live which God has bestowed upon this nascent life. To raise the question whether we are here concerned already with a human being or not is merely to confuse the issue. The simple fact is that God certainly intended to create a human being and that this nascent human being has been deliberately deprived of his life. And this is nothing but murder. A great many different motives may lead to an action of this kind; indeed in cases where it is an act of despair, performed in circumstances of extreme human or economic destitution and misery, the guilt may often lie rather with the community than with the individual. Precisely in this connexion money may conceal many a wanton deed, while the poor man's more reluctant lapse may far more easily be disclosed. All these considerations must no doubt have a quite decisive influence on our personal and pastoral attitude towards the person concerned, but they cannot in any way alter the fact of murder.[2]

These words of Dietrich Bonhoeffer, no matter the view we take of abortion, ought to prove somewhat shocking to contemporary Christians. The shock is not to do with his critical attitude to abortion as such, since critical attitudes, if less common than

---

[1] I owe a particular debt to the members of the Faculty of Religious Studies at McGill University in whose company I was able to spend a period of peace and quiet working on this essay during a recent sabbatical. I am most grateful for their generous hospitality, and especially that of my colleague Professor Doug Farrow. I am also grateful for the grant of study leave by the School of Humanities at King's College, London. Germain Grisez, Colin Gunton, Paul Helm, Peter Kashouris, Oliver O'Donovan and Francis Watson read and commented on a first draft and thereby enabled me to improve it, though in some cases by trying to be more precise about certain disagreements which remain.

[2] D. Bonhoeffer, *Ethics*, ed. E. Bethge, trans. N. H. Smith (London, 1955), 149–50.

when he wrote, are still familiar enough. What will shock those familiar with the current debate amongst Christians is his view that this critical attitude is so very obviously the right and proper one as to stand in need of no extended defence. Bonhoeffer's view is straightforward and easily stated. The motives and circumstances with and in which an abortion is performed will shape our understanding of the precise quality of the action, but they cannot alter 'the simple fact' that 'this is nothing but murder'. And then, with no more than a short footnote expressing sympathy for the Roman Catholic disapproval of the killing of the foetus even in cases where the mother's life is at risk, Bonhoeffer turns to other matters.

Anyone inclined today to state as a 'simple fact' that abortion 'is nothing but murder' would very likely be dismissed out of hand, but Bonhoeffer cannot be so easily dispatched. Bonhoeffer is generally reckoned to be one of the most significant theological thinkers of his generation and even of our century. Moreover he knew well enough that there were many who did not acknowledge the 'simple fact' of the wrongness of abortion; indeed, he was writing at a time when the German state was displaying a brutal disregard for human life which the German church had proved unable or unwilling to oppose. And yet, lacking neither skills of theological insight and argument, nor a sense of how afflicted was his own society by the moral chaos which would finally claim his own life, Bonhoeffer sees no need to develop an intricate or subtle line of argument on a matter which is in our day solemnly deemed on all sides, within and without the Church, to be difficult and perplexing – or if it is thought simple, what is thought simple is the case for rather than against abortion where the pregnancy results from rape, for example, or where the mother is herself little more than a child, or even where a baby will be 'unwanted'.

How can Bonhoeffer believe that the question of abortion is simple while knowing well enough that it is, as a matter of fact, contested? Plainly he did not subscribe to the maxim which an intellectually idle and complacent church regularly intones where it is riven by disputes, namely that such disputes are signs of 'profound theological differences'. The existence of profound theological differences is certainly a possible explanation for disagreement, but there are plenty of others. Disagreements in regard to almost any issue, from the most practical to the most theoretical, may have a source in such things as confusion, misinformation, inconsistency, prejudice, lack of imagination, and the like. Maybe we can, in the end, best explain a dispute within the church by reference to 'profound theological disagreements', but we can hardly allow ourselves to presuppose the fact of such profound disagreement, when the actual character of the disagreement can only be established by attending with the utmost care and concentration to the issues before us. Disagreement there may certainly be, but its cause is a matter for discernment not presupposition.

In this chapter we shall try to discern the shape and character of contemporary disagreements regarding abortion. We shall find, as a matter of fact, that the disagreement is not profound in at least two respects. In the first place, and for all its shrillness, we shall discover that the debate about abortion is marked more by certain crucial agreements than it is by radical disagreements. Furthermore and in the second place, we shall find ourselves forced to judge these agreements theologically questionable. This is to say, in other words, that the way in which the debate about abortion is framed is precisely such that its terms constrain Christian thought about abortion rather than allow its adequate expression. In so far as it tolerates this constraint, Christian thought is captive, albeit a willing or at least unwitting captive. Thus the recovery of a Christian understanding of abortion depends on the recovery of the freedom of Christian thought from its capture by dominant modes of discussion and debate. So the merit of Bonhoeffer's simple view will emerge only as we finally see through the current debate even if we must begin our journey by entering and reviewing this debate in the terms which it allows.

II THE CURRENT DEBATE

The current debate about abortion can be explored through a consideration of two related questions around which, in effect, it turns. First of all, does the status of the foetus matter and second, if it does, what is the status of the foetus?

(a) Does the status of the foetus matter?

To ask the question whether the status of the foetus matters will strike many as deeply odd. Of course it must matter, it will be said, whether the foetus is, so to speak, a 'thou' or a 'that'? Is not this why the question, for example, whether the foetus is a person is debated with such vigour?

We shall have cause to come back to that last mentioned question presently, but it is important to understand in the first place that if answers to that or similar questions do matter, they matter decisively only from certain points of view and that from other points of view, even if they do matter to some extent, they are by no means the end of debate nor even especially important to it. In particular these questions cannot be crucial for the moral theory which is known as consequentialism, and which has exerted a considerable influence in recent discussions of bioethics in particular and of public policy in general.

In popular terms, consequentialism is the doctrine that the ends justify the means and is associated with the names of Bentham and Mill. (Stated more carefully, it is the theory that actions are good or right, bad or wrong, in virtue, and solely in virtue, of their consequences, and further, that the morally best action in any situation is just that one which promises to maximise good consequences.) No action is as such, in and of itself, wrong. Whether or not an action is wrong is always an open or contingent question in the sense that one will in each and every case have to consider whether or not the action under consideration is likely to have, on balance, more good consequences than bad and whether it is, in particular, that one which offers the best such balance. If so, then the ends justify the means, and the consistent consequentialist will not entertain complaints which are based on the thought that there are some things which really ought not to be done no matter the good which may result – the thought which Augustine maintains when he argues that it is wrong to tell lies even for the sake of detecting heretics.[3]

Now it is easy to see that, for one who approaches the issue of abortion with consequentialist assumptions, questions about the status of the foetus can have no determinative significance. Perhaps the foetus is a person and perhaps (if these are thought to be different propositions) it can be said to possess a soul. But, since the killing of persons is, like any other action, in principle always on the agenda, abortion cannot just be ruled out but must always be considered amongst the repertoire of actions which may or may not contribute to the achievement of the most desirable state of affairs. Consistent exponents of such a position (and it may tell us something about the position that consistent exponents of it are sometimes hard to find) make themselves clear and understood by admitting that along with being open-minded about abortion they are necessarily and in principle open-minded about infanticide, for example.

Of course, it does not follow that because consequentialists are open-minded on the subject of abortion that they will always and invariably be in favour of it. Certainly, they would be suspicious of any strict prohibition of abortion, but then so ought they to be suspicious of any simply and uncritically permissive regime. There are severe problems with the sort of calculus of consequences which consequentialism presupposes. To determine that course of action, amongst all the alternatives, which offers the best balance of good and bad consequences, requires not only a remarkable ability to peer into an uncertain future, but also a not so much remarkable as questionable ability in comparing and weighing highly diverse outcomes – the problem of comparing cabbages and kings as it is sometimes characterised. But supposing for the moment and for the sake of argument that such difficulties can be surmounted – though they are considerable and arguably insurmountable – it cannot be assumed without more ado that such comparisons would favour abortion in every case in which it might be contemplated.

Certainly, it seems likely that the cases which were the stuff of

[3] Augustine, *Contra Mendacium* (*Against Lying*), PL40, 517–48, trans. H. Browne, in *The Nicene and Post-Nicene Fathers*, 1st. series, vol.III (Edinburgh, 1988).

the campaign for law reform (the teenager who has been raped, the hard-pressed mother of an already large family expecting a handicapped child and so on) will be deemed by a consequentialist analysis to be cases where abortions are warranted – just to take the first example, the already severely traumatised young girl, probably and understandably harbouring no feelings of love for the child she never wished for, will likely be said to have but a small chance of making a good mother or of giving the child a good start in life. Whatever one makes of that claim, however – and even here one may wonder whether its truth should be taken for granted quite as readily as it seems to be – the same analysis is unlikely to seem plausible in the case of the sort of abortions which have become increasingly common and indeed routine. A couple find themselves pregnant a few years before they intended to start a family. Or alternatively, they find themselves expecting a child with a minor handicap (such as hare-lip). Or, to take a third case, they find the child is not of the sex they wanted (meaning, in most cases, that it is a girl and not a boy). In none of these cases does it seem likely, prima facie, that the calculation would favour abortion. Of course, the couple are in different ways disappointed. Of course, they may regard the having of a child now as something of an inconvenience. Of course, they do not presently regard the child with the tenderness and sense of expectation which they might have had for a child other than the one they find themselves with. And maybe their sense of disappointment or inconvenience may subtly (or not so subtly) affect their future relationship with the child. But, to believe, even from a consequentialist viewpoint, that abortions are morally required in these cases, one would have to believe that the good which is likely to come to the child from his or her existence, however inauspicious its beginnings, and in addition the good which will come to anyone else who might care for the child in the place of the parents, are genuinely outweighed by any negative features of the case, so that, on balance, it would be better that the child should not be born – or at least one would have to believe, alternatively, that a greater good than would be produced by the birth of this child will come about through the birth of another that our hypothetical couple will have if they choose to have an abortion in this case but not otherwise. Now, either of these beliefs seems highly dubious even if we make the handicap a good deal more severe than we have imagined it. Thus, it might well be argued, though we shall not pursue the point in detail now, that even where a foetus is diagnosed as suffering from Down's Syndrome, the good of that child's existence is greater than any supposed burdens which this condition adds to the responsibilities and difficulties of parenthood. (And if this purported calculation seems to come out the other way, we would do well to pause to wonder whether the fact that the good of the child's existence is reckoned to be slight, and perhaps significantly less than that of other potential children, tells us more about the quality of care we give to the handicapped and our attitudes to them than it does about the undoubtedly objective limitations which handicap places on the possibility of human flourishing.) However that may be, in many other cases where abortions are presently sought it would seem that the good of the child's existence is greater than any disbenefits to itself or others, and thus that abortion is not warranted by consequentialist reasoning; and if that is so, it will also be that much harder to maintain as simply obvious that this good is one which is best traded for another and greater good which will result from the birth of another envisaged child. This is to overlook all such matters as the costs and traumas of abortion, the possible difficulties of conceiving, the risk that a future child might itself be severely handicapped and so on. The main point, however, is that consequentialism, often thought to provide a defence of the status quo, might well prove to be a restrictive rather than a straightforwardly permissive creed in relation to the general western norm of abortion on demand, were its recommended moral calculus attempted.

There is, of course, a respect in which the calculations we have been imagining are highly sensitive to particular elements in the situation, and this sensitivity begins to draw to our attention something of the difficulties in this whole way of thought for Christians (above and beyond the theoretical difficulties of which we must, in due course, make further mention). Suppose the various couples we have envisaged were far more

deeply averse to the birth of the child they have conceived than
we have imagined. Suppose, let us say, that they are so
profoundly and deeply materialistic that they are utterly dis-
traught at the possibility of their child being born before they
have completed the swimming-pool and games room they have
always wanted to build in their garden. Or suppose that,
priding themselves in particular on their looks and beauty, they
find the thought of having a child with a condition as mild as
hare-lip quite repugnant. Or suppose, in our third case, that,
for whatever reason, they so value a male child over a female
one, that the prospect of having a child of the 'wrong' sex causes
them very significant distress. And suppose further and in each
case that the consequentialist calculation is so crucially influenced or determined by these elements in the situation that
they are decisive in tipping the decision against the child's life.

What this brings to our attention is that consequentialist
reasoning is inclined, broadly speaking, to take our desires and
wishes as fixtures and fittings, as the givens of the case which
any moral calculus must take for granted. It thus invites us to
stand over any situation as observers, even ones in which we are
involved, making no judgment as such on the desires which are
perhaps crucial in determining the character of that situation
and the relative merits, in consequentialist terms, of the various
possibilities for action which lie within in. But, typically, the
stance of an uncritical observer is not one with which the
conscientious thinker will feel comfortable, and Christians in
particular are likely to balk at the relationship to one's desires
which this stance seems to presuppose.

Two points need to be made. In the first place, in so far as the
consequentialist calculus seems to take our desires for granted,
it overlooks the education and re-ordering of our desires which
Christianity teaches. 'Do not be conformed to this world' says
Paul, 'but be transformed by the renewal of your minds'
(Romans, 12: 2). And this renewal of our minds, which comes
about as we understand ourselves and the world in the light of
the gospel of creation, reconciliation and redemption which has
concerned Paul in the previous chapters of his letter, reorders
our beliefs and with that reordering, reorders our attitudes,

affections and desires. Thus, to go back to the cases we mentioned earlier, couples whose desire for an abortion depends on a desire for a swimming pool, for a 'perfect' child, or for a child of the 'right' sex (i.e., male), need to allow these desires to be schooled by Christian beliefs which might be expected, in different ways, to unsettle them.

But there is a second point which is important, and which comes into play even where the desires which have a part in determining the outcome of the consequentialist calculation are neither plainly, nor even arguably, disordered. Let us go back to the case of the victim of rape who finds herself pregnant. Amongst her desires variously affected by the birth of a child, might be a desire to go to university, or to take up a new and demanding job abroad, or to give more time to her writing, music or art. None of these desires is, on the face of it, improper. Even in a life which is in a very high degree morally conscientious, we might expect that such desires could and would and even should be satisfied in some way. But there is still something wrong, Christians might feel, with the invitation which consequentialism makes to us, even when our desires are the vital factors in the situation, to adopt the stance of observers and discern the best outcome by weighing in the balance the satisfaction of our desires alongside the satisfaction of any others. Bentham's famous slogan 'each to count for one and no more than one' is a proper plea against the temptation to which all moral agents are prone of thinking that their happiness should count for more simply on account of its being theirs! But the neutrality about my own happiness which prevents me counting it twice, becomes questionable when it seems to prevent me from wondering whether in some circumstances I should consider counting it less than once. Of course, when I am told that a decision favouring the claims of *a* over *b* will produce the best balance of consequences, I shall, if I think in consequentialist terms, favour this decision over any others. Even when I discover that I am *b*, I shall, if I am properly disinterested, continue to hold that this is the best outcome. But the minute that I discover that I am *a*, I immediately find myself invited, though not by consequentialism, to occupy another and

different position and perspective, in which the fact of my being
an agent possessed of moral responsibility asks me to consider
whether my desires should count for less than one. (And this is
why what are often called 'pastoral approaches' to moral
problems are so insufferably patronising, bidding me abandon
the perspective of a moral agent for whom sacrifice is a genuine
moral option and for whom the distinction between what is
forgivable or understandable on the one hand, and what is right
on the other, remains important.) None of this, of course, settles
the question of what course of action the victim of rape should
follow; it is to say, however, that there are certain further
questions she may well wish to pose in spite of consequentialism, which simply refuses them.

We have been giving the consequentialist approach a run for
its money, granting for the sake of argument its highly controversial assumption that, broadly speaking, ends may justify
means and also its equally controversial assumptions concerning the possibility of a moral calculus. We have seen how
this approach will tend to shape our thinking about the problem
of abortion, though we have also seen that a consistent consequentialism can by no means be assumed to be conservative
in relation to the present permissive regime. But we have
further seen that, even prior to examining its basic assumptions
directly, we discover problems with consequentialism as we
consider its failure properly to account for two aspects of moral
thought in relation to our desires which Christians, but not only
Christians, will wish to highlight: in the first place that these
desires may need 'schooling', and, in the second place, even
where they do not, that the responsibilities of moral agency
seem to invite us to adopt a relationship towards them more
subtle than unthinking neutrality. In both cases, what seems
wrong is the tendency to stand outside the situation as mere
observers, on the one hand treating desires as givens beyond
reform, and on the other forgetting that some of the desires
which constrain the situation are ours.

It is high time, however, to ask some questions about the key
assumption from which consequentialism begins. We have
already mentioned Augustine's insistence that it is wrong to tell

lies even for the sake of detecting heretics. In making this claim Augustine appeals in the first instance to the authority of Paul ('You should not do evil that good may come': Romans, 3: 8), but this appeal to authority does not prevent him developing a case which anticipates many of the arguments which have featured in modern-day disputes regarding the validity of consequentialism. In the end, however, Augustine's case against those who would tell lies for a good purpose comes down to this: to hold that it is sometimes right to lie is to hold that one may do evil that good may come; but this is to hold that if of the 'number of lewd Priscillianists [the heretics in question], some woman should cast her eye upon a catholic Joseph, and promise him she will betray their hidden retreats if she obtain from him that he lie with her, and it be certain that if he consent unto her she will make good her promise', we would be obliged to conclude that he should 'lie with her', so that there would be 'chaste adulteries', or thefts, or blasphemies, or whatever may be necessary to achieve the good end. But this, thinks Augustine, is absurd. Though 'It does indeed make very much difference, for what cause, with what end, with what intention a thing be done . . . those things which are clearly sins, are upon no plea of a good cause, with no seeming good end, no alleged good intention, to be done.'[4]

What is the force of this argument? Is it not simply, someone might say, an insistence that 'one should not do evil that good may come?' when this is exactly what is in dispute between consequentialism and its critics? The form of Augustine's argument here is that of a *reductio ad absurdum*, whereby the implications of a belief (in this case the belief that one may do evil that good may come and the implication that there might be good thefts, fornications and blasphemies) are held up as absurd. Now those thus challenged can, in principle, make a number of replies. They might maintain that the alleged implications of the fundamental principle, whether or not they are absurd, are not in fact implications of it. This, however, does not seem to be a promising strategy in this particular case.

---

[4] Augustine, *Against Lying*, 487.

Alternatively, if it is conceded that the implications really are implications, it will have to be contended that they are by no means absurd. Sure enough, it may be admitted, it seems surprising that there can be good thefts, fornications and blasphemies, but surprising conclusions are not the same as absurd ones.

The shift in moral opinion since Augustine's time, however motivated, does not help him here, and in presenting his argument to an audience of modern-day undergraduates (even perhaps to an audience of ordinands) one would probably be well advised to change his examples, since perceptions of various elements of the real and imagined cases have changed. Thus catching heretics is perhaps not thought to be a very pressing good end, and, more to the point, the existence of good thefts, and possibly even of good fornications and blasphemy, may be thought obvious rather than absurd. But the particular examples do not matter of course, for the principle that one may do evil that good may come will also yield the conclusion that, say, one may, for the sake of a greater good, discriminate against someone on ground of race or sex, that one might torture children, or that one might commit rape. And those conclusions are perhaps as likely to seem absurd to many moderns, as Augustine's examples seemed to many of his contemporaries.

Still, however, the determined defender of consequentialism may refuse to concede. Consequentialism is a moral theory which understands very well that its conclusions will seem absurd, and thus that its acceptance will lead to a reform of moral practice. It is hardly surprising that its conclusions will be opposed and resisted, its advocates will insist, but they are by no means shown to be wrong by such opposition.

The nature of this opposition must, however, be understood, since it can give an account of itself as something other than mere resistance to new ideas. Augustine's argument is, in essence and to translate it into our terms, that if consequentialism maintains that actions are good or bad solely in virtue of their consequences, then no action is, in principle, illicit. But, contrary to such an assumption, so Augustine and his modern allies claim, the belief that rape, racial discrimination and torturing children are always and ever wrong, is more certain than any claim about actions being justified by their consequences. That claim is, after all, a theoretical judgment which is itself neither self-evident nor supported by manifestly compelling argument. And even if the theoretical claim were better supported, so they might continue, at the least it has to be admitted that the relationship between moral theory and moral practice is more complex than any automatic favouring of the theoretical predilections of consequentialism seems to allow.

Take an analogy. Someone proposes a theory of what makes for good drama. On paper it looks a simple and persuasive account. But, when we start to apply this dramatic theory to plays we know, we find that it does not so much modify, deepen or nuance our critical judgments (which any good theory surely will) but radically overthrows them. Thus we find that according to this theory, *Henry V, Romeo and Juliet* and *Hamlet* are all to be reckoned bad plays; so too, let us suppose, the entire works of Racine, Chekhov and Molière. Now there is nothing here to compel the advocate of the theory to withdraw; like a government minister whose position has become 'unsustainable' as the press has it, the theorist may just 'tough it out'. It will, however, take a very strong preference for theory over practice for the theorist to stick to his or her guns and insist that these really are bad plays when the application of the theory is more likely to encourage us to wonder about its adequacy. For surely we properly trust our first-order judgments about what counts as a good play (even if we do not think these judgments are infallible), more than we trust any second-order theories about drama – which is just to say that our sense that *Hamlet* is a great play is considerably more secure than any theory about the nature of drama which we might spin.

Now the point of this analogy is to suggest the following. The claim that we may do evil that good may come is itself a second-order, theoretical judgment. But this claim comes into conflict with all sorts of first-order moral judgments: such as that one should not torture children, discriminate on grounds of race or sex, or whatever. There is, however, no reason to be forced into an abandonment of these first-order judgments by a second-order theory, which is itself less secure than those judgments. Indeed, there is every reason to refuse to be bullied by this unwarranted preference for theory over practice, albeit that one must rightly allow that the relationship between theory and practice in this area is a matter of some subtlety and needs careful handling. The problem with consequentialism, however, is just that it seems unaware of any such subtleties.

Although we have not mentioned abortion for a while, the discussion has been far from irrelevant to our subject. We began by asking the perhaps surprising question whether, in thinking about abortion, the status of the foetus matters. We pointed out that for the moral theory which holds that the ends justify the means, the status of the foetus could never be of decisive significance. It must always be an open question whether an abortion is justified in the circumstances, whether or not the foetus is a person, just because the killing of persons is itself always a possible course of action according to this point of view. We have sought to show, however, that there are certain good reasons for not accepting consequentialism, or at the least that its claims to our allegiance are far from obvious; hence the question of the status of the foetus becomes important, for the very reason that the taking of the life of a foetus might just be one of those means which no ends would justify. So the question of the status of the foetus cannot, it seems, be avoided.

Someone might still be forgiven for supposing that although not irrelevant in principle, the discussion has been something of a diversion in fact, just because apart from in departments of philosophy (or more commonly in departments of economics) consequentialists are rarely to be met with. Such a degree of intellectual quarantine would doubtless have been desirable, but the fact is that consequentialism has played a considerable role in shaping discussion about a host of moral questions even where those who seem to rely upon its presuppositions would be incapable of identifying or naming it. Thus one may discern the influence of consequentialism in the debate about abortion, as elsewhere, even when its assumptions are neither explicitly acknowledged nor adequately defended. Two examples will illustrate why the preceding discussion has been vital.

The first example will be recognised by anyone who has ever discussed the subject of abortion and has indicated even a passing willingness to entertain the thought that abortion is morally wrong as such and therefore should not enter into our thinking as an acceptable means to certain ends, no matter how good those ends may be. The defender of the status quo who refuses to give this thought a moment's reflection will certainly gain rhetorical advantage by descrying the 'extremism' of his or her opponents, and may even press the advantage by labelling their attitude 'absolutist'. And if this is not enough to win the day, one can develop the argument (one uses the noun loosely) by contrasting a 'negative absolutism' with an 'affirming prag- matism'; in some circles one can successfully round the whole thing off by further characterising the 'negative absolutism' as 'papist', though it is always as well to deploy this further refinement with a little caution for fear of sacrificing the advantage thus far gained with any who might harbour Roman Catholic prejudices.[5]

Of course, this will not do. The labels 'extremist' and 'absolutist' are certainly ones which no one will pick to describe their own position, but it is by no means clear that the rhetorical advantage which is gained by pressing these labels on those who think that abortion may be wrong in principle is anything other than rhetorical. After all, to revert to the earlier discussion, the committed consequentialist who thinks that non-therapeutic and harmful experimentation on unwilling human subjects may be justified can equally accuse all those who support the Nuremberg Code of being 'absolutists' and 'extremists', though it may be more difficult to make the label 'papist' stick in this case. Anyone *but* a consequentialist will be an absolutist in relation to certain moral principles, even if they disagree with some others about the scope of those principles – thus to change the example, it is hardly helpful, intellectually speaking, to accuse the out and out pacifist of being an 'absolutist' if one

---

[5] The reader is asked to note that the use of irony is not forbidden ministers of the Church of England.

wishes to maintain oneself that, let us say, the killing of prisoners of war is wrong. One might conclude, then, that the abolition of the label 'absolutist', while it would deprive some of a crutch, would serve the purposes of all those who are concerned that these matters should be subject to rational argument rather than to the crudest of rhetorical tricks.

If the use of the charge of 'absolutism' is typically an evasion which could only become something other than that by an acknowledged reliance on consequentialism and a willingness to defend its presuppositions, so too is the use of the slogan which asserts 'a woman's right to choose' if it is deployed as a bar to debate and not, as it might be, as a statement of a conclusion arrived at by means of an argument which can be brought out into the open, explicated and defended. On the face of it the slogan is no more than an assertion by members a particular group of a claim to be entitled to act in this matter as they alone determine; it is as if, that is to say, a case against slavery were met with the assertion of 'a slave-owner's right to choose'. But, in either case, a discussion of the rights and wrongs of *who* should take decisions in these matters presupposes that whatever is being chosen is the sort of thing which can properly be chosen, when that is just what is in question where the status of the slave or the foetus is a matter for dispute. And, if consequentialism is unacceptable, the rightness or wrongness of choosing an abortion will crucially depend on the answer to the question which we must now address: what is the status of the foetus?

(b) What is the status of the foetus?

For many, the question of the status of the foetus is where the debate about abortion really begins. Not only have they never heard of consequentialism, but they are not attracted by its doctrines. They will presuppose – and, so we have claimed, may presuppose with a certain propriety – that there are certain sorts of actions which ought not to be done no matter the intentions and ends one might have in view in doing them. Now we have already noted, in mentioning Augustine, that different individuals and societies may give different lists of such actions, but one likely candidate for inclusion in any list of 'thou shalt nots' is a 'thou shalt not kill'. Stated positively, many people would say that human life is sacred, and that its sacredness requires that it be accorded absolute respect. It is certainly right in general to consider the consequences of our actions, they might say, but never right to take human life even for the sake of very good consequences.

We can hardly fail to notice, however, that the 'thou shalt not kill' with which our society is most familiar occurs in the law code of a nation which eschewed neither war nor capital punishment. It would be a mistake to conclude too quickly that this is a blatant inconsistency; the very fact of its blatancy renders such an explanation somewhat unlikely. Indeed, it is better to suppose quite simply that 'thou shalt not kill' was understood rather more specifically than it is by those who take the view that the prohibition precludes both war and capital punishment. May be it was understood, that is to say, as prohibiting the killing of the innocent, for example, and thus as perfectly consistent with the practices mentioned.

It is not to the point to pursue the question as to which of these or other construals of the commandment is to be preferred. That there is a question to be pursued, however, points to the fact that a dispute about the rights and wrongs of abortion should not immediately be characterised as a dispute between those who accept and those who deny a doctrine of the sanctity of human life. Certainly we have seen that this way of characterising the situation will sometimes be appropriate: the consistent and hard-nosed consequentialist is, of course, obliged to deny any doctrine of the sanctity of human life just because such a doctrine would hold that human life (or innocent human life) is to be accorded an absolute respect. But the example of the previous paragraph suggests that there can be a dispute about the principle of the sanctity of human life even between those who accept it, a dispute not about its validity, that is to say, but about its scope. Thus those who argue that the foetus (or the foetus up to twenty-four weeks, prior to viability, or at whatever other point) falls outside the scope of the principle, like those who argue that convicted murderers fall outside its scope, are not to be accused immediately of doubting the validity of the principle as such. Indeed, one way of making sense of the law in relation to abortion in most western jurisdictions is just to see it as ruling on the scope whilst not questioning the validity of the principle of the sanctity of human life, since these jurisdictions typically signal a continuing commitment to that principle by leaving in place the crime of infanticide, for example.

The current and predominant legal position and its advocates and defenders cannot, then, be accused of simply denying the doctrine of the sanctity of human life; their position may make moral sense precisely in terms of the distinction between validity and scope to which we have alluded. Of course, it may not make moral sense. It may emerge that as a matter of fact there is a hidden inconsistency in the proposal to exclude foetuses, so that what should be treated in the first instance as a claim about the scope of the principle can, on second sight and after closer examination, be held to be a surreptitious rejection of it. That is to say that there are some attempts to establish the scope or bounds of a principle which have finally to be considered repudiations of it, since the case for the limitation is not morally comprehensible.

We could mark and illustrate the difference by contrasting the explication of a rule with the mere making of exceptions to it. Thus the rule that 'no pets are permitted within the college grounds' is explicated when we learn that guide dogs are permitted within the college, since we discover that the word 'pets' is construed, perfectly reasonably, as not covering certain working animals. But, if we learn that the bursar's dog is permitted in the college, we have not so much better understood the principle as simply learnt of an exception which, for whatever reason, is made to it. The exception is not completely mysterious, since the role and influence of bursars is generally such that we are not exactly surprised that it is made; but its existence is not explicable by reference to the rule's underlying rationale and is thus not, so to speak, morally comprehensible, and hence amounts to a repudiation of the rule, albeit one which may not threaten its general effectiveness.

Returning to the dispute about the scope of the principle of the sanctity of human life, we must give notice, then, that whilst we shall endeavour to treat the dispute as just that (that is, as a dispute about the proper explication of the rule between those who accept its validity), a failure to make moral sense of any proffered 'explications' will drive us to consider whether limitations of the rule's scope in relation to the foetus must, in fact, be deemed mere exceptions. To be specific, we may find ourselves forced to conclude that the limitations which are placed on the scope of the principle of the sanctity of life by the exclusion of foetuses from the protection it is usually reckoned to afford, are not morally compelling, however else they may be motivated.

One way in which the limitation is held to be justified is, of course, by maintaining that the protection which the principle requires is owed to persons, but that foetuses (or at least foetuses prior to viability, or whatever) are not persons and therefore are not within the principle's scope. Thus the question as to whether or not the limitation on the scope of the principle is acceptable is converted into the question 'is the foetus a person?'

It is, however, by no means obvious that the conversion of the question into this form actually constitutes a step towards its resolution. It could only constitute such a step if there were agreement not only on the principle that absolute respect is owed only to persons (which we may assume for the sake of argument), but also on the further and rather crucial matter of what it is to be a person, or at least on how this further question could be settled. And yet on both these points – on what it is to be a person, and on how the question of what it is to be a person could be settled – unanimity is not to be found.

On the question of what it is to be a person, we find on one side the view that from the moment of conception we have to do with a living and independent being (independent in the sense that it cannot be regarded as a part of the mother's body), the life of which can only be human; now since all humans are persons, the newly fertilised egg or embryo is a person. On the other side, we find the view that whilst the foetus is certainly alive and its life is human life, not all humans are persons. Typically it will be said that to be a person is to exercise certain functions and capacities characteristic of human life: it might be, for example, that the exercise of rational choice (which is what is usually meant by possession of autonomy), is picked out as the defining characteristic. Now a foetus is not capable of rational choice and is, therefore, not a person. (Obviously there are numerous variations on these two positions.)

Though both sides claim to agree that protection and respect is owed to persons, since they differ over what it is to be a person, this posing of the problem of abortion in these terms will only represent an advance if we have some means of agreeing on which of these accounts of what it is to be a person is to be preferred. No advance will be achieved whilst one side deduces from one set of premises (including the premise that all human beings are persons) that foetuses fall under the scope of the protection which the principle of the sanctity of life extends to persons, whilst the other side deduces from another set of premises (including the premise that only those presently capable of rational choice are persons) that they do not. But it is by no means obvious what these means would be; plainly it would be ridiculous to suppose that resort to a dictionary will allow us to chose between the two key premises (even if it provides evidence of what people have traditionally thought about the denotation of the word 'person'), since those who say that the foetus is or is not a person are not making a claim about how words are used, but rather about how they should be used. They are saying, in other words, that the word 'person', which is typically employed to mark out a subject of legal and moral standing, should or should not apply to the foetus. But the force of the 'should' in either case depends not on facts about language, but on facts concerning the foetus. Thus the debate is more helpfully posed not by asking ourselves whether the foetus is or is not a person, but by asking whether there is any difference or differences between the foetus and those human beings held uncontroversially worthy of protection by the principle of the sanctity of life which would render the denial of that same protection to the foetus morally explicable.

Of course, as has been said, there are any number of different candidates as answers to this question, some of which we have already encountered. We might think of these answers as on a continuum with the most exclusive answers at one end, and with the more inclusive at the other. Arranging them in these terms, some popular attempts to identify a difference which makes a difference, so to speak, might be rationality, 24 weeks or viability, sentience or the capacity to feel pain, or 14 days. We should look at each of these, albeit briefly, in turn.

The notion that because it lacks rationality the foetus is properly denied the protection which the principle of the sanctity of life demands in other cases has a certain simplicity to it, and also latches on to one aspect of certain common ways of thinking about the respect due to life in its different forms. Thus whatever view we may take about experimentation on animals, for example, at the very least most people would prefer that animals other than higher primates should be used where this is possible. This preference may have a number of roots, but one might lie in the sense that the relatively rich mental life of which chimpanzees, for example, are thought capable, renders their use objectionable where other animals would serve the purpose.

What this may suggest to us (though it would require a good deal more analysis and discussion if it were to do more than suggest it), is that the wrongness of taking a life may increase in proportion to the mental richness of that life. But even if it does suggest this, it is one thing to suggest that the possession of rationality may increase the wrongness of killing, and quite another to show that its absence could serve to excuse it in some cases or more generally to render it innocent. On the last point, not everything which seems to be deserving of respect and protection is rational, or even alive, or even for that matter presently in existence. Animals, plants, landscapes, ecosystems, works of art, historic buildings, corpses and future generations are just some of the items which it can be argued make claims, in different ways, for respect and protection;[6] and if this is so, it is by no means obvious that foetuses (not to mention new born

---

[6] The variety of moral claims is brought out tellingly in Mary Midgeley's 'Duties Concerning Islands' in *Environmental Ethics*, ed. R. Elliot (Oxford, 1995), 89–103.

infants, the severely mentally handicapped and the senile, since these too may be held to lack rationality), can properly be treated as disqualified from moral regard simply because they lack rationality.

Lack of rationality may, however, be thought to warrant not complete disqualification from moral consideration, but simply disqualification from the absolute protection which is accorded by the principle of the sanctity of life. After all it might be said, the fact that lots of things lacking rationality have a certain moral standing does not show that they should be accorded the moral standing normally attributed to human life. Rationality, it might be admitted, is not the foundation for all moral standing, but is precisely the foundation for the specific form of moral standing which is expressed by the principle that one should not intend the death of a human being, whereas one might, in certain circumstances and without denying their moral standing completely, intend the death or destruction of an animal, plant, building, and so on.

This claim – that rationality is a necessary condition for possessing the moral standing recognised by the principle of the sanctity of life – plainly has more to be said for it than the wider claim that rationality is a necessary condition for moral standing as such. It is not clear, however, that this more is enough to compel its acceptance. In the first place, it seems to overlook a fact of arguably some importance, namely that the foetus will, unlike animals, plants and buildings, come to possess the rationality typically associated with human life. In the second place, however, this stipulation of a condition necessary to gain the absolute protection normally accorded to human life (i.e., present possession of certain rational faculties) deprives, as we have said, the senile, severely mentally handi-capped and the new born of such protection. But it suffers from a further difficulty just in the fact of its being a stipulation; for whilst it may be that one cannot oblige someone, by appeal to universally accepted reasons, not to make this stipulation sup-posing they are willing to accept its implications, the fact is, however, that alongside it stand countless other possible stipula-tions, perhaps more exclusive (an IQ in excess of 100, for example), which seem to share with it its seemingly morally arbitrary character.

The drawing of the line at viability – commonly said to be attained presently at twenty-four weeks, though arguably attained earlier than this already, and certainly to be expected to be attained ever earlier as medicine develops – has a strong claim from the medical or legal point of view at least in the sense that if a line is to be drawn, it should certainly be drawn no later than this. It if were to be drawn later, then depending on the method of abortion, highly anomalous situations would arise, whereby a foetus could be delivered alive in one part of a hospital and left to die, where in another part of the hospital the same conduct might not only be considered as constituting bad medical practice but might also give rise to a charge of murder or manslaughter. The key difference between these cases would lie, presumably, in the wishes of the mother, but reference to parental wishes is hardly a secure or principled reference point for good medical practice or for the law of murder; thus viability commends itself as a place at or before which a line should be drawn.

The reasons for saying that if a line is to be drawn anywhere it should not be drawn any later than at this point in the foetus' development are not however, in themselves, reasons for saying that it should not be drawn earlier (or not at all). And whilst the moment of viability has, as we have noted, a certain legal and medical utility, it is far from clear that viability has any moral relevance, let along decisive moral significance. As regards its significance, all sorts of people are 'viable' only through their reliance on others, even if this reliance is not as intimate or extensive as the reliance of a foetus on its mother. It is hard to see how a failure to have reached the moment of viability should exclude foetuses from the protection of the principle of the sanctity of life, without also excluding these others, but more to the point it is even harder to see why viability should count at all. Again it is open to someone to stipulate that life can be taken with impunity where it cannot be sustained without assistance, or, more modestly, that such life does not deserve absolute protection even if it deserves some moral consideration; but though these creeds have certainly had an appeal for some of our century's more notorious regimes, it is far from obvious that weakness is to be regarded as disqualifying human life from protection.

The acquisition of a capacity for pain is sometimes held to be the point at which to draw a line. (The dating of this point is a matter of uncertainty and controversy which need not concern us; many would argue that twenty-three weeks is the likely stage at which the foetus develops the capacity for pain without thereby ruling out entirely the possiblity that it may be gained much earlier indeed.[7]) But again, as with rationality, the identification of a capacity for pain as *the* morally significant moment seems to confuse what may increase culpability with what is necessary to it. Certainly, the fact that a being suffers in its death is a factor in our assessment of the exact moral character of the killing, just as is its capacity for various forms of intellectual and social life. But a killing can plainly be wrongful even where no pain is suffered. Thus, the fact that the foetus does not feel pain cannot thereby be sufficient to show that its death is not a subject for moral criticism, nor even that while the foetus has some moral standing it does not deserve the protection accorded by the principle of the sanctity of human life.

Perhaps it makes a difference, however, that the early foetus rather than simply not feeling pain, is in fact incapable of feeling pain. The point would be that the foetus' incapacity in this respect serves to indicate that it is not a sentient being; thus, while it may be true that a killing can be wrongful even where no pain is suffered, it might be argued that it is wrongful, even though painless, just because the killing ends a sentient life. Where there is no pain because there is no sentience, so it might be said, the killing is not wrongful.

The problems with this argument seem to be twofold. In the first place, we can repeat in part the point we made in relation to the claim that rationality should function as a criterion of moral significance. Although sentience is, so to speak, a lower

---

[7] See, for some of the issues, the Parliamentary Office of Science and Technology's 'Fetal Awareness', POST, note 94 (London, 1997).

hurdle than rationality, it is still the case that as we review the list we gave then of things which might be held to make moral claims upon us without being rational we find some which are not sentient: plants, works of art and corpses, for example. Thus, it is far from obvious that the foetus does not deserve protection just because it lacks sentience. In any case, and in the second place, the foetus will possess sentience supposing it develops. Of course, if I were to kill it in the meantime I would have deprived the foetus only of a potential for sentience, but that defence of my actions seems weak, since we usually reckon it wrong to deprive people of capacities they will possess in the future, even if they do not possess them now. (It would be no defence to the charge that one had removed an eight-year-old girl's ovaries to insist that one had done her no harm since one had merely deprived her of her potential fertility.) But a deeper problem with sentience as a criterion for moral regard can be brought out by noticing another item on our earlier list: future generations. The nature of any obligation we may owe to future generations is a matter of some debate, but without going into that question we can at least remark that if we do owe an obligation to future generations (as current commitments to sustainable development, for example, suppose), it cannot be their present capacities which ground this obligation, since they have no present capacities. But then, if we do have an obligation to future generations in spite of their lacking present capacities including sentience, it is difficult to understand how the early foetus' lack of sentience should disqualify it from moral regard. It has a potential for sentience and for rationality in a much more straightforward sense than do non-existent future generations: if allowed to go to term a viable foetus will possess all those capacities we associate with fully developed human beings. Of course, if we kill the foetus now it will be none the wiser and will never come to regret our actions. But if we could not defend ourselves against the charge that our present life style threatens future generations by pointing out that we intend to life in such a manner that there will be no future generations, it is unclear why the same defence should be contemplated in the case of the foetus.

The difficulties even with as relatively inclusive a criterion as sentience must drive us to consider the claims made for fourteen days as the point at which what would now generally be referred to as an embryo rather than a foetus, should be afforded the protection of the principle of the sanctity of life. Such claims deserve our attention for two reasons. In the first place, although abortions typically occur much later than this, the question of the moral acceptability of abortions prior to fourteen days is a pertinent issue since its determination will be relevant to the acceptability of what are often thought of as forms of contraception but which either plainly ('morning-after' pills and chemical 'contraceptives', such as RU486) or generally (the IUD, or 'coil' as it is sometimes known) function as abortifacients. In the second place, the fourteen-day divide has assumed a certain significance as the point at which UK and other law prohibits experimentation on embryos, and if we are to make moral sense of the present legal settlement we shall need to reckon with this feature of the law as well as with the law relating to abortion as such.

Those who take the view that prior to fourteen days the embryo is not deserving of the protection demanded by the principle of the sanctity of human life tend to be impressed by a number of features of early embryonic development.

(a) Until about fourteen days it remains unclear whether early embryos will actually go on to become individual human beings – a particular embryo may become two (as in the case of monozygotic twins) or none (if it develops as a hydatidiform mole).

(b) Whilst the embryo is genetically unique from conception, and may be developmentally unique, so to speak, from around fourteen days, it is still a relatively undifferentiated organism, and certainly lacks many of the capacities we associate with fully developed human life, such as sentience.

(c) It seems that as few as one in five fertilised eggs actually develops to term. Furthermore many of those which are unsuccessful are genetically abnormal.

The significance of these considerations is by no means uncontroversial, however, and replies could be made as follows:

(a) The uncertainty about whether an early embryo will go on to become an individual human being or will become two or none, is just that: an uncertainty. In the present state of scientific knowledge we do not know what the outcome of the development of a particular embryo will be. It is, however, odd to argue from our uncertainty about whether something is true (i.e., whether the early embryo will finally become an individual human being) to its being false (i.e., that the early embryo is not an individual human being) or to its being permissible for us to act as if it were false.

(b) The fact that the early embryo is relatively undifferentiated and does not yet possess the capacities which we typically associate with fully developed human beings is not obviously significant for reasons we have previously explored.

(c) It is difficult to see what, if any, significance should be attached to the natural wastage of early embryos or to fact that many so lost are genetically impaired. The fact that infant mortality has often stood at very high levels, especially so in the case of the handicapped, does not cause us to doubt our duty to respect the sanctity of infant life in general, nor the sanctity of the life of the handicapped in particular.

Now those who are utterly convinced of the case for the moral significance of the fourteen-day divide could claim to behave conscientiously in supporting the practice of abortion and the use of abortifacients up to this point and no further. But it is extremely difficult to see what basis such utter conviction could have, since the replies to points (a), (b) and (c) are, at the least, grounds for thinking that the matter is unproven. Thus, a proper moral caution would seem to require that we make use of neither, for if the killing of a foetus is possibly wrong that possibility argues against killing, rather than providing a justification for it.

Am I claiming then, someone might ask, that abortion is always morally wrong and furthermore that it can be shown to be such by argument? The first half of the question had better be left until we have examined what the tradition has considered hard cases, but the second half of the question can be answered here and now. Looking back over the discussion, it will be seen that what has been maintained is that there are no differences between the foetus and those human beings typically held worthy of protection by the principle of the sanctity of life which are both morally relevant and plainly morally sufficient to justify making an exception of the foetus; that is to say, no differences which would render the denial of that same protection to the foetus fully morally explicable. This denial seems to be an arbitrary repudiation of the principle, then, rather than a morally comprehensible explication of its scope. So much argument can show. But were we to confront someone who denies the principle altogether it is clear that the appeal to consistency on which the argument thus far has depended can do no further work for us. When, for example, a modern philosopher (echoing Nietzsche) describes 'the idea of human dignity' as the 'moral effluvium of a discredited metaphysics',[8] the error, if there is one, is not one of logic alone. There is no inconsistency here, but rather the consistent application of a metaphysics and anthropology (i.e., a view of the world and humankind) which repudiates the valuation of human life, and individual human life, which belongs within, for example, the Christian tradition. Karl Barth wrote:

The last war, with all that led up to it and all its possible consequences, has posed afresh the problem of humanity from the particular angle of the question of the rights, dignity and sanctity of the fellow-man. Humanity stands at the crossroads. In its future development as humanity, will it be for man or against him? Behind the political, social and economic possibilities there stands always with the same urgency, if in different forms, the necessity of this decision.[9]

What Barth and Nietzsche both believed, for all their differences, is that that decision will only be made for the 'rights, dignity and sanctity of the fellow-man' if it takes its stand on a 'discredited metaphysics'.

We wondered to begin with whether we might make sense of the law in relation to abortion as it stands in most western

---

[8] J. Rachels, *Created From Animals: The Moral Implications of Darwinism* (Oxford, 1990), 5. For Nietzsche on this theme, see *The Anti-Christ*, trans. R. J. Hollingdale (Harmondsworth, 1968).

[9] K. Barth, *Church Dogmatics*, III: 2, trans. H. Knight et al. (Edinburgh, 1960), 228.

jurisdictions by seeing it as ruling on the scope whilst not questioning the validity of a principle of respect for human life, since these jurisdictions typically signal a commitment to that principle by continuing to criminalise infanticide, for example. But recall that in pursuing answers to the question 'what is the status of the foetus?', we have failed to make moral sense of the various grounds which might be offered as justifying exclusion of the foetus from the protection typically accorded to human life. Some of these grounds seemed morally irrelevant. Thus, although the foetus is not viable, this fact about it seems beside the point – one might as well say that it is small. Other grounds seem morally relevant, but not decisive; certainly the early foetus is not sentient, but sentience is arguably necessary neither for moral consideration in general nor for the particular moral consideration enshrined in the principle of the sanctity of life. When we add in the prohibition of experimentation on embryos after fourteen days the scene becomes more complicated, since if it is wrong to experiment on embryos after fourteen days it is far from plain how it can be right to abort them up to twenty-four weeks, unless we can make ourselves believe that the status of a foetus and its claim to protection are crucially determined by whether it is in a glass dish or in the womb. The law, and the medical practice it permits, presents a morally confused picture, which could, as we have acknowledged, be rendered consistent by a move in either direction, either for or against the foetus. Sometimes then, as Barth also observed, we may find ourselves giving thanks to God for the inconsequence of humankind.

III BEYOND THE CURRENT DEBATE

So far we have reviewed the debate about abortion in the terms in which it is commonly conducted. But we have already indicated that in these terms the argument is wrongly posed; thus the simple view taken by Bonhoeffer will commend itself to us not as a conclusion to that argument, but only as we come to understand why this way of framing the questions is, from a Christian viewpoint, highly problematic. The Church has no business simply entering this debate on the terms which the debate itself allows, just because, as we shall see, those terms do not facilitate the statement of the Church's distinctive point of view.

Though the debate about abortion can sometimes seem quite varied and complex, the sense of diversity is diminished when we take note of the fact that it is commonly characterised and thought about, and with some legitimacy, as a debate between essentially two positions which are identified by means of labels which serve as shorthand indications for the sets of assumptions, arguments and counter-arguments which we have outlined: 'pro-choice' and 'pro-life'. As we have seen, the pro-choice position, if it is to understand itself as rational and defensible rather than as a mere assertion of an unargued preference, is likely to depend on one or other of two leading assumptions (and, in addition, of course, on a number of subordinate arguments or claims). Either it must assume, with consequentialism, that the question of the status of the foetus is not decisive, since the best action is simply that which maximises good consequences, or, declining that route, it must assume that the foetus is not in fact deserving of moral consideration, or, if deserving of moral consideration, is not deserving of the absolute respect which would make it wrong to intend its death, but only of a moral consideration which seems to give way before any contrary claims. Thus, the mother has a right to choose. The pro-life position, on the other hand, will contest these claims and argue that the mother's rights, whatever they may be, cannot include a right to deprive another of his or her most basic right, namely the right to life.

From the point of view of the Church, however, there is a danger that these two positions could come to represent false options, even though the second is often advocated by those with sincere and strong Christian convictions. The danger is just that the affirmations of the pro-life case come to be determined to a certain extent by the denials of the pro-choice party, or at the least that the pro-life case will be interpreted in the terms of the pro-choice case to which it is dialectically related. In either case what is distinctive and important in a

Christian understanding of human life may be lost in this particular exchange (and especially so when the advocates of the pro-life position may think it prudent to present their case as being independent of any particular or acknowledged Christian convictions). To be more specific, since the pro-choice position regards the child as needing (but failing) to establish certain claims against the mother, the pro-life position may seem to take its stand on the existence of just such a legitimate claim, characterised as a right to life. But in seeming to concede the requirement laid down in the pro-life argument, and in meeting it with an assertion of the right to life, important Christian convictions are at risk of being lost.

The pro-choice conviction that a particular human life must, so to say, justify itself, calls into question the fundamental conviction that human life is a good and a gift of God. To take a critical attitude towards the foetus and to ask that it prove itself, and in general to regard humanity as an achievement or qualification and not as a simple and natural endowment, is to dispute this conviction, and to doubt the justification which human life has in its creation and redemption by God. (And, although the doubt is directed at another, and not at me, it is hard to see how the doubt, once active, can be contained; thus, to take the most immediate case, for a mother to adopt such a critical stance towards her own child seems to take a despising of the created order as close to a despising of the self as one can come without falling into the utter despair of self-hatred. For in this case it becomes clear that the alienation of self from other against which the command to love our enemies is directed, takes on a new and particularly stark form when even one's own child is found in the place of the stranger and enemy needing to rely on this command for its protection, a form in which the alienation of the self from other is on the verge of converting into a simple alienation from the self.)

Since, however, the assumption that the child needs to establish some particular claim is problematic, the assertion of the existence of a valid claim on the other side will be problematic in itself, regardless of the nature of the claim which is made. In addition, however, the particular claim which is in fact made on behalf of the child is, from a Christian point of view, dubious even though it aims at the child's protection. For the appeal to a 'right to life' not only seems to concede the need for justification, but does so by appealing to a certain regard for life which can have no basis in Christian thought. According to Barth, 'Everywhere life itself and as such is regarded as the actual ethical lord, teacher and master of man . . . In theological ethics the concept of life cannot be given this tyrannical and totalitarian function.'[10] For theological ethics, that is to say, life is not itself the ethical lord, but the gift of the Lord in whose service life is properly spent, and spent in two senses. Suicide is wrong just because it refuses to spend life in the service of God. Martyrdom is right just because it is willing to spend life, in a different sense, in the service of God. The rightness of spending life in the service of God, in the double sense, means, plainly enough, that what is crucial to a Christian understanding of life is not that life must always and ever be protected and served, but rather that life must always and ever be regarded not as our own, but as belonging to God. Against this understanding of human existence, insistence on a 'right to life' seems dangerously one-sided, and in this one-sidedness threatens to re-enforce the very attitudes which underlie the practice of abortion since it is just a too avid and unmoderated sense of the value of life (mistaking a penultimate for an ultimate good, in Bonhoeffer's terms) which motivates its protection at whatever cost, moral or otherwise.

One should not suppose that the best thing would be to position oneself between the advocates of a right to choose and the right to life (as self-proclaimed 'moderates' might conceive of themselves as doing). Placing oneself here may perhaps generate a certain sense of virtue since one can persuade oneself that one thereby partakes both of the fidelity to tradition which seems (but perhaps only seems) to belong to those who proclaim a right to life and also of the open-mindedness and sophistication which seems (but only seems) to belong to those who proclaim a right to choose. But, however that may be, the intellectual merits of

---

[10] K. Barth, *Church Dogmatics*, III: 4, trans. A. T. Mackay et al. (Edinburgh, 1961), 326.

this position are non-existent, since it does not represent a higher and principled synthesis of these two positions but a mere averaging of them in a refusal to make a judgment. There is nothing to commend such a stance to Christian thought, which far from seeking to stand between these two positions, should consider whether it must actually stand outside and over this particular dialectic with its danger of presenting false options, bearing witness to its own distinctive perspective.

A community which knows human life to be created, reconciled and redeemed in Jesus Christ will be a community which, in its acceptance of children, gives expression to its characteric virtues of faith, hope and love. With faith in the goodness of God's creation, a hope in his providential dealings with it, and a love appropriate to his regard for it, such a community would welcome children with a simplicity which is presupposed by Bonhoeffer's quick way with abortion. Once we have grasped this perspective, we can understand the very obviousness, as Bonhoeffer saw it, of the simple view and, furthermore, can understand the force of traditional Roman Catholic teaching in relation to certain hard cases.

According to that teaching, abortion is always wrong, though an action which will result in the destruction of the foetus may sometimes be licit since it is permissible, for sufficient reason, to perform an action in itself good or indifferent, which has a bad result which is foreseen, but not intended. Thus it would be licit for therapeutic reasons to remove a cancerous womb, even though this will result in the death of a foetus. In his recent Encyclical letter *Evangelium Vitae*, Pope John Paul II has reaffirmed this teaching, saying that 'direct abortion, that is, abortion willed as an end or as a means, always constitutes a grave moral disorder'.[11]

Let us imagine a case, however – it does not matter if it is uncommon or even unheard of, since its point is simply to display the presuppositions and implications of the teaching – in which mother and child will both die unless the foetus is aborted but which differs from the case described in the

[11] John Paul II, *Evangelium Vitae*, English trans. (London, 1995), 62.

previous paragraph in one particular respect. In this second case no other medical condition intervenes, so that if the death of the foetus is brought about, it will be directly intended, since it is the means of saving the mother's life, and not, as where the cancerous womb is removed, a foreseen but unintended side-effect of standardly indicated medical treatment. Now this difference, on this view, makes all the difference, so that in the second case the removal of the foetus from the womb would be regarded as wrong. Of course, the motives for such an action would be good ones, namely to save the one life which can be saved from the tragic situation which is about to unfold. But, to revert to our earlier language, this would amount to the doing of evil that good may come and this is illicit. There is a slogan which sums up the judgment in this case, which has a harsh ring to it but reveals the logic of the thinking plainly enough – 'better two deaths than one murder'.[12]

Any quick and ready dismissal of this view betokens a failure to grasp its philosophical and Christian seriousness. Philosophically, the doctrine in virtue of which the distinction between the two cases is made, the so-called doctrine of double effect, is one which has been and would be defended by any number of philosophers, with or without Roman Catholic convictions. Why? – because the doctrine represents an attempt to distinguish between the different sorts of responsibility which may attach to intended as against foreseen consequences or side effects, and some such distinction is arguably presupposed in the rejection of consequentialism and hence in the respect for those patterns of moral thought which motivate that rejection. But a summary dismissal of Roman teaching can also be accused of shallowness from a Christian viewpoint. Suppose a woman took the view that she could not and would not ask a doctor to kill her child either in the case we have imagined

---

[12] Readers should be aware that, though I have given a standard account of the doctrine of double effect, the noted Roman Catholic moral theologian Germain Grisez has a different interpretation dependent in turn on a different analysis of action. This allows him to offer solutions to the difficult cases discussed below distinct from those normally found in the Roman Catholic tradition, and similar in many respects to those given here. See G. Grisez, *Living a Christian Life*, vol. II of *The Way of the Lord Jesus* (Quincy, IL, 1993), 469–74 and 500–4.

(where, as a result, she and the child will die) or in the case where the refusal of an abortion will preserve the life of the child at the cost of her own. Is such a woman making a mistake of so crass a kind that we can dismiss her decision out of hand? Can we not understand the horror she might feel at laying a hand on her child, even if her unwillingness to consent to its being killed will result in the child's death and her own? If, without any false sentimentality, she feels herself called to express and witness to her commitment to this one who is her particular neighbour in this way, are we to say that she is quite simply and in a rather obvious way wrong? If we do say this – and a large number of Christians seem inclined to say it in their unthinking scorn of Roman Catholic teaching – we might just wonder whether we should not pause and try, perhaps with the help of a few novels if the Bible seems too distant, to enter the thought-world of those who actually believe that there are things worth dying for.

To find the Roman Catholic view philosophically and Christianly serious, however, is not the same as endorsing it without qualification. For, just as we can find a certain cogency in this position, so we can find a cogency and seriousness in other analyses of the situation in which the continuation of the pregnancy threatens the death of both mother and child, or of one or other. There are two lines of thought which are deserving of consideration, even if both need in turn to be subject to further questioning.

In the first place, although a foetus is not plausibly regarded as an aggressor (supposing that an aggressor is one who intends harm), none the less it may be that the general permissibility of acting in self-defence is of some relevance here. It might be maintained, for example, that the legitimacy of self-defence extends not only to those who threaten our lives intentionally, but also to those who endanger them unintentionally or inadvertently, and perhaps especially where the death of the unintending aggressor is in any case certain no matter what I do. Of course, to say that such action in self-defence might be legitimate is not to say that a woman who declined to act in self-defence would be blameworthy, for the consequence of recognising the Christian seriousness of traditional Roman teaching is to acknowledge the seriousness of such a refusal. It is to say, however, that the point of view here entertained – that the choice of the life of the mother over the life of the child where the latter poses a threat to the former – is not morally forbidden, even if it is not morally required, and has a claim to be taken seriously alongside the Roman Catholic position. (It should perhaps, be pointed out, that one ought not to accept attempts to enlarge this class of cases by those expansive construals of the notion of 'posing a threat to the life of' which are employed on behalf of the status quo as regards abortion; a literal construal of the notion has the distinct merit of allowing us to see what it is about these cases which causes us a sense of difficulty, namely that like is pitted against like. But, once we replace cases of life against life with cases of life against economic well-being, for example, the particular difficulty and poignancy of the situation is lost, and with it the particular force which this line of thinking might be reckoned to have.)

While the attempt to think through these cases in terms suggested by discussions of self-defence is worthy of careful examination, it is equally worthy of note that this line of thought may approach somewhat too closely reasoning of a sort we have earlier found wanting. The difficulty does not lie in those cases where the lives of mother and child will both be lost if action is not taken which could at least save the life of the mother; in those cases reasoning along the lines we have considered seems appropriate. The difficulty lies with those cases where only one or other could be saved. To bring into the consideration of such cases arguments having to do with rights to self-defence is once again to invite their treatment in terms appropriate to conflict resolution rather than to the relations of parent and child. It would be, as Luther might have it, to appeal to the laws which are made for the government of the earthly kingdom but have no place in the life of Christians, each one of whom is called to be – in his almost impious phrase – 'a Christ to my neighbour'.[13]

[13] M. Luther, *The Freedom of a Christian*, in many editions.

An alternative and better way of approaching these cases is suggested by Oliver O'Donovan.[14] According to O'Donovan, what is in danger of being overlooked in the traditional Roman Catholic analysis is that death has entered the situation of itself, so to speak. Mother or child, or mother and child, will die, whatever now happens. The physician who aborts a foetus in this situation has not chosen death, but only on whom death will fall. In some cases where the physician chooses that death will fall on the child, it may be that this is the only possibility besides its falling on both. If, however, the death of both may be prevented by death falling on either, the choice between mother and child may make reference to criteria which would none the less never justify a choice of a course of action which would itself bring death into the situation. (Thus, a physician might properly have regard to the mother's role, obligations and duties in saving the mother and not the child where one or other must die, even though, as we have argued, a regard for these factors would never warrant the choosing of abortion where death was not already present.) Nor need a regard to these features of the situation be unworthy in the mind of the mother, who as well as considering her call to be Christ to this neighbour, may have other neighbours to whom she already has such a vocation. Of course, she may still choose that the child's life should be preferred to her own where only one may be saved. But whether she makes this or the other choice, both seem choices which are explicable in Christian terms.

IV ASPECTS OF A GENEALOGY OF THE PRACTICE OF ABORTION

According to our argument thus far, society discusses abortion in ways which Christian thought cannot simply accept. To conceive this debate, as it typically is, as one concerning the right to choose or the right to life, creates a danger of its being misconceived. Bonhoeffer's simple view of these matters, so we have said, does not emerge from this debate, but presupposes a

[14] O. M. T. O'Donovan, *The Christian and the Unborn Child*, 2nd edn (Bramcote, Notts., 1975).

perspective outside it. But this perspective is the perspective on human life which comes from the Gospel, in which it is learnt that human life needs no further justification than the justification it has from God. Thus, though Christians may properly engage with the secular debate in an *ad hoc* and a pragmatic way – and indeed ought to do so in so far as this engagement may demonstrate some of the confusions and inadequacies of that debate even in its own terms and in so doing may encourage a questioning of current practice – they will do so knowing that the simple view will only gain understanding and acceptance as the Christian Gospel is itself understood and accepted.

There is one aspect of a pragmatic and *ad hoc* engagement with the current debate which we have not yet discussed, however, and which we cannot pass over just because it seems so unjustly neglected. Though we have set out in the first section of this chapter some of the questions which a critic might pose in the current debate without, as it were, going outside it, there are further points which might be put by the same critic not so much *within* the debate as *about* it and which may do something more to put it in question.

One distinct oddity of the debate about abortion lies in the relation which this debate seems to bear (or, in fact, not to bear) to practice, for the fact is that the practice seems independent of the argument. We should be precise about what we mean here. It is, of course, possible, as we have allowed, that arguments could be advanced in favour of current practice which would be perfectly consistent and, furthermore, might proceed from premises which could not be shown simply and uncontroversially to be wrong. The point now, however, is not to contest that claim, but to suggest that even if such a case has been made or could be made in principle, present practice has not obviously arisen out of any such arguments. Three aspects of the present situation seem to support this contention and we shall have to content ourselves with mentioning them, rather than developing them as fully as they might and ought to be.

In the first place, Noonan's claim of nearly thirty years ago – that there is a distinct 'indifference to fundamental questions' in public discussion of abortion – certainly seems to hold good now.[15] A telling sign is the fact that one would search *The Warnock Report* in vain for arguments to support the view that fourteen days is a morally significant moment in the development of the embryo, even though the *Report* claims to 'have attempted to argue in favour of those positions we have adopted' and even though this particular 'position' is central to the *Report*'s recommendation in favour of the practice of experimentation.[16]

In the second place and following on from this point, we have already had occasion to notice that the practice of most western jurisdictions presents, prima facie, something of a muddle in protecting the embryo from experimentation after fourteen days whilst offering no protection to the foetus in the womb for the subsequent twenty-two weeks or so. It would not be impossible to construct an argument to defend this dichotomy, but it is likely to require mental gymnastics of a fairly high order. On the face of it, argument is more likely to condemn rather than excuse current practice in this regard, and even if it did not, the argument which would provide the apology would be, as our last point suggested, *ex post facto*.

In the third place, let us note another respect in which the practice seems unrelated to argument. If our review of the debate in its own terms has suggested anything, it has suggested something of the difficulty of the issue judged from within that frame of reference – it would be only the most dogmatic of defenders of the status quo who could declare that the foetus is, without a shadow of doubt, unworthy of moral regard or consideration. But if that is so, were current practice to reflect the state of argument, we would expect it to be somewhat tentative and hesitant, whereas what we find is a rather confident, clear cut and decisive practice, the routinisation of which effectively denies the existence of moral difficulties regarding abortion. The practice seems to presuppose, that is to say, that the case for the acceptability of abortion is beyond any reason-

---

[15] J. T. Noonan, ed., *The Morality of Abortion* (Cambridge, MA, 1970), 'Introduction', xviii.
[16] *Report of the Committee of Inquiry into Human Fertilisation and Embryology, The Warnock Report* (London, 1984), paragraph 2.

able debate, whereas a review of the arguments in their own terms hardly suggests the possibility of such absolute conviction.

Just because it seems, for these three reasons, that the practice sits somewhat free of argument we may feel encouraged to ask a question which would not be inappropriate even if we had found a tight fit between argument and practice, but which seems especially appropriate here. What has driven the emergence of this practice in the modern West? We have spent some time considering what arguments might be constructed by way of justification for abortion, and have not only found most of the arguments wanting, but have said furthermore that, however one judges these arguments, they do not seem to have functioned as the basis for the practice. We might be led to suspect, then, that what has driven the practice are not arguments which declare that it is legitimate to meet the need for abortion, or to kill unwanted children, or to take the lives of those whose lives will be burdensome to them, or whatever, but rather the prior perceptions of a need for abortion, of the existence of unwanted children and burdensome life, and so on. (After all, we could imagine a culture which would be perplexed by the question whether it is permissible to kill unwanted children just because it finds the category of 'unwanted children' to be empty.) Reason has been overwhelmed, we might say, by categorisations, attitudes and expectations which are not themselves necessarily the children of reason, but products of diverse social forces – in the same way, argument about euthanasia may find itself simply overwhelmed by a culture which leads the elderly to identify themselves 'a drain on scarce resources', to think of dependence on care as 'undignified' and to regard any death which is not self-willed and controlled as 'demeaning'. In these circumstances, discussion about the propriety of doctors taking patients' lives will go on at the margins.

To venture an account of the genesis of the categorisations, attitudes and expectations associated with the practice of abortion is quite beyond this essay. But any such genealogy is likely to make reference to one important factor in the shaping of present mentalities which it is appropriate to pick out for mention here, even if we cannot complete the picture, for the sake of beginning to dispel the innocence of treatments of abortion which deal only with the world of reason. And we can get at this factor by looking at Friedrich Engels' early and important work *The Condition of the Working Class in England.*

As Engels sees it, the life of society has become, in fact, nothing of the kind. Instead 'isolation of the individual . . . narrow self-seeking, is the fundamental principle of our society everywhere' , though it is 'nowhere so shamelessly barefaced, so self-conscious as just here in the crowding of the great city. The dissolution of mankind into monads, of which each one has a separate essence, and a separate purpose, the world of atoms, is here carried out to its utmost extreme.'[17] And it is carried to this extreme under the compulsion of the development of capitalism, for which competition – the 'war of each against all'[18] – is the normal and proper condition of human life. But note, the development of capitalism creates not only a more perfect form of the competition of social classes, though it does indeed do that in securing the existence of the proletariat as a class of wage-labourers and of the bourgeoisie as the class of those who exploit such labourers; also and importantly the development of capitalism comes to determine the form and character of relationships within these classes. Engels writes:

Competition is the completest expression of the battle of all against all which rules in modern civil society. This battle, a battle for life, for existence, for everything, in case of need a battle for life and death, is fought not between the different classes of society only, but also between the individual members of these classes. Each is in the way of the other, and each seeks to crowd out all who are in his way, and to put himself in their place. The workers are in constant competition among themselves as the members of the bourgeoisie among themselves. The power-loom weaver is in competition with the hand-loom weaver, the unemployed or ill-paid hand-loom weaver with the man who has work or is better paid, each trying to supplant the other.[19]

Thus, 'In this country, social war is under full headway, every one stands for himself, and fights for himself against all comers,

---

[17] F. Engels, *The Condition of the Working Class in England*, trans. of 1886 revised (Harmondsworth, 1987), 69.

[18] Engels, *The Condition of the Working Class in England*, 142.

[19] Engels, *The Condition of the Working Class in England*, 111.

and whether or not he shall injure all the others who are his declared foes, depends upon a cynical calculation as to what is most advantageous for himself.'[20] Nor, by the way, should we expect the state to represent a real bar or check to 'social war': 'Free competition will suffer no limitation, no state supervision; the whole state is a burden to it. It would reach its highest perfection in a wholly ungoverned anarchic society, where each might exploit the other to his heart's content.'[21]

Now what the state will not check, the workers try to oppose; the workers, according to Engels, attempt to nullify this 'competition . . . among themselves' through association; 'hence the hatred of the bourgeoisie towards these associations, and its triumph in every defeat which befalls them'.[22] But such association takes other forms than nascent trade unions, and these others are no less a bar to the perfect and complete 'competition of workers among themselves' and thus no less subject to attack as the demands of competition are extended. These demands, for example, fuel, so Engels thought, the dissolution of the family which is achieved in a variety of ways: in the employment of children; in the necessity for women to work, and to work immediately prior to and straight after childbirth; in the high unemployment of men, and so on. And this dissolution of the family and of the community of interest which it represents is strikingly symbolised in a detail of working-class life in respect of children's dealings with their parents: 'When they get on far enough to earn more than they cost their parents from week to week, they begin to pay their parents a fixed sum for board and lodging, and keep the rest for themselves. This often happens from the fourteenth or fifteenth year. In a word, the children emancipate themselves, and regard the paternal dwelling as a lodging house, which they often exchange for another as suits them.'[23]

The forces of competition reach even here then, destroying this association and the community of interest which it sustains

[20] Engels, *The Condition of the Working Class in England*, 156.
[21] Engels, *The Condition of the Working Class in England*, 276.
[22] Engels, *The Condition of the Working Class in England*, 112.
[23] Engels, *The Condition of the Working Class in England*, 167.

just as surely as it seeks the destruction of other associations. The imperative to treat the other as 'mere material, a mere chattel'[24] touches even the family, recreating it in a form which meets the needs of competition.

We can hardly read this analysis of the outworking of the logic of capitalism through the re-ordering of the structure of social relations, including the social relations of the family, without being struck by the possibility of extending Engels' analysis to those developments in the form of the family with which we have been concerned. Where competition provides a dominant structure of social relations, and the 'war of each against all' is more and more generalised, and where the view of the other as a 'mere material, a mere chattel' is a presupposition and a consequence of these social relations, the fact that an unborn child can come to be thought of as a threat and a stranger should hardly surprise us. The family must bow to the needs of competition, and be fashioned by it, so that the practice of abortion, it might be claimed, is the practice of competition, born not of the logic of argument but of the logic of capitalism.

Of course, that such an analysis would have a part to play in a larger and more complete genealogy is here simply suggested, as we have said, without being established – nor have we begun to discuss the sort of qualifications and amendments which we might want to add to Engels' rather stylised picture. The important point is, however, that the refusal of most discussions of abortion even to entertain such a genealogy gives them an overly intellectualist character, since they seem to believe, in effect, that social relations, modern western medicine, the family and the like, are touched by nothing as base as economic forces, but have their character in virtue of pure reason. (Perhaps we should note in passing too, how often in these same discussions 'feelings' enter as an authentic and original datum which might serve as an arbiter in the debate, as if 'feelings' also stand outside the stream of history and social life.) We might find ourselves led to the view that the real genius of capitalism

---

[24] Engels, *The Condition of the Working Class in England*, 92.

lies not so much in fashioning the social world as it sees fit, nor even in persuading women to think that the dissolution of bonds of sympathy between children and parents, and indeed between parents, represents in some sense their liberation. Its real genius lies in concealing this achievement almost entirely from view. Christianity will bring this achievement out into the open, and in so doing will finally subsume any genealogy of the kind which it finds in Engels, even as it is willing to learn from it, in a richer and more fundamental genealogy of human alienation from God. In doing so, however, it too will place abortion in a social context which will be known as in need of a genuine liberation.

V WHAT ABOUT THE LAW?

Even if, with Engels, we do not expect that the law will stand effectively in the way of the generalising of competition, still we must turn to the question of what the law ought or ought not allow as regards abortion. It might be thought, however, that an answer to that question follows very quickly from what we have thus far said, but the matter is not quite so simple.

In general terms, from the fact that one takes the view that something is morally wrong, it does not follow immediately and without further argument that the law should take any note of it, and even where it should, it is by no means obvious what this 'taking note' – we use that phrase advisedly – should consist in. Greed, for example, is probably a vice more vicious than many others, but not obviously one the incidence of which the law could or should endeavour to affect. And even of a vice of which it is agreed that the law could and should take note, the form in which it should do so can be a matter of considerable difficulty and dispute. Take prostitution. If the law is to take a critical view of prostitution that view could be expressed in diverse ways. The law could provide for the punishment of prostitutes and their clients; it might punish neither of these, but only those who live off the proceeds of prostitution; there again it might punish no one at all, but could refuse to enforce any contracts for prostitution; or, to mention another possible option, with or without the last measure, it could simply express its disapproval by prohibiting the advertisement of prostitution.

The subtleties of whether and how the law might take note of the practice of abortion are often lost in popular debate, where a couple of suppositions seem unaffected by their doing without much in the way of argumentative support. The first supposition is that if the generality of abortions are morally wrong the law should certainly take note of abortions, and the second is that if it should take note of them it should do so in the very specific sense of criminalising abortion (though it may be unclear whether it is those who seek or those who perform abortions, or both, who are to be subject to the criminal law). Our point has been that the first conclusion really ought to be a conclusion, and that the second ignores the many options which lie between a studied neutrality and an outright criminalising of those seeking or performing abortions. The falsity of these options adds to the unreality of the debate, since those who argue for neutrality usually argue against criminalisation, whereas those who argue for criminalisation usually argue against neutrality – and this, to many, will seem like a choice between the devil and deep blue sea.

The exact form in which the law should take note of abortion, supposing that it should take note in some way, is not a matter which can be pursued here since, as the above example of prostitution must make clear, the final determination of this matter involves the consideration and weighing of a multiplicity of factors. But, since we are inclined to the view that the law should in some form or other take note of it, we have to deal with three considerations (they are not really well formed enough to be counted as arguments) which are often used against this claim and to support the status quo.

The first consideration points to the very widespread acceptance of abortion which has either grown up since or been revealed by the reform of the law. In England and Wales some 180,000 abortions were performed in 1996.[25] In the United States it is estimated that as many as 1,500,000 abortions take

[25] *Britain, 1998: An Official Handbook*, The Office of National Statistics (London, 1998).

place annually. Thus in these jurisdictions a very large number of women indeed will have an abortion in the course of their lives. Supposing, as is probably reasonable, that in many of these cases the women will have the support of their partners, friends or family members (though one must allow for the fact that some may be acting solely in deference to their partners' wishes), it seems to follow that a very sizeable portion of the population has come to regard abortion as a service which should be generally available. We may also suppose that of those who have not and will not have abortions, none the less a good number take the same view. Is it conceivable then, that the law could act (in whatever way) against what is now so widely regarded as a right? Would not any step towards criminalisation of abortions – even in relation to what we might think of as eugenic abortions on grounds of sex, for example – be so contentious given the strength of feelings on this matter, that a state which attempted to go in this direction would at the least bring the law into disrepute (since the criminalisation of abortion would, like the criminalisation of smoking on the streets of Paris, be effectively unenforceable), and might at the worst provoke civil disobedience and conflict?

A second consideration has to do with the situation which obtained before the reform of the law. Prior to the decriminalising of abortion, abortions still went on, but in a way which was, from any point of view, highly undesirable. Women were prey to unscrupulous and often unqualified back-street abortionists, whose lack of skill increased the risks of abortion and who had no interest in providing the counselling which might have led some women to decide against abortion. Thus criminalisation not only failed to prevent abortions, it may even have served in some cases to encourage them, and certainly it meant that whatever abortions were performed were performed in a way which no one could think acceptable.

A third consideration relates to the first, and maintains that any attempt to change the legally permissive view is in some sense undemocratic or unjust. This charge seems to allege one or other or both of two things. It may mean to maintain that since the majority view is that abortion should be permissible without let or hindrance, any view to the contrary, while it has a perfect right to a hearing, can have no right to seek to affect the legal situation prior to a shift in popular views. But it might be a bit stronger than that, since the point just made concedes that in principle a state could determine to prohibit abortion if there was majority support for such a prohibition, whereas some would want to claim that the state has no such prerogative. No one should be obliged to have an abortion, they might say, but equally no one should be prevented from having one. It is a matter of personal choice with which the state should not interfere. Hence, the law should simply be neutral on the matter.

Looking back at these arguments we might represent them as maintaining that it would be impossible for the law to act against the availability of abortion, or if not impossible then undesirable in practice, or if not undesirable in practice then wrong in principle. We should say something about each of these, taking them in reverse order.

The last argument – which says that it would be undemocratic to change the law without majority support, or, more strongly that even a majority would behave wrongly in amending the law – claims too much, or at least plainly relies on arguments of the sort we have encountered earlier and cannot simply be dependent on supposed truths of political theory. The point, to be blunt, is that the case for a prohibition of slavery, for example, would not be weakened by the observation that no one is compelled to keep slaves. If abortion is morally wrong, for reasons we have entertained, then the interest which the law may properly take in abortion is the interest it has in relation to slavery or infanticide. Of course there is disagreement, as we have said, as to whether abortion is a wrongful attack on life or not, and if it is not, then certainly the law has no obvious business in taking a view of it. But the proposition that the law has no business with abortion depends on the proposition that it is not a wrongful attack on life, and cannot be established simply by reflection on the limits of state power (unless, that is, one makes a case for the merits of anarchism).

If the law is entitled to an interest in the matter, would it be inadvisable, or indeed impossible, for it to alter the present practice as the first two considerations suggest? It is worth pointing out before saying anything else that the inadvisability or impossibility which is suggested here is in actual fact the inadvisability or impossibility of a regime of rather direct, simple and perhaps highly punitive criminalisation, whereas we have already suggested that the reform of the law allows any number of options between punishing those who seek or provide abortions and neutrality. Thus whatever force these arguments have against any move to criminalisation, they obviously possess much lesser force, or even none, in relation to these other options.

But, putting that highly important qualification to one side for the moment, let us consider what significance we should attach to the possible consequences of a change in the law which involved criminalisation. Remember that there were two points here – either that such a change would be, from any point of view, undesirable as resulting in higher maternal mortality without necessarily reducing (and possibly even increasing) the number of abortions, or if not undesirable in these terms, such as to bring the law into disrepute or to provoke mass civil disobedience because unenforceable and highly contentious.

The empirical judgments on which such claims depend are plainly difficult to substantiate, but for the sake of argument let us allow that they have a degree of plausibility. Should those who think abortion a wrong in some respects on a par with infanticide desist from any attempt at criminalisation in view of these scenarios, in one of which the numbers of abortions is unaffected and the suffering of women is increased, and in the other of which there is a breakdown in respect for the law going so far, perhaps, as to threaten the civil order? Grim as these possibilities are, it is by no means obvious how one should respond. Consider a parallel case. Suppose we take the view that discrimination on grounds of race is wrong, but recognise that in some societies it is deeply engrained. Imagine a move to criminalise it were met with bleak scenarios – an attempt to criminalise racial discrimination will have no obvious effect on its incidence and may even increase it since the passage of legislation could itself become a focus for resentment of minority populations; it may even be that this resentment will run so deep as to provoke blatant challenges to the state and its power and perhaps even violence towards minority groups. What should be done? Cases could be made for or against the passage of legislation, but at the least it is not obvious that the case against the legislation and in favour of the status quo is overwhelming. After all, one might be led to reflect in relation to the most extreme scenario, that the break down in the rule of law which is predicted could be regarded as a simple revelation of what is already in fact the case. 'Remove justice' writes Augustine, 'and what are kingdoms but gangs of criminals on a large scale? . . . For it was a witty and a truthful rejoinder which was given by a captured pirate to Alexander the Great. The king asked the fellow, "What is your idea, in infesting this sea?" And the pirate answered, with uninhibited insolence, "The same as yours, in infesting the earth! But because I do it with a tiny craft, I'm called a pirate: because you have a mighty navy, you're called an emperor." '[26] Piracy is a bad thing, but not obviously worse than state piracy; or, to put it simply, a rule of law which fails to protect the lives and rights of certain classes of a nation's citizens (be they the unborn or racial minorities) is as partial a rule of law as that which civil disobedience is itself likely to threaten.

v CONCLUSION

Whilst Christians quite properly have a concern for the provisions of the criminal law, it would be unrealistic to imagine that any likely or even conceivable changes in the law could serve of themselves to reverse the ever increasing resort to abortion in western countries. Nor, if our analysis is right, is argument likely of itself to succeed where legal reform would fail

According to Bonhoeffer in his rather dire circumstances, in meeting the threats to the simple Christian view not only of

---

[26] Augustine, *De Civitate Dei* (*City of God*), PL. 41, 13–804, trans. H. Bettenson (Harmondsworth, 1972), iv, 4.

abortion but of human life and existence in general, Christians had to take up the 'sharp swords' of simplicity and wisdom – the first consists in fixing 'one's eye solely on the simple truth of God at a time when all concepts are being confused, distorted and turned upside down'. And 'simplicity becomes wisdom', since 'the wise man is the one who sees reality as it is, and who sees into the depths of things. That is why only that man is wise who sees reality in God.'[27] But this, of course, is for Bonhoeffer, to see reality in Jesus Christ: 'It is in Jesus Christ that God's relation to the world is defined. We know of no relation of God to the world other than through Jesus Christ.'[28]

A church which saw reality through Jesus Christ would witness to the world through a way of life which would express those truths about human existence, its origin and its destiny, which are known in him. This way of life, in what is done as much as in what is said, would be welcoming of children, female as well as male, handicapped as well as unhandicapped, planned as well as unplanned. Such a way of life would find expression in countless practical endeavours, just as Christian witness always has, to support and assist those who are seeking to live the life of discipleship to which the Gospel calls us, aware as Bonhoeffer put it, that guilt in these matters 'may often lie rather with the community than with the individual'. In that life of discipleship there would be nothing of the despising of human existence, the despair in its course, and the estrangement of one from another, which presently characterise our dealings with the unborn, but not only the unborn. Instead, where there is faith, hope and love, there would be a life of joy in which abortion would not first of all be thought wrong, but would be quite simply, as Bonhoeffer says, unthinkable.

---

[27] Bonhoeffer, *Ethics*, 50.   [28] Bonhoeffer, *Ethics*, 321.

CHAPTER 4

Economic devices and ethical pitfalls: quality of life, the distribution of resources and the needs of the elderly

Some while ago I heard a senior administrator give a rather unsatisfactory lecture on the topic of the distribution of re- sources within the Health Service.[1] It was unsatisfactory not so much because the message of the lecture was that decisions in this area are extremely difficult to take; but because the speaker seemed to think that the repeated insistence of this point would do in lieu of an attempt to state the principles which govern or at least should govern the practice.

Decisions about the distribution of resources within the Health Service are important decisions for the obvious reason that the provision of funds for health care does not and could not meet all conceivable claims which might be made upon the budget. *The Beveridge Report* proposed that 'a comprehensive national health service will ensure that for every citizen there is available whatever medical treatment he requires in whatever form he requires it', but no matter how well funded, no health service could be comprehensive in this sense. Governments, civil servants and administrators are obliged, therefore, to allocate resources between the various specialisms deciding how much is to be devoted to neonatal care, how much to transplant surgery, how much to the care of the elderly, and so on. These decisions are no doubt extremely difficult, but this is all the more reason to think that we should seek to make them in an informed and principled way. It is not good enough to

[1] I am grateful to Charles Elliott, Luke Gormally, John Harris, Oliver O'Donovan and Nicholas Sagovsky for their criticisms of a draft of this chapter and to Basil Mitchell, Michael Lockwood, Solomis Solomou and Jane Wheare for discussions of the topic.

allow decisions as to the distribution of resources to be generated, so to say, from the interplay of tradition, interests, pressure groups and – what must now be added in the light of the policies of the last ten years or so – market forces, for where we allow these decisions to be 'generated' rather than consciously taken, we can hardly be confident that the result will be a morally acceptable, let alone an efficient, use of limited funds.

If it is the case that the distribution of scarce resources has been settled in an unduly *ad hoc* manner, then one must welcome attempts to bring principles to bear on the problem. Unfortunately however, among the various proposals for the rational distribution of resources within the Health Service, the one which is currently most influential ought to cause us considerable concern. For, under the guise of bringing properly informed evaluations to the problem of establishing priorities for health care, it threatens to impose extremely questionable moral assumptions on medical practice, and so to undermine medicine's traditional values and its characteristic commitments – such as to the care of the dependent elderly.

The proposal to which I refer has emanated from the Department of Economics at the University of York and is associated with the QALY (Quality Adjusted Life Year) and its inventor, Professor Alan Williams. Now the QALY is intended in the first place as a measure of the good which various health care activities achieve. But in combination with certain other assumptions, and making use of costings of different treatments, it becomes a means by which priorities in the distribution of resources can be settled, and it is clear that Williams and others have promoted the QALY as a solution to this particular problem. Williams writes:

The essence of a QALY is that it takes a year of healthy life expectancy to be worth 1, but regards a year of unhealthy life expectancy as worth less than 1. Its precise value is lower the worse the quality of life of the unhealthy person (which is what the quality adjusted bit is all about) . . . The general idea is that a beneficial health care activity is one that generates a positive amount of QALYs, and that an efficient health care activity is one where the cost-per-QALY is as low as it can be. A high priority health care activity is one where the cost-per-QALY is low, and a low priority activity is one where the cost-per-QALY is high.[2]

This is a proposal fraught with difficulties, not only moral but also technical or practical. Of the technical or practical problems Williams is not unaware, but of the moral problems he seems largely oblivious. To the practical difficulties I shall only allude, for I shall allege that even if, for the sake of argument, we concede the possibility of solutions to these genuine and deep difficulties, still we ought to conclude on moral grounds, that Williams' proposal has very little to commend it.

To begin at the beginning, it is worth recording the deep misgivings which even the very notion of the 'quality of life' can arouse.[3] It seems to lead us inexorably towards the judgment that some people have a low quality of life, a judgment which is to some reminiscent of the notorious concept of 'life unworthy of life' which was used to justify the abuse of the mentally and physically handicapped, the mentally ill and the elderly under the Nazi regime. To make such judgments, and to conclude as Williams does, that some states of existence register as less than zero on his scale (i.e., as states worse than death) is, it might be felt, the beginning of a slippery slope which may end, for example, in the practice of compulsory euthanasia for those unfortunate enough to be so assessed.

I do not for a moment underestimate the seriousness of the concern thus expressed, but I do think that in fact these worries can be allayed. Of course, the judgment that a particular person has such a low quality of life that death is preferable to further treatment, may be presumptuous and ill-informed, and it may even be taken as providing grounds for the killing of patients; were we to look at current practice in relation to the so-called 'care of the newborn', we would almost certainly come across instances of such dubious premises being employed in invalid arguments.[4] But should we reject the very

[2] Cited by M. Lockwood, 'Quality of Life and Resource Allocation' in *Philosophy and Medical Welfare*, ed. J. M. Bell and S. Mendus (Cambridge, 1988), 36.

[3] This was the experience of a Working Party at the Ian Ramsey Centre, Oxford, in its discussions of this topic.

[4] For examples, see some of the cases discussed by R. Weir, *Selective Nontreatment of the Handicapped Newborn* (New York, 1984).

possibility of quality of life judgments just because these might sometimes be misjudgments and, even if not misjudgments, might sometimes be misused? No doubt we should meet the judgment that such a patient has, in an absolute sense, a low quality of life, with a degree of suspicion. There are aspects of a patient's life which are inherently outside the scope of an observer's scrutiny. It will be replied, however, that we must acknowledge the legitimacy, or at least the necessity, of such judgments in certain circumstances. We shall surely not wish to quibble with the judgment which a sensitive and experienced medical practitioner might reasonably make in declining to pursue heroic measures on behalf of the incompetent patient who, let us say arrives in an intensive care unit after a major heart attack and such a judgment seems to be implicitly a quality of life judgment, and one moreover which is absolutely essential to the responsible care of the terminally ill, for example.

We might allow, therefore, that in very particular circumstances the judgment that a patient has a low quality of life, or even such a low quality of life that further measures to preserve life are inappropriate, is one which might be warranted. But we shall add two points. First of all, that to concede this is to concede very little to the case for either voluntary or involuntary euthanasia, which argues not that in such circumstances further measures to preserve life are inappropriate, but rather that in such circumstances measures intended to cause death are permissible. This, however, clearly requires a new argument: it is not, as such, required by the assessment of the situation. The second point would be that even those who feel some unease in presuming to measure the quality of life of a particular patient in particular circumstances, may none the less allow the propriety of the comparative judgments on classes of patients which decisions about allocation of resources may require. That is to say, those who hesitate to admit the claim that such and such a patient has a low quality of life, may yet accept the claim that one treatment does more than another (whether alternative treatments for the same complaint, or treatments for different complaints) to enhance the quality of life of a class of patients.

And that is all that is required for the use of the concept of quality of life to have a place in the debate over distribution.

If the suspicions I have referred to can, as I think, be allayed, we may acknowledge that the concept of 'quality of life' is a useful one, serving to denote an aspect of a patient's well-being which has always been of concern to good medical practice, even if it has only recently been so named. For in acting in the service of health, medicine has always sought to add to a patient's life both quantity and quality, that the patient may not just exist for three score years and ten, but genuinely flourish. Consciousness of quality of life serves to remind the medical practitioner of this fact and is thus an important aid to the profession's thinking. But what of the concept of a QALY? Can this have a similarly benign role?

To see the point of the concept we need to note that though, fortunately, in many cases medicine simply acts in the service of health without having to wonder about the relationship of quality and quantity of life (thus in treating diabetes or in offering kidney dialysis, the doctor will give the patient the chance not only of more life, but of better life), cases are not always that simple. Sometimes a treatment which adds to length of life may so affect the patient's hope of flourishing as to be unacceptable. Thus it may be that radical surgery offers the best chance of remission for a patient with advanced cancer but a remission so troubled by pain, discomfort or disability as to be a burden and not a benefit. Even in less extreme cases a choice between two forms of treatment may be complicated by the same sort of balance of considerations. An instance which is often cited is concerned with the treatment of laryngeal cancer. The choice for patients with advanced but localised laryngeal cancer is between surgery and radiotherapy. Surgery improves survival at the expense of impaired speech; radiation preserves speech at the expense of a decreased chance of survival. And to take another example, it may be – though the matter is, of course, controversial – that mastectomy offers the best prospect of long life to a patient with breast cancer, whereas a treatment which avoids such radical surgery is more acceptable on 'quality of life' grounds. The moral is clear and well put by two practitioners: 'we strongly believe that in cancer therapy equal emphasis should be given to the patient's quality of life as well as to objective measurements of tumour progression or regression'.[5]

The patient who has to choose between alternative therapies, or the administrator who has to decide which of two rival approaches to the treatment of the same disease or illness should be funded, will undoubtedly welcome the attempt which is represented by the invention of the QALY to render commensurable the two goods of quantity and quality of life. For the QALY is intended to determine what good a treatment does, weighing both quality and quantity of life together, and so to assist us in the difficult situations which sometimes confront us where quality and quantity conflict. In this respect the QALY may prove to be a useful device.

This said, we are, none the less, still a long way from the use of QALYs which Williams intends. However, if the first and most natural use of the concept of quality of life and of the QALY is, as we have said, in considering the merits of alternative courses of treatment open to the individual patient or in pursuit of limited funding, there is surely a temptation to carry it over to cases which are quite different and much more difficult, where the competition is not between alternative therapies for the same treatment but between entirely independent medical specialisms: between, for example, paediatrics and renal surgery, or between terminal care and gynaecology. For if in choosing between alternative therapies for the same treatment, we are naturally sensitive to the contribution each one makes to both quantity and quality of life, should not the administrator be sensitive to the same consideration in choosing between funding independent health care activities? And if so, is not the QALY the very device which will render distribution sensitive in the appropriate way, enabling us to settle the vexed question of priorities in health care? So Williams would contend.

If Williams' proposal for the distribution of resources is to be applicable even in principle – if, in other words, it is genuinely

[5] See T. J. Priestman and M. Baum, 'Evaluation of Quality of Life in Patients Receiving Treatment for Advanced Breast Cancer, *The Lancet*, April 1976, 899–901.

capable of making the comparisons it proposes as essential to rational decision making – then it must, of course, be able to measure both the costs and the benefits of treatment. That is to say, to achieve comparability of alternative health care activities two steps are involved. First of all the proposal requires that we assign different forms of treatment a 'QALY value' – that is, a value which represents the gain to the patient in both quality and quantity of life offered by treatment over against non-treatment. Secondly, it requires that we introduce into our considerations financial assessments of alternative treatments, for it is not just the QALY value – that is the benefit – of a treatment which is of interest to those concerned with the distribution of resources. They will also be concerned with the cost of achieving this QALY value. Thus, to take an example of a calculation done by Williams (and cited by Michael Lockwood[6]), a heart transplant is said to have a QALY value of 4.5 and home and hospital dialysis to have QALY values of 6 and 5 respectively. But the costs of these treatments are very different, and once this is taken into account heart transplants represent the best value for money: according to Williams the cost per QALY is £5,000 for heart transplants, but £11,000 and £14,000 respectively for home and hospital dialysis. Thus, in comparison with dialysis, heart transplants are, in Williams' terms, 'a high priority activity'.

In actual fact, both of these steps – the measuring of costs and the measuring of benefits – are far from straightforward. Since, however, my final conclusions do not depend on a challenge to the success of these two steps, I shall only pause to note some doubts about the validity and scope of the sort of calculations which Williams' proposal requires before going on to give attention to the more pressing moral difficulties which beset the policy Williams recommends.

The assessment of the relative priority to be accorded to different health care activities depends first on the calculation of the QALY value of various treatments. Calculation of a QALY value compounds expectations of quality and quantity of life

⁶ Lockwood, 'Quality of Life and Resource Allocation', 37.

given the treatment in question, over against expectations without treatment. Thus, in an example I have already given, the QALY value of kidney dialysis is the gain to the patient of so many years at such and such a quality above and beyond what can be expected without dialysis – and that expectation is, of course, for very little indeed. Now one element in the calculation is reasonably amenable to scientific assessment given sufficient research, and that is the increased expectation of quantity of life which various treatments yield. But the second element, the contribution made to quality of life, is by no means as easily assessed. The most commonly used scales of assessment (including the one relied upon by Williams) combine considerations of distress and disability, both of which are important aspects of what we refer to by the concept of 'quality of life'. There are, however, other aspects of it not included under these heads. And even were it feasible to widen the scope of the benefit to health which is allowed to count, most of us will sense that attempts to assign a value to a person's life under different circumstances are as likely to fall as far short of measuring what we intend by that rich concept 'quality of life' as IQ tests fall short of measuring that wide ranging intellectual ability and commonsense which we describe by the word 'intelligence'.[7]

Nor are the calculations employed to determine the cost of obtaining the QALY benefit easily made or uncontroversial. First of all, the notion of 'the cost of treatment' is not a simple one, for, even if one considers only the direct costs of treatment to the Health Service, economists would want to distinguish average cost and marginal cost, fixed costs and running costs.[8] Now, depending on which cost you choose as most important, you may get very different answers to the question of what a particular activity costs: Drummond and Mooney cite a diagnostic procedure of six sequential tests for detecting colonic

---

[7] John Broome makes the further point that 'It is a weakness of QALYs as a measure of good that they ignore many aspects of good, that is to that they are narrowly focussed on health considerations, whereas the value of good health to one person may be greater than to another, just because of other circumstances such as their material conditions'; 'Goodness, Fairness and QALYs' in *Philosophy and Medical Welfare*, ed. Bell and Mendus, 66.

[8] See P. Wiles, *Price, Cost and Output*, 2nd edn (Oxford, 1961).

cancer which was estimated to cost less than $2,500 for each case detected, whereas the marginal cost of carrying out six tests, as opposed to five, was $47,000,000. As they put it, 'clearly it is important to ask the right costing question'.[9] It surely is, but it is by no means clear which is the right question to ask or that the information needed to answer whichever question is the right one is available, for, as Williams points out, there is 'very little routine information on' capital costs.[10] Thus his estimates of the costs of various treatments are usually estimates of marginal costs.

These problems may be soluble. But there is another respect, according to Williams, in which the information on health costs which is readily available is 'not usually suitable as it stands for the efficiency calculus which is our central interest'[11] and this presents a graver difficulty. The limitation on available information is well illustrated by the policy of reducing the length of stay in hospital after treatment. This may or may not represent a saving to the hospital budget, but, as Williams comments, 'the patients' costs are being ignored in all this, as are the costs falling on non-hospital services, local authority social services, voluntary bodies, and friends and relatives who provide support'.[12] Williams is surely right that any calculations of the cost of treatment, no matter how cost is understood, which consider only what we might term the narrowly medical items – the cost of employing the surgeons, of providing a hospital bed, of offering an appropriate regimen of drugs and so on – have a certain unreality about them. There are many other costs associated with treatment or nontreatment, even if not directly charged to the health budget, which seem to have been arbitrarily excluded. To take an example: the contention that an operation at a hospital 50 miles from the patient's home is cheaper than the cost of the same operation at the local

---

[9] M. Drummond and G. Mooney, *Essentials of Health Economics* (Aberdeen, 1983), 4.

[10] A. Williams, 'Efficient Management of Resources in the National Health Service' in H. S. E. Gravelle and A. Williams, *Health Service Finance and Resource Management* (London, 1980), 68.

[11] Williams, 'Efficient Management of Resources in the National Health Service', 67.

[12] A. Williams, 'The Budget as a (Mis-)Information System' in *Economic Aspects of Health*, ed. A. J. Culyer and K. G. Wright (London, 1978), 88.

hospital, ignores the considerable cost which relatives may incur in using public transport in order to visit the patient. Or, to take another example, it may be that the average patient seeking a heart transplant is a middle-aged person with a family, and that this family may become a burden on the state if the patient is untreated and remains in poor health or worse. The average patient seeking a hip replacement may be a good deal older and have no such responsibilities, or at least none which are likely to be unfulfilled if he or she goes without treatment. If we are concerned to make a proper estimate of the costs of treatment and non-treatment so as to make a rational use of limited resources, ought we not to widen our calculations to consider costs such as these?

So Williams would suggest, it seems. But there are serious reasons to doubt both the feasibility and the desirability of construing 'costs' quite so widely. On the matter of the feasibility of so construing costs, one might think that the calculation of cost becomes meaningful at the expense of being practical when the notion of cost is widened beyond the direct charge on the health budget. But, more importantly, one will surely hesitate to broaden consideration of cost when to do so is to take a step in a direction which very obviously raises the spectre of making provision of health care dependent on supposed social worth.

I pause rather than dwell on the difficulties inherent in calculations of cost and benefit because even if simply as calculations they could be regarded as beyond suspicion, the use which Williams and others make of them is morally questionable. Of course, if we swallowed our doubts about the validity and scope of the measures of benefit and cost, then as calculations they would be unexceptionable and, as I have already acknowledged, of some interest. But Williams requires not only that we accept the validity of his sums, but also the use to which he puts them in proposing that a rational policy for the distribution of resources should aim at producing as many QALYs as possible. That is to say, he proposes that a policy for the distribution of resources should not only be sensitive to considerations of quantity and quality of life, but should be determined by an intention to obtain the maximum number of QALYs our money can buy. He proposes, in words I have already cited, that 'A high priority health care activity is one where the cost-per-QALY is low and a low priority activity is one where the cost-per-QALY is high.' Thus the QALY becomes a device which measures not just the contribution which various treatments make to quantity and quality of life, but also the relative worth of different health care activities, so that QALY maximisation is, according to Williams, a rational policy for determining the distribution of scarce resources.

Before I criticise that claim, it is worthwhile, I think, to consider in broad terms the implications which this 'rational policy' would have for the pattern of provision within the health service. One critic of Williams' proposals points out that 'it will usually be more QALY efficient to channel resources away from (or deny them altogether to) areas such as geriatric medicine or terminal care'.[13] I think that he is right, and that Williams' 'rational policy' has the same implications for the care of the mentally handicapped, for example, but for the moment I shall consider only geriatric and terminal care.

At first sight, it might not seem obvious that a policy of QALY maximisation will accord low priority to the care of the elderly. After all 'Old people need simple things' according to an article on 'Ethical implications in aging' in the *Encylopedia of Bioethics*, such as decent care for their eyes, teeth and feet.[14] They may, of course, need some basic help to allow them to remain in their homes, but even when they are no longer capable of living on their own they may require only relatively straightforward, albeit highly skilled and sensitive, nursing. Thus, in principle, the cost of providing for the care of the elderly is quite low and might be expected to come out reasonably well in a QALY calculation.

The point that we have overlooked, however, is the relatively low expectation of life of the elderly, and the fact that many of

[13] J. Harris, 'More and Better Justice' in *Philosophy and Medical Welfare*, ed. Bell and Mendus, 80.
[14] D. Christiansen, 'Ethical Implications in Aging' in *Encyclopedia of Bioethics*, ed. W. T. Reich (New York, 1978).

the services they need make absolutely no difference to that expectation. Such medical care of the elderly thus provides only an improvement in quality of life and an improvement which will be enjoyed for a much shorter time than if a similar benefit were to have been provided for a younger person. So, even where the provision of care for the elderly proves to be relatively cheap, it will yield a small return of QALYs compared with medical activity which either adds length to an otherwise healthy life or adds quality to a life with a long time still to run. This is not to say, of course, that *all* the services from which the elderly benefit will receive unfavourable assessment. According to some of the (inherently questionable) calculations which have been done, hip-replacement operations – a procedure often required in early old age – should have a high priority because they render significant benefit at low cost. But it is, I suspect, unusual for the care of the elderly to be so favourably assessed by a policy of QALY maximisation. For the most part, the relatively modest improvements or preservation of quality of life which much of the care of the elderly achieves is likely to be hard pushed to defend itself if asked to compete on these terms.

Professor Harris's point about the low priority QALY calculations will accord to terminal care is also sound. The work of a hospice is aimed not primarily at extending life but at making it more comfortable by palliative care. By the relief of symptoms, particularly by the relief of pain, patients are granted an opportunity to find peace and meaning in their last days, weeks or months, parting from relatives and friends in the best of circumstances. Such work increases a patient's quality of life and some aspects of that increase, such as benefit from the relief of pain, will be registered on the standard scales for measuring quality of life, though no such a scale is likely to be sensitive to the significance or value of appropriate human parting. To the extent, then, that the quality of life of the terminally ill is measurable, the hospice can enter into the competition for resources alongside any other health care activity by advertising the QALYs it produces; but in so far as it does not add years to life and adds quality only to those with low life expectancy, it can hardly enter the competition with great confidence of success.

To take seriously a policy of QALY maximisation would result, so it seems, in a considerable devaluing of the care of the elderly and of the terminally ill. Does it follow, then, that our present provision in these areas, often thought in many respects inadequate, is in fact an irrational use of resources which ought properly to be deployed elsewhere in our health service? So we should believe if we accept Williams' contention that a rational policy for the distribution of resources is one which maximises QALYs or health.

It is probably already apparent that Williams' proposal is, broadly speaking, a utilitarian one. It will be apparent too, perhaps, that thus far we have been engaged in the initial skirmishes which always take place with utilitarians, skirmishes aimed at suggesting first of all that the claim to have measured the benefits and burdens which are in question, as is necessary to their calculus, has more than something of pretence about it, and secondly that the policy they recommend is seriously counter-intuitive.

We must, however, do more than skirmish, and unambiguously deny a principle which is central to Williams' proposal. We must contend, in other words, that *the strength of a patient's or class of patients' claim to health care is not, in any straightforward sense, proportionate to the benefit which will be achieved by the treatment of that patient or class of patients, even though it is not irrelevant in certain circumstances to take note of such benefit.* And we make this contention against Williams' policy just because we acknowledge what Williams cannot acknowledge or accommodate, and that is a commitment to justice – to make a point which is standardly made against utilitarians.

What, however, do we mean by 'justice' and what does it demand in this sphere? Were you to browse in a book shop along a shelf of currently available texts which might provide the answer, your eye might first rest in delight on John Lucas's *On Justice*, with the title's seeming promise of a clear account of the concept. John Rawls' *A Theory of Justice* might cause some anxieties as to the complexity of the problem, and Karen

Lebacqz' *Six Theories of Justice* would increase them. But those anxieties would know almost no bounds were you to spot Alasdair MacIntyre's *Whose Justice? Which Rationality?*

In fact, John Lucas's book does not pretend that the concept of justice is, so to speak, a simple or unitary one. Concerning the principles which should govern distribution of any good, Lucas writes that 'Although . . . reasons based on the individual's deeds and agreements are in some way pre-eminent, reasons based on individual need, status, merit, entitlement or right are all, in appropriate circumstances, the proper basis of apportionment. How much weight should be given them will depend partly on the nature of the good, partly on the purposes of the association that has the disposal of the good in question.'[15] And it is MacIntyre's contention, going further than Lucas perhaps, that there are many concepts of justice, each one having its origin in rival social and cultural traditions and only capable of validation by the assessment of the intellectual adequacy of the tradition to which it belongs.[16]

If Lucas and MacIntyre are right, then there is no simple answer to the question which we posed earlier: what is justice and what does it demand in this sphere? Justice will be understood differently and demand different things according to different conceptions of it. And, if that is the case, then it is beyond the scope of a chapter on the distribution of resources to justify fully the particular conception of justice to which it appeals. All that can be done within such a chapter, I suspect, is to elaborate the concept in such a way that those who have an alternative account of justice – or none at all – begin to understand the force of the one which is offered. Fortunately, however, at least one of the concerns which is central to the conception of justice I shall give, is a concern which Williams claims to share, as will emerge in what follows. Thus in criticising his proposals as failing to accord with that conception of justice, I shall be offering a criticism which, by his own standards, he ought to take seriously.

---

[15] J. Lucas, *On Justice* (Oxford, 1980), 164–5.
[16] A. MacIntyre, *Whose Justice? Which Rationality?* (London, 1988).

Justice has two major concerns, one to do with fairness and the other to do with need. Neither concern is one which QALY maximisation can cope with, for in making maximisation of benefit the sole ground of distribution this policy cannot countenance the fact that there may be claims to health care which derive strength not merely from the degree of benefit which their satisfaction will realise.

We may speak first of all of fairness, which requires at its most basic level, treating like cases alike, so far as possible.[17] A policy of QALY maximisation, however, since it is concerned only that the good of health be maximised, is inherently insensitive to the question of how that good is allocated between individuals. That is to say, it would prefer a larger benefit for a few over against even only a slightly smaller benefit for many. To take an example: it would prefer to treat nine AIDS patients with slightly better and slightly more expensive drugs and leave one with no treatment (producing remission for each of the nine of 14 months, i.e., a total gain of 10 years 6 months), to treating all ten with a marginally less good but cheaper alternative supposing that that drug produced a remission of only a year for each patient (i.e., a total gain of ten years). And yet in the face of such a distribution of benefits and burdens the untreated patient would quite reasonably complain that he or she was being treated unjustly. There are some distributions of benefits and burdens which are properly regarded as unjust, no matter that we are assured that the distribution produces the maximum amount of the good which we are concerned to secure. For we should, so far as possible, treat like cases alike. Of course, if we changed the example we have just given, so that the gain from treatment by the slightly more expensive drug is considerably more significant than we have imagined it to be, then it might be right to treat only nine of the ten patients, and indeed we could imagine that this is what the patients themselves would want, provided they had a fair chance to be selected for treatment, by means of a lottery perhaps. But then

---

[17] A thorough critique of a policy of QALY maximisation as unfair is found in John Harris's 'EQALYty' in *Health, Rights and Resources: King's College Studies 1987–8*, ed. P. Byrne (London, 1988), 100–27.

we should have ensured fairness, in another way, bearing further witness to the point that a policy of QALY maximisation, which is intrinsically insensitive to our concern to treat like cases alike, offends against a principle which must be basic to any acceptable distribution of scarce resources.

Fairness is important, and QALYs no doubt offend against it, but a good deal of the debate about the moral implications of Williams' policy for the distribution of resources has been concerned with the question whether QALYs are not only unfair in general but discriminatory in particular against the elderly – whether, that is, they are, as it said, 'ageist'. This is, I shall suggest, though important, not the main point to make against Williams' proposal. For even were expectation of life excluded from consideration of the problem of distribution, still the claims of the dependent elderly and the terminally ill to treatment would not be properly recognised by Williams just because, given his understanding of need, their need for treatment is small.

It is true, as I have been concerned to argue, that under a policy of QALY maximisation, the elderly will do extremely badly. But one cannot conclude that this in itself is evidence of unfair discrimination and Michael Lockwood thinks that though a policy of QALY maximisation is open to criticism as unjust, the claim made for example by Harris, that the policy would involve such discrimination against the elderly in particular, is unsound.[18]

Lockwood makes the obvious point that there is no improper discrimination involved in preferring some people to others provided the grounds for doing so are relevant to the choice being made. Thus, it is not sexist to prefer strong people for a job which requires physical strength, even if this means that women are not likely to be selected. For women are not rejected because they are women, but because they do not meet a legitimate criterion employed in considering candidates for the job in question. In the same way, a health policy which has a built-in preference for those with a high life expectancy does

[18] Lockwood, 'Quality of Life and Resource Allocation', 47f.

not discriminate against old people as such. It just so happens that a policy of distribution which is sensitive to life expectancy will tend to favour the young, in the same way that a selection procedure sensitive to physical strength will tend to favour men – though there are in fact some circumstances, according to Lockwood, in which the QALY approach would favour an older over against a younger patient.

As a defence of the QALY policy against this particular objection, however, this answer is, as it stands, inadequate. Preferring people with physical strength does not discriminate against women as such only if the job is of a sort which properly demands physical strength. If the same criterion were used in selecting candidates for, let us say, an academic position, then it would be judged to be discriminatory. It thus begs the question in favour of the QALY policy to say that it is not discriminatory as such when just what is in dispute is whether or not a policy for the distribution of resources for health care ought to be sensitive to life expectancy. The question is whether in preferring those with a higher life expectancy (and thus, in most cases, the young), the QALY approach employs a criterion which is patently appropriate to the distribution of resources. Nor is it to the point in rebutting the charge of discrimination merely to note that there are some circumstances in which it so happens that the policy might actually favour the elderly, such as in choosing between the treatment of a young person with a terminal disease from which he or she will shortly die and the treatment of an older person who has a life expectancy of another ten or so years. It would hardly serve to show the non-discriminatory nature of a policy for the selection of police officers favouring those with four grandparents born in Britain to point out that it did not pick out ethnic minorities as such, and that in some peculiar cases it might actually help them.

The charge that a policy of distribution on the basis of QALY maximisation is discriminatory can only be answered by an argument which shows that life expectancy or age is a factor to which such distribution ought to be sensitive. And it would need to be an argument sufficient to deal with a counter-argument which appeals to our indebtedness to the elderly for their past contributions to society, thus claiming for them a privileged entitlement to proper health care. Now there is such an argument which is widely canvassed and which Harris and Lockwood call the 'fair innings argument'. If it works, it would, according to the latter, not only justify a policy of preferring the young to the old but also show that a policy of QALY maximisation is, if anything, insufficiently discriminatory in relation to the elderly. This argument says that the fact that the elderly have already had a 'decent innings' provides a reason for giving scarce resources to the young who have yet to enjoy a comparable spell (though it is usually not specified how many years constitutes a decent innings). The suggestion is that it would be unfair to treat someone who has enjoyed a full life in preference to one who has not. Thus, even if a policy of QALY maximisation happened to favour an older patient in very particular circumstances, this argument, based so it seems on considerations of fairness, insists that the younger patient be preferred.

Whilst there is something in this argument, it needs some fairly careful qualification. Harris is probably right in his contention that 'We should remember that the fair innings argument is only plausible in extreme emergency when hard choices have to be made.'[19] One such emergency might arise where a choice has to be made between two victims of an accident both of whom arrive at an intensive care unit which has space and equipment for only one more patient. Here it *might* be right to choose a young patient for treatment, over against an elderly patient, where both will die without it, so that there may be circumstances in which we would reckon there to be no unfairness in taking age or life expectancy as a relevant factor in making some medical choices. But it is one thing to recognise such a point, and quite another to concede the whole case to those who hold, as in effect advocates of a policy of QALY maximisation do, that in all circumstances claims to medical care are dependent, in some degree, on life expectancy. Certainly Williams' proposal could not be warranted merely by the consideration of hard cases of the sort just mentioned, for

[19] Harris, 'EQALYty', 119.

outside these extreme situations it would almost certainly be thought unfair to consider differences of say, a year or two in life expectancy as a relevant factor in determining entitlement to treatment.

A policy of QALY maximisation would be unfair in a variety of ways and unfair in particular to the elderly. But then it might be replied that in all sorts of ways the present pattern of distribution of resources is itself manifestly unfair, and does not treat like cases alike. Some years ago, Dr Julian Tudor Hart wrote an article in *The Lancet* in which he argued that the situation was even worse than that, and he formulated what he termed 'the inverse care law', which held that 'the availability of good medical care tends to vary inversely with the need of the population served'.[20] Nearly ten years after he wrote, the then Secretary of State for Social Services (Patrick Jenkin), received the *Report of the Working Group on Inequalities in Health*, subsequently known, after its Chairman, as the *Black Report*. In considerably greater detail than Hart provided, the Report demonstrated the deep social inequalities in the provision of health services within Britain – and demonstrated it so clearly that the Secretary of State, rather than have the *Report* properly printed and distributed by his department, made available only some 260 duplicated copies during the August bank holiday week of the year in question when the Establishment was in deepest recess. (The tactic came to nothing, however, since it was quickly perceived that a report which the government reckoned to be dangerous must be worth reading, resulting in considerable publicity for it and its eventual publication as a Pelican book.[21])

Since the present distribution of resources for health care is inequitable, criticism of Williams' proposal should not be taken as a justification of the *status quo*. But against Williams' proposal it must be recorded that it would produce unfairnesses of its own – albeit probably not unfairnesses which would correlate

[20] J. T. Hart, 'The Inverse Care Law', *The Lancet*, 1971, 1-i, 405–12.
[21] *Inequalities in Health: The Black Report*, ed. P. Townsend and N. Davidson (Harmondsworth, 1982). See also J. Le Grand, 'The Distribution of Public Expenditure: The Case of Health Care', *Economica*, 45 (1978), 125–42.

as closely with social class as do the present ones – and so cannot be regarded as a satisfactory solution to the problem we are trying to address.

Justice, so I have said, is not just a matter of fairness. It has another aspect, and that is the recognition of need. To distribute goods fairly is to distribute to like cases in like degree, but need in turn justifies – makes just – a distribution which is not an equal split between all the parties who would benefit, but which takes note of the fact that some of those who would benefit have greater need than others, to health care or whatever else is in question.[22] It may be, for example, that a certain patient would benefit in a variety of ways from a kidney transplant, even though kidney dialysis, which he or she presently receives, will ensure moderately good health for the foreseeable future. But certainly this patient, even if he or she could be said to need a kidney transplant, could not be said to need it in quite the same way that someone needs a liver transplant, without which they will be dead in a matter of days. And the greater the need, the greater the claim on resources.

Can a policy of QALY maximisation make any sense of the obligation that just distribution should recognise need? Williams seems to think that it can, and in a discussion of the proposals for the reform of the Health Service he defends what he terms an 'egalitarian perspective' which holds that the objective of the Health Service is to meet needs, and to do so as efficiently as possible. What however, is meant by need? He comments that 'Need is a slippery concept which I am going to take to mean "capacity to benefit" for I cannot see how anyone can really "need" anything that will not do them any good. Doing good in health care means increasing people's life expectancy and/or improving their quality of life by reducing health-related disability and distress. So improving the efficiency of the NHS means generating as much of these benefits as

---

[22] This is a key point in Michael Lockwood's criticism of QALYs in his paper 'Quality of Life and Resource Allocation', and I have drawn extensively on his argument in what follows. He does not stress sufficiently, however, the problem which respect for the claims of need creates for this particular approach to the allocation of resources.

possible, given the resources (human, material, and financial) that are available.'[23]

The confusions in this statement ought to be manifest. Whilst it might be true that no one has a need for treatment which will do them no good, so that to have a need for treatment one must have a capacity to benefit from it, it does not follow that everyone who has a capacity to benefit from health care has a need for it. If I am sufficiently vain I may benefit from cosmetic surgery to improve the shape of my perfectly normal, if not perfect, nose, but it is by no means obvious that I have a need for such surgery. Furthermore, and more importantly, it is not the case that need is proportional to capacity to benefit, as Williams seems to think in proposing that a commitment to meeting needs entails the maximising of benefit. Were need proportional to capacity to benefit, then the policy of QALY maximisation which puts the claims of the terminally ill or the dependent elderly near the very bottom of the pile could not be faulted on these grounds, just because few benefits accrue to patients treated in these circumstances. Since, however, the need of the terminally ill patient for palliative care is quite clearly greater than the 'need' of the patient for cosmetic surgery, or the need of the patient we imagined as wanting a kidney transplant (no matter that the QALY calculation would probably be in favour of the last two over the first), we can see

---

[23] A. Williams, 'Creating a Health Care Market: Ideology, Efficiency, Ethics and Clinical Freedom', *Occasional Papers of the Department of Economics, York*, 1989, 8. A. J. Culyer offers an essentially similar definition and seems to draw the same implication from it, namely that 'the health services exist to minimise need or, what is the same thing to effect the maximum increase in the health status of the client population'; see A. J. Culyer, 'Needs, Value and Health Status Management' in Culyer and Wright, *Economic Aspects of Health*, 10. Drummond and Mooney seem to endorse this approach to the understanding of need. Need, they say, cannot be determined 'objectively'. 'It is a relative, dynamic, value-laden concept. "Need", as Cooper remarked, "is in the eye of the beholder". Some needs will yield large benefits if met, some will be expensive to meet. Need should be met in different ways and to different extents and weighed up in terms of the costs and benefits of different courses of action.' See Drummond and Mooney, *Essentials of Health Economics*, 18. And Williams's colleague, Alan Maynard, also regards 'the allocation of health care resources on the basis of need or maximising improvements in health status (QALYs)' not as alternative policies, but as different descriptions of the same policy. See his 'Markets and Health Care', in *Health and Economics*, ed. A. Williams (London, 1987), 196.

that Williams offers not a recipe for meeting need, but a device which systematically fails to recognise it.

The question must be asked, however, whether the recognition of need can be built into a feasible policy for the distribution of resources. In the first place, we can imagine the point being put that all those who would benefit from health care in fact need it, give or take certain contentious claimants, such as those seeking cosmetic surgery, for example. So, far from providing grounds for discrimination, consideration of patients' needs merely intensifies the dilemma involved in distributing scarce resources. Is there any way, then, in which we can distinguish between the claimants for health care as more or less in need?

Need does seem to admit of degrees, though not in the way Williams supposes, for there are certain sorts of needs which stand out from the crowd of general and lesser needs as making a particular claim upon us. They are, for example, the needs of those whose lives are endangered by illness or injury, the needs of the dependent elderly, the needs of the seriously handicapped, and the needs of the terminally ill.

Now, the claim which some of these needs make on health care is a claim which the advocate of QALY maximisation might pretend to explain. If you think of need as capacity to benefit, then the need of someone with acute appendicitis is one which will be recognised just because the treatment of such a patient will show up well in QALY calculations. But, in this way of thought, the other needs I have mentioned will receive no special recognition. Indeed, the needs of the terminally ill, the dependent elderly, and of the mentally and physically handicapped will be, as I have said, low priority needs, for the meeting of them will inevitably represent a poor return in QALY terms.

The misunderstanding of need, which a policy of QALY maximisation involves, might have been avoided had attention been given to the simple fact that, though care of the dependent elderly, of the terminally ill, or of the mentally and physically handicapped, produces a 'poor return', this does not undermine the commitment of those engaged in the giving of such care.

The nurse who devotes a year of patience and sympathy of quite heroic proportions to enabling a stroke patient to achieve some modest goal such as being able to button a shirt, does not do so because he or she has made the mistake of supposing that perhaps far greater things were possible which might have rendered the endeavour worthwhile if they had been achieved. Indeed, the devotion to such care is surely founded on the insight that the slight amelioration which these conditions admit of, far from being a reason for thinking care so directed to be problematic, dubious or marginal, as the QALY maximiser must suppose, is instead the explanation of the peculiar and particular strength of the claim which it makes upon us and our resources. This might, at first sight, seem paradoxical, but it is not really so. The point is that in these particular circumstances, where we can do very little, we have a special obligation to do what we can.

The question which the advocate of QALY maximisation will ask, namely 'why should we invest so much in what promises so little return?', is one which evidences a failure to recognise the demand made upon us by the existence of those whose needs are so patent partly because human endeavour can do so little to meet them. Thus we should see in the attempt to meet those needs as best we can, not an inefficient or unproductive use of resources, but rather something which is at the heart of humane medicine as it is at the heart of a humane, or we might just say human, society: that is, the expression of a sympathy which asserts a desire to maintain, and does indeed maintain, our kinship and community with those who, through the approach of death or through physical or mental deprivation, stand in different ways on the edges of the most limited and perhaps the most obvious of communities, namely the community of those who are fit, strong and productive.[24]

[24] Just as the supposition, that the rationale of trying to meet the needs of the most needy lies in the prospects of success, conceals from view the true nature of the values which medicine, perhaps unknown to itself, expresses in the care of the dependent elderly and the mentally and physically handicapped, so too does the attempt to portray the case for proper provision for the old as a matter of prudence, since we shall all, one day, be old. For an example of such a strategy, see N. Daniel's *Am I My Parents' Keeper: An Essay in Justice Between the Young and the Old* (Oxford, 1988).

Paul Ramsey has written that 'to comprehend the depth and scope' of the biblical notion of justice, 'it is necessary first to *distinguish* two kinds of justice – God's judgmental righteousness and human justice – and then to *relate* them decisively together, so that the meaning of God's righteousness acting in judgment . . . becomes normative for human justice'.[25] Were we to allow ourselves to speak now in a theological voice we would refer to this work amongst the elderly and the handicapped as expressive of a fidelity towards them in which we rightly see a reflection of the trustworthy fidelity of God himself towards human kind; fidelity to the elderly on our part, so understood, is an attempt to allow our justice to approach, as its required pattern, the justice of God. We would say, further, that the commitment of some to the care of the elderly and the handicapped is a response to a divine vocation to reflect in this sphere of human life the continuing and unbroken fidelity of God, just as the vocation to marriage, for example, seeks to express it in another. So that we shall find ourselves insisting that this work is to be valued not only in and of itself, but also because the expression of solidarity and fidelity which it involves is a sign or reflection of, and thus a faithful response to, the gracious work of God in keeping faith or community with us in Jesus Christ.

To return from where, in other circumstances, we might have begun, we may repeat the claim that in considering need, justice has an eye for the most needy. In traditional portrayals, the figure of justice wears a blindfold. The blindfold symbolises justice's impartiality, an impartiality which suggests that justice treats all who make claims upon her equally. And this, in part, is right as I have wanted to say in speaking of justice as fairness. But justice, properly speaking, peaks under the blindfold and sees cases of need. And, in particular, justice is partial to the very needy and gives a priority to their claims upon her, so that we can indeed say that the claims which, for example, the dependent elderly, the handicapped and the terminally ill make upon us are primary amongst the claims of all those in need.

Is it possible to be more exact, however? Can the claims of

---

[25] P. Ramsey, *Basic Christian Ethics* (Chicago, 1950), 4.

need and of the very needy be ranked, so that our administrators are given a clearer guide in setting priorities? Perhaps there is more to say than I am capable of saying, but I doubt that even at the end of discussions more insightful than these, a graph or a table could be produced which would take us beyond what has thus far been said, namely that we cannot regard the claims of those in need, and in especial need, as merely some claims among the claims of all those to whom we might do good.

But then the question comes back all the stronger. Can the administrator who must allocate scarce resources accommodate considerations of this sort? Are we not still a long way from offering a workable account of the principles which should govern the distribution of resources? Our discussion suggests that, though, in principle, we should do the most good we can, we must also bear in mind an obligation to treat like cases alike, and recognise the claims of need. But to this, the proponents of QALY maximisation can be expected to protest that they are looking for something altogether sharper, and indeed we find Williams complaining of opposition to his proposals that 'There is no shortage of rhetoric about "equality" and "need", but most of it is vacuous, by which I mean it does not lead to any clear operational guidelines about who should get priority and at whose expense.'[26]

Now I have not denied that we need to provide a proper answer to the question 'who should get priority and at whose expense?', and I have agreed that we cannot rest content with the present pattern of distribution of health care. Nor am I unaware of the increasing strains which will be placed on the health budget by, for example, the sharp rise which is expected over the next fifty years in the proportion of the population over the age of seventy. The question will thus become the more pressing. Even so I would insist that Professor Williams' protest against his critics gets things the wrong way round. Reflection on the problem of the distribution of scarce resources has to begin by considering what values or principles must be re-

[26] A. Williams, 'Ethics and Efficiency in the Provision of Health Care' in *Philosophy and Medical Welfare*, ed. Bell and Mendus, 111.

spected in any scheme which could commend itself as morally acceptable. Then we shall have to go on to think about the different problem of how we could give effect to these principles and values in practice, in itself a very serious and important task. It is, none the less, a secondary task, so that it is to turn the matter on its head to suppose that we should allow the demand for clear operational guidelines to determine what values can or cannot be allowed to enter into our deliberations. The desire for administrative clarity is a legitimate one, but such clarity ought not to be achieved by discounting values, such as justice, which make the task of devising guidelines more difficult. We are under no obligation to prune our values in deference to a desire to make our moral lives more susceptible of 'rational' arrangements. Indeed, the obligation is the other way round. It is not that our values must be set aside if they prove recalcitrant in the hands of tidy-minded administrators, but rather that a 'rational' distribution of resources has no claim on our attentions unless it expresses our values, unless it has struggled, for example, to relate the claim that health care should be efficient to the claims of those in need, rather than solved the difficulty by ignoring an element of the dilemma.

A further point must be made, however, and that is that one detects in Williams' discussions of this problem not so much a reasonable demand for 'clear operational guidelines' as an unreasonable demand for an algorithm. Of course, administrators must have clear guidelines which allow them to ensure that their decisions respect whatever principles are regarded as central to a sound policy for the distribution of resources. They cannot be expected to act according to such principles if, for example, the principles are hopelessly unclear or contradictory. But, if those principles are not at fault in this respect, it does not follow that administrators lack clear guidelines just because the stated principles do not suggest the sort of simple algorithm which Williams offers with his proposal to maximise QALYs. Williams is foisting on us a very particular paradigm of what it is to offer guidelines, and one which in all sorts of areas of life we reject. To take just one example, judges presented with a statute which forbids unreasonable noise would not complain that unless they are given an instruction which relieves them of the need for judgment – such as 'all noise over ten decibels is unreasonable' – then they lack clear guidelines. In the same way, administrators who are asked to distribute resources with an eye on fairness and need, as well as on benefit, have no ground of complaint just because they are being asked to exercise a certain amount of judgment rather than merely to do sums.

In answer then, to Williams' complaint, I would claim that these discussions have provided at least the outline of a policy for the distribution of resources and that we have said rather more than the anecdotal administrator with whom we began. 'It is very difficult' is not the basis for a policy, and I have tried, in pointing to the claims of justice which require that we treat like cases alike and give prior claim in health care to cases of need, to offer an account of some of the constraints which a policy for the distribution of resources must acknowledge if it is to be more acceptable than Professor Williams' unsatisfactory proposals. Of course, I have not tried to work out the implications of this policy in detail, nor do I suggest that it would be easy to do so. But it may just be that there are no easy solutions, of the sort some economists might like, to the vexed problem of the distribution of resources. Whether or not that is the case, we should certainly not allow a desire for administrative simplicity to override the claims of fairness and need which any policy for the distribution of limited resources must respect if it is to commend itself to our moral reason. Instead, we should require that such a policy endeavour to reflect the values which are characteristically expressed in the practice of medicine, including the values which are expressed in the care of the elderly.

CHAPTER 5

Why and how (not) to value the environment[1]

I INTRODUCTION

According to a widely used definition, pollution is 'the introduction by humans into the environment of substances or
energy liable to cause hazards to human health, harm to living
resources and ecological systems, damage to structures or
amenity, or interference with legitimate uses of the environment'.[2] In reflecting common uses of the word 'pollution' the
definition also reflects the different, and sometimes competing,
rationales for its regulation. Thus, on the one hand, it indicates
that by 'pollution' some are put in mind principally of what, in
affecting the natural world, does harm to humans (and specifically to their 'health', and to the 'legitimate uses of' and the
'living resources' and 'amenity' they find in the environment).
On the other hand, however, it recognises that others use
'pollution' to describe not only what adversely affects humans
through affecting the environment, but to describe in addition
what, quite simply, adversely affects the environment; thus
there is reference to harm not only to 'living resources' but also
to 'ecological systems', and to damage not just to 'amenity', but
also to 'structures' (not, as it might have been, 'structures of
value to humans').

The existence of competing rationales for protection of the
environment reflected in this definition has been the stuff of

[1] An early draft of this chapter was prepared for the Royal Commission on Environmental Pollution and parts of it were also given as lectures at Imperial College,
London and at the European Environment Agency in Copenhagen. In all cases it
benefited from criticisms and discussions.
[2] M. Holdgate, *A Perspective of Environmental Pollution* (Cambridge, 1979), 17.

much of the debate in the field of environmental ethics over the last few decades, certainly as it has been received outside the discipline itself. Thus it has seemed that the debate has been dominated by the question as to whether we should value the environment for the sake of human interests alone, or for the sake of the environment itself (or at least for the sake of some other of its constituents in addition to humans). Should the prevention of pollution be concerned with the prevention of damage to 'health', 'living resources', amenities and so on, or in addition, or primarily, be concerned with the prevention of harm to 'ecological systems'? Should our environmental policy be anthropocentric, as it is put, or non-anthropocentric – that is, roughly speaking, should it accord value to the environment as it is instrumental to human purposes, interests or needs, or for itself?

In this chapter I shall argue that this debate, which has been perceived as central to environmental ethics, is, in a number of respects, misconceived:

(i)   Both advocates and opponents of anthropocentrism have tended to assume a problematic conception of the human good.

(ii)   Both advocates and opponents of anthropocentrism have tended to assume a problematic notion of moral obligation.

(iii) The debate itself has served to suggest that the issue between advocates and opponents of anthropocentrism is central for contemporary environmentalism, when, as a matter of fact, this debate about why we should value the environment is and can be nothing more than a pleasant side-show where practices of valuation (the 'how' of valuing the environment) effectively preclude certain reasons for valuing the environment (anthropocentric as well as non-anthropocentric) from being taken seriously.

For these charges to make sense and be substantiated, something of an overview of the debate between anthropocentrism and non-anthropocentrism will be required. To begin with we shall ask (in section II) how far anthropocentrism may, whilst being wholly anthropocentric, provide a basis for wide-ranging environmental regulation. We shall then (in section III) look at the attempt to widen or extend the scope of an anthropocentric approach by maintaining that animals or plants or perhaps ecosystems, are themselves properly objects of moral concern and can be seen to be so on the basis of a reflective and unbiased application of criteria which are said to warrant regard for humans. These two sections will lay the foundations for the argument (of section IV) that the debate has been guilty of the first two misconceptions and furthermore that the contrast between anthropocentrism and non-anthropocentrism is itself unhelpful. We shall then (in section V) contend that influential practices of environmental valuation in actual fact only take account of certain reasons for valuing the environment (both anthropocentric and non-anthropocentric in the terms of the earlier debate) in such a way as to misrepresent them.

II ANTHROPOCENTRISM AND ITS SCOPE

The term 'anthropocentric' is usually employed to describe any code of environmental ethics which holds that moral duties are properly owed only to humans and that whilst we may certainly have duties *concerning* the environment, we do not strictly have duties *to* it. Such a code may well express environmental concern, but what may appear as a concern for the good of the environment will in fact be a concern for the good of the environment only in so far as that is good for humans. And to be concerned for the environment only as it is good for something else, is to view it instrumentally; that is, not as an end in itself, but only as a means to the good of a different end. This is a way of thought which, of course, the very term 'environment' itself suggests, since to label non-human nature thus is to identify it simply as the context for human life. As a context for human life it is instrumentally valuable, but in and of itself it lays no claims upon us. Any duties we may seem to have in relation to it, or to the 'resources' or 'stock' it contains, are in reality duties owed to other humans.

Anthropocentric concerns for the environment have a long history and, as Keith Thomas argues, are evidenced in such traditional practices as the instituting of close seasons for fishing or hunting, the prohibition on the felling of young trees and so on.[3] Though such simple measures are straightforwardly prudential they have roots in a wider pattern of thought which provided a basis in principle for a more far-reaching environmentalism, to use our terms. 'We are but stewards of earthly treasures' a sixteenth-century preacher declared, 'and therefore must one day be called to account'.[4] Such a thought was commonplace: the earth had been created by a good God for the sake of humankind, but humankind is responsible for using these gifts wisely and well, that is, with a view to the needs of other humans, both now and in the future. And such wisdom could even include what might have been thought to be a typically modern concern, namely concern for the preservation and protection of other species, each of which, so eighteenth-century natural theologians would maintain, has a utility within God's purposes and design, however difficult it might be to fathom in some cases.

'Much modern environmental thinking', writes Thomas, 'takes the form of finding new secular justifications for this older religious position'. To put the point another way, many contemporary approaches to the environment commend an attitude of stewardship, purportedly independently of the theological beliefs which were, and indeed are, taken to mandate such a stance.[5] No matter the basis for this contemporary commendation of stewardship, these modern anthropocentric positions, like their theological predecessors, should not be supposed to be inimical to environmental concerns (even if the

---

[3] See Keith Thomas, 'Introduction', *Ethics and the Environment*, ed. C. C. W. Taylor (Oxford, 1992) and, more fully, his *Man and the Natural World* (New York, 1983).

[4] Thomas, 'Introduction', 6.

[5] This is not the place to take exception, as one should, to the widespread contemporary appeal to the notion of stewardship as expressive of a theological regard for the environment. Suffice it to say that the typical argument for a benevolent human dominion in place of a despotic human dominion fails to see the theologically questionable character of any claim to human dominion over nature, whether benevolent or otherwise. To take an analogy; it is certainly far from negligible that the British Empire, as opposed say, to the Mongol Empire, was, on the whole benevolent; but a question might quite properly be raised as to the existence of empires, not just as to their character.

label 'anthropocentric' applied to environmental attitudes has increasingly in popular usage a pejorative tone) since it can be seen at once that an anthropocentric viewpoint may provide a widely persuasive warrant for far-reaching environmental protection. (Indeed, many of the foundational documents of modern environmentalism are anthropocentric in tone, even if they are not obviously conscious of making any philosophical commitments. Thus the *Declaration of Principles* from the United Nations Conference on the Environment in Stockholm in 1972 states that 'Man . . . bears a solemn responsibility to protect and improve the environment *for present and future generations*', and again, that 'the natural resources of the earth including the air, water, land, flora and fauna, and especially representative samples of natural ecosystems must be safeguarded *for the benefit of present and future generations*'.[6] And the *Brundtland Report* of fifteen years later reveals a similar perspective with its reference to 'ecological capital' in the heading 'Species and Ecosystems: Resources for Development'.[7]) Anthropocentrism, properly understood, then, is not necessarily a licence for ruthless exploitation of the natural world, but may offer a reason for treating it with a degree of care and caution – and this for the simple reason that where human well-being is reasonably held to be by no means independent of the well-being of the environment, human self-interest will itself dictate a concern for the interests of others than humans alone. So it is that Passmore, an advocate of an explicitly anthropocentric approach, has been attacked by an opponent as a sheep in wolf's clothing![8]

Reasons of human self-interest can doubtless be found for

[6] United Nations Conference on the Environment, Stockholm, 1972, *Declaration of Principles*, 1 and 2, reprinted in *Reflecting on Nature: Readings in Environmental Philosophy*, ed. L. Gruen and D. Jamieson (Oxford, 1994), 179–82.

[7] United Nations World Commission on Environment and Development, *Our Common Future* (The Brundtland Report) (Oxford, 1987).

[8] Passmore's claim, in *Man's Responsibility for Nature: Ecological Problems and the Western Tradition* (New York, 1974), is that it bids to recognise the interests of, or accord rights to, animals, plants or other elements of the environment depend on misunderstandings of the nature of interests and rights, and that there is no need for a 'new environmental ethic', since the resources of the tradition of moral reflection are sufficient as a basis for dealing with contemporary problems and issues. See, more briefly, J. Passmore, 'Attitudes to Nature' in *Nature and Conduct*, ed. R. S. Peters (New York, 1975), 251–64.

seeking to ensure clean air and water, the conservation of soils, the preservation of forests, and so on. The question is, however, what is the shape and limit of the concern for the natural world which such self-interest dictates? Only in the light of an answer to that question can another more basic question be addressed; that is, are there concerns for the natural world which are missed (or if not missed, at least mischaracterised) by anthropocentric considerations?

The exact scope of the environmental concern warranted by attention to human self-interest will depend upon answers to a number of subsidiary questions, some of them empirical, some more plainly philosophical. The following might be mentioned as among the most important:

(i)   How finely tuned a system is the environment? Is it to be expected, that is to say, that changes in the distribution and prevalence of plant and animal species, or to particular habitats or aspects of the wider environment such as the climate, in which humans have no direct interest, will, through the subtle interplay of environmental and ecological relationships, threaten aspects of the environment crucial to human interests?

(ii) Whether it is finely tuned or not, what is our ability to predict the consequences of our actions in relation to the environment? It might be believed, that is to say, that though human well-being is to a considerable degree independent of the well-being of individual species or habitats, for example, we are incapable of reliably determining where this independence pertains and where it does not.

(iii) If the human self-interest which motivates environmental concern includes the interests not only of those presently alive but also of future generations, what account is to be given of the character, limits and demands of this responsibility to the future?[9]

(iv) With what confidence can we presently determine not only

---

[9] For an introduction to some of the issues, see *Obligations to Future Generations*, ed. B. Barry and R. Sikora (Philadelphia, 1978) and *Responsibilities to Future Generations*, ed. E. Partridge (New York, 1981).

the needs of the future, but also the part which particular species of animal or plants, non-renewable resources, habitats, or whatever, may have in meeting those needs? Can we know of any seemingly insignificant species or habitat (e.g., a species whose numbers are already so small that its extinction will make no appreciable difference, or because, though not small in numbers, a closely related species can be expected to fill its ecological niche, or a habitat which supports no unique species, nor any other species in significant numbers), that it will not become of particular value in a future we can only partially anticipate (either in scientific research or in supporting other forms of life under changed climatic conditions, and so on)?

And – perhaps most importantly of all:

(v) If concern for the environment should properly serve only the good of humans, how shall we specify that good? Is that good, for example, simply the aggregate of individual goods or does it have a communal aspect? And is this human good, whether individual or social, primarily, or even exclusively, a good of consumption?[10] To be blunt, does the value of mountains lie in their being a source of minerals (and thus demand an ethic of resource conservation), or in their being objects of beauty and wonder (thus suggesting an ethic of preservation)?

As these and other questions and issues are addressed and settled, anthropocentrism will take quite different forms, resulting in perhaps quite different prescriptions as to what would constitute a proper policy in relation to the natural world. Without pausing, however, to engage in a careful identification and categorisation of different versions of anthropocentrism, we repeat the question posed earlier: that is, are there concerns for the natural world which are missed, or if not missed, mischaracterised, by an anthropocentric approach? What our considerations thus far suggest is that a contrast between

[10] The view that it is, has been labelled 'economism' which is said to hold that 'we are agents of *consumption*, motivated by consumer *preference* living in a world of *resources*'; see *The Ethics of the Environment*, ed. A. Brennan (Aldershot, 1995), 'Introduction', xxiii.

anthropocentric and non-anthropocentric ethics, whilst being sharp in theory, may not be so very sharp in practice. A simple but reflective concern for human well-being, that is to say, can plainly come to embrace a large part of the environmental agenda. Indeed, once we take account of the point that an anthropocentric concern will be a concern for the good of future generations, that human well-being is not a concern simply for narrowly material or financial interests, but for such goods as beauty and tranquillity, and so on, and thus that concern for human well-being requires not only conservation of forests and fish stocks but also the protection of landscapes, ecosystems and wildernesses, we might wonder what, if anything, is at stake in this argument.

Whatever convergence there may be between these different approaches, it seems unlikely, however, that this convergence will be either exact or, even where it seems so, other than somewhat misleading. Anthropocentric environmentalism, that is to say, is unlikely to take on all the concerns of a typical environmentalism, or, if it does, may significantly misrepresent them. These two points must be explored in turn.

In the first place, though, as has been said, the exact scope of an anthropocentric environmentalism will depend on the resolution of a variety of questions, some of which have been identified under (i) to (v), it seems unlikely that a plausible resolution of those questions will result in an anthropocentric ethic which matches in its concerns and policies the concerns and policies of a typical non-anthropocentric environmentalism; for even if the interests of humans and of the natural environment are not always simply opposed, there are surely cases where they are not simply compatible. Take a case which may be far from uncommon. A proposed development will affect a particular habitat and in so doing will threaten with extinction various species of flora and fauna. Of course, the various questions which have been mentioned as determining the shape of an anthropocentric ethic will have to be answered in turn before a decision can be taken as to whether a development should proceed; but it seems doubtful that plausible answers to them will, in all cases, count against the development. Thus, (i) the species which will be eradicated, far from being crucial to the functioning of the particular habitat in which they are found, may – perhaps as a result of their present rarity – be peripheral to the maintenance of its character; and this may be so plainly the case that (ii) there is no difficulty in predicting a virtual null-effect from their disappearance (apart from the particular extinctions themselves). Of course, a responsibility to future generations (iii) makes a difference; but, however that responsibility is spelled out, it is difficult to see how a loss of species with no practical significance for the needs of the present generation can be prohibited by reference to the needs of a future one. Certainly our ability to anticipate the needs of the future is fallible (iv), but such fallibility could not of itself prohibit any action likely to result in an irreversible change to the environment, whether through loss of species or otherwise. A proper caution about effecting change is not to be identified with a requirement to maintain the status quo.

There remains the point (v) that if we are to be sure of what is required of us in pursuing an anthropocentric environmentalism, we must have an account of the human good which is to be served. Here it might be thought that an anthropocentric objection to the planned development can finally be grounded; not, of course, if the human good is thought of solely in material terms, but certainly if is noted, for example, that as a matter of fact humans generally happen to value and enjoy a rich diversity of species and prefer that they should be maintained. Is not this just one way in which anthropocentrism might converge with environmental concerns which have a different rationale?

The problem with such an anthropocentric justification for the preservation of other species is that it seems to be parasitic off what must be an independent and non-anthropocentric justification. Suppose for the moment the anthropocentric case for the preservation of species takes its stand on, as we have put it, what humans happen to value, enjoy or prefer. Putting aside any doubts about how general is the preference for a rich diversity of species, the question is why this is a preference which should be respected. In general, people will maintain that they prefer to travel to work by car than by train, but where this preference is one which proves socially inconvenient or harmful, it would generally be thought perfectly rational and acceptable to seek to overcome the preference, and not only by making train travel more attractive, but also by spending money on advertising aimed simply at making it seem more attractive! Why would a policy aimed at overcoming a preference for a rich diversity of species not be acceptable, even if that preference were also proving socially costly, in this case in creating opposition to a proposed development which will bring widespread benefits to a community? The answer must lie not in the bare fact of there being a preference, but in the nature of that preference. This is a preference, that is to say, which is right for people to have; which is to say, in fact, that what is worthy of respect is not the *preference* that humans happen to have for a rich diversity of species, but that which the preference relates to, namely the rich diversity of species itself. In other words, the seeming convergence between an anthropocentric case for environmentalism and typical environmental concerns is not, in fact, a convergence – the anthropocentric case at this point must actually presuppose the propriety of respecting the existence of other species as such (and thereby cease to be purely anthropocentric) or fail to carry weight. (This is not to say that environmental concerns which can't be justified anthropocentrically can be justified. It is just to say that if they can be justified, that justification does not seem to be anthropocentric.)

In the second place, and related to the point just made, even if anthropocentrism is reckoned to justify the same prescriptions as a non-anthropocentric environmentalism, it does so only whilst misrepresenting them. Even if it seems possible, contrary to what has just been said, to portray environmental concerns as concerns for a human good, they would thereby be fundamentally misconstrued. What is lost in the anthropocentric perspective is the quite simple thought that certain ways of treating the environment are not only ill-advised or imprudent humanly speaking, but quite simply wrong. However hard we push the anthropocentric view, and however much it yields by way of serious environmental concern, we are surely left with the sense that the project of rendering the anthropocentric view environmentally friendly resembles the project of seeking to ensure the proper treatment of slaves by labouring the doubtless valid point that the well-being of slave owners is by no means independent of the well-being of slaves: even if it is generally true that there is a coincidence of interest, the case for ensuring the well-being of slaves is misrepresented if is portrayed as a function of the well-being of their owners. As Rolston puts it, 'the deeper problem with the anthropocentric rationale, beyond overstatement, is that its justifications are submoral and fundamentally exploitative even if subtly'.[11] Arne Naess puts it more bluntly when he labels conventional environmentalism 'shallow', in overlooking the fact that 'the well being of non-human life on earth has a value in itself . . . independent of any instrumental usefulness for limited human purposes'.[12]

III THE EXTENSIONIST CASE AGAINST ANTHROPOCENTRISM

Whether because it does not take up all its concerns, or because, even where it does, it mispresents them, an anthropocentric ethic seems to be at odds with an environmentalism which reckons with the existence of duties to, and not just concerning, the environment – certainly this is presupposed by the various cases which have been made against anthropocentrism. Now, though these cases seem to yield quite different codes, they share the conviction that anthropocentrism is in error in recognising the well-being of humans alone as the proper object of moral concern, and the well-being of entities other than humans only as these contribute to human well-being. They claim, that is to say, that the boundaries of moral concern or obligation should be placed more widely and adopt a common tactic in arguing that the basis of moral regard for

[11] H. Rolston, 'Duties to Endangered Species' in *Environmental Ethics*, ed. R. Elliot (Oxford, 1995), 62.
[12] A. Naess, 'A Defence of the Deep Ecology Movement', *Environmental Ethics*, 6 (1984), 266. In addition, see 'The Shallow and the Deep, Long-Range Ecology Movements', *Inquiry*, 16 (1973), 95–100, and 'The Deep Ecological Movement: Some Philosophical Aspects', *Philosophical Inquiry*, 8 (1986), 10–31.

humans, properly and impartially considered, requires an extension of that regard to other classes of being. Three commonly canvassed 'extensionist' alternatives to anthropocentrism take the higher animals (zoocentrism), living things (biocentrism) or ecosystems (ecocentrism), as proper objects of moral concern, in addition to human beings. It will be appropriate to look briefly at each of these claims in turn.

The most influential defence of the notion that animals are worthy of moral consideration is associated with Peter Singer (though Stephen Clark and Tom Regan are also significant advocates of related but importantly different points of view).[13] In *Animal Liberation*, Singer, presupposing the thesis that an action is good or right in so far as it maximises utility (here understood as pleasure and the absence of pain), argues that in determining morally good courses of action there is no sound reason for excluding from consideration the suffering which may be caused to non-human animals – to exclude animals simply because they are animals is a form of of discrimination ('speciesism') which is objectionable in the same way as say, racism and sexism. It follows that for Singer harm to animals cannot be justified simply by parading the benefits to humans which may result from it; it would have to be shown that the benefits to humans outweigh the harm done to the animals. Singer's position, however, whilst it agrees with those of Regan and Clark in regarding animals as morally considerable, is significantly weaker in the protection it offers to animals (and, of course, to humans). According to Regan, for whom the higher animals are possessors of rights as individual subjects of life, experimentation on animals is straightforwardly illicit; as bearers of rights they are wrongly treated, as would be humans, if used as unconsenting experimental subjects, no matter the benefits which such experimentation may reasonably be expected to bring. Singer's consequentialism can make no such objection to experimentation in principle.

In whatever form it takes, however, zoocentrism, though it widens the concerns of an exclusively human ethic, has to face

[13] P. Singer, *Animal Liberation* (New York, 1975); S. Clark, *The Moral Status of Animals* (Oxford, 1977); T. Regan, *The Case for Animal Rights* (Berkeley, 1983).

essentially the same questions which were posed to anthropocentric environmentalism, namely whether there are concerns
for the natural world which are missed or mischaracterised
even by a zoocentric ethic. On the first point, take an oft cited
example of conflict between zoocentrism and environmentalism: 'On San Clemente Island, the US Fish and Wildlife
Service and the California Department of Fish and Game
planned to shoot two thousand feral goats to save three endangered plant species, *Malacothamnus clementinus, Castilleja grisea,
Delphinium kinkiense*, of which the surviving individuals num-
bered only a few dozens.'[14] Such a case is presumably by no
means rare: the culling of large numbers of introduced animals
must quite often be necessary for the sake of returning an
ecosystem to something of its previous and perhaps greater
biodiversity or simply for the sake a preserving certain rare
species. But it is doubtful that such a course of action could be
acceptable to ethical codes which focus on animal suffering or
animal rights.[15] Moreover, and this is the second point, even
where there is no such conflict, and the good of animals and the
good of the environment are reckoned to require a common
policy, it is not the case that the good of the environment is
pursued for the sake of the animals. There is a wider environmentalism, whether or not it is defensible, which has an
independent concern for the good of something other than
sentient creatures alone.

A sense of such limitations encourages the advocacy of
biocentrism, which, as its name suggests, regards capacity for

---

[14] See H. Rolston, 'Challenges in Environmental Ethics', in *The Environment in Question:
Ethics and Global Issues*, ed. D. Cooper and J. Palmer (London, 1992), 140.

[15] It depends, of course, on how such an ethic is worked out in detail; if sentience is
reckoned to be merely a sufficient but not a necessary condition for moral considerability, a form of zoocentrism might be compatible with environmentalism. But then
there would cease to be any point, perhaps, in identifying the position as zoocentrism. Regan is explicit in acknowledging the opposition between his own
position and environmentalism: 'If . . . we had to choose between saving the last two
members of an endangered species, or saving another individual who belonged to a
species that was plentiful but whose death would be a greater prima facie harm to
the individual than the harm that death would be to the two, then the rights view
requires that we save the individual'; *The Case for Animal Rights*, 359.

life (and not just sentience) as the basis for moral standing.[16] Biocentrism argues that the link which is typically made in both anthropocentrism and zoocentrism between moral value and sentience is mistaken. It is not capacity to experience, but rather capacity to flourish which counts, and any organism, be it an animal or a plant, which has the capacity to flourish may be said to have an interest in so doing which ought to be respected.[17]

Now, while the basic criterion of moral standing favoured by biocentrism leads it to recognise the claims on our moral attention made by a wider class of entities than is allowed by either anthropocentrism or zoocentrism, like them it has to face the question as to whether it represents, and properly represents, environmental concerns. The difficulty lies in the fact that it remains focused squarely on the claims of individuals and is able to represent a concern for species and ecosystems, only as such a concern serves the good of those individuals. But plainly it does not necessarily serve the good of individuals as such; that is to say, a concern for the preservation of a particular species, whilst it certainly serves the good of some individuals of that species, may, as a matter of fact, require action contrary to the interests of other individuals of the same species (perhaps the culling of the sick), or against the good of other individuals of other species (perhaps the culling of certain predators or competitors). Environmentalism, in other words, typically favours rarity and biodiversity, even where this favouritism may subordinate the interests of organisms held to be morally considerable by biocentrism.

[16] Cases for biocentrism are advanced by P. W. Taylor in his *Respect for Nature: A Theory of Environmental Ethics* (Princeton, 1986) and also by R. Attfield in *The Ethics of Environmental Concern* (Aldershot, 1994). In addition, see K. Goodpaster, 'On Being Morally Considerable', *Journal of Philosophy*, 78 (1978), 308–25.

[17] The problems for such approaches posed by Philimore's parody of Coleridge are not unfamiliar to their advocates ('He prayeth best who loveth best, All things both great and small; And streptococcus is the test, I love him best of all'); and Taylor and Attfield have elaborate, though opposed, proposals for adjudicating the conflicts which may occur for those who set out to respect the interests of living things. Both maintain, in effect, that 'Moral considerability does not entail equal moral significance. So, moral significance is, if you like, a measure of degree of considerability'; Elliot, editor's 'Introduction' to *Environmental Ethics*, 13. (Philimore's parody is cited by S. Clark, *How to Think About the Earth* (London, 1993), 130.)

It is natural enough, then, for interest to turn in the direction of ecocentrism – the view that rain forests, oceans, grasslands, ecosystems, or nature as a whole, are proper objects of moral regard and consideration as themselves possessed of interests and a capacity to flourish. Such a position is defended by Lawrence Johnson, who can be seen as developing and taking further the biocentric viewpoint which claimed that the concepts of 'well-being' and 'interests' can be applied as well to plants as to sentient animals. Johnson contends that these concepts have application not just to individuals, but to collectives such as species and ecosystems. And, since this is so, these collectives must themselves possess moral standing.[18]

We need to be clear that this particular version of ecocentrism is extensionist; that is, that it proceeds by claiming that the grounds which explain regard for humans (and animals and living things in general) also licence regard for the larger systems of which they are a part. There are other versions of 'ecocentrism' which likewise stress the importance of such collective entities, but not on the basis of extensionist considerations. These positions tend to have in common a regard for A. Leopold's *A Sand Country Almanac: With Essays on Conservation from Round River* as the inspiration for the new ecocentric outlook which is thought to be needed to address our environmental plight, but in justifying this outlook, his disciples diverge.

In *A Sand Country Almanac*, Leopold advocates a so-called 'land ethic' which 'enlarges the boundaries of the community to include soils, waters, plants, and animals, or collectively the land'.[19] 'A thing is right', he declares, 'when it tends to preserve the stability and integrity of the biotic community; it is wrong when it tends otherwise'.[20] The tensions in the theoretical basis of Leopold's approach are plain enough from the juxtaposition of these maxims. The first, in speaking of an enlargement of the boundaries of the community, seems to endorse the extensionism defended by Johnson. But there again the second seems

[18] L. E. Johnson, *A Morally Deep World* (Cambridge, 1991).
[19] A. Leopold, *A Sand Country Almanac* (New York, 1949), 204.
[20] Leopold, *A Sand Country Almanac*, 224–5.

to posit an entity, 'the biotic community', the well-being of which is not an addition to the class of things demanding moral consideration, but that which all actions must serve. This claim – not that the biotic community counts on the same basis as other moral considerable items, but rather that for whatever reason it counts, it trumps other claims to moral regard – can be found in the work of J. Callicott and H. Rolston, though they develop their ideas differently.[21] Callicott is clear on this point: 'An environmental ethic which takes as its *summum bonum* the integrity, stability, and beauty of the biotic community is not conferring standing on something *else* besides plants, animals, soils, and waters. Rather, the former, the good of the community as a whole, serves as a standard for the assessment of the relative value and relative ordering of its constitutive parts and therefore provides a means of adjudicating the often mutually contradictory demands of the parts considered separately for *equal* consideration.'[22]

Objections to these different forms of Leopoldian eco-centrism are themselves slightly different. Against Johnson it can be argued that the attempt to stretch extensionism as far as he does is highly implausible; that is, whilst the notions of 'well-being', 'flourishing' and 'interests' may, with some conviction (and on the basis of a long tradition of Aristotelian thought), be employed in relation to animals and plants, it is far from obvious that they can be applied to ecosystems, biospheres, deserts, or whatever. 'One problem here' writes Brennan, 'is knowing just what the good of the biosphere is if it is something

---

[21] J. Callicott, *In Defense of a Land Ethic* (Albany, 1989) and H. Rolston, *Environmental Ethics: Duties to and Values in the Natural World* (Philadelphia, 1988).

[22] Callicott, 'Animal Liberation: A Triangular Affair', 44. According to Callicott such 'holism' (i.e., preference for the systems, collectives or wholes of which individuals are a part) is somehow demanded by a biological outlook: 'Rather than imposing our alienation from nature and natural processes and cycles of life on other animals, we human beings could reaffirm our participation in nature by accepting life as it is given without a sugar coating. Instead of imposing artificial legalities, rights and so on on nature, we might take the opposite course and accept and affirm natural biological laws, principles and limitations in the human personal and social spheres'; 'Animal Liberation: A Triangular Affair', 54. Rolston appeals to a similar naturalism: 'The individual is subordinate to the species, not the other way round . . . The appropriate survival unit [i.e., the species] is the appropriate level of moral concern'; H. Rolston, 'Duties to Endangered Species', in *Environmental Ethics*, ed. Elliot, 71–2.

different from the sum of the goods of all the individuals living within it'.[23] We could focus on this difficulty by wondering about the status of the word 'stability' in Leopold's original slogan; in what sense can the good of the biotic community consist in its stability? Certainly this stability might be thought of as a good from a number of different perspectives *within* this community, but it is difficult to see that this stability constitutes the good (as opposed to the simple persistance) of the object (the biotic community) under discussion.

Against the unqualified, non-extensionist holism found in at least some of the writings of Callicott and Rolston other objections come to mind. Callicott's original formulation of his position was charged with misanthropy; as he comments in a later preface to an earlier article, 'a target ratio of one bear for every two people seems a bit extravagant'. But ecocentrism has also been labelled 'ecofascism' – and the preference for the good of the whole over the good of the individual in both Callicott and Rolston is enough to explain the point of the charge, though there is in addition Callicott's praise for the ethos of the Stone Age in which 'population was routinely optimized by sexual continency, abortion, infanticide, and stylized warfare'.[24] Whatever the problems with extensionism, it at least has the merit of not inviting us to trade what is said to be one form of moral insensibility for what is quite definitely another.

IV THE REPUDIATION OF EXTENSIONISM

In the last two sections we have considered the scope of anthropocentrism and the claims chiefly of different versions of extensionism. We might thus seem to be intending a contrast between anthropocentrism and its critics. The survey, however, has been meant to serve a claim about the shared presuppositions of these positions, presuppositions which, so we shall claim, show this debate to be in certain and important respects misconceived.

[23] A. Brennan, 'The Moral Standing of Natural Objects' in *The Ethics of the Environment*, ed. Brennan, 52.
[24] Callicott, 'Animal Liberation: A Triangular Affair', 30.

We should note to begin with that extensionism, no matter whether it is judged in some degree persuasive, has seemed to many a curiously wrong-headed strategy for the defence of a genuinely environmental ethic. Unlike anthropocentrism, it does not claim that we have duties concerning the environment only in so far as these are mandated by regard for human interests; it does, however, in claiming that we have duties to the environment, do so on the ground of the alleged likeness in certain key respects (the possession of interests, the ability to flourish, or whatever) between elements of the environment and humankind. But to present respect for nature as a form of extended humanism, whatever merits it may have in some respects, seems to misconstrue at least something important in our attitudes towards nature, which has to do with its existing over against us as radically other and different.[25] Extensionism, far from noting or reckoning with this otherness, seems persuaded by a certain ethical monism, which presupposes one ground of moral obligation. It is just because of this presupposition that it endeavours to find this ground in, and a hence similiarity between, a diverse range of objects. In so doing, at least as its range increases, it at one and the same time strains our credulity in alleging likenesses between rather different things, whilst overlooking the possibility of a diversity of grounds for moral regard and thus of a moral sensitivity to these differences.

If this is so, the question becomes why a strategy of extensionism has been found appealing? In her article 'Duties Concerning Islands', Mary Midgley alleges that 'a blight in this area' has been spread by the social contract model of moral obligation which sought to explain the existence of certain rights and duties by reference to the interests or consent of the parties involved.[26] This explanation of certain duties in contractual terms has, however, come to be treated as the basis of any legitimate moral claim, so that it has seemed at the least highly problematic to suppose that rights could be attributed or

[25] See B. Williams' 'Must a Concern for the Environment Be Centred on Human Beings?', in *Ethics and the Environment*, ed. Taylor, 60–68.
[26] M. Midgley, 'Duties Concerning Islands' in *Environmental Ethics*, ed. Elliot, 91.

duties owed to those who could not understand or claim them or be thought to have an interest in their being observed. Midgley contends, however, that the intellectual pretensions of the contract model to serve as a general model of moral obligation should be resisted – we should remind ourselves that we naturally recognise a whole range of obligations, very few of which can be treated even with a degree of plausibility as 'quasi-contractual relations between symmetrical pairs of rational human agents'.[27] Midgley lists nineteen candidates for moral consideration, including the dead, the permanently insane, so-called 'human vegetables', animals, plants, works of art, inanimate but structured objects, cities, countries, oneself and God. As she comments:

As far as importance goes, it is certainly possible to argue that some of these sorts of beings should concern us more and others less: we need a priority system. But, to build it, *moral* arguments are required. The various kinds of claims have to be understood and compared, not written off in advance. We cannot rule that those who, in our own and other cultures, suppose that there is a direct objection to injuring or destroying some of them, are always just confused and mean only, in fact, that this item will be needed for rational human consumption.[28]

Now, if Midgley is right, the appeal and the error of extensionism are at once apparent. The appeal of extensionism is just that it proposes to defend regard for animals, trees, rainforests, or whatever, in terms which are acceptable to what Midgley calls the social contract theory; that is, it argues that animals, trees, rainforests, and so on, are, at least by analogy, individuals with interests (however implausible or stretched the analogy seems to be). But the error is just to accept this theory's pretensions to intellectual hegemony. Thus, as we said at the outset, the whole debate has been founded on a misconception, whereby both advocates and opponents of anthropocentrism have together assumed a problematic notion of moral obligation.

Something of the recognition of a variety of grounds of moral obligation in the context of thinking about the environment is illustrated by an account of the criteria used in selecting and

[27] Midgley, 'Duties Concerning Islands', 101.
[28] Midgley, 'Duties Concerning Islands', 97–8.

grading the United Kingdom's sites of special scientific interest.[29] Here the importance of a site is said to depend on size (or
extent), diversity, naturalness, rarity, fragility, typicalness, recorded history, position in an ecological/geographical unit,
potential value (in conservation terms) and instrinsic appeal.
Given this diversity, it seems highly improbable that there
should be some general account of why each of these claims
makes a claim upon us in terms of some more general theory,
nor does such an account seem necessary. To suppose that we
are somehow prohibited from recognising the legitimacy of
these claims until they can be accounted for in terms of some
other higher reason or theory is, on the one hand, to threaten
an infinite regress (for this higher or more general reason might
be regarded as unwarranted itself until itself warranted by a
higher reason or theory, and so on) and, on the other hand, to
misunderstand the nature of moral theory in relation to moral
obligations – moral theory may serve to interrogate, elucidate
or articulate obligations we acknowledge, but does not itself
provide a prior standard against which each and every moral
obligation must first prove itself.

The other misconception we mentioned as underlying the
debate was one concerning the human good, and that too can
now be explained. We have already referred to the crucial
significance of the account to be given of the human good in
determining the scope of anthropocentrism. Whatever disagreement there may be on that point, however, both parties to
the debate we have described, just by entering into it on the
terms allowed, may seem to take it for granted that humans and
the environment should be thought of as at odds with one
another, with non-anthropocentrism disagreeing with anthropocentrism in proposing a more highly moral, altruistic or
selfless way of coping with the conflict. But again, in so far as
this is a fundamentally shared framework for debate, it should
be challenged.

Recall the point made against economism that it mistook the
goods constitutive of human well-being. Thus it may be that

[29] *A Nature Conservation Review,* ed. D. Ratcliffe (Cambridge, 1977), 3–14.

someone thinking in accordance with this perspective and wondering why he or she should recognise a duty to the environment, is like the person who, to use an example of John O'Neill's, wonders 'why have friends?' or 'why should I do good for my friends?' To have friends belongs to human flourishing, and it belongs to friendship that one values one's friends for their own sake. So it may be that 'for a large number of, although not all, individual living things and biological collectives, we should recognise and promote their flourishing as an end in itself. Such care for the natural world is constitutive of a flourishing human life. The best human life is one which includes an awareness of and practical concern with the goods of entities in the non-human world.'[30]

But, if O'Neill is right, it would be misleading, I think, to regard this simply as a point against anthropocentrism, rather than as a point against much of the debate concerning it, since if human well-being consists in part in enjoyment of the well-being and flourishing of the natural world, the anthropocentric/non-anthropocentric contrast begins to break down. We could get at this point by an analogy. Suppose we were to ask whether the duties and obligations parents have towards their children are egocentric or non-egocentric – that is, do they care for their children and their children's well-being for their own sake or for the sake of the children? Doubtless, in some cases and in some particular situations, one or other of the two answers we are offered by this contrast would describe the motivation of the parents, but in the generality of cases to choose either account would mischaracterise what is going on. Most parents just do not think in these terms, and if, forced to choose, they would be inclined to choose the non-egocentric account, this is surely only because it seems to offer the least unsatisfactory of the two. But both seem unsatisfactory for the reason that the link between the good of the parents and the good of the child is such that to oppose and contrast them misrepresents their relationship. In what would be thought of as a satisfactory relationship between children and parents, the

---

[30] J. O'Neill, 'The Varieties of Intrinsic Value', *The Monist*, 75 (1992), 133.

good of the parents in some sense consists in the good of the child. How is this so? It is so just because the good of parents, as parents, consists in having happy and flourishing children; that is, in having children who realise and express their potential. But if parents have an interest in the latter, it is not 'in their interest' in the narrow sense. Thus the good of parents and children is too closely bound up, where it is properly understood, for the contrast egocentric/non-egocentric to make much sense.

The parallel point in relation to the environment would be that where human well-being is reckoned to consist in part in the appreciation of the well-being and flourishing of the natural world, it will be unhelpful to ask whether a concern for the well-being of the environment is for the sake of those who are concerned for it or for the sake of the environment itself, or to think of the latter concerns as in some way especially selfless or altruistic. A proper account of human well-being, it might be argued, would allow us to understand something of the unreality of the contrast which the debate in environmental ethics has tended to assume.

V HOW HOW PRECLUDES WHY

Of the three misconceptions which I have associated with the debate between advocates and opponents of anthropocentrism, it remains to deal with the third – this is the misconception which the seeming earnestness of the debate encourages, that the dispute is central for contemporary environmentalism. I shall claim, on the contrary, that debates about why we should value the environment are, in effect, sidelined by the use of methods of valuation (the 'how' of valuing the environment) which cannot adequately represent certain reasons of a moral kind – anthropocentric as well as non-anthropocentric – for valuing the environment. Thus, in so far as both anthropocentric and non-anthropocentric environmentalism typically hold that we have certain types of moral obligations in relation to the environment (for example, to preserve it for future generations or simply to preserve it), they will properly share a concern about the articulation and representation of moral obligations towards the environment in the process of policy formation, whether or not they differ in their understanding of the nature of those obligations.

It might be thought that the debate is relatively insignificant, or even trivial, for another and quite different reason, namely that the commitment of the world's leading nations at Rio and Kyoto to sustainable development has effectively settled the 'why' question. The question as to why we should value the environment may still be debated as a theoretical one, so it might be said, and doubtless a variety of answers will continue to be given to it. But for all practical purposes, it could be claimed, the answer is established and widely agreed: the environment should be protected for the sake of sustainable development.

Let us put to one side any questions about how serious is the commitment to sustainable development. Even taking this commitment at face value does not, however, settle the debate about why we should value the environment since the broad objectives or goals of sustainability are not sufficiently clear for one to suppose that this commitment has done away with the need for any further argument or discussion. And to understand that this is so is to understand something of the appeal of the types of economic analysis which we shall presently criticise.

It is a by now a commonplace that the concept of sustainability can be understood and used in numerous ways.[31] Increasingly it is thought best to see the commitment to sustainable development as simply a commitment to set policy in the light of the three related concerns indicated by the original definition. 'Development which meets the needs of the present without compromising the ability of future generations to meet their own needs' is, that is to say, development pursued in consciousness of the claims of equity and of the environment and in consciousness of the complexity of the relationship between these three constraints or principles.

[31] See e.g., J. Pezzey, *Sustainable Development Concepts: An Economic Analysis*, World Bank Environment Paper No. 2 (Washington, 1992) and 'Sustainability: An Interdisciplinary Guide', *Environmental Values*, 1 (1992), 321–62.

The complexity of the relationships between development, the pursuit of equity and the good of the environment, could be represented in a diagram which had each of these objectives standing as points of a triangle. The sides of the triangle could be represented by lines with arrowheads at either end. Each line would then signify the relationship of serving and threatening, and, pointing in both directions, gives us six (or, if we prefer, twelve) claims about the connections between development, the pursuit of equity and the good of the environment. These are as follows:

(i)   The pursuit of development both serves and threatens the protection of the environment. The sense in which development threatens the environment hardly needs explanation, since countless examples come to mind. The way in which development may serve the protection of the environment is, however, less obvious perhaps. There are, none the less, a number of connections to be made, of which the most important in this context is that since poverty is itself sometimes a cause (as well as an effect) of environmental degradation (in particular through the use of resources to meet short-term rather than long-term needs) then development could quite definitely serve environmental protection by enabling that judicious use of resources against which dire necessity militates.

(ii) Moving round the triangle to 'protection of the environment' we may now reverse the previous claim and note that the protection of the environment may both serve and threaten development. Again the sense in which the protection of the environment may conflict with aspects of development by constraining it is obvious enough, and it is the other relationship which deserves comment. The thought here, however, is not itself difficult or obscure: it is that development, even over the space of one generation, presupposes and relies upon, at the very least, a sure supply of such basic resources as clean air, water or soil, and indeed of other renewable and non-renewable resources. Thus the protection of the environment is not invariably inimical to the pursuit of development, but is presupposed by development if it is not, even in the short term, to risk the destruction of the basis on which it stands.

(iii) Staying at the 'protection of the environment' corner, the next contention is that the protection of the environment both serves and threatens the pursuit of equity. Such protection can plainly be seen to serve the pursuit of equity once we allow for our reponsibilities to future generations; that is, the protection of the environment and of its renewable and non-renewable resources, is essential if we are not to compromise 'the ability of future generations to meet their own needs'. But if the protection of the environment serves to prevent that 'asset stripping', so to speak, which expresses an inequitable attitude to future generations, that same protection may threaten the pursuit of equity in relation to the existing generation. The point here is that the burdens of protecting the environment may fall disproportionately on some, and perhaps disproportionately, in particular, on those who are already disadvantaged. Thus, to take an example, the protection of biodiversity may require action especially from countries whose richness in flora, fauna and ecosystems may be inversely proportionate (and not always coincidentally) to their GNP; and nearer to home, a strategy for the conservation of non-renewable energy resources through increases in duty may fall hardest on the poorest sections of society.

(iv) Moving to the corner labelled 'pursuit of equity', we now note that setting our sights on this goal may both serve and threaten the protection of the environment. The pursuit of equity may serve the good of the environment in two ways. In the first place equity towards future generations will, as we have seen, require the protection of the environment. And in the second place, again as we have seen, if environmental degradation is sometimes not only a cause of, but itself caused by, poverty, a juster distribution of the world's goods will, indirectly, serve the good of the environment. But the pursuit of equity equally threatens the protection of the environment for reasons already alluded to – the provision of the basic necessities of life for the poor of the

world would seem to mandate the development of agri-
cultural and industrial activities which are likely further to
endanger remaining environmental goods.

(v) If the pursuit of equity has this dual relationship with the
protection of the environment, so does it also with the goal
of development. That is to say, that the pursuit of equity
both serves and threatens development. It threatens it in
the sense that equity is concerned not with development as
such, but with development which is fair; thus equity may
require that we should prefer development which produces
a just distribution of goods over development which simply
maximises those goods and is heedless of their distribution.
(This point has relevance for equity both within and
between generations.) But the pursuit of equity also serves
the goal of development, though the sense in which it does
this is altogether less obvious than the sense in which it
conflicts with it. None the less, just as development which
pays no regard to the good of the environment endangers
the very conditions which it presupposes, so too development which is blind to the claims of equity may be
thought to risk its own existence for the very reason that
the secure and dependable social conditions which development requires are themselves to some extent imperilled
by grossly inequitable patterns of distribution and
consumption.

(vi) The last claim takes us back to development from where we
began, and consists in the contention that development
both serves and threatens the pursuit of equity. What has
already been said should make this relationship clear
enough: development may serve the just satisfaction of the
needs of the developing world, but may also, if carried on
without check, simply perpetuate or increase current inequalities.

To point to the complex web of relationships between development, equity and the environment which the concept of
sustainable development indicates without determining, only
serves, however, to bring to attention the appeal of the practices
of valuation to which we shall, in due course, none the less take

exception. To say that we have duties towards animals, plants, landscapes and ecosystems, or towards the environment in general, seems to make especially urgent an understanding of how these claims can be related to, or ranked against, other claims and considerations which properly figure in the shaping of public policy.

On the face of it, economic analysis, and cost–benefit analysis in particular, might seem an ideal way out of the difficulty we have identified. Public policy must be set in the light of a variety of considerations and concerns, some of the most important of which are identified by the concept of sustainable development. How shall we decide the weight to be given to each of these concerns, and thus the overall policy recommendation? Cost–benefit analysis promises a means of bringing the diverse elements of the situation under a common measure and hence, by rendering them commensurable, a means of arriving at a determination of the best way forward. It is no wonder then, that there has been much official interest in the use of these techniques.[32]

A detailed account of the practice of cost–benefit analysis is not here to the point, since we are chiefly interest in its theoretical presuppositions, which it shares with economic appraisal in general, even where the latter is more informal. According to Robert Laslett, 'CBA attributes a social value to everything affected by a project. Some things are negatively affected (costs) and some are positively affected (benefits). CBA adds up the costs, and the benefits. It takes the resulting estimate of the costs away from the benefits. It gives a social decision rule: economics says a project who benefits exceed its costs is worth considering, while one whose benefits are less than its costs is not.'[33] Now there are a number of features of

[32] In the UK, for example, this is evidenced by such documents as the Department of the Environment's *Policy Appraisal and the Environment* (London, 1991) and the Treasury's *Appraisal and Evaluation in Central Government* (London, 1997), the so-called 'Green Book'.

[33] R. Laslett, 'The Assumptions of Cost Benefit Analysis' in *Environmental Valuation*, ed. K. G. Willis and J. T. Corkindale (Wallingford, 1995), 5. For a fuller account following the same lines, see R. Layard and S. Glaister, *Cost Benefit Analysis*, 2nd edn (Cambridge, 1994), 1 2. The documents from the UK government are based on the same approach. Thus the Treasury's *Appraisal and Evaluation in Central Government*

such an understanding of cost-benefit analysis as providing a 'social decision rule' which could be challenged, and would indeed be challenged by many economists – thus we find Arrow and others saying that 'Contrary to the views of some, benefit-cost analysis is neither necessary nor sufficient for designing sensible public policy.'[34] Our purpose, however, is not to examine all aspects of this rather ambitious account of the proper role of cost-benefit analysis, but to consider just one aspect of the difficulties with taking it seriously: that is, the inability of cost-benefit analysis to capture the moral values typically expressed in connection with the environment.

Cost–benefit analysis faces two major sets of problem. The first set of problems is essentially practical, and relates to the ability of cost–benefit analysis to gather the information it needs to compare and contrast different courses of action and outcomes. The second set of problems has to do with the principles of cost–benefit analysis and centres on the question as to whether such analysis represents, or rather misconstrues, environmental values. Plainly the second set of problems is the more important, but the first set needs at least to be mentioned.

The first problem for cost–benefit analysis – that of gathering the information it needs – itself has two apects. In the first place, the analysis will be beset by the uncertainties which affect any attempt to peer into the future (and in particular to peer into the future of systems as complex, sensitive and imperfectly understood as ecosystems and, for that matter, economies). Thus, to take an example, suppose we ask ourselves about the costs and benefits involved in limiting emissions of SO_2 to such and such a level. The determination of figures on both sides of the equation will be afflicted by a range of

asserts that 'If *all* costs and benefits could be valued, the preferred option would be the one with the highest "net present value" (NPV), defined as the difference between discounted benefits and discounted costs' (2.31). Again it asserts (at 4.64) that 'Central government expenditures should normally be appraised in terms of their net present value (NPV), or net present costs. The "decision" rule for a given project is . . . to maximise the NPV, or minimise the net present cost, subject to account being taken of those impacts which cannot be valued.'

[34] K. J. Arrow, et al., *Benefit–Cost Analysis in Environmental, Health, and Safety Regulation: A Statement of Principles* (Annapolis, 1996), 3.

uncertainties: about the precise effects of SO_2 emissions on humans, animals, plants and ecosystems, and hence about the specific consequences of reductions; about the various possibilities which may emerge for reducing the emissions as technology develops; about the exact implications for industry of bearing greater costs; and so on. Arrow et al. make this simple, but far-reaching point when they note that 'In many cases, benefit–cost analysis cannot be used to prove that the economic benefits of a decision will exceed or fall short of the costs. There is simply too much uncertainty in some of the estimates of costs and benefits to make such statements with a high degree of confidence'.[35]

The second practical difficulty, and an aspect of the question as to the ability of the analysis to gather the information it needs, is this: if cost–benefit analysis is to determine the best way forward, it must not only face such uncertainties, but also be able to render alternative outcomes commensurable by assigning to them readily comparable values. That is, the analysis requires not only that we predict a range of outcomes, but that to each of them we attach specific and common values. Thus it is not enough to know that, say, the reduction in SO_2 emissions will, to whatever degree, aid the preservation of historic buildings, give certain plants a better chance of flourishing, threaten the viability of certain industries, improve human health in a number of respects, and so on; if the results of the sums in the cost–benefit analysis are to determine or at least suggest the right course of action, values would need to be assigned to each of these consequences or possible consequences so that a direct comparison could be made.

There is, of course, no existing common measure for many of the goods and harms which are in question, and in particular when it comes to environmental matters – thus if at least the main costs and benefits associated with planting a ten acre field with cabbages are ascertainable and can be expressed in monetary terms, where those ten acres are not just a normal field presently in cultivation, but a site of special scientific interest,

[35] Arrow et al., *Benefit-Cost Analysis*, 5.

the measuring on a common scale of the costs and benefits involved in taking the field into cultivation becomes altogether more problematic. To get round the fact that many of the important 'costs' at stake when humans affect the environment (such as the cost of destroying a site of special scientific interest) lack the market values which render many goods readily commensurable, various devices relying on so-called revealed preferences or contingent valuation have been devised, the purpose of which is to provide the proxy 'market values' which are needed for the cost–benefit analysis to proceed. With these notional market values to hand, the now achieved commensurability permits a determination of the net benefit (or, as it may be, net cost) of the project under consideration.

Even those who do not question the principles of cost–benefit analysis may doubt the satisfactoriness of this particular move – the level of such caution would depend on a judgment as to whether the various methods of determining revealed preferences or a contingent valuation really do capture the valuation which people make of the goods or benefits in question. At this level, debate may centre on such issues as the proper design of questionnaires, the amount of information which is needed to elicit real preferences, and so on. Depending on how the debate goes, the participants will express different degrees of confidence in the figures which emerge, in some cases counselling a considerable caution in placing reliance on them. No matter this point, however, this is essentially a debate about the techniques of cost–benefit analysis and their refinement. Thus, those who admit only the existence of these difficulties, while acknowledging that uncertainties about environmental effects and their valuation give the numbers a certain 'softness', will none the less think that this is, in principle, the right way to approach the resolution of environmental questions and will think it highly desirable that continuing attention be given to different and better means of generating proxy market values to express environmental concerns.

When, however, Beckerman and Pasek conclude that 'an attempt to represent people's valuations of the environment in the same terms as their valuations of ordinary market goods would be a simple category mistake',[36] we have moved from problems with the practice of cost–benefit analysis to its very principles. This conclusion, which is by no means original to them, rests on the contention that certain moral obligations or values have a character and logic which is different in kind from the character and logic of preferences.[37] Cost–benefit analysis, in aggregating all costs and benefits, overlooks this distinction and thereby treats such values as if they were simply preferences. Hence it does not serve as an adequate means of recognising such environmental concerns, but only of systematically misrepresenting them.

One way to approach the issues at stake in this discussion is to consider the variety of ways in which one might explain or deal with a phenomenon associated with the different methods of contingent valuation, either those surveys aimed at establishing willingness to accept or those seeking to determine willingness to pay. This, it should be stressed, is *not* simply to make a point about the unsatisfactoriness of contingent valuation and its attempts to assign monetary values to different environmental outcomes or states of affairs. It is, in fact, to make a point about cost–benefit analysis in general and in principle, since the critique of contingent valuation which follows is a critique of the consequentialist presuppositions which are merely rather starkly revealed in contingent valuation, but are common to economic appraisal as it is usually conceived.

Asked to name a figure they would accept in return for allowing certain changes in the environment, some respondents say that they would be unwilling to accept anything or specify an infinite sum. Others, when asked to express their willingness to pay for a certain environmental good, either name an infinite amount or decline altogether to do so, registering discontent with this line of questioning. Now the well-documented exist-

[36] W. Beckerman and J. Pasek, 'Plural Values and Environmental Valuation', *Environmental Values*, 6 (1997), 69.
[37] Mark Sagoff has, in particular, been influential in explicating the distinction between values and preferences; it is his notion of a confusion between the two as involving a category mistake which is taken up by Beckerman and Pasek and by many others: see, *The Economy of the Earth* (Cambridge, 1988), esp. 92–5.

ence of such respondents naturally poses a problem for these surveys, since the inclusion of an infinite amount on one side of the equation settles the matter rather decisively; hence answers of this kind are often just excluded, sometimes with observations as to the irrationality, unreasonableness, fanaticism or emotionalism of those who give them.

Whilst the discounting of these answers is vital for those who wish to defend the usefulness of these surveys, it is plainly a highly problematic manouevre as it stands. After all, it is simply question-begging to suppose that the refusal to answer the questions set by the surveys in the terms they allow, reveals a wilful or obstinate irrationality.[38] Such a refusal may just as well express a sense that the questions themselves are in some way badly posed or straightforwardly objectionable – as would a refusal to answer the questioner who insists on a simple 'yes' or 'no' in reply to the question 'are you still beating your wife?'

But in what way are the questions of a cost–benefit analysis badly posed? What might it be that those who decline to accept the terms of these surveys are getting at? In answering this question we see that the problem is not a problem specifically with contingent valuation, but with the most basic assumption of cost–benefit analysis and economic appraisal in general, namely that values can somehow be treated or represented in the same terms and on the same metric as one can represent preferences.

Let us take a question which asks about my willingness to accept the destruction of an ancient woodland. Those who decline to name a figure, or who want an infinite sum, are surely getting at the point that the woodland cannot be valued in the way the question presupposes. They react, in other words, as many people would if they were asked how much they would be prepared to take for betraying their country or their friends. To say that there is no such sum, or that it would have

---

[38] Of similar moves in relation to other 'difficult' responses to contingent valuation, A. Holland comments: 'It is notable that what all these hypotheses have in common is that they impugn the wits and/or self-knowledge of those involved while leaving the credentials of the methodology intact.' See, A. Holland, 'The Assumptions of Cost–Benefit Analysis: A Philosopher's View', in *Environmental Valuation*, ed. Willis and Corkindale, 26.

to be infinite, is to say that the protection of the woodland or loyalty to my country and friends are not just preferences I happen to have, but rather that the protection or loyalty express, and are required by, certain values; and whilst things I just happen to prefer I may sell or give up as I see fit (as I might dispose of an interest in a piece of property), things which are valued cannot be thought of, or dealt with, in quite that way. We might even say of the woodland that it is invaluable – not that it is without value, but that it is beyond value in any straightforward sense.[39]

What is at fault, then, is the basic assumption of cost–benefit analysis that moral considerations can be treated as, and thereby 'weighed' against, other benefits. Suppose we are considering whether to increase fishing or logging in or around the Amazon basin and someone objects that such a practice would be unjust or inequitable because it would infringe the rights of native tribes. It is of the essence of a proper understanding of the claims of equity that the rights of the natives are not 'weighed' against the prospects of catches of fish or hauls of timber, whether or not such weighing makes use of monetarisation. Certainly I can weigh my preference for developing my fishing business against my preference for developing my logging business, but once I attempt to factor into the weighing and balancing 'equitable treatment of the natives of the Amazon basin' I have misunderstood and misconstrued the character and the logic of the claims of equity. The misunderstanding would be plain enough in such a case if the prospective developer replied to the complaint that his or her proposals treated the native tribes inequitably by saying that the complainants did not realise quite how big the catches of fish and hauls of timber would be!

It should be made clear again that the point we are making here – namely that, in effect, cost-benefit analysis overlooks the important distinction between preferences and values, treating

[39] See John Foster's remarks on the complexity of the language of value in his introduction to *Valuing Nature?*, ed. Foster (London, 1997), 2–3. This an especially useful collection of essays, providing a more sustained and adequate discussion of practices of environmental valuation than has been possible here.

all our commitments as simple preferences, albeit with varying degrees of strength – is a point about cost–benefit in general, and not only about contingent valuation in particular. Contingent valuation's discomfort with certain sorts of responses to its enquiries is simply an instance of the general inability of cost-benefit analysis to acknowledge this distinction. Nor is this a matter of the use of words: nothing turns on whether we use the two words 'preferences' and 'values', or choose some others. What matters is that the distinction between two types of consideration, indicated by these two words or by whatever terms we care to use, be marked and respected; the charge against cost–benefit analysis is just that it fails to allow for the distinct character of a commitment which is expressive of a value as against one expressive of a preference. Hence the commensurability it reckons to achieve is in fact a systematic misrepresentation of characteristic patterns of thought about the environment (and of other matters which raise questions of value), excluding from consideration ways of valuing the environment which are not allowed for and cannot be captured by its own methods and presuppositions.

Once we have marked and understood the distinction between values and preferences, those who refuse to participate in, or co-operate with, contingent valuation surveys or are suspicious of cost–benefit analysis in general, cannot be regarded as guilty of confusion or irrationality; unwillingness to go along with such surveys is, rather, a sign of a sense that cost–benefit analysis, while it seems to promise to provide an overarching framework for our thinking about environmental questions, excludes from consideration vital aspects of the thinking it pretends to capture. It cannot capture vital aspects of that thinking just because we value environmental goods morally (no matter whether we reckon we have duties to or concerning the environment); hence these commitments do not and cannot enter our thinking simply as so many preferences which must compete with, and take their place alongside, other preferences. This is not to say that these commitments cannot be argued with in rational discussion and debate; but just because these 'preferences' are really values they cannot be treated in the way we handle preferences, and in particular those socially inconvenient choices which typically arise from no such deep commitment.

If then, we accept Beckerman and Pasek's conclusion that 'An attempt to represent people's valuations of the environment in the same terms as their valuations of ordinary market goods would be a simple category mistake' and hence the critique of the notion that cost–benefit analysis can provide the right means for adjudicating public policy in this area, the problems which this method of economic analysis promised to solve remain no less acute. As Beckerman and Pasek point out, the critics of cost–benefit analysis and of contingent valuation have to recognise that it is still necessary to make choices in the public sphere between different and competing policies and options not least, but not only, because of constraints on resources. How then, are these decisions to be made? If cost–benefit analysis does not provide an adequate method of settling these questions, what method or process should be preferred?

This question is especially pressing since it cannot be taken for granted that any recognition of the problems of cost–benefit analysis will thereby result in more adequate regard for the ethical concerns of environmentalists; after all, whatever is wrong with economic evaluation of environmental goods in theory, in practice it at least ensures that something of the valuation which is placed upon them figures in the sums that are done. It is clear from the argument thus far that, since the problems with cost–benefit analysis are problems of principle and not of practice, it is vain to suppose that further efforts aimed at refinements in the methodology of environmental valuation will solve the difficulties. If the criticisms here rehearsed are valid, then the very elements of the situation which render decision-making in relation to the environment so vexed – namely the claimed existence of moral obligations which such decision-making should respect – by their nature defy representation in these terms. None the less, there may seem to be a pragmatic case for claiming that this misrepresentation should be tolerated. Even if economic valuation is not fully adequate, that valuation may well be enough to ensure, for example, the protection of a particular piece of countryside against a proposed development.

The real problem with this way of going on is that even where it is undertaken pragmatically, it threatens to undermine or corrupt the patterns of thought which are misrepresented. That is to say, if for short term advantage in winning their case environmentalists do not protest at the inadequacies of a cost-benefit analysis or economic appraisal which, as it happens, comes up with the result they favour, they risk in the long term the virtual unintelligibility of the valuations of the environment which they hold to be the right ones and which will not always happen to coincide with economic valuations. (We are making a point parallel to the one we were making about the dangers of non-anthropocentrism trading off anthropocentrism.)

A way of registering the problems with cost–benefit analysis which avoids this difficulty might seem to be to require of any such analysis that it leaves out of its formal and quantified assessment all those elements of the situation which cannot adequately be captured by its methods. Thus it would not seek to find a monetary value for, let us say, the loss of avocets which may result from the implementation of a scheme to drain marshes in Norfolk, but would simply include this and like considerations at the bottom of the balance sheet which is then to be passed to whomsoever must take the decision. (Note, by the way, that these considerations are highly unlikely to be pointing all in the same direction – in the case we have imagined the draining of the marshes might lead to higher levels of rural employment and in so doing to the viability of previously threatened hamlets and villages, and the loss of these, no less than the loss of avocets, surely defies satisfactory monetary valuation.) The decision maker is then presented with an analysis which neither misconstrues these moral elements, as they would be misrepresented if they were represented through contingent valuation or revealed preferences, nor conceals the fact which a supposedly more complete economic analysis might – that decisions in relation to the environment can never be based on science and economics alone, whatever role these disciplines must play, but always, as questions about values, require the exercise of practical judgment and decision.

Such a way of presenting cost–benefit analysis, however, represents an insufficiently radical response to the problem which has been identified. In the first place, the proposal for 'business nearly as usual' seems to overlook the fact that once it is acknowledged that the balance sheet must be presented with all sorts of unquantified and incommensurable extras, especially when they may be on both sides of the equation, the balance sheet loses a good deal of interest or significance. Suppose I have to choose between two jobs with essentially similar patterns of responsibility and intrinsic interest, but with very different patterns of financial reward. One pays more now, but the other promises better rewards in mid-career. One offers an excellent pension, the other will require me to make my own arrangements. One provides a company car whilst the the other allows loans on generous terms for such a purchase. A comparison of the two in economic terms, adding, subtracting and discounting as necessary, will be of considerable interest to me in this situation, but only until I add in the further consideration that the one job will require me to move house and so disrupt my children's schooling, while taking the other, though not requiring a move, will entail that I continue to live at some distance from aged relatives who, as a matter of fact, live close to where I would live if I pursued the other option. It is difficult to envisage in this situation that the 'balance sheet' would hold my attention more than momentarily – the hard decision cannot be conjured out of the numbers, but only out of careful reflection and deliberation on the wider issues.

There is a second respect, however, in which the presentation of cost–benefit analysis in a properly modest and limited form is insufficient to meet the difficulties of the situation. If it is the case that decisions in relation to the environment are typically of such a kind as to require the resolution of difficult questions of value, then the social acceptability of those decisions will in turn depend upon their being taken in such a way as to foster consensus. Now it is clear that cost–benefit analysis, in its ambitious form, is in this respect the problem and certainly not the solution – even if, contrary to what we have argued, it properly measures and represents environmental 'preferences', it leaves those preferences intact, so to say, and just as it discounts or disguises the need for practical judgment neither does it serve to facilitate agreement in such judgment. But cost–benefit analysis in its more modest form, whilst it admits that there is a surplus element in these matters, which cannot be settled by economic analysis alone, does nothing to consider how agreement in judgment might be secured. That is to say, it allows – rightly – that cost–benefit analysis cannot function as an arbiter of social choices, but has no account as to how that arbitration should occur. Thus something more is needed than business nearly as as usual, whatever place economic analysis of certain kinds may have in certain kinds of cases.

Nothing said here has been intended to deny that costs matter. It has simply been denied that economic analysis can properly handle how they matter alongside and against other things that matter. But what can? The answer in broad terms is practical reason, exercised in judgment and dependent upon deliberation.[40]

According to Onora O'Neill's account, 'Judgement guides the move from indeterminate principles towards one rather than another particular policy or action . . . by heeding the requirements and recommendations of a *plurality* of practical principles. Judging is not a mysterious ability to leap from principle to particular, but a process of deliberating.' Deliberation she continues:

is in some ways like solving a design problem. In designing a stove, for example, numerous distinct constraints must be met. The stove must be made of available materials; the heat it yields must be accurately controllable; its energy consumption and waste must be held down; safety standards must be met; the stove must be affordable and attractive to those who are envisaged as purchasers. These design criteria constitute a set of constraints and standards none of which

---

[40] For suggestive thoughts in this direction see R. Grove-White and O. M. T. O'Donovan, 'An Alternative Approach' in *Values, Conflict and the Environment*, ed. R. Attfield and K. Dell (Oxford, 1989), 73–82. This subtle and important essay is a dissenting comment on a flat-footed attempt to produce a 'rational' approach to the environment.

can be met perfectly, but which also cannot always or perhaps generally be traded off against one another: the stove that does not heat fails even if it is very, very safe.[11]

Thus 'judgement is indeed, as Kant said, a "peculiar talent". It is a talent because it follows no algorithm: there are no complete rules for the application of rules. It is not a matter of deducing comprehensive instructions for action from relatively indeterminate principles. Rather, it is a question of seeking to find ways of meeting the multiple constraints and recommendations of a plurality of principles.'[12]

Economics tries to replace the task of practical reasoning and deliberation with a technique. It is a technique, we have argued, which distorts the values which it claims to represent and measure, and compounds the error by trying to creep up, so to speak, on the values which are at stake. It thus not only misrepresents the values that are held, but fails to understand that it is the very process of reasoning and deliberation which it seeks to dispense with which may cause these values to emerge fully and coherently into view, to be tested and challenged by competing and opposed values, and thus to contribute to the framing of a policy which has general support.

VI CONCLUSION

This chapter has not answered the two questions it has been concerned with, namely why and how to value the environment. It has rather said that one common way of posing the first question has been somewhat unhelpful, and that one common way of answering the second prevents account being taken of some likely answers to the first.

If the concept of sustainability has value it is not because it provides a solution to the difficulties of policy-making in this area. It fails to provide an answer not because it is vague in some reprehensible way, but rather because it is adequate, we might say; not adequate if by that we mean an algorithm which

[11] O. O'Neill, 'Principles, Judgments and Institutions' in *Laws, Values and Social Practices*, ed. J. Tasioulas (Aldershot, 1997), 69.
[12] O'Neill, 'Principles, Judgments and Institutions', 71.

will dispense with the need for the exercise of judgment in formulating a policy, but rather as a reminder of the chief concerns to which any policy must relate. The concept of sustainable development can be seen as providing an account of the chief amongst the 'multiple constraints' and 'plurality of principles' in the light of which we typically seek to determine environmental policy. The constraints represent the framework of values which define, to some extent, the limits of our actions and projects and policies – these actions and policies must seek to respect these constraints. Thus these constraints establish, in effect, a presumption in favour of certain types of action and policy, so that if we take the view that the Antarctic should not be exploited for its minerals or for any other purpose, but should remain as close to being an untouched wilderness as it presently is, we do not do so on the basis that this represents the best balance of benefits against costs – the destruction of the Antarctic, and perhaps of other irrecoverable and unique landscapes, ecosystem or species is to all intents and purposes practically unthinkable. Such destruction does not enter into our thinking as one of a range of possibilities open to us in pursuing other goals and projects. This does not necessarily mean that the loss of these goods is something which we would, in actual fact, never tolerate. If a unique and ecologically rich wetland area needs to be drained to prevent intolerable levels of malaria in a neighbouring settlement, it might be that we would accept the loss of such a wetland. This would not, however, involve any simple repudiation of the presumption in favour of the wetland, but rather a recognition of its defeasibility in certain extreme situations of tragic conflict. The fact that the wetland would, on balance, make the best site for an airport would not, in contrast, defeat the presumption in its favour.

The charge of vagueness is often, in actual fact, just a complaint that the concept of sustainable development cannot function as a simple rule for decision making. And, of course, those who promote the claims of cost–benefit analysis as providing a rule for decision-making will allege the advantages of such analysis in enabling us to reach a clear and unambiguous policy recommendation.[43] But, given the argument of the previous sections, this 'advantage' is only achieved by systematically misrepresenting or discounting essential elements of fully informed and responsible decision-making. What is needed, however, is not that we should make our decisions easy by ignoring factors relevant to their determination, but rather that we should seek to ensure that the processes by which the decisions are taken are sensitive to all the criteria which properly deserve consideration. The case for making 'sustainable development' the overarching concept in thinking about the setting of environmental standards is that it helps us to do precisely that: it points to the need for the setting of such standards to take account, in particular, of the three goods of development, equity, and environmental protection, without, by the way, excluding any others. It does not tell us precisely how we are to take account of those goods or how we should relate them one to another, but that, it might be argued, belongs not to conceptual analysis but to political thought, deliberation, judgment and practice, whereby a society identifies the objectives which technocratic and expert thinking cannot themselves determine.

[43] Those who thus complain are likely to be advocates of what is known as 'weak sustainability', which is sometimes represented as encapsulating a constant natural capital rule   it maintains, in effect, that the overall stock of capital (widely construed and including both man-made and natural capital) should remain constant over time. Weak sustainability, then, constrains development on the basis of an equity rule, but, since it treats man-made and natural capital as freely substitutable for each other, denies any protection as such to the environment. It is, in effect, that is to say, a form of cost benefit analysis subject to one prior constraint.

CHAPTER 6

On not begging the questions about biotechnology

I

The Report of the Committee to Consider the Ethical Implications of Emerging Technologies in the Breeding of Farm Animals (hereafter the *Banner Report*), seeks to address the questions raised by the application to animals of the broad range of techniques of biotechnology.[1]

Such a sentence, for all its seeming innocence as a factual description of the *Report*, will doubtless trouble philosophically minded readers. Those who have been brought up *After Virtue*,[2] so to speak, can hardly fail to be aware that amidst the moral fragments of western thought no questions about biotechnology are straightforwardly 'the' questions about biotechnology. MacIntyre's sequel to *After Virtue* asks *Whose Justice? Which Rationality?*, and here we might echo the point by asking 'whose questions?'[3] The heirs of Aristotle, Thomas Aquinas and Descartes will, for example, with their different views of animals, ask different sets of questions of the new technology.

The *Banner Report* can be distinguished from certain related reports, so I shall argue, in that it shows itself to be aware of what we might term the embeddedness of questions in metaphysical and moral theories. Naturally, it takes a view as to what

---

[1] *Report of the Committee to Consider the Ethical Implications of Emerging Technologies in the Breeding of Farm Animals* (London, 1995).
[2] A. MacIntyre, *After Virtue: A Study in Moral Theory*, 2nd edn (London, 1985).
[3] A. MacIntyre, *Whose Justice? Which Rationality?* (London, 1988).

questions are raised by biotechnology as regards, for example, the status and protection of animals, but it does so quite consciously and with a degree of argument appropriate if not for philosophers, then at least for Government Ministers to whom the *Report* is addressed. To be specific, the *Report* challenges the tendency to assess the new technologies solely in terms of questions of risk and benefit, and contends that this tendency uncritically privileges a particular philosophical position. Instead, it proposes a policy and system of moral evaluation which allows and requires questions of a different sort. This system of moral evaluation, so I shall conclude, calls into doubt the current pattern of regulation of the use of animals, and provides a basis for its examination and reform.

In this chapter I shall focus on genetic manipulation as the technology which has been at the centre of controversy. In the first place, I shall illustrate the rather unselfconscious tendency in certain recent reports dealing with genetic engineering to presuppose philosophical theories which suppress particular questions. The reports I shall mention are not concerned, or not concerned exclusively, with genetic modification of animals, but this does not matter for my purpose, which is to demonstrate how a certain narrowing of debate in bioethics occurs as a result of often undeclared, and certainly undefended, philosophical presuppositions. I shall then set out the principles which the *Banner Report* enunciates and on which it is based. I shall contend that these principles provide a more satisfactory framework for the regulation of the new technology than the framework used in these other reports, and shall consider the significance of these principles, in the context of current UK legislation, for the practice of genetic engineering in relation to animals. I shall then go on to indicate briefly something of the broader question which theology should put to biotechnology, but which would be excluded by the way of approaching these matters which sees them as requiring a balancing of benefits and burdens.

II

The knowledge which is yielded by the recent advances in genetics renders possible essentially three projects of indirect or direct genetic engineering.

(i)   In the first place, it allows for the more effective selection of progeny according to genotype. This can be thought of as *indirect* genetic engineering, since it does not involve the direct alteration of a gene but does effect the shaping of genetic inheritance. The possibility of effective selection may, then, depend merely on a breeding programme which makes use of knowledge of the genetic character of the 'parents', where this knowledge allows choices to be made for and against the occurrence of certain genotypes; with the growing understanding of the links between particular genes and traits, this knowledge will yield an increasingly powerful means of predicting and determining the characteristics of progeny in plant and animal breeding.

(ii) In the second place, selection for specific genotypes may occur after, rather than before, breeding has taken place. Again, this does not involve direct genetic engineering, but rather the use of knowledge of the genotype of progeny to allow choices to be made for or against particular types through cloning, through the implantation only of certain embryos where there has been *in vitro* fertilisation, or through the abortion of unwanted offspring after *in utero* testing.

(iii) In the third place, direct genetic engineering (i.e., that which involves altering genes as opposed merely to selecting them on the basis of knowledge of actual or likely genotype) may occur either through manipulation of somatic cells with a view to changing the characteristic expression of an organism's genes or, more radically, through the manipulation of the germ line itself.

If the science which has put into our hands these various possibilities is dazzling in its dogged rigour and sophistication, the same cannot be said of much of the moral reflection which has followed the scientific developments, declaring the newly feasible advancing of certain ends, or the means by which they are pursued, to be either acceptable or unacceptable. The moral reflection found, for example, in three recent reports is, for the most part unsystematic and superficial, to such an extent that one is forced to say of these reports not simply that the answers they give are problematic, but that their very framing of the questions to be treated is itself questionable. Specifically – and they have this in common – they demonstrate a tendency to suppose that an ethical analysis of the new technology is exhausted by a prudential consideration of its potential risks and benefits, when this supposition in fact serves to conceal from view many ethical concerns. (One suspects, by the way, that this view of the matter would be more widely and vigorously expressed – or at least, more sympathetically entertained – were it not for the fact that the consensus which seems to emerge from the supposed moral discussion of these issues in these three reports is not one to which the pragmatically minded research scientist or medical practitioner is likely to object. As a matter of fact, this consensus proposes what might well be regarded, from this point of view, as a satisfactory division of the spoils – that is to say, it makes some concessions to those who would restrain or limit the practice of genetic engineering, but not such concessions as might seriously hamper either the advance or application of research. This consensus could be broadly characterised as countenancing widespread genetic screening and abortions within certain limits, somatic cell therapy subject to the usual principles governing experimental procedures, and, for non-human organisms, genetic manipulation even of the germ-line where any harms associated with their production or release of such organisms can be regarded as warranted by the expected gains. There are things which, at least for the present, this consensus does not countenance – most obviously the manipulation of the germ line in humans. But, since the technicalities of germ-line manipulation are considerable, the constraint can hardly be thought unduly onerous, at least for the time being.)

The *Report of the Committee on the Ethics of Gene Therapy* (hereafter the *Clothier Report*) is remarkable for its very limited engagement with the questions raised by the practice of genetic manipulation in humans.[4] This limitation is twofold, having to do with both the scope and the depth of the discussion.

It might be thought that a perfectly satisfactory explanation of the scope of the *Clothier Report* can be given by noting its terms of reference. These were:

> To draw up ethical guidelines for the medical profession on treatment of genetic disorders in adults and children by genetic modification of human body cells; to invite and consider proposals from doctors wishing to use such treatment on individual patients; and to provide advice to United Kingdom Health Ministers on scientific and medical developments which bear on the safety and efficacy of human gene modification.[5]

Since the Committee was asked for advice on the 'treatment of genetic disorders . . . by genetic modification of body cells', the fact that the *Report* has next to nothing to say regarding either the use of genetic manipulation with a view to enhancement of certain traits or germ-line therapy, is perhaps unsurprising. But, as the *Report* itself makes clear,[6] the Committee did not judge itself to be strictly bound by these terms of reference, but free, in fact, to go beyond them. However, having declared itself free to consider either of these topics, the Committee discusses neither, and limits its discussion to somatic cell therapy, saying that, given the novelty of the techniques involved, this therapy should be regarded as a form of research involving human subjects, and as such properly bound by the regulations which govern experimentation. On the other matters, it merely declares, first, that 'In the current state of knowledge it would not be acceptable to use gene modification to attempt to change human traits not associated with disease', and second, in relation to germ-line manipulation, that 'there is at present insufficient knowledge to evaluate the risks to future generations'.[7]

As well as being limited in scope, the *Report* is limited in the depth and seriousness of its discussion. Central to its recommendations is that, whereas somatic-cell therapy to alleviate a

[4] *Report of the Committee on the Ethics of Gene Therapy* (London, 1992).
[5] *The Clothier Report*, 1.3.   [6] *The Clothier Report*, 1.7.
[7] *The Clothier Report*, 4.22 and 5.1.

disease should be permitted on the same basis as other medical research, such research should not be allowed into the enhancement of human traits. But the distinction between the two is not without difficulties. In the first place, the distinction is just not that easy to make since the concept of disease, which is crucial to the distinction, needs considerable analysis. Without this analysis, one is left in doubt as to what exactly is permitted and what is not. Suppose, however, that a distinction between enhancement and treatment is satisfactorily drawn. There is, in the second place, a problem with the moral weight it is supposed to bear. Why should research into the enhancement of human traits be forbidden, notwithstanding that it could be subject to the very same conditions as regards consent, feasibility, and so on, which govern research into the alleviation of disease? At one point in the *Report* it is declared, as we have seen, that the attempt to modify human traits by genetic manipulation would not be acceptable 'in the current state of knowledge'. This suggests, although it does not explain, a pragmatic and rather limited objection having to do with the risks which might be involved in such a project, and seems to have nothing to do with 'the profound ethical issues that would arise were the aim of gene modification ever to be directed to the enhancement of normal human traits', to which issues the Committee declares itself to be 'alert'.[8] What are 'these profound ethical issues' and would they arise where the normal human trait to be enhanced was, let us say, immunity to viral infection? The *Report* has nothing to say in answer to such manifestly pertinent questions.

If we ignore for the moment the seemingly stray reference to 'profound ethical issues', the *Clothier Report* illustrates very well the tendency to which I have referred, to consider the new technology almost solely in terms of categories of prudence, benefit and risk. It is prudent that somatic cell therapy, given the risks which may be involved in any novel treatment, should be governed by the protocols which relate to experimentation. Somatic cell enhancement or manipulation of the germ-line,

---

[8]   *The Clothier Report*, 2.16.

for whatever end, are, however, held not to be prudent 'in the current state of knowledge'. The dominance of the vocabulary of prudence and risk is, however, even more evident in two other reports I shall mention. And here the consequences of that dominance becomes absolutely clear – the utter exclusion of the possibility of certain moral questions from a debate which has been framed (and one uses the word in its pejorative sense) in this way.

According to the report from a working party set up by the BMA, *Our Genetic Future: The Science and Ethics of Genetic Engineering*, 'biotechnology and genetic modification are in themselves morally neutral. It is the uses to which they are put which create dilemmas. The challenge which faces us is to try to achieve an optimal future: one which maximizes the benefits of genetic modification and minimizes the harms.'[9] This conception of the 'challenge which faces us' in virtue of our ever-expanding understanding of genetics is essentially the same as that which is found in a book written by J. R. S. Fincham and J. R. Ravetz in collaboration with a working party of the Council for Science and Society, entitled *Genetically Engineered Organisms: Benefits and Risks*.[10] They, too, think the challenge, as the title indicates, is that of maximising benefits and minimising risks. Given this conception, it is hardly surprising that, like the BMA working party, Fincham and Ravetz find the chief difficulty for the application of genetic understanding to lie in our lack of a complete knowledge of the consequences of our interventions and manipulations. It follows then, that in principle the dilemmas in this field, to which the BMA report refers, are really the familiar difficulties which arise when we must act with imperfect empirical information. As the BMA report puts it:

Our predicament would be a great deal simpler if we could simply ask, in respect of any proposed development, questions such as 'Is it safe?', 'Will it enable us to find cures for genetic diseases?', and 'How much will it cost?', and receive unequivocal answers. Unfortunately

---

[9] The British Medical Association, *Our Genetic Future: The Science and Ethics of Genetic Technology* (Oxford, 1992), 4.
[10] J. R. S. Fincham and J. R. Ravetz, *Genetically Engineered Organisms: Benefits and Risks* (Milton Keynes, 1991).

life is not so straightforward. The totality of scientific knowledge which we should like to have when making judgements about the future is rarely available. Consequently, the judgements which need to be made, and the decisions which need to be taken, are complex, contestable, and often incomplete. Until we have answers to these questions it is not possible to form settled views about the acceptability of some developments.[11]

The characterisation of the 'challenge' which faces us in coping with the new biotechnology (as that of maximising the benefits and of minimising the harms) and of our 'predicament' (as that of doing so in a situation of imperfect knowledge), shared by these two reports, has an air of common-sense about it. None the less, we should reject it as begging important moral questions. Specifically it will be argued that the tendency of both reports to locate the contestability of decisions about the application of genetic knowledge in the empirical realm, and in particular in the realm of uncertain futures, betrays an albeit unconscious (or at least undeclared) commitment to a highly questionable moral framework.

Two things must, however, be said by way of clarification, for it is not being contended that the considerations which dominate these reports have no place in the discussion. First of all, there can be no doubt that the determination of the likely outcomes of alternative courses of action represents an element, and an important element, in many or most moral decisions. It follows, of course, that any uncertainty about these outcomes may be at the root of controversy and disagreement. Thus, to take an obvious example, a dispute as to whether capital punishment really serves as a deterrent, may underlie a difference of opinion as to whether or not it should be permitted. Similarly, a dispute as to whether a genetically engineered organism will or will not affect the ecology of the environment into which it is proposed to release it, may be the source of a disagreement between those who advocate its release and those who do not. But such disagreements would be essentially non-moral and trivial in comparison with the deep ethical disagreements which may occur in practical reasoning – a

[11] BMA, *Our Genetic Future*, 5.

disagreement here, perhaps, over whether the state has a right to take life, or whether the natural ecology of an area is as such deserving of protection from human interference or change.

In the second place, it may also be that a consideration of likely outcomes is the only issue at stake in certain decisions as to the use or application of biotechnology. It might be argued, for example, though it is likely to be contested, that the only issue which arises in relation to the production and release of a genetically modified plants is an issue of prudence. Now there may be disagreement over whether that production and release is indeed prudent – a disagreement which may in fact be complicated by a dispute as to what constitutes a risk, or a risk worth taking (these last two being quite plainly ethical, not empirical issues). But, in principle, the dispute might be no more than a straightforwardly empirical disagreement between those with a common prudential concern for genetic diversity and human safety.

But, if we allow for the sake of argument that sometimes a disagreement about genetic engineering will have this aspect alone, it can hardly be supposed that this circumstance will be characteristic of all the questions which the new genetics will cause to arise. Take, for example, the controversy which might be expected to surround the application of genetic knowledge, by whatever means, to broadly eugenic ends. According to the BMA report:

Using the science of genetic modification to produce a 'master race', or to select children with particular attributes, is unacceptable. Even if parents are entirely free to reproduce as they choose, considerable social and ethical problems could arise if we eventually reach the currently remote possibility of being able to choose not just the gender but also some of the physical, emotional, and intellectual attributes of our children. If it became commonplace, for example, for parents to choose a boy as their first child, then this might well make it even harder to diminish sexual discrimination in our society.[12]

The reasoning here is uncertain, but the opposition seems to focus on the practice's undesirable consequences. Similarly, Fincham and Ravetz are inclined to portray possible controver-

----

[12] BMA, *Our Genetic Future*, 209.

sies in these terms. Thus, having concluded that for those who
are do not object to antenatal diagnosis on the basis of 'religious
principles', the practice 'would seem to offer only benefit', they
take note of the fact that 'even some who are not absolutely
opposed to abortion may still be worried by the possibility that,
given too much information about the unborn child, some
people might resort to abortion for reasons unconnected with
predicted handicap', and instead having to do only with a
preference for male over female children. They comment that:

Most people would probably consider aborting a fetus or discarding
an embryo because of its gender far less defensible than doing so
because it was destined to suffer from a crippling handicap. Apart
from anything else, to give free rein to parental choice in this matter
might jeopardize the approximate numerical equality of the sexes,
which it is clearly desirable to maintain.[13]

In fairness, we should note the 'apart from anything else' by
which Fincham and Ravetz qualify the giving of this particular
reason for opposing abortion on the basis of sex, since it at least
leaves open the possibility that this 'anything else' would reveal
the authors to have greater insight than they here display. For,
in entertaining an objection to this practice based solely on a
prediction of future consequences, Fincham and Ravetz, along
with the BMA report in its consideration of selection in general,
betray the distinctly odd standpoint from which they approach
these matters. For suppose we were persuaded, *contra* the BMA,
that, as a matter of fact, sex-selection would cause the diminution of sexual discrimination. Or suppose, *contra* Fincham and
Ravetz, we took the view that numerical inequality between the
sexes was desirable – it would, after all, give a certain power to
the sex about whom the BMA is so anxious. Are we to suppose
further, that all but 'religious' objections to sex selection would
melt away in the light of the desirability of the envisaged
outcome and thus that any controversy about this practice must
reside in differences over the likely consequences of this intervention? Could it not be that someone might hold the selection
of children (by sex or any other characteristic) to be wrong in

[13] Fincham and Ravetz, *Genetically Engineered Organisms*, 117.

and of itself as a simple refusal of the fact that children are gifts and not acquisitions?

The inclination of these two reports to think of our predicament in making use of genetic knowledge as to do with the ensuring of good outcomes in circumstances of empirical uncertainty, is a way of thinking which seems to neglect or exclude the possibility of genuine and deep moral disagreements over and above the prudential consideration of risk; that is to say, the conceptualisation of the challenge presented by the new technology as being that of balancing benefits and harms, converts what were thought to be ethical, into essentially empirical, disputes. It thus rules out the very sort of disagreement one would anticipate in the matter, for example, of sex selection (regardless of the method of selection), and in relation to genetic engineering too – a disagreement which centres on the question as to whether these practice are objectionable not in virtue of the balance of consequences, but in virtue of particular effects or even simply as such. Is genetic engineering in relation to animals, for example, wrong as fundamentally disrespectful, or as causing them harms to which they ought not to be subject, no matter the benefit?

But from where does the way of thought and conceptualisation which dominates these reports come? If its only warrant were from common-sense, one might happily pass by with a warning against following such guides in these matters. But one suspects a certain indebtedness in these reports, albeit indirect, to consequentialism, which continues to exert an undue influence in the field of bioethics.

Consequentialism holds that actions are good or bad, right or wrong, solely in virtue of their consequences and more specifically that a good action is one which, in the given circumstances, will maximise overall benefits. Specifying or defining a benefit (and, of course, a harm, burden or cost) becomes all-important for such a moral theory, and spawns a variety of consequentialist approaches to the resolution of ethical questions. (One might note, then, how surprising it is that both the BMA Report and Fincham and Ravetz treat the notions of burden and benefit as if they did not require careful analysis but are intuitively plain and in order.) But, no matter the variety, consequentialist theories have this in common, namely that they think of all moral problems as in reality problems about the maximisation of a good. This way of thought thus transforms moral dilemmas into problems of a more familiar sort, for the difficulties involved in moral decisions become the difficulties of calculation which are involved in making prudent choices of all sorts, moral or not: shall I buy a dishwasher or a freezer? Would it be better to go to York by train or car? This transformation is not, however, without its own problems, for it seems to overlook the distinctive quality and character of genuine moral dilemmas. When we are confronted by such dilemmas, we have a sense that the difficulty is not simply one of calculating the probabilities of certain outcomes and comparing their desirability. It is rather the difficulty which occurs, for example, when a particular and worthy end can be secured only by a seemingly prohibited means, or when one recognises the claim made by two (or more) obligations where the fulfilment of one necessarily entails reneging on the other or others.

Of course, consequentialism contests the existence of such dilemmas – a good action just is that action which maximises beneficial consequences, so that a sense of difficulty which does not derive from empirical uncertainty can stem only from confusion, supposing, that is, that the notion of benefit is not itself contested. But consequentialism is itself a controversial moral theory, and one ought not to accept, without a good deal of argument, its understanding of moral decisions. Certainly, one ought not to allow either the BMA Report or Fincham and Ravetz to foist upon us the seemingly innocent picture of our challenging predicament as that of balancing benefits and burdens in a state of imperfect knowledge, without an awareness of the underlying commitments from which it stems. As it is, we can say of these reports, before we even consider their answers, that they are unsatisfactory in the very questions they do (or more to the point, do not) pose. Specifically, for no reason which can be found in either report, they decline to ask questions about these practices which society at large is asking – such as whether they are intrinsically objectionable and impermissible.

III

The underlying and undeclared philosophic commitment of these recent reports prevents them from posing the questions about genetic engineering which are raised by those who do not share these very particular commitments. But, if, as we said at the outset, there is no neutral account to be given of the questions to be put to biotechnology, how is society to proceed in forming public policy? More immediately, how is a committee charged with advising Ministers to proceed in framing its advice?

The *Banner Report* notes, on the basis of the many submissions it received, that:

> though they may not use this language, many people have intrinsic objections to the use of the emerging technologies. They may well be concerned about the effect of these technologies on animal welfare, genetic diversity, the environment, the pattern of farming and rural life, etc., but their concerns would not be exhausted by a considera-tion of these matters. For as well as worrying about the effects of the new technology, they feel a distinct unease about its very use.[14]

Furthermore, even some of those who did not express what could be described as an intrinsic objection, expressed objec-tions to various, particular perceived consequences of the application of biotechnology which were clearly not ones which they would reckon could be outweighed by associated benefits – this was the case in relation to many of the objections having to do with animal welfare. Now, even had the Committee been persuaded of the philosophical merits of consequentialism, it is difficult to see how a workable and acceptable public policy could be established which, on the basis of such a philosophy, would simply refuse to entertain intrinsic objections and, in addition, would maintain that any harm could, in principle, be outweighed by sufficient goods. Thus, without feeling the need for sustained engagement with the philosophical problems of consequentialism, the *Banner Report* sets out a policy based on a quite different set of assumptions.

These assumptions are contained, in effect, in the three

[14] *The Banner Report*, 3.3.

principles the *Report* enunciates, and which provide the basis for its proposals for the direction of future practice. The three principles are as follows:

(a) Harms of a certain degree and kind ought under no circumstances to be inflicted on an animal – a principle which provides the rationale for various current prohibitions relating, for example, to non-therapeutic operations on farm animals such as tongue amputation in calves, tail-docking in cattle and so on.

(b) Any harm to an animal, even if not absolutely impermissible, none the less requires justification and must be outweighed by the good which is realistically sought in so treating it. This is the principle which underlies, in effect, the Animals (Scientific Procedures) Act 1986, which sets out to ensure that animals are used in experimental work only where the end result of the experiment can reasonably be expected to be commensurate with the harm which the animal is likely to suffer.

(c) Any harm which is not absolutely prohibited by the first principle, and is in the particular circumstances considered justified in the light of the second, ought, however, to be minimised as far as is reasonably possible. This principle, which says that all reasonable steps should be taken to minimise the harm caused even by procedures which are justified when tested against the first two principles, gives rise to codes such as the Bovine Embryo Collection and Transfer Regulations 1993, which seek to ensure good practice in regard to those particular techniques.

Well, it might be said, if these principles already underlie the existing animal legislation within the UK, what is the point in enunciating them and, indeed, proposing them as a framework in which to evaluate the use of animals? The point is that though these principles can be found to underlie aspects of the contemporary regulatory regime they do so in a rather haphazard fashion; that is to say, though they surface from time to time in various pieces of legislation, codes and so on, it cannot be said that they are applied systematically and rigorously across the board to the whole range of issues which ought to be governed by such principles. Indeed, very broadly speaking we could characterise the present state of affairs by saying that the first principle (the straightforwardly prohibitive one) has some (but limited) application in relation to farm animals, whereas the second principle (the cost–benefit one) is (though, not exclusively) significant in relation to laboratory animals. The importance of this point is that whereas the cost–benefit analysis tends to allow a good deal of research which might be questionable if the prohibitive principle applied, the prohibitive principle tends to allow certain practices which might be questionable in relation to the cost–benefit analysis. Put it another way – on the farm, animals lack the protection of a form of cost–benefit test; in the lab, they lack the protection of something like the test contained in the first principle.

The present situation has an unmistakable hint, therefore, of a strategy of divide and rule – the different principles give rise, within the domains in which they operate, to various provisions which doubtless do much to prevent harm to animals, but, by being divided, do far less than they otherwise would. It is not, of course, that one would wish away either of these principles, or the provisions which they warrant. What the framework recommended by the *Report* requires, however, is that these principles, together with the third, should apply consistently in all cases.

What is the significance of this proposed framework for the regulation of genetic engineering? Are the harms it threatens to do to animals ones which ought to be ruled out straightaway under the first principle; or, even if they are not of that kind, are they such that the goods which are sought in practising genetic engineering are insufficient to outweigh them?

If things were black and white it would, of course, be a lot easier. If the effects of genetic modification were invariably deleterious for an animal's welfare, or if the very use of genetic modification expressed a contempt for animals and a disregard for their natural characteristics (as some objections to genetic engineering maintain), a system of regulation might be devised which would aim to prevent all genetic modification. (And, if one believed that about genetic engineering, one would not be deterred in advocating its prohibition by the argument which is so often trotted out, that we ought not to take unilateral action on this or any other welfare question, since to do so would simply be to export our welfare problems, since farmers on the continent will now produce for the British market what British farmers are prohibited from doing. Doubtless the same arguments could have been used 150 years ago by those who opposed legislation to prohibit child labour, and they would have been as unpersuasive then as they are now.) If, on the other hand, genetic modification were invariably neutral in relation to an animal's welfare, or conducive to it, and could never be used in ways which are fundamentally objectionable, then no regulations would be needed.

As it is, however, genetic modification cannot be regarded as a single moral entity – some genetic modification may be intrinsically objectionable as manipulative of an animal's good, some not; some may be neutral in relation to an animal's welfare, some may actually result in an improvement, and some may do severe harm. Transgenesis may give us, that is to say, the notoriously deformed Beltsville pigs (modified with a human growth hormone), or it may give us the seemingly (and I underline the word 'seemingly') unaffected Edinburgh sheep (producing a human protein in their milk as a result of the incorporation of a human gene). The trick in any system of regulation then, is to discriminate between the acceptable and unacceptable uses of genetic engineering. Does the present regulatory regime do that?

The key element in the present regulation of genetic engineering in relation to animals is the Animals (Scientific Procedures) Act, 1986 (hereafter 'ASPA'). This has at its heart the provision that 'in determining whether' to grant a licence for so-called regulated procedures, 'the Secretary of State shall weigh the likely adverse effects on the animals concerned against the benefit likely to accrue as a result of the programme' (ASPA, 5(4)). The interpretation of this clause is a matter of some difficulty and it has not been tested in the courts.

On one interpretation the clause does not require the Secretary of State to engage in, or be constrained by, what we might think of as a narrowly conceived cost–benefit assessment. That is to say, that though he or she must 'weigh' the cost to the animals against the benefit from the programme, the clause does not require the Secretary of State to grant a licence where the benefits outweigh the costs or, for that matter, to withhold one where the reverse is the case. And it is interesting to note that recent Secretaries of State have announced that, as a matter of policy, they will not grant licences for work for particular uses of animals, or of particular animals, notably uses of the great apes. Now this latter move, for example, cannot be understood, it could be argued, as an application of a cost–benefit assessment (since it simply could not be known that in no programme would the benefits exceed the costs), but only as an expression of a principle that certain uses of animals, or types of animals, should not be allowed no matter the benefits. On this line of interpretation, then, the Secretary of State has wide powers and discretion which could, in principle, be used to prohibit genetic engineering or certain uses of it for reasons other than to do with the perceived balance of benefits and burdens it may offer.

On another interpretation, the Secretary of State's duty is, in all cases, to carry out a cost–benefit assessment, more narrowly conceived. Now it is obvious that the weighing and balancing which is required on this interpretation is a highly intuitive matter. We do not have a scale which tells us how to compare unmeasurable quantities of animal suffering against unmeasurable quantities of human well-being. But here there is a more mundane difficulty, of the type which the BMA report and Fincham and Ravetz are inclined to think exclusively significant in this field. There is, that is to say, an empirical problem in making the required judgment – the effect of modifications is highly resistant to prediction, and may in any case emerge not immediately, but only as heterozygous offspring are produced, or as animals are subjected, outside laboratory conditions, to the varied conditions and pressures of contemporary systems of production. Thus though, on this interpretation, the Secretary of State must weigh the likely adverse effects on the animal against any likely benefit, the present inability of researchers to predict or control the expression of a gene makes such a task more than problematic, and so renders uncertain the effectiveness of this provision in preventing harm to animals.

It is clear that in the light of the principles it adopts, the *Banner Report* must judge the cost–benefit test, narrowly conceived, to be morally insufficient on its own, whether or not such a test has these further problems of application. The *Report* maintains that there are certain things which might be done to animals which are impermissible no matter the good which may result. Hence, it would judge the ASPA more acceptable on the first interpretation, and thus more adequate to the regulation of genetic modification.

There is, however, a further refinement since there is, as a matter of fact, a further provision in this legislation which, in effect, introduces a more obviously deontological element into the picture, at least as regards genetic modification. Section 15(1) requires that any protected animal which, at the end of the regulated procedures 'is suffering or likely to suffer adverse effects', must be killed and cannot be released from the Act's control. There is no qualification on this requirement – the Secretary of State cannot consider, in other words, whether the benefit of goods over harms would warrant the continued suffering of an animal. This means that even were the Secretary of State to grant a licence for an experiment which produced transgenic animals whose welfare was seriously impaired, the harm done to the modified animals would prevent their being released from the control of the Act and passing into commercial conditions. And, since the purpose of any modification is to produce a transgenic line, this provision effectively blocks the achievement of such a purpose where there are 'adverse effects'.

As the *Banner Report* notes, however, the interpretation of the phrase 'adverse effects' is a crucial matter in judging the significance of these provisions. The *Report* recommends, therefore, that the Home Office give an account of this phrase, and of the methods by which the existence of adverse effects are established. In making this recommendation, it had in mind two principal concerns. In the first place, that 'adverse effects' may not be construed sufficiently widely to include within its scope what might be deemed intrinsically objectionable modifications, and in the second that the matter of the existence of adverse effects may not be the subject of an appropriately rigorous and wide-ranging review of an animal's condition. Until there is clarity in relation to these issues, and the others already mentioned, the adequacy of the Act in relation to the problems posed by genetic modification is not finally settled.

In principle, the existing UK legislation provides the basis for quite stringent control of genetic engineering of animals. Indeed, the effect of sections 5(4) and 15(1), depending on their interpretation and application, is to introduce what I have referred to as the prohibitive principle into a piece of legislation which has at its heart a principle which might seem to derive from a quite different approach to the problem of the treatment and use of animals – the approach favoured by those reports which I have criticised as implicitly begging some important moral questions. If that principle is found to be already embedded in the regulatory regime, then it could be said that as things stand, animals produced by transgenic modification are more thoroughly protected than animals produced by conventional means. After all, conventional breeding, and other techniques such as embryo transfer and artificial insemination (unless they are specifically regulated), could, intentionally or unintentionally, adversely affect the welfare of farm animals and are not even subject to the so-called 'cost–benefit' analysis which is required before the licensing of a proposed programme of genetic modification – thus, breeding programmes which have produced oversized turkeys with considerable welfare problems are not subject to regulation of this kind. Whilst, then, it seems that an appropriate structure of regulation may be in place in relation to genetic engineering, much remains to be done to ensure that anything like such adequate provisions apply to other, less newsworthy procedures.

IV

The general point, regardless of the details of the particular case, is just that an appropriate structure of regulation, in relation to any and all of these technologies, be they applied to animals, plants or humans, can arise only where the real ethical questions are acknowledged and elucidated, not simply ignored or excluded. And, if that is to occur, we shall have to be ready to decline the all-too-common invitation to frame the questions to be put to these technologies as ones having to do only with the balancing of benefits and burdens.

Theology, in particular, so we might note briefly in conclusion, will have particular grounds for declining this invitation – grounds, that is to say, for wondering not just about the balance of benefits and harms which may result from the application of these techniques, but about their particular effects or, more fundamentally still, about the very character of what humans intend with certain uses of genetic engineering and the like.

What are these grounds? We can begin to grasp something of what they might be if we can understand why Karl Barth should have begun his treatment of what he calls 'special ethics' (in part 4 of the volume of the *Church Dogmatics* devoted to the doctrine of creation) with a reflection on the observance of the sabbath.[15] Barth begins here for the simple reason that the Christian moral life is to be understood, in virtue of the facts of creation, reconciliation and redemption, as first of all a life of freedom, signified by the rest of the sabbath day. The freedom of this day comes, in part, from knowing that nature, our own and nature as such, confronts us not as a raw material on which we must impose our purposes or which must submit to our projects if it is to have form or meaning, but that it is, in contrast, a nature which, in virtue of its being created, possesses form and meaning. We might make the point in another way by insisting that when God rested on the seventh day, it should not be supposed that he did so on account of tiredness. That the rest of the sabbath is not the rest of weariness, is plain enough from the fact that humankind, which has done no work, is invited to join God in the sabbath – in restful contemplation of the good work of God which finds its completion here when God is with and for his creation, and in particular with and for humankind.

---

[15] K. Barth, *Church Dogmatics*, III: 4, trans. A. T. Mackay et al. (Edinburgh, 1961), 47.

But, if we now turn back to the problem of genetics and genetic manipulation, we cannot fail to note that it is not uncommon to find supposedly Christian reflection on human efforts at genetic amelioration entertaining the thought that such efforts may be approved of as completing what God (through want of energy?) did not complete. The language of humankind as 'co-creators' is typically deployed, usually without much evidence that consideration has been given to the significance and character of the act of creation as it has been understood within the Christian tradition, not least through its understanding and interpretation of the sabbath. Maybe the concept of 'co-creators' has a place; but, unless it is closely related to an understanding of the creator with whom some sort of partnership it claimed, it serves only to provide to projects which may repudiate rather than embrace the created order an air of pious respectability.

To ask about the compatibility of projects of genetic manipulation with that belief in the fact of creation and its goodness which belongs to the credal core of Christianity, is to take up a line of questioning of a sort not covered by the pragmatic and prudential comparison of benefits and risks which is the favoured mode of engagement with these issues. For what this line of questioning wonders is not just whether projects, for example, of perfective (as opposed to therapeutic) genetic engineering will have a balance of good over bad consequences, but rather whether they express a fundamentally mistaken attitude towards human being in the world, an attitude which will be overcome only as we learn what it means to keep the sabbath as a day on which humankind is called to a knowledge and love of the order which God himself knows and loves.

CHAPTER 7

'Who are my mother and my brothers?': Marx, Bonhoeffer and Benedict and the redemption of the family

I

We have in recent times multiplied significantly the occasions on which the question 'who are my mother and my brothers?', taken quite literally, could have a use.[1] Prior to our day, it can have had few very obvious applications. Of course, we can imagine that it might have had a use for foundlings when the circumstances of their earliest days became known to them. And various utopians (such as Plato in his *Republic*) have dreamed of a time when the question would be asked by many, if not all, children. But, apart from such dreams, some ingenuity was required to devise employment for the question.

In our day, such ingenuity has been rendered unnecessary. The various practices of donation of gametes have brought into being a whole class of foundlings, for whom this question, 'who are my mother and my brothers?' has immediate use and purpose, expressing that radical dissociation and alienation which has been wished upon them by the utopian dreamers of our times. And these children, the offspring of anonymous donors or of surrogates, may yet be joined by others, born from eggs harvested from the dead or the unborn – for, if the Human Fertilisation and Embryology Authority presently judges us unready for these developments, it gives the distinct impression

---

[1] I am grateful to Ben Quash, Tim Jenkins, Markus Bockmuehl and Peter Kashouris for their comments on a draft of this chapter and for the discussion of it which took place at a meeting of the Society for the Study of Christian Ethics.

of biding its time whilst 'sentiment' catches up with 'rational' thought.[2]

How is it, we might ask, that we have come to give this question such wide, new currency? How is it that we have deliberately set about creating foundlings, who with their posing of this question, pose in a most dramatic and pressing way the further question of how we understand the character and form of the family, in relation to which they are so ambiguously placed?

II

The doubtful honour of first using the word 'reproduction' in its usual modern sense is accorded by the *Oxford English Dictionary* to John Wesley – who, it should be said, used the word only to protest at its use. Writing in 1782, Wesley complained of the French naturalist Georges Buffon that 'he substitutes for the plain word *generation*, a quaint word of his own, *reproduction*, in order to level man not only with the beasts that perish, but with nettles or onions' – the point being, presumably, that to equate human generation with reproduction is to overlook the fact that humans give birth to what cannot properly be regarded as copies (or reproductions) of themselves, but only as radically other selves; they have not reproduced another 'I' , but participated in the generation of a 'Thou'.

Whatever Buffon's intentions may have been, we would surely accord him too much significance if we were to suppose that the usage which he introduced could itself and alone effect,

---

[2] The HFEA is the UK body established by statute to oversee, and advise the Governent on aspects of the use of the new technologies of reproduction. See the HFEA's *Donated Ovarian Tissue in Embryo Research and Assisted Conception: Report* (London, 1994). To the use of ovarian tissue from cadavers in infertility treatment it finds 'no objection in principle' (para. 19), but thinks that 'more . . . should be done to find out about the psychological consequences for the recipient couple and particularly for the prospective child' (ibid.). The use of fetal ovarian tissue is said to raise 'difficult social, medical, scientific and legal [but not ethical?] concerns' (para. 20). Again, psychological consequences for the offspring are picked out as the main ground for anxiety. But, if the psychological difficulties in either case do not depend on some ethical base, are they not ultimately corrigible? Certainly the HFEA shows no sign of entertaining an objection 'in principle' even to the use of fetal material.

however it may have assisted, the levelling which Wesley feared. This surely gets things the wrong way round – the novel usage more likely evidences a shift in understanding which has already been in part achieved, rather than itself creating, *ex nihilo,* that shift in understanding. (We might make the same point about the introduction of the word 'termination' to replace the plain word 'abortion'.) Wesley may have been right to protest at the usage, but behind that protest must lie, at least implicitly, another protest at the diverse forces which were achieving the levelling which the new coinage evidenced rather than created. But what forces were these?

Coincidentally, the *Oxford English Dictionary* records another neologism for 'reproduction' which effectively proffers an answer to our question – this time from the English translation of *Capital,* where Marx asserts that 'the conditions of production are also those of reproduction'.[3] By 'reproduction' Marx means to refer not to the biological process by which the human race is perpetuated, but to the process whereby a society converts some of its products back into means of production. But later commentators have noted that, even if Marx did not in the context mean to assert what the sentence might be taken, out of context, to say – that is, that human reproduction has an historically specific mode or character, and that this mode or character is a reflection or function of the condition of the means of production – such an assertion is precisely a consequence of his general position.[4]

---

[3] K. Marx, *Capital,* trans. Moore and Aveling (London, 1878), II, 578.

[1] It has to be said, however, that Marx was not thoroughly consistent in thinking of human reproduction in these terms. Critics complain of a certain 'naturalism' in Marx's thought about the family and about relations between the sexes, in virtue of which some patterns of social life are treated, rather uncritically, as essentially determined by nature and not by history. Thus, although Marx insists in *Capital* that: 'it is just as stupid to regard the Christo-Teutonic form of the family as absolute, as it is to take the same view of the classical Roman form, or of the classical Greek form, or of the Oriental form' (*Capital,* 4th edn, trans. E. and C. Paul (London, 1974), 529), elsewhere, to give a single instance, he seems simply to assume that monogamy will prevail under communism. See the discussion, for example, in S. Himmelweit, 'Reproduction and the Materialist Conception of History' in *The Cambridge Companion to Marx,* ed. T. Carver (Cambridge, 1991), 196–221, whose point, in any case, seems to be that what is really needed is not an attempt to understand the conditions of reproduction as determined by the conditions of production, but rather to understand

The project which Marx and Engels set out most clearly for the first time in *The German Ideology*, must, that is to say, apply to the family. Here Marx and Engels announced the anti-idealist slogan under which they would work, that 'It is not consciousness that determines life, but life that determines consciousness'[5] – understanding by 'life', specifically economic life as expressed in the form of the means of production. Thus, they set about the project of comprehending the various configurations of social life as connected with, and created by, different modes of production – declaring that 'one cannot speak at all of the family "as such" '[6], and, true to this insight here and in later works (such as Engels' influential *Origin of the Family, Private Property and the State*), tracing the form of the family through its communal, feudal and bourgeois forms.

According to the *Communist Manifesto*, 'the bourgeoisie cannot exist without continually revolutionising the instruments of production, hence the relations of production, and therefore social relations as a whole'.[7] In the social revolution which follows the revolution in production, 'The bourgeoisie', so it is alleged, 'has torn away from the family its sentimental veil and reduced the family relation to a mere money relation'.[8] It was this family, the bourgeois family, whose 'abolition' Marx and Engels prophesied and prescribed, sweeping complaints to one side with the observation that:

> Bourgeois phrases about the family and child-rearing, about the deeply felt relationship of parent to child, become even more revolting when all proletarian family ties are severed as a consequence of large-scale industry, and children are simply transformed into articles of trade and instruments of labour.[9]

The understanding of the relationship between the form of the family and the outworking of the developmental laws of

---

social life as the result of the dual influence of the conditions of human reproduction and of the production of material goods.

[5] K. Marx and F. Engels, *The German Ideology*, vol. v of *Collected Works* (Moscow, 1976), 37.
[6] Marx and Engels, *The German Ideology*, 180.
[7] K. Marx and F. Engels, *Manifesto of the Communist Party*, in K. Marx, *Later Political Writings*, ed. and trans. T. Carver (Cambridge, 1996), 4.
[8] Ibid.
[9] Marx and Engels, *The Communist Manifesto*, 17.

bourgeois economic organisation here outlined, rendered Marx and Engels all the more sensitive in their more empirical work (and especially in Engel's *Outlines of a Critique of Political Economy* and *The Condition of the Working Class in England*) to features of family life which are to them, so to say, symptoms, but which the 'untheorised' will most likely pass over as mere phenomena. Thus, to take one example, Engels notes that:

> It is a common practice for children, as soon as they are capable of work (i.e., as soon as they reach the age of nine), to spend their wages themselves, to look upon their parental home as a mere boarding house, and hand over to their parents a fixed amount for food and lodging.[10]

In virtue of the theory, however, this is not merely noted, but explained or comprehended. Engels finds here the system of free trade exerting its grip, for this system can only operate on the basis of the separation of interests: thus 'the last vestige of common interests, the community of goods in the possession of the family, has been undermined by the factory system'.[11]

What, we might wonder, should we make of the phenomenon we have already noted – what we might describe as the free trade in gametes – in the light of Marx and Engels' analysis? Since 'the system of production is at the same time the system of reproduction', it might plausibly be regarded as no mere phenomenon, but as the further expression of the underlying imperative of the economic forces of modern capitalism – the transformation of children into 'simple articles of commerce' and a further step in the dissolution of the family. For it is an implicit characteristic of the practice of donation of gametes that parents show themselves willing to treat their offspring or potential offspring as surplus goods, rendering them thereby, rather unambiguously, a commodity.[12] This 'commodification of children' also explains the rather curious fact that the dead

---

[10] F. Engels, *Outlines of a Critique of Political Economy*, vol. III of Marx and Engels, *Collected Works* (Moscow, 1975), 423–4. And see also, F. Engels, *The Condition of the Working Class in England*, trans. of 1886 revised (Harmondsworth, 1987).

[11] Engels, *Outlines of a Critique of Political Economy*, 423–4.

[12] Marx used 'commodity' in a technical sense to describe something with both a use and exchange value; I use it here in its more usual sense to refer to something viewed or treated as a raw material or product.

and unborn have come to be regarded, quite seriously, as putative parents. For those who can exercise no responsibility for their children can, of course, be deemed appropriate parents of them, if children, like commodities, are held, quite simply, to be alienable.[13] Nor should we be surprised to find these developments in the social relations of the family taking place, veiled, as Marx and Engels would put it, by the 'holy concept of it in official phraseology and universal hypocrisy'[14] – in this case, veiled by the HFEA's much vaunted, though essentially shallow, concern for the need to 'assess the likely psychological effects' on a child and 'on wider family relationships', 'of knowing that it was born from an egg derived from a cadaver or from an aborted foetus'.[15]

From within a materialist conception of history, the family can not but be seen as an evolving historical product, shaped by the development of the means of production and the wider social relationships to which they give birth. But, even if we do not fully accept such a conception of the dynamic of history, are doubtful of the schema which Marx and Engels impose on their data in telling their story of the evolution of the family, think that that data is itself to some extent dubious,[16] and prefer a different 'eschatology' (as Barth puts it[17]) to the one which dialectical materialism proffers, this analysis serves to remind us that to treat the family, whether in its present or in an earlier form, as a natural given, standing outside the forces of history,

[13] The point that to 'undertake to become the parent of a child in order to alienate one's parental relation to another, implicitly converts the child from a person to a commodity' is made by O. M. T. O'Donovan, *Begotten or Made?* (Oxford, 1984), 37. The phrase 'commodification of children' comes from M. A. Field's *Surrogate Motherhood* (Cambridge, MA, 1988), in which she argues that the use of the laws of contract or property to settle the fate of human subjects, be they frozen embryos or new-born infants, can only encourage the view (which, so O'Donovan claims, is already implicit in the practice) that we are here concerned with chattels.
[14] Marx and Engels, *The German Ideology*, 180.
[15] HFEA, *Donated Ovarian Tissue in Embryo Research and Assisted Conception: Public Consultation Document* (London, 1994), para. 23.
[16] The data used by Engels in his *Origin of the Family, Private Property and the state* is borrowed in large part from L. H. Morgan's *Ancient Society*. A critique of Morgan's anthropology, with a none the less sympathetic treatment of Engels' work, is provided by E. B. Leacock in her introduction to the *Origin of the Family, Private Property and the State* (London, 1972).
[17] K. Barth, *Church Dogmatics*, III: 2, trans. H. Knight et al. (Edinburgh, 1960), 388.

persisting as a natural good no matter what, is not so much innocent as foolish. We may tell other stories about the genesis of the family in its contemporary form and with its contemporary ethos, about the levelling which Wesley feared, and about the development of the free trade in gametes – the point is, however, that some such story is waiting to be told, since the family, left to itself so to say, cannot but be shaped and conditioned by the diverse forces to which it is subject.

III

It is for this very reason that when Bonhoeffer spoke of marriage and the family as one of the divine mandates, he was careful to distinguish his understanding of mandate from the terms 'institution' and 'order' – which were, of course, not without a particular vogue in certain theological circles in Germany in the 1930s. 'The term "mandate" ', so he writes:

must . . . be taken to imply the claiming, seizure and the formation of a definite earthly domain by the divine commandment. The bearer of the mandate acts as a deputy in the place of him who assigns him his commission. In its proper sense the term 'institution' or 'order' might also be applied here, but this would involve the danger of directing attention rather towards the actual state of the institution than towards its foundation, which lies solely in the divine warrant, legitimation and authorization. The consequence of this can all too easily be the assumption of a divine sanction for all existing orders and institutions in general and a romantic conservatism which is entirely at variance with the Christian doctrine of the . . . divine mandates.[18]

'What is required here is . . . a return to a genuine sub-ordination to the divine mandate and restoration of genuine responsibility towards the divinely assigned task.'[19] Unless Christianity undertakes the 'claiming, seizure and the for-mation of a definite earthly domain', that domain will serve a different *dominus* (or we might say 'Führer') from the one the Christian acknowledges. Indeed, Bonhoeffer goes so far as to

---

[18] D. Bonhoeffer, *Ethics*, ed. E. Bethge, trans N. H. Smith (London, 1955), 254.
[19] Bonhoeffer, *Ethics*, 180.

say, that 'It is only from above, with God as the point of departure, that it is possible to say and to understand what is meant by the Church, by marriage and the family, by culture and by government.'[20]

That the Lutheran Bonhoeffer should make this point so very forcefully – the point that these 'institutions' can come to serve their true Lord only as they are claimed, seized and formed by the Word of God – should not surprise us; the openness of the Lutheran Church of the thirties to, as the *Barmen Declaration* put it, 'yet other events, powers, historic figures, and truths as God's revelation', 'besides this one Word of God', had convinced him of the need for utter seriousness and clarity in relation to the question of Christian 'formation', or 'conformation' as he would rather say.[21] It also led him to reflect on the causes of the Lutheran Church's so rapid a loss of its own integrity. Part of his analysis of this centred on the 'fatal misunderstanding'[22] to which the preaching of justification by grace alone was always open. The danger is that in this preaching 'a true understanding of the mutual relation between grace and discipleship'[23] is lost, so that 'the Christian life comes to mean nothing more than living in the world and as the world, in being no different from the world, in fact, being prohibited from being different from the world for the sake of grace'.[24] Thus:

the price we are having to pay today in the shape of the collapse of the organized church is only the inevitable consequence of our policy of making grace available to all at too low a cost. We gave away the word

[20] Bonhoeffer, *Ethics*, 255. A report on the family from a working party of the Church of England's Board for Social Responsibility, *Something to Celebrate* (London, 1995), entirely innocent of such thoughts, is quite at a loss to know what theology might have to contribute to a consideration of the form and character of the family, and the simple blessing of what currently pertains is the only role which it can find for the Church. If this is not a form of 'romantic conservatism' it is its historicist counterpart; but the theological methodology of this report, in so far as it can be said to have one, is none the less the methodology of of the German Christians. See my brief critique of the report, 'Nothing to Declare', *The Church Times*, 16 June 1995.

[21] *Barmen Declaration* of 1934, trans. D. S. Bax, *Journal of Theology for Southern Africa*, 47 (1984), 1, reprinted in E. Jüngel, *Christ, Justice and Peace* (Edinburgh, 1992). For the distinction and discussion of 'formation' and 'conformation' see *Ethics*, 60–6.

[22] D. Bonhoeffer, *The Cost of Discipleship*, trans. R. H. Fuller (London, 1959), 40.

[23] Bonhoeffer, *The Cost of Discipleship*, 47.

[24] Bonhoeffer, *The Cost of Discipleship*, 42.

and sacraments wholesale, we baptized, confirmed and absolved a whole nation unasked and without condition. Our humanitarian sentiment made us give that which was holy to the scornful and unbelieving. We poured forth unending streams of grace. But the call to follow Jesus in the narrow way was hardly ever heard.[25]

Bonhoeffer regards this, of course, as a corruption, not an explication, of Luther's message. But for this corruption Luther may himself have laid the seeds, with an anti-nomianism which is sometimes more striking than the dialectical qualification to which it is usually subject. However that may be, according to Bethge, the 'tireless search, upon which [Bonhoeffer] had been engaged ever since he wrote *Sanctorum Communio*', and which was to continue with, in particular, *The Cost of Discipleship* and *Life Together*, was, in effect, a re-examination of 'the Reformers' habitual condemnation of faith as an *"habitus"*', which means that all interest in its dimension of existence is, by definition, rooted in evil'.[26] The Church, Bonhoeffer insists, must find '*Lebensraum*', not only in her liturgy and order, 'but also for the daily life of her members in the world'[27] – and, in particular, in those 'earthly domains' which are claimed by the family, culture and government as they exercise the mandate which they are given in the divine command.

But what, to be specific, is the mandate given to the family? What is the commission with which it is charged? Here, unfortunately Bonhoeffer does not help us, since his intended treatment of the mandates in the *Ethics* breaks off unfinished before he reaches the family. It is true that he has told us in a preliminary discussion of the mandates in an earlier section that:

through marriage men are brought into being for the glorification and service of Jesus Christ and for the increase of his kingdom. This means that marriage is not only a matter of producing children, but also of educating them to be obedient to Jesus Christ . . . [I]n marriage it is for the service of Jesus Christ that new men are created.[28]

[25] Bonhoeffer, *The Cost of Discipleship*, 45.
[26] E. Bethge, *Dietrich Bonhoeffer*, trans. and ed. E. Robinson (London, 1970), 372.
[27] Bonhoeffer, *The Cost of Discipleship*, 228.   [28] Bonhoeffer, *Ethics*, 183.

This point, however, would hardly have represented his complete account of the subject – even if, although wholly traditional, it certainly needs to be made, particularly, as Stanley Hauerwas would point out, in a society so corrupted by its moral confusions that even believers feel diffident about seeking to raise their children as Christians! But there would surely have been more to what Bonhoeffer would have wanted to say. After all, very little is said or implied here regarding the good of marriage or the family as such, and they are treated instead simply as instrumental in the production of other values – like a factory, we might say, rather than like a college or university where the end 'product' is not all.

If, however, Bonhoeffer does not give us a full account of the meaning of the life of the family, elsewhere he provides us with an account of the proper form of its life, albeit that he does so almost incidentally. In *Life Together*, his reflection on the pattern of life of a Christian community seeking to live out its discipleship of Jesus Christ, he quite consciously has the family in view. Reflecting, for example, on the different instances of common life amongst Christians, he remarks quite simply that 'Others have the privilege of living a Christian life in the fellowship of their families.'[29] Thereafter, he takes it for granted that the life of the Christian family will be structured by the practices of prayer, praise and confession which order the Christian community.

But to tell us how the family should live is not directly to tell us what is the 'mandate' or 'commission' which belongs to the family. We have an account, that is to say, of the practice of its life and thus of the means by which, as Bonhoeffer understands it, the 'claiming, seizure and formation' of this earthly domain is accomplished, but not the theory which lies behind the practice – a theory which would tell us how this practice would seize this domain, and thus perhaps what the significance and consequence of this 'claiming, seizure and formation' would be. What theory might this be? I am going to propose that we can

---

[29] D. Bonhoeffer, *Life Together*, trans. J. W. Doberstein (London, 1954), 10.

understand the theory of this practice by reflecting on another account of 'life together', the *Rule of St Benedict*. For, in virtue of a certain commonality of concerns, the *Rule of St Benedict* gives us the clues we need if we are to understand how the practice of community life which Bonhoeffer commends for the family, enables and effects its 'claiming, seizure and formation'.

IV

There are, I shall contend, three features of the *Rule of St Benedict* with which we must reckon if we are to make sense of the form of life which it lays down. I shall note these features one after another before trying to interpret their conjunction.[30]

The first aspect of the *Rule* with which we must come to terms is that it is most definitely a rule for a shared or social life and as such marks a resolution of the tensions implicit in earlier monasticism, principally in favour of its communal elements. It is easy for us to overlook this fact, perhaps not least because Benedict himself disguises to some extent what he is really about with his expression of great regard for the eremitical tradition (associated especially with the fierce asceticism of the desert and the great St Anthony of Egypt) and with his suggestion that his monks are actually in training for the solitary life – this is 'but a little rule for beginners'.[31] But, whilst expressing the seemingly merely pragmatic caution that the life of the hermit is something which can only be attempted by those who are 'well-armed' after 'long probation in a monastery',[32] and can never be the first step in the religious life, he conceives the

---

[30] A fuller defence of my interpretation of the *Rule* than is possible here would make detailed reference to the work of A. de Vogüé; see, in particular, *La Règle de St. Benoît*, *Sources Chrétiennes*, 181–6 (Paris, 1971–2); *The Rule of St. Benedict: A Doctrinal and Spiritual Commentary*, trans. J. B. Hasbrouck (Kalamazoo, 1983); and *Community and Abbot in the Rule of St. Benedict*, trans. C. Philippi, 2 vols. (Kalamazoo, 1979 and 88). In addition see G. Holzherr's commentary on the *Rule*, trans. by monks of Glenstal Abbey as *The Rule of St. Benedict: A Guide to Christian Living* (Dublin, 1994).

[31] *Rule of St. Benedict*, trans. J. McCann (London, 1976), 73. This and subseqent references are to the chapters of the *Rule*.

[32] *Rule of St. Benedict*, 1.

religious life in such a way that it is hard to see that the life he favours does or could serve the other.[33]

The very name for the type of monks Benedict favours – 'cenobites' – reveals what is at stake here, since the notion of a cenobitic monastic is something of a contradiction in terms. The word 'cenobite' comes from a Latin word itself formed from two Greek words: 'koinos', common, and 'bios', life. The word 'monastery', on the other hand, has its root in the Greek 'monos', alone or single. Thus, the conjunction of the two in the notion of a cenobitic monk, gives us the paradoxical category of a solitary who pursues the common life. Cassian, to whom Benedict is indebted, knows of the tension between the solitary and the cenobitic ideals although, claims McGinn, he 'did not work out a clear and coherent solution to the relationship of contemplative absorption in God and active love for the monastic brethren';[34] Benedict, it could be argued, both knows of the problem, and resolves it in favour of the communal ideal, albeit whilst paying his respects to the alternative tradition.

Evidence for this development, according to Owen Chadwick, is found in a number of details in the *Rule* which might easily be passed over.[35] Take for example, the place of silence. For Cassian – whose writings were a source for Benedict, and who with Basil is picked out alone among the 'Catholic Fathers' for particular mention when Benedict comes to list works which might take monks further towards perfection than can his rule[36] – silence was related to contemplation. In his conception of the monastic life, long hours of silence in the cell were an essential part in the practice of that contemplation of God which was the monk's first task. But note that contem-

---

[33] See O. Chadwick, *John Cassian*, 2nd edn (Cambridge, 1968), who demonstrates the many continuities between Benedict's and Cassian's thought whilst noting, however, that 'the idea of continuing in the monastery until death was changing the old relation between the community and the anchorite, the old distinction between the obedient and the contemplative. The Rule is the confession of humility that all men are in truth beginners' (155).

[34] B. McGinn, *The Foundations of Mysticism*, vol. 1 of *The Presence of God: A History of Western Christian Mysticism* (London, 1992), 226.

[35] O. Chadwick, *The Making of the Benedictine Ideal*, the Thomas Verner Moore Memorial Lecture for 1980, St Anselm's Abbey (Washington, 1981).

[36] *Rule of St. Benedict*, 73.

plation (*contemplatio*) is not a word Benedict uses, and his understanding of silence is severely practical – it is required as Chadwick puts it, 'not to hear the whisper within, but the exposition from lectern or pulpit'.[37] It is required too by humility – the key virtue of the monastic life, as we shall see – but the silence of the day is filled with activity, not with long periods for contemplation. 'Idleness is the enemy of the soul' says Benedict, not the door to spiritual growth, and 'the brethren, therefore, must be occupied at stated hours in manual labour, and again at other hours in sacred reading'.[38] Even the cell, which was, as Chadwick puts it, 'the sacrament of the interior life',[39] has given way to the dormitory: 'if it be possible' says Benedict, 'let them all sleep in one place'.[40] There is another detail in this regard, to which Chadwick does not draw attention, but which is in some ways just as noteworthy as these others. So far is it from being the case that solitariness is of the essence of the life of the monk, its imposition functions as the chief punishment at the Abbot's disposal. 'The brother who is guilty of a graver fault shall be excluded both from the table and from the oratory. Let none of the brethren consort with him or speak to him. Let him work alone at the task enjoined him and abide in penitential sorrow.'[41]

It would be wrong to think that the consolidation of the communal ideal is evidenced only negatively, so to speak, by the disregard for certain principles of practice and organisation previously safeguarded. Positively speaking, Chadwick finds in the *Rule* and its provisions a more developed sense of the good of the common life than is to be discerned in its immediate sources. Thus, 'Not only shall the virtue of obedience be practised by all towards the abbot, but the brethren shall also obey one another, knowing that by this road of obedience will they go to God.'[42]

The contrast between Benedict and his predecessors should

---

[37] Chadwick, *The Making of the Benedictine Ideal*, 14.
[38] *Rule of St. Benedict*, 48.
[39] Chadwick, *The Making of the Benedictine Ideal*, 10.
[40] *Rule of St. Benedict*, 22.
[41] *Rule of St. Benedict*, 25.   [42] *Rule of St. Benedict*, 71.

not be pressed too hard – prior to Benedict, the monastery had already ceased to be simply a 'training school for hermits', to use Chadwick's words, and, after him, the existence of the seventy-third chapter ('That the Full Observance of Justice is Not Established in This Rule'), with its references to the 'Conferences' and 'Institutes', 'continued to remind the Benedictines of Egypt and of Cassian'[43] – a reminder which was crucial for the development of Cistercian practice. Our first point, however, is that, whatever may be said of earlier or later conceptions of the monastic life, the *Rule of St Benedict* is quite determinedly a rule for a common life.

A second feature of the *Rule* which we must now note is one which, unlike the first, can hardly fail to come to our attention even on a first reading: that is, the central place given to 'humility', which, with self-denial, Hume properly identified as one of the 'monkish virtues'.[44]

Chapter 7, 'Of Humility', is itself the longest in the *Rule*; in addition, the *Rule* returns to the theme again and again in what follows. Humility, we are told, is a 'ladder', by which we may ascend 'unto heaven'; it has twelve degrees (though the choice of the number twelve seems a pious, rather than an analytical, demand) and through these degrees the monk must climb. He must begin by keeping 'the fear of God before his eyes', mindful of the evil in his heart. Then he must come to the second degree – 'that a man love not his own will, nor delight in fulfilling his own desires'. So he may pass to the third: that 'for the love of God', he 'may subject himself to his superior in all obedience', and to the fourth, that 'meeting in this obedience with difficulties and contradictions and even injustice, he should with a quiet mind hold fast to patience, and enduring neither tire nor run away'. Then there is the fifth degree: that he 'humbly confess and conceal not from his abbot any evil thoughts that enter his hearts, and any secret sins he has committed'. The sixth is that he be 'content with the meanest and worst of

---

[43] Chadwick, *John Cassian*, 156.

[44] D. Hume, *An Enquiry Concerning the Principles of Morals*, ix, part 1 in *Enquiries Concerning Human Understanding and Concerning the Principles of Morals*, ed. L. A. Selby-Bigge, 3rd edn, rev. P. H. Nidditch (Oxford, 1975).

everything, and esteem himself, in regard to the work that is given to him, as a bad and unworthy workman'; the seventh that he should believe in 'his inmost heart' what he declares when he declares himself 'lower and of less account that all others'; the eighth that he do 'nothing except what is commanded by the common rule of the monastery and the example of his superiors'. And so to the ninth, tenth, eleventh and twelfth: that he should be humble in word and manner, speaking only when questioned, 'not prompt and ready to laughter', but speaking seriously in 'few and sensible words', with head and heart downcast.

We can give a correct, but superficial – though for the moment adequate – answer to the question as to why the virtue of humility occupies so central a place by saying that it is the prerequisite for the practice of obedience which is for Benedict another defining characteristic of his monks. They are not anchorites or hermits, as we have already learnt; but neither are they 'Gyrovagues' or 'Sarabaites' – the former being monks who wander from monastery to monastery, the latter being altogether more mysterious. What these monks are said to have in common, and what Benedict finds contemptible, is that they live in accord with no very specific principles whatsoever. Thus, 'their law is their own good pleasure: whatever they think of or choose to do, they call holy; what they like not, that they regard as unlawful'.[45] Benedict's monks are not to live thus but according to a rule, and a rule which regulates and disciplines, through the office of the abbot as well as through the rule itself, almost their every move – what they eat and drink and wear; when they sleep and when they rise; what they read and do; when and how they pray; even the nature of the special abstinence they might adopt for the observance of Lent. The *Rule* is addressed, that is to say, as the Prologue specifically declares, 'to thee . . . whosoever thou mayest be that renouncing thine own will to fight for the true King, Christ, does take up the strong and glorious weapon of obedience'.

Unlike those Gyrovagues and the mysterious Sarabaites,

---

[45] *Rule of St. Benedict*, 1.

then, who are 'given up to their own wills',[46] Benedict's monks, placed in this 'school of the Lord's service', obedient to the *Rule* and the Abbot as its authoritative interpreter, aspire not to 'living by their own will, and obeying their own desires and passions, but [to] walking by another's judgment and orders'.[47] So it is that the *Rule* considers humility the central virtue of the monastic life.[48]

There is a third feature of the *Rule*, which, like the second, will strike even the casual reader, and this we may note quite briefly. It is the centrality which it accords to worship: 'the work of God' as it is tellingly called. The main body of the *Rule* contains long and detailed prescriptions relating to worship – thus we have chapters on 'The Divine Office at Night', 'How Many Psalms are to be Said at the Night Office', 'How the Night Office is to be Said in Summer', 'How the Night Office is to be Said on Sundays', 'How the Office of Lauds is to be Said', 'How Lauds Shall be Said on Ordinary Days', 'How the Night Office is to be Performed on Saints' Days', 'at What Seasons Alleluia is to be Said', and so on. And, in case the point is missed, we receive the forceful and unambiguous injunction – 'Let nothing. . . be put before the work of God.'[49]

We have before us, then, three features of the *Rule of St Benedict*. The *Rule* is a rule for 'life together', it assigns a pivotal place to the virtue of humility, and it makes worship *the* central practice of the common life. How shall we relate and interpret these elements? Our claim will be that for Benedict humility is central just because it is the crucial social virtue, and that worship is the practice in which humility is both presupposed and grounded. How is this so? To understand the connections we need to look over Benedict's shoulder to Augustine, and to Augustine's analysis of human sin and the history to which it gives birth.[50]

---

[46] Ibid.   [47] *Rule of St. Benedict*, 5.

[48] Benedict's treatment of humility is not unproblematic – a fuller discussion would question the notion of the ladder of humility, and the seeming paradox of seeking to make progress in humility.

[49] *Rule of St. Benedict*, 43.

[50] This analysis also lies behind the development in Augustine's own understanding of the nature of the monastic life from a contemplative to a more communal ideal; see, J. M. Rist, *Augustine* (Cambridge, 1994), 205ff.

In Augustine's treatment of the story of Adam and Eve in Book xiv of the *City of God*, pride is identified as the original sin.[51] The evil act of taking the apple contrary to the commandment of God was necessarily preceded by an evil will. But what tempted the will to disobedience and thus to evil? Man, says Augustine, was 'delighted' by the promise of the serpent, 'you will be like gods'; thus it was pride which enticed him to disobedience, a 'longing for a perverse kind of exaltation'. 'In pride [they] made themselves their own ground.' Now, if pride is the original vice, humility is the virtue which is opposed to this vice. In pride, the mind turns away from God and towards the self. In humility, the mind clings to God as humankind's one true good – so 'obedience can belong only to the humble'.[52] Thus the way of redemption is 'first humility, second, humility, third, humility'.[53]

According to Rist, 'Plotinus associated pride with a perverse love, a love of one's own powers, a wish to be one's own master . . . Characteristically [however] Augustine adds a social dimension to Plotinus' insight.'[54] For pride and humility, these two opposed loves, have established, 'speaking allegorically',[55] two cities. 'The earthly city was created by self-love reaching the point of contempt for God, the Heavenly City by the love of God carried as far as contempt of the self.'[56] And the earthly city, the city of self-love, has for its founder the fratricide Cain, whose sin is repeated by Romulus the founder of Rome, 'the capital of the earthly city of which we are speaking'. Why did Romulus murder his brother? – plainly because 'anyone whose aim was to glory in the exercise of power would obviously enjoy less power if his sovereignty was diminished by a living partner'. Why did Cain murder Abel? Not because Abel threatened his exercise of power, 'for Abel did not aim at power in the city

---

[51] Quotations are from Augustine, *De Civitate Dei* (*City of God*), PL. 41, 13 804, trans. H. Bettenson (London, 1972). In addition to Book xiv, see xii, 6.

[52] Augustine, *City of God*, xiv, 13.

[53] J. Burnaby, *Amor Dei: A Study of the Religion of St Augustine* (London, 1938), 190, quoting *De Peccatorum Meritis et Remissione*.

[54] Rist, *Augustine*, 189.   [55] Augustine, *City of God*, xv, 1.

[56] Augustine, *City of God*, xiv, 28. And see also xix, 12: 'Pride is a perverted imitation of God. For pride hates a fellowship of equality under God, and seeks to impose its own dominion on fellow men, in place of God's rule.'

which his brother was founding. But Cain's was the diabolical envy that the wicked feel for the good simply because they are good, while they themselves are evil.'[57] The hostility of Cain and Romulus is at root, however, the same: it was the pride of Cain which could not bear the reproach of Abel's goodness, and the pride of Romulus which could not tolerate any diminution or sharing of his sovereignty. The love of self necessarily sets one against another and is the root of the division of the earthly city against itself and against the City of God. Only the virtue of the heavenly city, humility, can create a true peace. 'Where there is humility, there there is love' says Augustine.[58]

Barth's analysis of human sin in his reflections on 'The Pride of Man' also makes a connection between the fundamental sin of pride and human conflict. True to Barth's declared principle of founding anthropology on Christology, he knows of human pride only from knowledge of the humility of the Son of God. But on that basis one can say that 'Sin in its unity and totality is always pride', and in particular the pride in virtue of which humankind becomes, absurdly, 'the servant who wants to be lord'.[59] Furthermore, 'The humility of faith and obedience demanded of man as the creature and covenant partner of God is completely crowded out by its disorderly opposite.'[60] And, again, this disorder between God and man will take a social form:

At once the created world in which this takes place, and within it the relationship of man and man in particular is forced to suffer with it. It cannot be otherwise. Wanting to act as lord in relation to God, man will desire and grasp at lordship over other men, and on the same presupposition other men will meet him with the same desiring and grasping.[61]

The sin of pride is the end of fellowship; the breach of peace with God is the breach of peace between humankind. Thus, in the Garden of Eden the man who had greeted the woman with that great cry of joyful recognition and solidarity, is now

[57] Augustine, *City of God*, xv, 5.
[58] Rist, *Augustine*, 191, quoting *In Epistolam Ioannis ad Parthos Tractatus*.
[59] K. Barth, *Church Dogmatics*, IV: 1, trans. G. Bromiley (Edinburgh, 1956), 413 and 432.
[60] Barth, *Church Dogmatics*, IV: 1, 485.
[61] Barth, *Church Dogmatics*, IV: 1, 436.

separated and isolated from her by both shame and mutual recrimination.[62]

If, then, to return to Augustine, 'Humility is highly prized in the City of God and especially enjoined on the City of God during the time of its pilgrimage in this world'[63] – if, that is to say, humility is the condition for genuine sociality, or true peace, to use Augustine's phrase – we can now make full sense of the privileging of this virtue, so to speak, in Benedict's *Rule* for 'life together'. But what shall we say of worship, which is accorded so central a place in this life?

Humility, we need to stress, is not merely a sentiment (using 'sentiment' in that vulgar modern sense, as naming a feeling or emotion which is essentially unrelated to beliefs about what is the case), but is fundamentally cognitive.[64] It is an expression, that is to say, of an understanding of the order of reality and one's place within it. Thus, according to Rist, for Augustine, humility:

has primarily two sorts of reference: to a recognition that man is not God but that he depends on God for his existence, and to a recognition that in his fallen state he needs the help of God's 'humility', God's being willing to serve others, as shown above all in the Incarnation. At bottom, humility is honesty about the human condition.[65]

But this 'honesty about the human condition' is, in a way which Rist does not here bring out, crucially determined by the fact that it arises from a hearing of God's 'Yes', and only within that 'Yes' of his 'No' – not a matter of man knowing his *need* of God's 'humility', but his knowing of the *actuality* of that humility. Arising thus, human humility cannot be a matter of 'discouragement or shame or humiliation',[66] but only of courage and joy. Founded on this understanding of the order of reality, it is a humility, that is to say, which answers the 'Yes' spoken by God in Jesus Christ, with its own 'Amen', this 'Amen' being, to borrow from a well-known title, 'the service of God' demanded

[62] Barth, *Church Dogmatics*, IV: 1, 466.
[63] Augustine, *City of God*, xiv, 13.
[64] For a treatment of some of the 'moral emotions' in these terms, see G. Taylor *Pride, Shame and Guilt* (Oxford, 1985).
[65] Rist, *Augustine*, 190.
[66] Barth, *Church Dogmatics*, IV: 1, 488.

by 'the knowledge of God'.[67] Thus, the order of reality which shapes humility makes it a humility which gives voice to worship. So of this worship we may affirm – whatever else we may need to add to this affirmation – that it is the practice which presupposes, is required by, expresses and instils, the understanding of the human condition enshrined in the virtue of humility.

The connections between the three elements of sociality, humility and worship in the *Rule of St Benedict* are to be understood, so I have argued, in the following way. The *Rule* makes humility the key virtue, for the sake of the common life: it is the overcoming of self-love on which depends the very possibility of the life of the City of God which, unlike the earthly city, realises a true peace. This humility is, however, at once expressed and formed by the community's worship. Worship is the practice appropriate to humility, and thus at the heart of its 'life together'. In worship, which occupies so much of its waking hours and so much of its energies, the monastic community stands properly before its creator, and standing properly before its creator, may stand in the right relationship to others, knowing them thus as *fellow* creatures.

V

Our diversion by way of St Benedict was intended to help us with the question which was raised by the practice of family life as commended by Bonhoeffer. If the family is a worshipping community, if it is in this that the 'claiming, seizure and formation' of this earthly domain consists, how is it that this practice accomplishes this 'seizing', and what, furthermore, will be the significance and consequence of its 'claiming'? How, in the light of this practice, may we conceive the mandate and commission which it is called to take up? Our answer, in the light of our dialogue with Bonhoeffer and Benedict, will be that the Christian family properly serves the state.

Put abstractly, this claim is not specifically Christian. After

---

[67] K. Barth, *The Knowledge of God and the Service of God* (London, 1938).

all, when Aristotle protested in Book II of the *Politics* against Plato's proposed abolition of the family (at least for his guardians), he did so not for the sake of the family, so to say, but for the sake of society – thus he might be contrasted with Schleiermacher who, picturing the privacy of the family as a haven from the vicissitudes of the public sphere, might be expected to use this as a ground for protecting the family from abolition on account of its being a private, not a public, good.[68]

Plato had proposed the abolition of the family (in Book V of the *Republic*) for the sake of the unity of the state. This unity, so he claims, will be best achieved when the words 'mine' and 'not mine' can be used by each citizen in reference to the same things; thus, men must share women, and women men, and the children will be 'mine' to all.[69] Aristotle objects in a variety of ways, but most interestingly by alleging that Plato's proposals will have quite the reverse effect from the one intended:

This community of wives and children seems better suited to the husbandmen than to the guardians, for if they have wives and children in common, they will be bound to one another by weaker ties, as a subject class should be, and they will remain obedient and not rebel. In a word, the result of such a law would be just the opposite of that which good laws ought to have, and the intention of Socrates in making these regulations about women and children would defeat itself. For friendship we believe to be the greatest good of states and the preservative of them against revolutions; neither is there anything which Socrates so greatly lauds as the unity of the state which he and all the world declare to be created by friendship . . . [But] in a state having women and children common, love will be watery; and the father will certainly not say 'my son', or the son 'my father'. As a little sweet wine mingled with a great deal of water is imperceptible in the mixture, so, in this sort of community, the idea of relationship which is based upon these names will be lost; there is no reason why the so-called father should care about the son, or the son about the father, or

[68] See F. Schleiermacher, *Predigten über den christlichen Hausstand*, trans. as *The Christian Household: A Sermonic Treatise*, D. Seidel and T. N. Tice (Lewiston, NY, 1991), 47: 'From this maze of activities, from this manifold of projects and precautionary measures, from this annoying commerce with all the vain and selfish emotions of a worldly muddled crowd, to where else can that person of piety withdraw who wants to keep tranquillity and peace of mind than, first of all, into the narrow circle of one's household.'

[69] Plato, *Republic*, trans. F. M. Cornford (Oxford, 1941), Book v, 464.

brothers about one another. Of the two qualities which chiefly inspire regard and affection, that a thing is your own and that you love it – neither can exist in such a state as this.[70]

According to Aristotle, friendship 'is both what holds the city together and the main reason for its existence'.[71] And since certain social structures are vital to the fostering of friendship, these structures must be maintained.

Aristotle's particular lesson about the role of marriage and family in cementing and unifying a state was one which Christians were not unwilling to learn: both Augustine and Aquinas, for example, justify exogamy as enlarging those affinities and ties on which human society depends.[72] But Aristotle's more general insight, that the family serves the state, is also one which was never lost to the Christian tradition. Thus we find W. Perkins in his *Christian Oeconomie: Or a Short Survey of the Right Manner of Erecting and Ordering a Family, According to the Scriptures* mindful that 'marriage was made and appointed by God himself to be the fountain and the seminary of all other sorts and kinds of life, in the Common-wealth and in the Church'.[73] And, according to George Herbert, the country parson makes 'his children . . . first Christians and then Commonwealth's men; the one he owes to his heavenly Country, the other to his earthly, having no title to either, except he do good to both.'[74]

The notion that the family serves the state is, however, given a particular twist in Christian thought, for the Christian family – the family, that is to say, which has been seized, claimed and formed by the Word of God – serves the state by witnessing, like other Christian communities, to it, but also thereby, against it. The sociability which it instantiates and propagates, that is to

[70] Aristotle, *The Politics*, translated B. Jowett (Oxford, 1905), Book II, iv.

[71] R. F. Stalley, 'Aristotle's Criticisms of Plato's *Republic*' in *A Companion to Aristotle's Politics*, ed. D. Keyt and F. D. Miller (Oxford, 1991), 193.

[72] Augustine, *City of God*, XV, 16 (see also, XIX, 16); St Thomas Aquinas, *Supplement* to *Summa Theologiae*, 3a, trans. Fathers of English Dominican Province (reprinted Westminster, MD, 1981), q. 54, art. 3.

[73] W. Perkins, *Christian Oeconomie: Or a Short Survey of the Right Manner of Erecting and Ordering a Family, According to the Scriptures* (Kingston, 1618), III.

[74] G. Herbert, *The Country Parson*, ed. J. Wall (New York, 1981), X.

say, has its own quality which renders its witness, judged from the outside, subversive.

So it is that Barth writes that:

> the decisive contribution which the Christian community can make to the upbuilding and work and maintenance of the civil consists in the witness which it has to give to it and to all human societies in the form of the order of its own upbringing and constitution. It cannot give in the world a direct portrayal of Jesus Christ, who is also the world's Lord and Saviour, or of the peace and freedom and joy of the kingdom of God. For it is itself only a human society moving like all others to His manifestation. But in the form in which it exists among them it can and must be to the world of men around it a reminder of the law of the kingdom of God already set up on earth in Jesus Christ, and a promise of its future manifestation. *De facto*, whether they realise it or not, it can and should show them that there is already on earth an order which is based on the great alteration of the human situation and directed towards its manifestation.[75]

But, since it shows them this alternative order, does not the Christian community thereby 'ask the pagan polis to remedy its state of disorder and make justice a reality'?[76] Certainly the monastery puts the world in question by its practice of hospitality ('let all guests that come be received like Christ'); by its repudiation of private property (a 'most wicked vice'); by its recognition of the prior claims of need ('before all things and above all things care must be taken of the sick'); and, ironically, by its witnessing to the possibility of a form of community which is not dependent on the natural ties of blood and kinship, but in which, transcending the possibilities and limitations of simple, human community, each calls the other 'brother' or 'father'.[77] And must we not say that the Christian family, formed as a Christian community, may itself take part in this attestation?

The most sustained and thorough modern reflection on the specific character of this attestation is found in what will perhaps prove to be the most significant body of moral theology

---

[75] Barth, *Church Dogmatics*, IV: 2, trans. G. Bromiley (Edinburgh, 1958), 721.

[76] Cited in E. Busch, *Karl Barth: His Life from Letters and Autobiographical Texts*, trans. J. Bowden (London, 1976), 216.

[77] *Rule of St. Benedict*, 53, 33, 36 and 63.

in the second half of the twentieth century, namely the writings of John Paul II. Two Apostolic Exhortations are particularly important for our concerns: *Familiaris Consortio*, an attempt to understand the 'apostolate of the family', and the later, but logically prior work, *Christifideles Laici*, a systematic reflection on the ministry of the laity built around, in what is now characteristically papal style, a particular text ('You go into the vineyard too'; Matthew, 20: 4) and its associated rich biblical imagery, of vine, branches and fruit.[78]

At the heart of both of these documents is an attempt to reflect upon the claim of Vatican II's *Lumen Gentium*, that through baptism the lay faithful are 'sharers in the priestly, prophetic and kingly office of Christ' and hence in the threefold ministry of the Church. According to *Familiaris Consortio*, the Christian family's participation in the Church's ministry can also be understood in these terms; indeed, though it speaks more generally of the family as essentially 'a community of life and love' and as having a fundamental mission 'to guard, reveal and communicate love',[79] it is in treating this participation in the life and mission of the Church – priestly, prophetic and kingly – that it seems to find the most fitting characterisation of the family.

The family, we are told, shares in the prophetic office of the Church as 'a believing and evangelising community'. It fulfils this role, 'by welcoming and announcing the word of God',[80] becoming thereby a genuine community of persons, united in love, hope and joy and thus 'a sign of the presence of Christ'.[81] It shares in the priestly office of the Church as 'a community in dialogue with God.' Grounded in baptism and the eucharist and in common prayer, renewed through repentance and united in its self-offering, the family consecrates itself and its life to God. And it shares in the kingly role of the Church as 'a community at the service of man'. It performs a particular

---

[78] John Paul II, *Familiaris Consortio*, English trans. (London, 1981); *Christifideles Laici*, English trans. (London, 1988). References will be to paragraph numbers.
[79] John Paul II, *Familiaris Consortio*, 17.
[80] John Paul II, *Familiaris Consortio*, 51.
[81] John Paul II, *Familiaris Consortio*, 54.

service in witnessing to what the Pope has called more recently 'the Gospel of life'.[82] But, in setting its face against the murderous rejection of children in abortion, it merely takes up one aspect of the general kingly mission which belongs to the people of God and which commits them to seek and serve 'justice, reconciliation, fraternity and peace among human beings'.[83] Thus 'in ordering creation to the authentic well-being of humanity, in an activity governed by the life of grace, they share in the exercise of the power with which the Risen Christ draws all things to himself and subjects them along with himself to the Father, so that God might be everything to everyone'.[84]

There are details in all this which would cause us more than a pause. We might not agree with the Pope's understanding of what the ordering of 'creation to the authentic well-being of humanity' means in relation to the practice of contraception, for example. We might want to be careful in specifying just how the Church, the lay faithful and the family share in Christ's priestly offering. We might hesitate at the account we find here of how the sacrament of marriage, in addition to the sacraments of baptism and eucharist, actually nourishes the couple in their Christian life. We might wish that the Pope had not allowed his passion and fervour to get the better of his theology when he tells us that 'the future of the world and the Church passes through the family' and apostrophises 'young men and women' as 'the future and hope of the Church and the world'.[85] But, when we have entered all such caveats, we have to say that taken together these two Exhortations represent a serious attempt to understand what it might be for the family to recollect itself, to live after the Spirit and not after the flesh, to envision itself in the light of the Gospel, and hence to fulfil that duty of attestation which belongs to the redeemed family as its vocation and mandate.

---

[82] John Paul II, *Evangelium Vitae*, English trans. (London, 1995).
[83] John Paul II, *Familiaris Consortio*, 48.
[84] John Paul II, *Christifideles Laici*, 14.
[85] John Paul II, *Familiaris Consortio*, 75 and 86.

VI

The land east of Eden is not simply a land in which humankind wills to live apart from God, but is the land in which creatures, living apart from God, live apart from and against each other. It is the 'far country' into which the prodigal goes – a land, that is to say, in which humankind finds not liberty, but only starvation and degradation and toil, for when one inhabitant turns in his or her need to another, as the prodigal turned 'to a citizen of that country', he or she is met, as the prodigal was met, with that utter denial of fellowship which sees in human neediness an opportunity for advantage – 'and the citizen of that country. . . sent him into his fields to feed swine' (Luke, 15: 15).

It is here, too, that the family dwells. It did not stay behind in Eden but entered this other land, the first sin of which, as Augustine reminds us, was the sin of Cain against Abel. This is a land in which brother struggles against brother (Jacob and Esau), in which father is set against son (Saul and Jonathan), and son against father (Absalom and David); in which the dream of one (Joseph), that he should take 'the role of the central monad before which all the others are destined to do obeisance',[86] is actually the dream of all.

The one who took upon himself the degradation and humiliation and suffering of life in the far country, that he might make, on behalf of humankind, the journey back to the Father which humankind would not, and could not, make, poses the question – 'who are my mother and my brothers?' With this question he invites us to doubt that about which the world is certain – the identity of his mother and his brothers – and invites us so to do on the basis of his sure knowledge of that about which the world is unsure – the identity of his Father. But the invitation to doubt is but a step towards the possibility of knowledge of the true order of things – 'Whoever does the will of my Father in heaven is my brother, and sister, and mother' (Mtatthew, 12: 50). For it is from this Father that 'every family in heaven and on earth is named' (Ephesians, 3: 15).

---

[86] Barth, *Church Dogmatics*, IV: 1, 433.

John Paul II writes in *Familiaris Consortio* that 'by praying with their children, by reading the Word of God with them and by introducing them deeply through Christian initiation into the Body of Christ – both the Eucharistic and the ecclesial body – they [parents] become fully parents, in that they are begetters not only of the bodily life but also of the life that through the Spirit's renewal flows from the Cross and Resurrection of Christ.'[87] Not fully, but for the first time – for if we take Jesus' question and answer with utter seriousness, we shall say that it is only where the family is called into question by the observance of the will of God that my mother and brothers can be my mother and brothers; that it is only where this question is asked and this answer received, that we are summoned from the degradation and humiliation and suffering of life in the far country, of which the creation of foundlings is but an aspect. All are summoned from this far country; but perhaps especially those who, humanly speaking, find themselves unable to give an answer to this question.

[87] John Paul II, *Familiaris Consortio*, 39.

CHAPTER 8

Five churches in search of sexual ethics[1]

As surely as God is faithful, our word to you has not been Yes and No. (2 Corinthians, 1: 18)

Unlike Paul's word to the Corinthians, the word of the House of Bishops of the Church of England in their statement entitled *Issues in Human Sexuality* certainly seems like Yes and No – or rather No and Yes.[2] For an attempt has been made to balance a fairly traditional approach to the problems of sexual ethics, and thus a fairly traditional critique of homosexual relationships, with a relatively tolerant pastoral policy. Thus, while the Bishops are 'unable to commend the [homophile] way of life . . . as in itself as faithful a reflection of God's purposes in creation as the heterophile', they 'do not reject those who sincerely believe it is God's call to them' (5.6) – though in their 'considered judgment the clergy cannot claim the liberty to enter into sexually active homophile relationships' (5.17).

In speaking this No and Yes, the Bishops can hardly have expected that their statement would be well received, no matter any merits it may have and no matter that they have spoken in moderate tones and evidently with a genuine pastoral concern. For with this No and Yes and the attempted mediation between two points of view, the statement is surely destined to satisfy the advocates of neither, who would prefer to hear Yes or No as the case may be, but certainly not both. Those, in other words, who

[1] I am grateful to Wolfram Kinzig, Markus Bockmuehl and John Lucas for their comments on a draft of this chapter.
[2] House of Bishops of the Church of England, *Issues in Human Sexuality: A Statement by the House of Bishops* (London, 1991). References to this statement will be to paragraph numbers, and will appear in the text.

welcome the initial critique of homosexual relationships are unlikely to welcome what seems to be the liberty which is allowed in practice, and those who welcome the liberty in practice are unlikely to welcome the initial critique. And, though these opposed camps will agree on little else, they will surely be united in portraying the distinction between clergy and laity as revealing intolerable tensions in the settlement proposed. Thus the statement will have an immediate appeal only to those who suppose that it is the historic destiny of the Church of England to stand roughly in the middle and between extremes, saying Yes and No, when to either side stand churches which say only the one or the other. And, certainly, the Church of England does stand in this position on this issue, judging from various statements and reports which have emerged recently from other denominations.

A clear and unequivocal No is spoken, for example, by the United States Catholic Conference in a conservative statement entitled *Human Sexuality* and issued in 1991.[3] It reaffirms traditional Roman Catholic teaching in the field of sexual ethics, says of 'homosexual genital activity' that it is 'immoral' and counsels the way of chastity as the only morally licit course for the homosexual.[4] On the other side, a Yes is spoken, for example, by the report of a Working Party of the United Reformed Church of 1991, entitled *Homosexuality: A Christian View* which 'is not prepared to describe homosexual activity as intrinsically sinful in principle' and so holds that the possibility of a homosexual relationship ought not to be denied even to ordained ministers.[5] Even more clearly and unequivocally the same word is proclaimed by the *Report of the Special Committee On Human Sexuality*, received, but not endorsed, by the General Assembly of the Presbyterian Church of the USA in 1991.[6] For, what the Working Party of the United Reformed Church put rather negatively (namely, we are 'not prepared to describe

[3] United States Catholic Conference, *Human Sexuality: A Catholic Perspective for Education and Lifelong Learning* (Washington, 1991).
[4] United States Catholic Conference, *Human Sexuality*, 55.
[5] United Reformed Church, *Homosexuality: A Christian View* (London, 1991), 5.
[6] The Report, with a response, is published by the Office of the General Assembly of the Presbyterian Church as *Presbyterians and Human Sexuality* (Louisville, 1991).

homosexual activity as intrinsically sinful in principle'), the Presbyterian Special Committee states unambiguously and positively: 'Coming of age about sexuality requires affirming a diversity of responsible sexualities in the church, including the lives of gay men and lesbians.'[7] Only with the *Report of the Commission on Human Sexuality*, presented to the Methodist Conference in 1990, do we find a church occupying much the same ground, it seems, as that on which the Bishops of the Church of England stand.[8] But even then there is a difference: for, whereas the statement from the Bishops says No and Yes, the report from the Methodist Commission says neither Yes nor No, since it declines to rule on the question of whether physical homosexual relationships are sinful and should be held to constitute a bar to the ordained ministry.

Were the Bishops right to speak their distinctive No and Yes – right, that is to say, on the basis of some coherent moral theology, rather than simply as expressing the supposed genius of the Anglican church for seeing the two sides of every issue? In order to answer that broad question we must first answer some others. Specifically, we must ask if the statement's critique of homosexual relationships is warranted, and thus is to be preferred to the agnosticism of the Methodist statement and to the acceptance of homosexual relationships implied in the report from the Working Party of the United Reformed Church and proclaimed in the report from the Special Committee of the Presbyterian Church. If it is not warranted, then there is little more to say. If, however, it is, then we must ask why this No is balanced with a Yes – whether, in other words, the Bishops are right, over against the Roman Catholic Bishops of the USA, to allow the liberty of practice which they allow to the laity. And then we must further ask whether this liberty, if properly allowed to the laity, is properly denied to the clergy.

'[H]omophile orientation and its expression in sexual activity', so the Anglican Bishops claim, 'do not constitute a parallel and alternative form of human sexuality as complete within the terms of the created order as the heterosexual' (5.2).

[7] General Assembly of the Presbyterian Church, *Presbyterians and Human Sexuality*, 5.
[8] Methodist Conference, *Report of the Commission on Human Sexuality* (Peterborough, 1990).

Again, 'Heterosexuality and homosexuality are not equally congruous with the observed order of creation or with the insights of revelation as the Church engages with these in the light of her pastoral ministry' (5.2). Now I have referred to this side of the Bishops' statement as expressing a No, but the more we study what is said here, the more we wonder what exactly is meant, and we can only wish that the Bishops had been more frank. When they tell us that heterosexuality and homosexuality are not 'equally congruous' with the order of creation and with revelation, do they mean to say that homosexuality is not equally congruous because it is simply not congruous at all? When they tell us that homosexuality is a less complete form of sexuality than heterosexuality do they not mean to say that homosexuality is incomplete? Do they mean, in other words, to say No clearly and unambiguously, or do they mean instead the rather more equivocal No which their words might be taken to suggest? Perhaps they feared that an unequivocal No would have sounded too harsh, and certainly had the Bishops said their No thus, rather than as ambiguously as they have, it would probably have been taken to be denying what ought not to be denied, and what they doubtless had no intention of denying, namely that homosexual relationships can instantiate qualities of faithfulness and commitment altogether lacking in many heterosexual unions. Or perhaps they were not sure whether they really meant their No, for certainly the case they make on its behalf, as it stands, lacks sufficient force to justify it fully.

Their case against the acceptance of homosexual relationships as 'in all respects on a par with heterosexual marriage' (5.17) rests, so it is alleged, on insights drawn from revelation and from the order of creation. Now on the matter of the meaning of scriptural texts, the Bishops seem to take a traditional line. In the Scriptures, so they say, 'Sexual activity of any kind outside marriage comes to be seen as sinful, and homosexual practice as especially dishonourable' (2.29).

We might quibble with the details of their account, and with the rather uninspired approach to the Scriptures in general, but the main point to note is that the Bishops appear to be discounting the recent wave of radical exegesis which denies that the central biblical texts bear the meaning they attribute to them, exegesis which has clearly weighed with the authors of the reports from the Methodist, United Reformed and Presbyterian churches. This exegesis holds either that there is no condemnation of homosexual relationships as such in the New Testament, but only of 'homosexual acts committed by apparently heterosexual persons' (thus Boswell in *Christianity, Social Tolerance and Homosexuality*[9] on the first chapter of Romans), or that there is condemnation but only of homosexual relationships of a very specific, and specifically exploitative and promiscuous, sort (thus Scroggs in *The New Testament and Homosexuality*[10]).

In rejecting this exegesis, and in holding that according to the New Testament 'homosexual practice is dishonourable', the Bishops find themselves in good company. The noted Pauline scholar E. P. Sanders, for example, though not averse to radical reinterpretation of scriptural texts, maintains in his recent book *Paul* that both 1 Corinthians, 6: 9 and Romans, 1: 26f. do indeed represent, as has usually been thought, clear condemnations of homosexual practice.[11] But, having taken this clearly defensible line, the Bishops go on to observe that the 'biblical consensus presents us with certain problems' (2.29). In particular 'we need to note', they say, 'the question raised by Paul's aetiology of homosexual practice' (2.28). Now they do not specify at this point in the statement what this question is, but in the Introduction they have posed the general hermeneutical issue which is surely troubling them here: 'What are the consequences for scriptural interpretation of critical scholarship or new scientific knowledge or new sensitivities arising from changing experience?' (1.3) In this instance the question which they seem to have in mind takes the following form: if Paul did not know of the fact of homosexual orientation as a, so to say, given condition, does his 'blanket' condemnation of homosexual

---

[9] J. Boswell, *Christianity, Social Tolerance and Homosexuality* (Chicago, 1980), ch. 4.

[10] R. Scroggs, *The New Testament and Homosexuality* (Philadelphia, 1983).

[11] E. P. Sanders, *Paul* (Oxford, 1991), 110–13, and see also R. B. Hays, 'Relations Natural and Unnatural: A Response to John Boswell's Exegesis of Romans 1', *Journal of Religious Ethics*, 14 (1986), 184–215.

practice, to use Sanders' word, have any bearing on current ethical deliberations? It is a pity that, having alluded to this question and having noted 'the problem we face in seeking light from Scripture in this complex area of human sexuality' (2.28), the Bishops do not venture an answer. For, when we are assured at the close of the chapter entitled 'Scripture and Human Sexuality' that the 'biblical consensus . . . is quite clearly the foundation on which the Church's traditional teaching is built' (2.29), we are left in some doubt as to whether the Bishops suppose these foundations to be of sand or of rock. It is clear, that is to say, that according to the Bishops' reading of Scripture, homosexuality is less congruous with the insights of revelation than heterosexuality, but unclear whether these insights really are insights in their eyes and thus whether lack of congruity with them should cause us any concern.[12]

In answer to the question they implicitly pose, the Bishops could have made the following points. In the passage in question, in the first chapter of the Epistle to the Romans, Paul views homosexual behaviour as a particular manifestation of the general moral blindness which afflicts humankind as a result of its 'primal rebellion' against God.[13] It is because of this rejection of God that pagans have 'exchanged natural relations for unnatural'. In this sense, then, Paul has 'an aetiology of homosexual practice', though it is not to be supposed, however, that this mythic aetiology is in any sense in competition, as it were, with contemporary scientific theories of homosexual orientation, genetic, Freudian or whatever. As a matter of fact, Paul's picture, which involves 'a corporate indictment of pagan society, and not a narrative about the "rake's progress" of particular individuals',[14] is perfectly compatible with any one of these scientific theories and thus with an aetiology of homo-

[12] For a slightly more detailed treatment of the exegetical controversy see my 'Directions and Misdirections in Christian Sexual Ethics: A Survey of Recent Books' in *The Epworth Review*, 19 (1992), 95–108. The debate is placed in a wider and more adequate context in my essay on 'Sexualität' in *Theologische Realenzyklopädie* (Berlin, forthcoming).

[13] Hays, 'Relations Natural and Unnatural', 189.

[14] Hays, 'Relations Natural and Unnatural', 200.

sexual practice which makes reference, as his does not, to the state or condition of being a homosexual. Further, since as the Bishops themselves note in a later chapter, 'neither a genetic nor a psychological explanation for a person's condition can itself say whether a condition is good or bad, nor does a genetic origin mark a particular condition as in accordance with the undistorted will of God' (4.2), it is plain that the question of the aetiology of homosexual practice has no decisive bearing on the debate as to the morality of that practice. Thus, if 'we need to note the question raised by Paul's aetiology of homosexual practice' – namely, can the biblical consensus be taken seriously given the supposedly deficient scientific knowledge of Paul and others? – we need to do so only to note also that the question can be answered with a clear and unequivocal Yes.

Had the Bishops thus answered the question which is raised by implication in their treatment of the Scriptures, they would have spoken with greater clarity than they have on the significance of the congruence, or lack of it, between homosexuality and the 'insights of revelation'. They might also have seen the link between their examination of the scriptural prohibitions and the more broadly theological issues to which they properly devote some attention. For the real question to be put to the 'biblical consensus', as they call it, is surely a question about the availability or otherwise of a theological anthropology which makes sense of it and so renders the prohibition of homosexual relationships, theologically speaking, meaningful.

No matter that they do not explicitly make the link between the scriptural and the theological investigations, it is to questions of theological anthropology that the Bishops turn after their treatment of the Scriptures, alleging here a lack of congruence between homosexuality and 'the observed order of creation' (5.2). But although this is the right issue to introduce at this point, it has to be said that their handling of it is less than assured theologically, as I shall presently explain.

Assured or not, the treatment of the concept of the order of creation ought to be welcomed as at the very least indicating a sense of the importance of a theme in Christian ethics which the present era is inclined to forget. For a Christian ethics which takes seriously the fact that the Gospel of Jesus Christ is a gospel of the world's redemption, and not of escape from it, cannot but inquire with the utmost seriousness as to the nature and form of the order of creation which it was God's will not only to create but also to redeem. And it cannot but treat this order as morally significant, holding that it is part of the Christian life to live obediently and joyfully in the God given order for which Christ died and rose.[15]

There is much more to be said, much of which will, no doubt, be controversial, but we can quite confidently assert that Christian ethics in general, and Christian sexual ethics in particular, ought not to avoid an engagement, such as the Bishops attempt, with the theological issues here at stake.

Unfortunately, the other reports to which I have referred, with the exception of the statement from the Roman Catholic Bishops, seem unaware of the issue, as if the doctrine of creation, and more specifically the doctrine of humankind, are remote from the ethical questions which are their primary concern. Thus, the statement from the Working Party of the United Reformed Church has nothing to say on this subject, just as the report presented to the Methodist Conference seems to suppose it has exhausted relevant theological material when it has treated all but only those biblical passages which make rather obvious mention of questions of sexual conduct, going on at once to sections dealing with sociological, biological and psychological studies of the subject. How are we to explain the disregard for what we might have expected to be found interesting in a Church report, namely the *theological* study of the subject? One suspects that here the authors are guilty of a rather narrow 'biblicism' which they would doubtless condemn in some of its other manifestations, for they seem not to understand that there might be purpose in studying the Bible not just for its rather infrequent specific references to issues of

---

[15] This theme is, of course, especially important, if not always obviously so, in the ethics of Brunner, Barth and Bonhoeffer. In Bonhoeffer's *Ethics*, for example, it is found in his treatment of what he calls 'the penultimate' in a chapter entitled 'The Last Things and the Things Before the Last'. The most important contemporary treatment of this theme and of its significance for Christian ethics in general is found in Oliver O'Donovan's *Resurrection and Moral Order* (Leicester, 1986).

sexual ethics, but for the sake of an altogether broader theological anthropology. Were the Presbyterian report to be judged by its rhetoric and not by its substance then it could be supposed that it reveals a degree of insight on this matter. It has some fine sounding phrases which might unwittingly be taken to indicate a proper regard for the importance of theological anthropology – there is talk, for example, of 'God's gift of sexuality in creation' and an insistence that 'we ought not to call "bad" what God has called "good"'.[16] But, like so much in this report, these words are revealed as mere rhetoric as soon as we begin to look for evidence that their sentiments have found thoughtful application. For the authors of this report have not stopped to ask the crucial question as to the exact nature or character of 'God's gift of sexuality in creation'. And, since they have not asked and answered this question, their commitment to 'the full flourishing of all creation' can only be regarded as, morally speaking, vacuous. For how will we know what this 'flourishing' consists in if we do not first establish what is proper to the created order as created? Does sexual differentiation, for example, belong essentially to God's gift? As far as one can tell, the report seems to suppose that it does not, preferring instead to speak of an abstract sexuality which is unshaped by sexual differentiation and the created relatedness which sexual differentiation implies. Indeed, it suspects that all attempts to accord significance to sexual differentiation are forms of 'patriarchal heterosexism', which is said to depend crucially on what are clearly taken to be the mistaken notions of the 'romanticised fusions of "two persons in one"', and of a 'gender dualism, in which neither partner functions sexually or socially as a fully integrated person, but rather as a fragmented complementary half'.[17]

According to Karl Barth's rather more serious engagement with the doctrine of creation in volume 3 of *Church Dogmatics*, what God has called good is humankind created, as he puts it, as fellow-man, and that primarily in the relationship of man

[16] General Assembly of the Presbyterian Church, *Presbyterians and Human Sexuality*, 76.
[17] General Assembly of the Presbyterian Church, *Presbyterians and Human Sexuality*, 26 and 15.

and woman. To be created in the image of God means for the Book of Genesis, so Barth alleges, to be created male and female, and it is in the creation of woman, with and for the man, that both creation accounts see the completion and perfection of God's work. Furthermore, he argues, we can assert (on the strength not only of the Book of Genesis but also on the basis of the rest of the Old and New Testaments which find such meaning and significance in the man/woman relationship) that it is in the duality of male and female that humankind is determined in its creaturely being as the covenant-partner of God; that is to say, that this earthly determination of humankind as man and woman corresponds to the divine determination of humankind for covenant with God. So that 'the fact that [man] was created and exists as male and female will . . . prove to be not only a copy and imitation of his creator as such, but at the same time a type of the history of the covenant and salvation which will take place between him and his creator'.[18] And since here and typically God 'commands [man] to be what he is', it only 'remains for [him] to confirm this natural dualism'.[19]

Barth's account of what belongs essentially to God's good creation requires careful and critical study, but it requires neither careful nor critical study to see that, over against the position adopted in the Presbyterian report, we have here an attempt to allow the doctrine of creation to shape an approach to the problems of sexual ethics. With its disparaging references to the 'romanticised fusions of "two persons in one"', the Presbyterian report, by contrast, reveals an indebtedness not to the main themes of theological thought but to the presuppositions of a popular and thoroughgoing individualism which balks at the idea that men and women are made for fellowship and thus are, as individuals and alone, in some sense incomplete. Once we note this indebtedness we shall hardly be surprised by what ought otherwise to surprise us in this report, such as its stressing of the need for 'positive affirmation of the role of

[18] K. Barth, *Church Dogmatics*, III: 1, trans. J. Edwards et al. (Edinburgh, 1958), 186 7.
[19] K. Barth, *Church Dogmatics*, III: 4, trans. A. T. Mackay et al. (Edinburgh, 1961), 116 and 121.

masturbation in human sexuality'.[20] For, whereas masturbation is not and cannot be characteristic of *human* sexuality – supposing, that is, that that adjective is understood theologically rather than sociologically and thus as referring to our essential relatedness – but only of human alienation, individualism will quite naturally regard it as altogether the most normal, and indeed perhaps the most satisfactory, form of sexual expression.

For all the encouraging phrases which suggest a concern for the flourishing of creation, it turns out then, that the Presbyterian report really has no such concern since it has no conception of what belongs to the created order and what does not. The implications of this fact for the treatment of the problems of sexual ethics is made abundantly clear to the thoughtful reader, albeit not to the report's authors, by the repeated contention that 'Homosexuality . . . should be approached as a justice issue',[21] for whatever this means, it is quite plainly an eschewal of what a proper respect for the doctrine of creation tells us is primary, namely the question of the conformity of this or any other form of human sexuality to the order in which God created us.

Happily, the Bishops' statement knows of the ethical importance of these questions about the congruence between homosexual relationships and 'the order of creation'. It is unfortunate, however, that it treats them less than adequately, and in particular in a curiously untheological manner. Here we might make a criticism which applies equally to the statement from the Roman Catholic Conference of the United States. That statement starts promisingly enough with the claim that 'The mystery of what it means to be human incarnate, embodied, and therefore sexual is bound up in the mystery and purpose of God, who is the author of all life, and love itself.'[22] But, if this is right – if the mystery of what it is to be human is bound up in the mystery and purpose of God, and thus bound up with knowledge of Christ in whom 'all things were created' and 'are hid all the treasures of wisdom and knowledge' (Colos-

---

[20] General Assembly of the Presbyterian Church, *Presbyterians and Human Sexuality*, 33.
[21] General Assembly of the Presbyterian Church, *Presbyterians and Human Sexuality*, 53.
[22] United States Catholic Conference, *Human Sexuality*, 7.

sians 1: 16; 2: 3) – then our anthropological inquiry must be quite consciously and consistently theological. 'Your life is hid with Christ in God' (Colossians, 3: 3), and, if so hid, will not be revealed to those who look elsewhere for wisdom. And yet both the Anglican Bishops and the Roman Catholic Conference seem to prefer the altogether more shaky ground of philosophical speculation to the *terra firma* of theological knowledge. There is in the Roman Catholic document, for example, no sustained development of the theological anthropology on which sexual ethics should be based, though there are hints on the basis of which a beginning might be made. All too often it seems that the Bishops are more ready to trust 'those basic moral laws inscribed in the human heart and conscience' rather than specifically theological wisdom. Similarly the Bishops of the Church of England, as we shall see, seek to answer a question which they have properly phrased in theological terms (about the congruence between homosexuality and the order of creation) by way of inquiry which forgets its theological bearings and wonders about the congruence between homosexuality and the order of nature, an order which they take to be naturally known. It is this shift which explains why here too, as in the treatment of Scripture, the No of this statement is less than fully convincing.

According to the Bishops, 'moral theology employs [the word "natural"] to describe those types of human conduct which are in harmony with the will of God as discernible from creation as opposed to those which violate that will and which are "unnatural"' (4.13). Now there is a certain ambiguity in what is meant here by 'discernible from creation'. Does the discernment of the natural presuppose a true knowledge of God's creative will (and thus knowledge of Jesus Christ), or is this discernment independent, so to speak, of such revealed knowledge and hence itself purely natural knowledge? The ambiguity is, however, resolved in favour of the latter option – and so in agreement with the approach of the Roman Catholic Bishops – judging from the example and argument which follow. Thus, as an example of moral discernment, we are told that it is unnatural in this sense to tell a lie, 'because if God created a world in which accurate communication is possible we may properly assume that his overall purpose was to enable us to give and receive the truth' (4.13). And then, applying the same style of argument to the issue in hand, it is noted that human sexuality serves the purposes of procreation and that 'it would be highly unreasonable to argue that it was not the will of a creator that this should be so' (4.14). It is noted, furthermore, that only the interaction of male and female genital organs makes procreation possible, so 'that too must be part of God's purpose for at least the great majority of humankind' (4.14). The conclusion follows, that 'In short the biological evidence is at least compatible with a theological view that heterosexual physical union is divinely intended to be the norm' (4.14).

Whether or not this argument is persuasive, its point is by no means obvious. For the argument's conclusion, which is so very modest, is not the one that we were surely led to expect and seems to be presupposed at later points in the statement, namely that homosexuality is unnatural and thus contrary to the will of God. It is the much weaker conclusion that the biological evidence is compatible with a theological view which regards heterosexual relationships as the norm. This is a weak conclusion in two senses. In the first place, as I have said, it is not identical with the claim that homosexuality is contrary to the will of God, since quite clearly not everything which is contrary to a 'divine' norm, or 'abnormal', is unnatural in the sense of being contrary to the will of God – as the Bishops recognise in the case of some lies and would surely acknowledge in the case of celibacy, for example. We should thus need further argument to show that homosexual relations are, as a matter of fact, contrary to the will of God. But it is a weak conclusion in a second respect, in that it claims only that the biological evidence is *compatible* with the view that heterosexual unions are to be regarded as the norm. In other words, it seems to allow that there may be other ways of specifying the norm which are consistent with the biological evidence. Perhaps the evidence is compatible with the view, for example, that the divinely intended norm is procreative heterosexual union, or perhaps with the view, since successful procreative sexual inter-course is so uncommon, that non-procreative sexual activity, heterosexual or otherwise, is the norm. So even the weak contention that homosexual relationships are contrary to the norm is, according to the sort of argument the Bishops seem to advance, only weakly supported by the evidence.

If it is thus that we are to discern the will of God in the created order, then we might fairly judge the project to be unfruitful. Certainly we should conclude that this dim, faint and insecure discernment of God's will in relation to human sexuality by no means warrants the No to homosexual relationships which the Bishops seem to pronounce on the basis of this argument combined with the evidence from Scripture. But then we should also say that the Bishops might have spoken more clearly if they had developed and relied upon the theological anthropology at which they hint and had not relied for guidance on purely philosophical argument. If the ordering of the male to the female and vice versa is known as the will of God for humankind – and not just as a 'norm' – it is known as such not apart from the theological sphere, but in this very sphere. It is known, in other words, if it is known, in the light of an anthropology such as that explored with great profundity by Barth in his magisterial treatment of the doctrine of creation – which is to say that the Bishops were right to raise a question about the congruence between homosexuality and the created order, but wrong to try to answer it in the manner they have. Had they taken a different route their No would, perhaps, have been more adequately supported.

The Bishops' No to homosexual relationships in the section of their report which constitutes a theoretical treatment of sexual ethics seems both equivocal and, as regards the argument presented in the statement, unwarranted. Now it has to be said of the Yes to homosexual relationships, in the section of the report which contains recommendations for pastoral practice, that it, too, is an equivocal word. The question which critics have addressed to this section of the statement is why, having said No in theory, the Bishops seem to pronounce a Yes in practice, at least for the laity? And why, if for the laity, not for the clergy too? But under examination the seeming tensions between the two sections of the statement, and between the treatment of clergy and laity, dissolve. For this Yes is not really a Yes: all that the statement says, in effect, is that where in good conscience a person disagrees with the teaching of the Church and its call to abstinence, and chooses instead to live in a committed homosexual relationship, such a person should not be excluded from the fellowship of the Church; thus, 'while unable, therefore, to commend the [homophile] way of life . . . as in itself as faithful a reflection of God's purposes in creation as the heterophile, we do not reject those who sincerely believe it is God's call to them' (5.6). It is impossible for the Church, we have been told, 'to come with integrity to any other conclusion' than that homosexual relationships do not 'constitute a parallel and alternative form of human sexuality as complete within the terms of the created order as the heterosexual' (5.2). But, while believing this, and in consequence that a call to homosexuality cannot be the call of the God of this created order, the Bishops none the less believe that someone can, in good faith, believe otherwise, albeit mistakenly, and should not be rejected if they do so believe and act upon that belief.

Such a conclusion will not, of course, satisfy the critics of traditional teaching. Even an earlier report from a Working Party of the Board for Social Responsibility, entitled *Homosexual Relationships*, seems more radical in holding that sexual abstinence is too demanding a requirement to place on all those of homosexual orientation and that in certain circumstances 'individuals may justifiably choose to enter into a homosexual relationship'.[23] In the present statement, there is no suggestion that this choice is justifiable, but only that those who have taken a morally wrong decision ought not for that reason to be 'rejected', to repeat the word used in the statement. But, since the Church of England neither excommunicates nor, in effect, imposes any penitential discipline on what it takes to be its erring members, the promise not to reject homosexuals seems to add nothing to existing practice, unless we take it as a welcome signal of a determination to ensure that practising homosexuals are not singled out for the more informal 'disci-

---

[23] Board for Social Responsibility of the Church of England, *Homosexual Relationship: A Contribution to Discussion* (London, 1979), 52.

pline' which certain congregations no doubt exercise in excluding some from fellowship.

Once we understand that the Yes to the laity is not really a Yes, the No to the clergy is not in the least contradictory. For, in holding that conscientious dissent may or must be tolerated from the laity, the Bishops are not obliged to hold that such dissent may or must be tolerated amongst the clergy, for the clergy stand in a different relationship to the teachings of the Church, with a particular commission and obligation to expound those teachings. Thus their dissent on a matter which is judged central to the life and witness of the Church places them in an invidious position, which perhaps neither they nor the Church should tolerate. This is not a matter of the religious being subject to counsels of perfection which do not apply to the laity, for the Bishops do not say that it is right for the laity to have homosexual relationships and wrong for the clergy, but only that where the clergy have such relationships they, unlike the laity, create a scandal which consists in the fact that one whose authority is derived from the authority of the Church challenges that very authority.

To say that the distinction which the Bishops make between the clergy and laity, far from being absurd, has more than a little to commend it, is not to say that there are no further questions which might properly be raised about the stance they adopt. Obviously not every disagreement with what the Bishops call 'the mind of the Church on matters of faith and life', even where the disagreement is open, constitutes a matter of such seriousness as to place a dissenting member of the clergy in a questionable position, and we obviously need some principles which will allow us to make requisite distinctions. One might have thought, for example, that dissent from the articles of the creed is manifestly more scandalous to the Church than is dissent on matters of sexual ethics, notwithstanding that the world judges otherwise. But then, if disagreement about sexual ethics often rests, as I have suggested, on disagreement about, or forgetfulness of, Christian doctrine, perhaps dissent on this issue is, in fact, equally scandalous.

Those who are commissioned and authorised by the Church

to proclaim its teachings cannot simultaneously claim the right to dissent from those teachings. If that is the rationale underlying the distinction in pastoral practice as between clergy and laity, then the Bishops should not have allowed sentences to creep into the statement which suggest, at least *prima facie*, another, and less satisfactory, rationale. At times it really does seem as if the Bishops are endorsing two standards: 'From the time of the New Testament onwards it has been expected of those appointed to the ministry of authority in the Church that they shall not only preach but also live the Gospel' (5.13) – as if the Church expects of the laity only that they should hear but not also live that same Gospel. Such an objectionable notion can surely not have been seriously entertained by the Bishops, and it is regrettable that they did not expunge the sentences which might be taken to suggest it.

In effect, *Issues in Human Sexuality* is a report of a Working Party and the joins, so to say, are bound to show from time to time. The very same comment could be made about the other reports mentioned here, though not of the statement from the Roman Catholic Conference, which has a greater fluency and coherence than is found in the others. This is, of course, probably explained by the fact that the Roman Catholic Church has a rather distinctive notion of what it is to establish the 'mind of the Church', and one more likely, perhaps, to guarantee consistency and clarity if not necessarily truth. This is not the place to adjudicate between the competing notions, but this much should be said: that Working Parties can too easily confuse the task of establishing the mind of the Church with that of reporting what is in the minds of church people. And then there is an inclination to say Yes *and* No on a particular issue, not because this is what Scripture, reason and tradition demand, but because this is what the spirit of the age demands. But, where this occurs, the Church is no longer in search of sexual ethics, but has given up the search in a faithless despair at possessing here or elsewhere what is its promised inheritance – the mind of Christ.

CHAPTER 9

Prolegomena to a dogmatic sexual ethic

I

Christian ethics is Christian ethics in so far as it is dogmatic –
that is, in so far as it allows its form and content to be shaped by,
and tested against, the affirmations of Christian doctrine.[1]
More fully we may maintain that Christian ethics is founded
upon and arises from the threefold knowledge of God and
humankind as creator and creature, reconciler and sinner,
redeemer and heir of God's good future, given in the life, death
and resurrection of Jesus Christ. Thus it is the task of Christian
ethics to understand the claiming of humankind which is
implicit within its gracious election as a threefold imperative;
specifically Christian ethics may speak of the Gospel of Christ
as containing within itself the threefold command of God the
creator, the reconciler and the redeemer. As the command of
the creator, the command of God commands us to be what we
are. As the command of the reconciler, the command of God is
directed against the disorder of our present existence. As the
command of the redeemer, the command of God directs us to
the good future which God intends, and thus to what we shall
be.[2]

Christian sexual ethics, to turn to the subject of this chapter,
will properly be developed on the basis of this self-understanding,

[1] I am grateful for comments from participants at a conference on Ethics and the
Doctrine of God at King's College when this paper was given in an early version. I
also benefited from discussion when I lectured at the Evangelisch-Theologisches
Seminar, in the University of Bonn.
[2] This conception of the nature of Christian ethics, learnt from Karl Barth, is explained
and defended in chapter 1.

learning, that is to say, to understand and represent life in this sphere as determined by knowledge of the claim made upon us by the grace of God shown in Jesus Christ. It will thus expound three principal theses, displaying Christian sexual ethics as the command of the creator addressed to the creature, as the command of the reconciler addressed to the sinner, and as the command of the redeemer addressed to the heir of God's good future. The task of this chapter will be to give an indication, albeit a preliminary one, of the character and shape of a sexual ethic which understands itself thus, and also thereby to differentiate that ethic from those non-Christian or avowedly Christian codes, which do not pose and answer the question of sexual ethics within this dogmatic framework.

II

Our first thesis then, is that, in knowing humankind as creatures of a good creator, Christian sexual ethics will affirm, as Barth has it, that the ethical question in this sphere is 'essentially a question of things that are natural and right'.[3] With this affirmation sexual ethics is recalled to an important element of its proper task: the discernment and proclamation of what we are as the initial word of God's command in the realm of sexual ethics.

For this claim and its implications to be fully understood, however, we shall need to do two things. First of all, we shall seek to identify and understand the explicit or implicit denial within sexual ethics of the authority of the 'natural' against which the thesis sets its face; here we identify objections to the very concept, or to its authority, arising from metaphysics or, more commonly, from metaethics. We shall look at each of the denials in turn as they manifest themselves both in secular and supposedly Christian forms. In the second place, we shall give attention to the problem of the discernment or characterisation of the natural which obviously arises for any ethic which asserts its authority; here we shall have cause to maintain that this

---

[3] K. Barth, *Church Dogmatics*, III: 4, trans. A. T. Mackay et al. (Edinburgh, 1961), 120.

discernment is properly a theological task, since what is known as natural cannot, as a matter of fact, be securely naturally known.

The metaphysical denial of an authoritative nature is hardly surprising in secular thinkers who may be expected to take what Hans Jonas refers to as 'the Darwinian view', in which:

man bears no eternal 'image' but is part of universal, and in particular of biological, 'becoming'. His 'being' as it actually turned out is the unintended (and variable) product of unconcerned forces whose prolonged interplay with circumstances have 'evolution' for their joint effect but nothing (not even evolution as such) for their aim . . . He is an accident, sanctioned merely by success.[4]

To be sure, even on this view of things, the secular thinker is unlikely to eschew all talk of human nature or to disallow reference to this nature in ethical deliberation, though it will probably be spoken of with nothing more than a certain matter of factness. He or she may even admit that this nature must continue to shape, as it surely has shaped, human sexual relations in general and the institution of marriage, let us say, in particular. After all, it would be no more sensible to recommend a pattern for marriage which ignored the 'laws of human nature' (the fact of limited human altruism, for example, that men and women often want children, and so on) than to write a sex manual which ignored the laws of gravity. But, just as the respect that we accord to laws of nature is only the grudging respect which we accord to necessity, so too the respect which is here accorded to the laws of human nature will be no more than that; and in so far as it is feasible to contemplate the reform of the so-called laws of human nature it will indeed be less than that. Thus, far from human nature being thought of as a given which demands our respect, it will come to be conceived of as no more, perhaps, than a too resistant matter which may be subjected as we see fit and are able, to our projects and plans. Of course, as we have said, anthropology will still have a place in ethics, since we may be obliged to accept what is humanly natural for present purposes and build human

[1] H. Jonas, 'Contemporary Problems in Ethics from a Jewish Perspective' in *Philosophical Essays* (Chicago, 1974), 170.

relationships accordingly; but, given this metaphysical position, there is no reason why we should not, at the same time conspire to fashion a humanity rid of these fetters. To halt, or even to pause, at this boundary out of reverence for human nature is to accord to human nature a status it does not deserve; the notion of reverence for human nature is thus to be assigned to the very category to which James Rachels assigns 'the idea of human dignity' which is, he alleges, 'the moral effluvium of a discredited metaphysics'.[5]

Alongside the denial in metaphysics of an authoritative nature, we must also place the denial of such a nature which comes from meta-ethics or moral philosophy, and which is advanced, at least implicitly, by consequentialism with its refusal to allow moral significance to actions in and of themselves. Consequentialism holds, of course, as its name suggests,

---

[5] J. Rachels, *Created From Animals: The Moral Implications of Darwinism* (Oxford, 1990), 5. Something of the difficulties for sexual ethics which flow from the metaphysical repudiation of the moral significance of human nature is revealed in Thomas Nagel's 'Sexual Perversion', *The Journal of Philosophy*, 66 (1969), 5–17. Nagel sets to one side the emotivist analysis of the use of the concept of 'perversion' as simply expressing disgust (since the fact that something is perverted is usually offered as an explanation of the disgust, not as simply another way of expressing it) and considers what other analysis might be offered. He seeks to understand perversion as a failing of sexual activity to satisfy a particular condition found in 'paradigm cases of sexual desire', namely that in such cases there is a complex relation between the perceptions of the partners, whereby the perception of another as desirable is associated with that other's perception of being desired and of the first's perception of the other as perceiving that s/he is desired, and so on. Where such complex reciprocity of awareness and intention is impossible or at least unlikely (such as would be the case, says Nagel, in bestiality or paedophilia) then we have instances of perversion, but where it is perfectly possible (as with homosexuality, oral sex and so on) we do not. This is not the place to engage fully with Nagel's argument, but we should note the central difficulty with it, which Nagel does not seek to conceal. What is the significance, morally speaking, of the fact that not all sexual activity instantiates a characteristic which Nagel finds in what he terms 'paradigm cases of mutual desire'? The problem is just that the presuppositions required to ground a *moral* theory of perversion are not ones which a secular thinker typically wants to embrace. Of course, the secular thinker can offer an account of what is deemed to constitute paradigmatic sexual activity, but the authority of such an account remains in question. But then what we might think of as the trials of the liberal conscience will begin, since a need will probably be felt to go further than one does in describing paedophilia as simply less 'paradigmatic' than other types of sexual activity. But to go further one will probably have either to rely on certain empirical claims (such as that paedophilia is always coercive) which may or may not be true, or illicitly to assume the normative assumptions which were supposedly eschewed (for example that paedophilia is wrong just because it prevents the development of 'normal' sexual relations).

that actions are good or bad, right or wrong, solely in virtue of their consequences and, further, that in any given situation the best action is that one which maximises whatever are identified as good consequences. No action is, in itself, right or wrong, be it breaking a promise, telling a lie, or being unfaithul to a friend. In themselves these actions are, so to say, morally neutral. It is only in the light of their particular consequences that they take on an ethical character. But if this is the case – if, that is to say, actions in and of themselves, have no moral quality – then the consequentialist necessarily denies the authority of a human nature with which they may or may not accord.

The radical consequences of this position in relation to sexual ethics were well understood by that great prophet of the modern age, Jeremy Bentham. Bentham had long attacked asceticism and made pleas for what he termed 'sexual nonconformity', but in an 'Essay on Pederasty' he went further and argued for the innocence of what we would term 'homosexuality'.[6] 'I have been tormenting myself for years', he declares, 'to find if possible a sufficient ground for treating them [i.e., 'these irregularities of the venereal appetite which are styled unnatural'] with the severity [both in law and in morals] with which they are treated at this time of day by all European nations: but upon the principle of utility I can find none.'[7]

Naturally enough as a consequentialist – i.e., as one who holds that actions are good or bad, right or wrong, solely in virtue of their consequences – he reviews the alleged consequences of homosexual relationships which have been held to provide grounds for the disapproval of them. Montesquieu's contention that the practice is 'debilitating' is judged to lack evidential support.[8] The charge to which 'Mr. Voltaire appears inclined in one part of his works to give some countenance' that it is 'prejudicial to population' is held to be dubious:[9] the fact

[6] This essay was published some twenty five years ago from amongst his posthumous papers and is reprinted in *Philosophy and Sex*, ed. R. Baker and F. Elliston, revised edn (Buffalo, NY, 1984), 354–69.
[7] Bentham, 'An Essay on Pederasty', 354.
[8] Bentham, 'An Essay on Pederasty', 356–9.
[9] Bentham, 'An Essay on Pederasty', 359.

that something would be prejudicial if practised exclusively is not a reason for punishing its every occurrence and 'if we consider the time of gestation in the female sex we shall find that much less than a hundredth part of the activity a man is capable of exerting in this way is sufficient to produce all the effect that can be produced by ever so much more. Population therefore cannot suffer till the inclination of the male sex for the female be considerably less than a hundredth part as strong as for their own.'[10] In any case, this objection 'could not with any degree of consistency be urged in a country where celibacy was permitted, much less where it was encouraged'.[11] For 'if . . . out of regard to population it were right that paederasts should be burnt alive monks ought to be roasted alive by a slow fire'.[12] And, to the further complaint that it somehow 'robs women' of their rights – by depriving them of the opportunity of marriage, for example – he answers that, judging from the history of the practice of paederasty amongst the Greeks, 'there appears not any great reason to conclude that, by the utmost increase of which this vice is susceptible, the female part of the species could be sufferers to any very material amount'.[13] Thus he concludes that 'In this case . . . as in so many other cases the disposition to punish seems to have had no other ground than the antipathy with which persons who had punishment at their disposal regarded the offender',[14] an antipathy 'grounded only in prejudice'.[15] There is no reason, then, upon the principle of utility, for regarding these 'unnatural vices', either in law or in morals, as vices.

Bentham's argument here, applied more generally, would doubtless serve, as he realised, to call into question a whole range of traditional attitudes to sexual conduct. More importantly, however, consequentialism's commitment to the moral neutrality of acts can be regarded as having furnished at least some of the constituents of the soil in which has flourished

---

[10] Bentham, 'An Essay on Pederasty', 360.   [11] Ibid.
[12] Bentham, 'An Essay on Pederasty', 360–1.
[13] Bentham, 'An Essay on Pederasty', 365.
[14] Bentham, 'An Essay on Pederasty', 366.
[15] Bentham, 'An Essay on Pederasty', 368.

perhaps the most characteristic of modern concepts governing this sphere, that of casual sex.

Casual sex is, one supposes, a bit like a casual remark – you did not really mean anything by it and it is not to be taken at all seriously. Thus the phrase implies that, even if sexual intercourse has a normal meaning or significance, it none the less has no essential meaning or significance, for the act is capable of being performed in such a way that it implies nothing at all. It is true enough that our culture is familiar with the thought that sexual relations may 'take on' – again a telling phrase – greater significance in a deep and romantic attachment. But the significance is an addition to the act derived from the context, from the intentions of the agents or perhaps from the act's consequences, rather than being inherent in it. The significance is, if you like, a bit like a sun roof on a new car – it is not a standard feature, but is, so to say, an optional extra. Plain sex has, in itself, no connotations other than those we choose, individually or socially, to attribute to it, and in that sense may be quite as trivial as, if not more trivial than, shaking hands.

The notion of casual sex, as we have just tried to characterise it, is not solely endebted to consequentialist ideas, but it can be seen readily enough that a metaethical thesis concerning the moral neutrality of acts provides the notion with certain support or encouragement. For the consequentialist, sexual acts, like all acts, are merely movements of bodies, capable of being judged morally only when we peer into the future to determine the results which flow from them. With the advent of relatively effective contraception and means of avoiding, preventing or curing sexually transmitted diseases, however, 'the results which flow from' sexual acts are likely to seem negligible. Thus, consequentialism fosters the notion of casual sex and presents a meta-ethical obstacle to the acceptance of the idea that certain sexual acts are in and of themselves wrong, or as we might prefer to say, 'demeaning', that is, contrary to the meaning which sexuality has within human nature properly understood – the very idea which, as we have already seen, finds itself under attack from the metaphysical questioning of a normative ontology and thus the notion of 'human nature properly understood'.

The moralist's refusal of a deontology, and the metaphysician's refusal of a normative ontology (whatever the logical or historical connections may be between these two), together or separately, provide grounds for rejecting vital elements in the traditional understanding of human sexuality as well as in its critiques not only of homosexuality, but also, for example, of masturbation or bestiality, since those critiques are likely to make reference to what belongs to human nature and to assume that departure from this nature is morally significant not only in virtue of any bad consequences it might have. (Of course, this is not to say that critiques of these practices might not be sustained on other grounds, or even to say that they should be sustained at all, but just that, where the metaphysical or meta-ethical critiques are accepted, they can no longer be sustained on the usual grounds.) But, then, we ought to notice too that the simple extension of straightforwardly consequentialist reasoning to these issues, which is doubtless culturally the most significant basis for repudiation of certain traditional attitudes, would have exactly the same character as Bentham's reasoning applied to homosexuality, namely it would merely assume, rather than show, that any disagreement with the deliverances of the principle of utility is, so to say, in bad faith and arises from antipathy. For Bentham's reasoning, it should be clear, amounts to nothing more than question-begging restatement of the moral assumptions of consequentialism, namely that actions are good or bad solely in virtue of their consequences.

The point of these remarks, however, is not simply to register the weakness of Bentham's argument in a particular essay – or, to put it another way, its force only against those who share his consequentialist assumptions – but to make us aware of a modern attitude no less characteristic than the one which is expressed in the concept of casual sex, and that is the assumption that any views in relation to sex which are at odds with a belief in the moral neutrality of acts must arise from antipathy. It has been the genius of consequentialism so to insinuate its meta-ethical assumptions into the modern mind as being simple common sense and uncontroversial truisms that alternative viewpoints, and in particular those belonging to the Christian tradition, are rendered almost entirely opaque. In other words, where it is assumed that it can only be prejudice or 'antipathy', to use Bentham's word, which motivates any concern for sexual conduct which is not strictly required by consequentialist thought, the result will be a baffled misunderstanding of alternative codes and of traditional Christian teaching in particular. Thoroughly convinced of the thesis that actions are, in and of themselves morally neutral, the contemporary observer, influenced by such assumptions, can only suppose that any moral criticism of an action which makes no sense in broadly consequentialist terms makes no moral sense whatsoever. Thus, this modern observer typically displays his or her modernity by seeking not a charitable cognitive explanation of the attitudes of our Christian forebears, but by feeling compelled to explain these attitudes in terms of a sociological or psychological pathology which usually makes reference to the 'horror of sex', and more recently the misogyny, which is discovered at every turn to have afflicted all ages but our own now happy and enlightened era.[16]

---

[16] L. W. Countryman's *Dirt, Greed and Sex: Sexual Ethics in the New Testament and their Implications for Today* (London, 1989) is an example of a blank incomprehension of the past, instilled by the assumption of certain metaethical presuppositions, posing as exegesis. According to Countryman, the sexual ethics of the Old Testament are to be understood as shaped principally by twin commitments to what he terms a 'purity code' and a 'property ethic'. It is, he argues, the property ethic which primarily governs the Old Testament consideration of, for example, incest, prostitution and adultery, and the purity code which primarily governs consideration of, for example, bestiality, homosexuality and intercourse during menstruation. The New Testament, so Countryman argues, follows the Jesus of the Gospels and declares the end of the ethic of physical purity. Thus, he concludes, the New Testament is, for example, indifferent to homosexual behaviour. Now this account of matters is fraught with problems, but most relevant to our immediate discussion is Countryman's attempt to explain what he means by a purity code and how its rules are to be distinguished from those which have another source. According to Countryman, this is, in fact, quite a simple matter: 'what marks particular sexual acts as violations of purity rather than of some other ethic is that the acts are deemed repellent in and of themselves, like snails or slugs on a dinner plate. One rejects them because they seem self-evidently unacceptable, not because of an identifiable concrete harm which they threaten to a society or to a person participating in them' (18). Thus it follows, since the Gospel has, as he alleges, declared 'the end of the ethic of physical purity', that it

The denial of an authoritative natural order which has in secular thought two forms, metaphysical and moral, also takes these forms in supposedly Christian thought. We cannot, however, regard the denial of this order as compatible with the principle dogmatic presuppositions of Christianity, but rather see in this denial, in either of its forms, the essence of what Augustine opposed in his defence of marriage against the Manichees – that is, the rejection of the belief that we are, in our natures, the creatures of a good God.

'allows no rule against the following, in and of themselves: masturbation, nonvaginal heterosexual intercourse, bestiality, polygamy, homosexual acts, or erotic art and literature' (243) – though, as Countryman points out, 'like other sexual acts' they may become wrong, so to say, extrinsically, in virtue of their identifiable harmful consequences.

Where has Countryman learnt this distinction which he takes to the Old and New Testament? Countryman declares that it is the task of Christian theology to 'seek, with the help of the past, to understand the present in its own terms and proclaim the gospel in ways pertinent to it' (238). We see here, however, an attempt by Countryman not only to understand the present on its own terms, but also to understand the past on its (the present's) own terms too! For he attempts to understand these texts by means of a distinction which is only too plainly dependent on the philosophical assumptions of Bentham, Mill and modern liberalism: namely, that a rule is either aimed at the prevention of an 'identifiable concrete harm' or must arise from an antipathy. With these assumptions in hand, Countryman need hardly trouble to await the *judgment* of the Old or New Testament on purity codes. For, once we discover, by the merest introduction to the study of other places and times, 'that what has long seemed self-evident with regard to sexual ethics – that certain acts are right in and of themselves – is in fact the reflection of purity values we have drawn from our culture' (18), we are well on the way to knowing that any purity code, whether it relates to eating pigs or to sleeping with them, is merely, so to speak, a matter of taste. Not surprisingly, Countryman is not a little uncomfortable with some of his conclusions – at least subconsciously. He can hardly bring himself to declare bestiality a matter of complete and utter indifference, and comments instead, that 'where it is the casual recourse of the young or of people isolated over long periods of time from other humans, [it] should occasion little concern. It is probably too isolated a phenomenon to justify strong feelings' (244). But this makes no sense at all given his previous discussion. Either bestiality, which is, according to Countryman, morally neutral in and of itself, causes some further identifiable harm or it does not. If it does not cause such harm, then it should occasion Countryman little concern whether it is a 'casual recourse of the young or of people isolated over long periods of time', or is instead a settled taste of grown-ups with otherwise normal human relationships – unless bestiality, like sightseeing, is the sort of thing which becomes harmful when it reaches a certain level of popularity. But, whatever he says on this issue, our main point holds – the book demonstrates the genius of consequentialism in so insinuating its theoretical commitments into the popular consciousness that even exegetes, instead of noting a conflict between biblical and contemporary views, read the former out of the latter and so circumvent the need for the former's explication, let alone any debate with them.

Sometimes the denial of the goodness of the created order emerges in a not obviously self-conscious espousal of what we might think of as a metaphysical thesis – thus, to take an example, J. J. McNeill in *The Church and the Homosexual* insists that 'the call of the Gospel to man is not one of conforming passively to biological givens; rather that call is to transform and humanize the natural order through the power of love'.[17] Thus, when he further asserts that 'what it means to be a man or woman in any given society or culture is a free human cultural creation',[18] this is not, we may suppose, a state of affairs which is in any sense to be regretted as it might be if the natural order were possessed of some good which this or that 'cultural creation' were in danger of obscuring or distorting. The natural order needs grasping and humanising just because, presumably, it lacks any inherent good apart from this grasping and humanising. Thus, if one were to ask whether it has been grasped and humanised well or badly, it is plain that McNeill will not allow that that 'well' or 'badly' can be determined in relation to some ontological reference point. It is just because of this, we may presume, that McNeill declares that 'the only ideals involved in all questions of sexual orientation are the great transcendent questions of justice and love'.[19]

If in Christian ethics the denial of the authority of the natural order sometimes arises under the influence of metaphysics (and in the case of McNeill, one suspects, under the influence in particular of the sort of historicism which gained a certain popularity as a result of the influence of Teilhard de Chardin), more often the denial of this authority is determined by meta-ethical assumptions. Typically, as the treatment of secular philosophy may lead us to expect, the dominant thought will be

---

[17] J. J. McNeill, *The Church and the Homosexual* (London, 1977), 102–3. McNeill seems driven to this claim, as the quotation suggests, by understanding the claims of 'nature' in severely reductive terms; 'one learns the purposes of nature', so he tells us, 'by an impersonal and objective reading of the biological laws governing the sexual operations of the human body' (102). Of course, McNeill could find such understandings of the natural order easily enough, but it is unfortunate that an objection to certain understandings of the natural order is taken to be an objection to the authority of the natural as such.

[18] McNeill, *The Church and the Homosexual*, 104.

[19] McNeill, *The Church and the Homosexual*, 148.

that acts in general, and sexual acts in particular, cannot be wrong in and of themselves, but only in virtue of their consequences and additionally, perhaps – where the sway of a thoroughgoing consequentialism is not absolute – in virtue of the intentions with which they are done.

James Nelson will serve as an example of this fairly common pattern of thought, in spite of the fact that his declared principles lead us to expect something else altogether – thus he tells us that 'genital sexual expression should be evaluated in regard to motivations, intentions, the nature of the act itself, and the consequences of the acts',[20] thereby signalling a commitment to moral evaluation which at least includes a deontological element. But, no sooner has the principle been announced, than his practice belies it, for Nelson confesses that he finds 'it extremely difficult to label whole classes of acts as inherently right or wrong, since moral quality hinges so heavily on what is being communicated to the persons involved in the particular relationship and context'.[21] Such an approach, however, as Gilbert Meilaender and others have pointed out, so isolates the nature of an action from its moral evaluation as to fail to take seriously the human embodiment which Nelson so frequently claims to honour. On his view, actions of bodies are not, it seems, actions of persons. Instead, moral agents so float above their bodies, as it were, that they can make the doings of these bodies mean whatever they want them to mean. Ironically, of course, such a sexual ethic displays a dualism of body and self which is unknown to the tradition which Nelson persistently accuses of dualism, for in that tradition the assessment of the morality of an agent's conduct was not independent of a consideration of the nature of his or her acts.[22]

Whether inspired by metaphysical or meta-ethical presuppositions, those who deny the moral significance or authority of

[20] J. Nelson, *Embodiment: An Approach to Sexuality and Christian Theology* (London, 1979), 127.

[21] Nelson, *Embodiment*, 128.

[22] G. Meilaender, *The Limits of Love: Some Theological Explorations* (University Park, PA, 1987), 121ff. The popular influence of thoughts such as McNeill's and Nelson's is evidenced in the report, *Presbyterians and Human Sexuality*, discussed in the previous chapter.

the natural may aptly be identified as the new Manichees. In presupposing either that the natural is possessed of no moral significance, or that actions are morally neutral apart from a consideration of the balance of their consequences and perhaps a consideration also of our intentions in performing them, these new Manichees, like the old ones, presuppose that our bodily life is not possessed of a form or character which comes from the hand of a good God. But, against both the metaphysical and the meta-ethical forms of the denial of the existence or authority of human nature, we may ask what account their proponents can give of the creation, contending with Brunner that:

The world, that which is not 'I', is not something material, needing to be shaped and moulded by us. To think it is betrays an impertinent, arrogant habit of mind springing from the delusion that man is a god. The world is not a shapeless mass of matter, it is not a chaos which we have to reduce to form and order. It was formed long ago: it is given to us in a rich variety of form. In its *form* the will of God is stamped upon that which exists. We ought to understand this existing shape or order as the expression of the Divine Will . . . We are to range ourselves within this order.[23]

To mention Brunner is, however, to bring us face to face with the problem to which we have already alluded, of the discernment or characterisation of the natural. And we shall notice straightaway that the penultimate sentence of the statement we have just quoted – 'We ought to understand this existing shape or order as the expression of the the Divine Will' – displays the very ambiguity on the point at issue which Barth consistently, and rightly, found in Brunner's handling of these questions.

According to Brunner, the order we are called to respect does not consist only in 'our natural existence, but also . . . [in] our historical existence.' Thus, when he claims that 'Reverence for the Creator, whose work, in spite of all human perversion, is the one existing reality, demands as our first reaction obedience to the existing order, and grateful acceptance of the goodness of the Creator in the orders, through which alone He makes it possible for us to serve our neighbour, and, indeed, to live at

---

[23] E. Brunner, *The Divine Imperative*, trans. O. Wyon (London, 1937), 124 5.

all',[24] he means by the 'orders' something more than the mere biological givens of human existence. He means, in fact, 'those existing facts of human corporate life which lie at the root of all historical life as unalterable presuppositions, which, although their historical forms may vary, are unalterable in their fundamental structure, and, at the same time, relate and unite men to one another in a definite way'.[25] Brunner names five such orders: the family, the state, culture, the church and the economic order, and concludes that 'the Command of God comes to us related to these orders of reality . . . [and] can be perceived in and through them'.[26]

Barth's protest against Brunner, at its most sharp in his 'Nein!', lacks precision, as O'Donovan has pointed out, in distinguishing the epistemological and ontological issues,[27] but what Barth intended to object to in Brunner's suggestion that God's will 'can be perceived in and through' the created orders was the slurring of the distinction between the proposition that the good is natural to humankind and the quite different proposition that the good can be naturally known. To take a specific example relevant to our concerns, in relation to marriage Brunner claims that 'Matrimony is a "natural" ordinance of the creator because the possibility of and the desire for its realisation lies within human nature and because it is realised to some extent by men who are ignorant of the God revealed in

[24] Brunner, *The Divine Imperative*, 214.
[25] Brunner, *The Divine Imperative*, 210.
[26] Brunner, *The Divine Imperative*, 93.
[27] O. M. T. O'Donovan, *Resurrection and Moral Order* (Leceister, 1986), 86–7: '[I]n the great theological attack upon Natural Law which [he] spear-headed . . . the ontological and epistemological issues were never properly differentiated.' Thus, 'in his pursuit of an uncompromised theological epistemology Barth allowed himself to repudiate certain aspects of the doctrine of creation (such as "ordinances") which ought never to have fallen under suspicion'. Barth might be taken to admit just this point and to show a better understanding when he writes, some fifteen years after the earlier controversy, that 'What seems to be Brunner's basic idea [in *The Divine Imperative*] is sound and must not be rejected: "The Divine Command is not a law which hovers above our actual existence without any connexion with it; it is the command of the God who has created our actual existence."' He properly insists, however, on the existence of an epistemological difficulty: 'what I do not understand is from what source and in what way Brunner claims to know these orders' (*Church Dogmatics*, III: 4, 20).

Christ.'[28] Now those words 'to some extent' signal Brunner's intention to distance himself from what he takes to be classical versions of natural law, which hold, according to him, that 'Nature, i.e., the divine order of creation, is entirely accessible and adequately intelligible to reason.'[29] Yet, in spite of Brunner's awareness of a need for caution, the distancing seemed to Barth insufficient, for having made his qualifications about the orders of creation Brunner maintains 'nevertheless [that] through the preserving grace of God they are *known* also to natural man as ordinances that are necessary and somehow holy and are by him *respected* as such',[30] and, again, that in the orders, 'although in a fragmentary and indirect form, it is God's will that meets us. Even a man who does not know God perceives in them something of the Will of God.'[31] But, as Barth points out:

No doubt there are such things as moral and sociological axioms which seem to underlie the various customs, laws and usages of different peoples, and seem to appear in them with some regularity. And there certainly seems to be some connection between these axioms and the instinct and reason which both believers and unbelievers have indeed every reason to allow to function in the life of the community. But what are these axioms? . . . If we consulted instinct and reason, what might or might not be called matrimony? Do instinct and reason really tell us what is *the* form of matrimony, which would then have to be acknowledged and proclaimed as a divine ordinance of creation? . . . And who or what raises these constants to the level of commandments, of binding and authoritative demands,

---

[28] E. Brunner, 'Nature and Grace' in *Natural Theology*, E. Brunner and K. Barth, trans. P. Fraenkel (London, 1946), 30.

[29] Brunner, 'Nature and Grace', 46. Essentially the same qualifications on the use of the notion of the orders of creation can be found in the earlier work, *The Divine Imperative*. Thus, there we are told that, though 'the orders themselves are the subject of a purely rational knowledge', 'The ultimate, real meaning of these orders can only be perceived where God is recognized as creator and redeemer, in faith, through his Word' (*The Divine Imperative*, 220). The same qualification is repeated in 'Nature and Grace' when Brunner balances the claim that the orders 'can be recognised as necessities and as goods by natural man', with 'the critical point' that 'only by means of faith can their significance be perfectly understood and therefore it is only by means of faith that they can be realised according to the will of Him who instituted them' ('Nature and Grace', 30).

[30] Brunner, 'Nature and Grace', 31.

[31] Brunner, *The Divine Imperative*, 221.

which, as divine ordinances, they would have to be? Instinct and reason?[32]

According to Barth, then, an anthropology which follows this path in discerning the natural will be unsure and uncertain, or where it is sure and certain its confidence will reflect no more than the cultural presuppositions of its exponents – and this is exactly what one has to say of Brunner's treatment of marriage in general, and in particular of his claims in regard to 'the problem of order':

Both [man and woman] are called to be persons, to live in love, in the same degree, but in different ways. The man is the one who produces, he is the leader; the woman is receptive, and she preserves life; it is the man's duty to shape the new; it is the woman's duty to unite it and adapt it to that which already exists. The man has to go forth and make the earth subject to him, the woman looks within and guards the hidden unity. The man must be objective and generalize, the woman must be subjective and individualize; the man must build, the woman adorns; the man must conquer, the woman must tend; the man must comprehend all with his mind, the woman must impregnate all with the life of her soul. It is the duty of the man to plan and to master, of the woman to understand and unite.[33]

Barth does not pursue such a route to knowledge of the natural, but insists instead that:

To be aware of this order [of creation] we do not leave the closed circle of theological knowledge. We do not in some way read off this order where we just think we find it. We do not understand it at all as an order which can be discovered by us, but as one which has sought us out in the grace of God in Jesus Christ revealed in His Word, disclosing itself to us as such where we for our part could neither perceive it or find it. We not merely suppose it; we see it and know it. We do so in the secret of revelation and faith, but in this way really and authoritatively.[34]

Barth develops an account of the order of creation and hence an anthropology in volume 3 of the *Church Dogmatics*. Understanding creation in the light of the covenant to which it is

---

[32] Barth, 'No!' in Brunner and Barth, *Natural Theology*, 86.
[33] E. Brunner, *Man in Revolt: A Christian Anthropology*, trans. O. Wyon (London, 1939), 358–9.
[34] Barth, *Church Dogmatics*, III: 4, 45.

directed, it is necessary, so Barth argues, to understand human being as being in fellowship:

Humanity, the characteristic and esential mode of man's being, is in its root fellow-humanity. Humanity which is not fellow-humanity is inhumanity. For it cannot reflect but only contradict the determination of man to be God's covenant partner, nor can the God who is no *Deus solitarius* but *Deus triunus*, God in relationship, be mirrored in a *homo solitarius*.[35]

Understanding humanity thus, we may in turn make sense of the sexual differentiation which is the focus of both accounts of creation in Genesis as the creaturely counterpart to the determination of humankind for God which is known in Jesus Christ. Thus, if human being is being in fellowship, it is specifically and concretely being as man or woman, or, more accurately, as man and woman; the command of God is that we should live out and affirm the differentiation and connexion in which we are created and which is ordered and witnesses to, and measured by, the union of Christ and the Church:

We have to say both that man is necessarily and totally man *or* woman, and that as such and in consequence he is equally necessarily man *and* woman. He cannot wish to liberate himself from the differentiation and exist beyond his sexual determination as mere man; for in everything that is commonly human he will always be in fact either the human male or the human female. Nor can he wish to liberate himself from the relationship and be man without woman or woman apart from man; for in all that characterises him as man he will be thrown back upon woman, or as woman upon man, both man and woman being referred back to this encounter and co-existence.[36]

It would take us to beyond the scope of this chapter to trace in detail Barth's anthropology in general, and its bearing on sexual ethics in particular. The point to be noted here, however, from what can be no more than a brief indication of the direction which Barth takes, is that, in maintaining that the first question in this sphere is 'essentially a question of things that are natural and right', Barth presupposes neither that the question can properly be answered outside theology, nor that

[35] Barth, *Church Dogmatics*, III: 4, 117.
[36] Barth, *Church Dogmatics*, III: 4, 118.

the theologian should be troubled by finding theology's answer at odds with others which might be given to it from outside this realm. Indeed – to make that last point with some emphasis – it can be observed that even between Barth and Foucault, to name two who may be thought unlikely companions, there need be no great difficulties. For, though the purpose of Foucault's *History of Sexuality*[37] is to claim that the natural and the unnatural are cultural constructs and that, as one of Foucault's disciples expresses it, 'almost any imaginable configuration of pleasure can be institutionalized as conventional and perceived by its participants as natural',[38] Barth has no reason to reject Foucault's epistemological scepticism about 'the natural', but only to reject it as ontologically decisive. Christianity, that is to say, need not deny the ideological character which Foucault finds in human knowledge in this sphere, nor Foucault's contention that within the *human* understanding of human nature there are only alternative ideologies, alternative ways of organising and constructing our desires, none of which has a indubitable claim to a privileged status. While Christian sexual ethics must assert the existence and authority of the created order, knowledge of the form and character of that order may be reckoned to be irreducibly theological. (Which is why so much of the popular debate in the the churches about the naturalness or otherwise of homosexuality simply misses the point.)

III

Our second thesis is that the Command of God must be heard, in this sphere as in any other, not only as the word of the

---

[37] M. Foucault, *The History of Sexuality*: vol. I, *An Introduction* (London, 1978), vol. II, *The Uses of Pleasure* (London, 1986), and vol. III, *The Care of the Self* (London, 1986), all trans. R. Hurley. Foucault's proposal for a *history* of sexuality expresses the essential thought which animates his project, namely that 'sexuality must not be thought of as a kind of natural given which power tries to hold in check, or as an obscure domain which knowledge tries gradually to uncover. It is the name that can be given to a historical construct: not a furtive reality that it is difficult to grasp'; *An Introduction*, 105.

[38] J. J. Winkler, *The Constraints of Desire* (London, 1990), 17. See also D. M. Halperin, *One Hundred Years of Homosexuality: and Other Essays on Greek Love* (London, 1990), for lucid reflections on, and application of, Foucault's central theses.

creator, but as the word of the reconciler addressed to the sinner, calling humankind back from the disorder in which we presently stand. In this fallen world, that is to say, God's command is heard not simply as a call to be what we are, but as a heteronomous command – that is, as one which bids us return to an order which is experienced as an imposition, and thus as asserting what seems to be an alien claim. God's command finds us in revolt against the created order, and thus addresses us, so we shall say, in a word of judgment which announces our restoration and liberation in Christ.

If Manichees are the opponents of the first thesis, that 'it is a question here of what is natural and right', it is plainly Pelagians who are the opponents of the second thesis, that the call to what is 'natural and right' is a liberating judgment on what is presently the case, for, if the Manichees beset 'human nature' with 'detestable censure', the Pelagians heap on it 'cruel praise'.[39] Of course, Pelagians did not deny the existence of sexual sin, nor even of wrongful sexual desires, any more than they denied the existence of other sins or sinful desires. What was characteristic of their position was an unwillingness to explain the existence of such sinful desires by any reference to human nature, thinking that to do so amounted to joining the Manichees in their 'detestable censure' of it. Their conviction was, says Brown 'that man's nature was certain and fundamentally unchanging'.[40] This conviction, that the basic drives and powers of human nature were themselves good, and hence that sin could not be explained by reference to that nature, went hand in hand with the notion that sin sat lightly, so to say, on humanity. According to Brown, the Pelagian view was that though 'the powers of human nature had, admittedly, been constricted by the weight of past habits and by the corruption of society', 'such constriction was purely superficial'.[41] Thus, since the burden of sexual sins, as of any others, was a burden of habit and imitation, not one which touched our natures, it

[39] Augustine, *De Nuptiis et Concupiscentia* (*On Marriage and Concupiscence*) PL 44, 413 74, trans. P. Holmes and R. Wallis, *Nicene and Post-Nicene Fathers*, 1st series, vol. V (Edinburgh, 1991), ii, 9.
[40] P. Brown, *Augustine of Hippo* (London, 1967), 365.   [41] Ibid.

could be shaken off with more or less ease. To suppose otherwise, so Julian of Eclanum would charge, is not only to fall back
into Manicheeism, but to encourage moral laxity – to mention
two of the objections which Augustine answers in *Contra
Julianum*.[42]

Augustine seeks to find a way between the 'censure' of the
Manichees and the 'praise' of the Pelagians: 'Man's nature owes
nothing to the Devil. But, by persuading man to sin, the Devil
violated what God made well, so that the whole human race
limps because of the wound made through the free choice of
two human beings.'[43] Julian, as Augustine sees it, faces a
dilemma – he must either praise this 'limping', giving 'most
shameful approval'[44] to concupiscence, or he must condemn it.
If he will praise it, why does he commend celibacy and its
glorious battles? But, if he condemns it, and admits that
concupiscence is an evil, then he can only resist the conclusion
of the Manichees by admitting in turn that evil may arise even
in good natures, 'for this is what they assert, that evil can be
produced only from evil, and their whole vicious sect is built
upon this foundation'.[45] Thus, against Manichees and Pelagians
alike Augustine asserts:

man's safety and the salvation of his nature consists in this, not that
the flesh and the spirit, as though by nature hostile to each other as
the Manichaean foolishly thinks, may be separated, but that they may
[contrary to what the Pelagian thinks necessary] be healed of the fault
of discord and be in harmony. For this it is to be delivered from the
body of this death: that what is not the body of death may become the
body of life, death itself dying in it; an end of discord, not of nature.[46]

Manichees are wrong to thing the flesh evil, whereas Pelagians
are wrong to think it is not disordered or that its ills are of such

[42] Augustine, *Contra Julianum* (*Against Julian*), PL 44, 641–880, trans. M. A. Schumacher
    (Washington, 1957), iv, 2, 4 ('Who ever theorized that "the conjugal relationship was
    invented by the Devil"?') and ii, 8, 30 ('[Y]ou dare say in your heart that when men
    hear you they are inspired to virtue, but when they hear these others, men of such
    quality and importance, Cyprian, Hilary, Gregory, Ambrose and other priests of the
    Lord, they are overcome by despair and give up the pursuit of perfection.')
[43] Augustine, *Contra Julianum*, iv, 16, 83.
[44] Augustine, *Contra Julianum*, ii, 6, 15.
[45] Augustine, *Contra Julianum*, i, 9, 43.
[46] Augustine, *Contra Julianum*, ii, 3, 6.

a kind that we can ourselves accomplish our deliverance – as Augustine ruefully observes, 'Not even when the virtue of chastity stands unshaken is there no sickness by which the flesh lusts against the spirit.'[47] At first sight, it might seem that, far from being at odds with our highly Augustinian second thesis – that the command of God is not only a command to be what we are, but, in this fallen world and in relation to our fallen sexuality, will appear as a heteronomous command, announcing judgment and promising liberation – much modern secular thought is so close as to represent no less than a vertitable *preparatio evangelium*. Indeed, if we are looking for the simple presentation of a dialectic of judgment and liberation, which does of course represent an element central to our second thesis, then we need look no further than those two great masters of suspicion, Marx and Freud. It is, of course, something that we find in them such a dialectic, and in this they contrast favourably with some of those who aspired, as they did not, to stand in the Christian tradition. Thus, we might prefer Marx and Freud to Tolstoi, let us say, who here is no better than a Manichee, since he knows only of judgment, but nothing of liberation.[48] And we shall

---

[17] Augustine, *Contra Julianum*, vi, 18, 57.

[18] The utter bleakness of Tolstoi's understanding of human sexuality is starkly expressed in his *Kreutzer Sonata*. In this story, the sensuality of a particular marriage leads first to infidelity and then to murder; what his later comments make clear, however, is that the vicious character of this marriage displays what he takes to be the tendency of all marriages which do not exclude entirely indulgence in sensual pleasures. '[T]here is no basis in the true Christian doctrine for the institution of marriage.' See Leo Tolstoi, 'Postface to *The Kreutzer Sonata*' in *The Kreutzer Sonata and Other Stories*, trans. D. McDuff (Harmondsworth, 1985), 277. 'There never has been and there never will be', he asserts, 'a Christian marriage, just as there never has been nor can there be a Christian ritual (Mt vi. 5–12; John iv, 21), Christian teachers and fathers (Mt xxiii, 8–10), Christian property, or a Christian army, justice or state. This was always understood by the true Christians of the earliest times, and by those who lived thereafter. The Christian ideal is the love of God and of one's neighbour; it is the renunciation of self for the service of God and of one's neighbour. Marriage and carnal love are, on the other hand, the service of oneself and are therefore in all cases an obstacle to the service of God and men – from the Christian point of view they represent a fall, a sin. The contraction of marriage cannot promote the service of God and men even when the partners have as their aim the propagation of the human species' (276). Thus, those already married 'should strive together to free themselves from temptation, to make themselves pure, abstain from sin, and replace conjugal relations, which are opposed to the general and particular service of God

prefer them, too, to those latter-day Pelagians, who know nothing of either judgment or liberation, and who thus stand to learn from Marx and Freud that human sexuality needs liberating and that it needs liberating from something more than the ties of a thread or a string, but in actual fact from something like the 'chain of sexual desire', forged from links of 'iron', which subjected Augustine to the 'harsh bondage' of which he speaks in the *Confessions*.[49] Be that as it may, however, what we find in Marx and Freud is not the *same* dialectic of judgment and liberation that we should properly find in Christian thought, but is, in each, one in which the liberation is finally a little too easily and, as one might expect, humanly won.

The case of Marx and Engels is more obviously unsatisfactory than is the case of Freud. Consistent with their methodology Marx and Engels take seriously the historically and socially specific character of the family, arguing, for example, that under the conditions of bourgeois economic organisation marriage becomes a scene of human alienation, in which the wife is seen as 'a mere instrument of production' and the relationship between the two parties is both exploitative and oppressive.[50] So far so good one might say, at least in principle, for with this analysis Marx and Engels provide, in effect, an account of the fallen character of human sexual relations. And yet with their next move they seem to discount the character and depth of this fall, for, as if pulling a rabbit from a hat, they simply declare that with the freedom and equality in social relations which will prevail under communism the relationship between the sexes will itself become free and equal and that genuinely loving monogamous unions will arise, and not the 'conjugal partnership of leaden boredom, known as "domestic

---

and men, replace carnal love with the pure relations that exist between a brother and a sister' (280). Tolstoi's conviction, shaped by an acquaintance with Shaker ideas, that any other form of married life is contrary to the demands of the Gospel, was also backed by a belief, developed under the influence of various American medical manuals counselling sexual restraint, that abstinence is demanded by a regard for human health (268).

[49] Augustine, *Confessiones (Confessions)*, PL 32, 659–868, trans. H. Chadwick (Oxford, 1991), viii, 6, 13 and 5, 10.

[50] K. Marx and F. Engels, *Manifesto of the Communist Party*, in K. Marx, *Later Political Writings*, ed. and trans. T. Carver (Cambridge, 1996), 17.

bliss"' which is typical of the Protestant bourgeoisie.[51] But why will such unions arise and why will monogamy prevail under communism? Because, according to Engels, 'sexual love is by its nature exclusive'.[52] This move betrays, as many critics have pointed out, a certain 'naturalism' in Marx and Engel's thought about the family and relations between the sexes, in virtue of which some patterns of social life are treated, rather uncritically, as essentially determined by nature and not by history.[53] And it is just this naturalism which allows too easy a promise of liberation to accompany the judgment on existing forms of social life, since it grounds Marx and Engel's simple optimism about sexual relations under communism – the sort of optimism, by the way, which Marx and Engels would surely reckon utopian and unscientific if they found it in forms of socialism they elsewhere criticise for failing to understand the nature of the true determinants of social life. Marx and Engels are, then, as Foucault would complain, insufficiently radical, just because their belief in the social determination of sexuality is constrained and threatened by a dialectic of liberation.

Freud, like Marx and Engels, deserves a fuller and more careful treatment than can be given here, but would, like them, have to face related charges of naturalism and optimism. If human sexual life is subject to judgment (as it is in a theory which sees repression as the dynamic force shaping the varieties of human sexual dissatisfaction, anxiety and perversion), and if further the therapeutic resolution through analysis of internal Oedipal conflicts and the like is conceived as a liberation won not without a certain struggle, involving something more than the simple 'trying harder' which only the most naïve of Pelagians can ever have judged sufficient to cope with sexual or other sins, still the liberation is too easily won, and just because

---

[51] F. Engels, *Origin of the Family, Private Property and the State*, trans. A. West (London, 1972), 134.

[52] Engels, *Origin of the Family, Private Property and the State*, 144.

[53] Arguably, Lenin betrays the same presuppositions when he insists that 'freedom of love' (meaning freedom 'from the serious element in love', 'from child-birth' and 'freedom of adultery') 'is not a proletarian but a bourgeois demand'. See his letter to Inessa Armand, in V. I. Lenin, *Collected Works*, vol. xxv (Moscow, 1966), 180 1.

of Freud's underlying naturalism. As one commentator notes, 'the logic of emancipation' is the same in Marx and Freud – individuals 'reappropriate basic capacities (Marx) and inherent dispositions (Freud) that have been externalised, alienated, distorted and suppressed', through an elimination of domination which 'enables transparent insight into true needs, so that individuals, reconciled with their biological natures, will live freely and harmoniously with one another'.[54] Of course, in relation to both Marx and Freud, it is the very image of liberation to which Foucault would object.[55] But, though Christian thought will not object to the notion of liberation as such, it may none the less share Foucault's sense that in both cases the liberation which comes about through the triumph of the natural not only treats the natural somewhat uncritically, but, so Christian thought may add, in so doing reaches back behind the Fall with somewhat too much of the ease of the Pelagians. Specifically in Freud this liberation is conceived as a task of recollection and thus as a form of self-knowledge, albeit that arriving at this knowledge requires the assistance of another, after the manner of Plato's *Meno*. But, as Kierkegaard points out in his *Philosophical Fragments* in relation to the matter of knowledge of God, on a Christian rather than a Socratic conception the learner needs to be given not simply an 'occasion' to learn the truth, but the 'condition'.[56] And what is true of such knowledge is true of a knowledge of the natural as comprising the human good – the judgment and liberation which such

---

[54] D. Ingram, 'Foucault and Habermas on the Subject of Reason', in *The Cambridge Companion to Foucault*, ed. G. Gutting (Cambridge, 1994), 219.

[55] As J. W. Bernauer and M. Mahon put it (in 'The Ethics of Michel Foucault' in *The Cambridge Companion to Foucault*, ed. Gutting), for Foucault 'the story of Oedipus . . . is not essentially a deep truth about ourselves "but an instrument of limitation and compulsion that psychoanalysts, since Freud, utilize in order to calculate desire and make it enter into a familial structure which our society defined at a determined moment." Rather than a deeply hidden content of the unconscious, as Freud would have it, Oedipus is "the form of compulsion which psychoanalysis wants to impose on our desire and our unconscious." Rather than the fundamental structure of human existence, as Freud maintains, Oedipus is an instrument of power, "a certain type of constraint, a relation of power which society, the family, political power establishes over individuals"' (149).

[56] S. Kierkegaard, *Philosophical Fragments*, ed. and trans. H. V. and E. H. Hong (Princeton, 1985), 14ff.

knowledge represents requires the provision of a condition and not just an occasion, namely the transformation of both heart and mind.

If the denial of our second thesis in the secular realm finds expression in thinkers with whom we may none the less profitably engage and from whom we may expect to learn much (even if we are unwilling to learn everything they would like to teach us), when we turn to Christian thought the engagement with contemporary versions of Pelagianism is altogether less inviting. This is because we detect it not so much in high-level and carefully articulated positions in moral theology, but rather in the low-level and often-times implicit assumptions which pass for common sense in the controversies and disagreements of the day. Here, in a distinctly twilight world of intellectual undergrowth, no matter any rhetoric of judgment and liberation, the notion that this judgment and liberation concerns human nature as such and without exception will not be taken with great seriousness, and a conception of the fallenness of human sexuality is likely to give place to, at best, a treatment and categorisation of essentially discrete sexual sins. Augustine, it will be muttered, as by Julian, is unduly pessimistic.[57] And, just as 'no irreversible Fall of Man, [but] only a thin wall of corrupt manners stood between Julian and the delightful innocence of man's first state',[58] so for latter-day Pelagians, their diagnosis of our situation will be essentially optimistic, and, by the way, remarkably similiar to the diagnosis which underlies the nostrums of popular sex therapy – that there really is nothing wrong with human sexual relations which cannot be put right by adequate instruction in the basics of biology, the acceptance of a few enlightened attitudes and a certain resolute and determined athleticism.

When Don Quixote meets at the door of an inn with 'two young women, ladies of pleasure as they are called', 'who

---

[57] To mention just two examples: according to McNeill, *The Church and the Homosexual*, 'St Augustine went so far as to identify all sexual attraction and pleasure with sin' (94), and L. S. Cahill refers to 'an Augustinian and unbiblical negativity toward all sexual activity', in *Between the Sexes: Foundations for a Christian Ethics of Sexuality* (Philadelphia, 1985), 124.

[58] Brown, *Augustine of Hippo*, 382.

seemed to him to be two beautiful damsels, or graceful ladies, who were taking their pleasure at the castle gate', he, 'with courteous demeanour and grave voice' thus 'accosted' them: 'Fly not ladies, nor fear any discourtesy; for the order of knighthood which I profess, permits me not to offer injury to any one, much less to virgins of such high rank as your presence denotes.'[59] The *naïveté* with which contemporary Pelagian miscontruals of Christianity greet 'human sexuality' seem similarly comic,[60] but the edge is rather taken off the comedy when one reflects that Pelagianism, old or new, is, in its mistaking the nature of sin and thus in failing to take it at all seriously, deeply unevangelical, in the sense of being a denial of the Gospel – a point which emerges clearly as we consider a rather specific instance of a Pelagian rejection of our second thesis at a particular point in the debate about homosexuality.

More than forty years ago now, D. S. Bailey argued that traditional teaching in regard to homosexuality was defective in thinking of it as a way of acting whilst knowing nothing of 'inversion', as he termed it, or as we might say, in knowing nothing of the state or condition of having a sexual desire only for others of one's own sex.[61] For Bailey, the discovery that homosexuality was in this sense a condition meant that the having of homosexual desires could not as such be accounted a sin, even if it remained open to argument that acting upon those desires would indeed be sinful. But suppose that we approach this area of debate with the essentially Pelagian thought that sin is a matter of choice and persuade ourselves further, as Bailey was not persuaded, that not only the having of these desires but acting upon them is not a matter of choice. Now we arrive at a defence of homosexual conduct almost by

[59] M. de Cervantes, *Don Quixote*, trans. C. Jarvis, ed. E. C. Riley (Oxford, 1992), 31.
[60] It is perhaps best to pass over in complete silence the further level to which this *naïveté* goes in a crop of what we might term sexual spiritualities. Here the age-old tendency to treat human sexual life as if it were – at least in some of its aspects – a sphere of Eden-like innocence in which we do not need reconciliation, is taken a step further, and human sexual life is held to be not simply innocent, but itself revelatory of the divine. Thus, according to James Nelson, the incarnation obliges us to 'take our body experiences seriously as occasions of revelation'; see: *Body Theology* (Louisville, 1992), 9. For all their faults, even the Pelagians were not guilty of this.
[61] D. S. Bailey, *Homosexuality and the Western Christian Tradition* (London, 1955), x-xii.

way of a syllogism: sin is a matter of choice; homosexual conduct is not a matter of choice; therefore homosexual conduct is not a sin.[62] It would be a mistake to reply to this perhaps never articulated, but often implicit syllogism, by arguing that, as a matter of fact, homosexual conduct is always a matter of choice, even if the having of homosexual desires is not. And it is a mistake not just because such a claim could only be defended with considerable difficulty, but rather because to set about defending it suggests an acceptance of the Pelagian terms within which the issue is being posed.

Certainly, the claim that homosexual conduct is always or generally a matter of choice is difficult to defend, and that for two reasons. In the first place, the notion of 'choice' on which the claim depends may be suspected of being rather thin to say the least – after all, in relation to certain actions, even when they are described as 'choices' by those who have taken them, we would reserve the right in the light of social and cultural analysis to deny that the decision was anything but constrained. And, in the second place, even if it is maintained that this is not how it is in contemporary western society with regard to homosexual conduct, it is easy enough to imagine a society in which such conduct could not be regarded as in any very interesting sense chosen. But the more important point is that, on whatever side one comes down in relation to the minor premise in the syllogism, to enter into avid debate about it is, in effect, to concede the propriety of the framing of the debate in Pelagian terms, since it is the thoroughly Pelagian major premise which excites interest in the question here being pursued as to whether homosexual conduct is really a matter of choice.

Rather than entering into a debate as to whether homosexual conduct is chosen, then, it would be better to challenge the very

---

[62] We might suspect such a hidden syllogism in, for example, the argument of a report from a Working Party of the Board for Social Responsibility, entitled *Homosexual Relationships* (London, 1979), which holds that sexual abstinence is too demanding a requirement to place on those of homosexual orientation and therefore that in certain circumstances 'individuals may justifiably choose to enter into a homosexual relationship' (52).

direction of the inquiry by insisting that, as it depends on a Pelagian conception of the nature of sin, it depends on a notion of sin which is utterly wrong-headed and inadequate. What needs to be said is that we shall approach the questions of sexual ethics properly only when we come to them with a better sense of the fact that the dialectic of judgment and liberation is actually addressed not just to bad choices, but even or especially to those inclinations and traits of character which impel us towards actions in such a way that those actions hardly seem to appear before us as choices. Perhaps we reckon that this class of inclinations and traits of character is a small one, and judge so from our personal experience. If so, we should thank God, but should also read a few novels, starting perhaps with *Anna Karenina*, and go on to reflect that we shall certainly need to understand sin with resources richer than those provided by the category of 'bad choices' before we can begin to come to terms with the really rather widespread phenomena of child abuse, rape, pornography, prostitution and the like. We shall never come to terms with them whilst we implicitly say with Caelestius, 'It is the easiest thing in the world to change our will by an act of the will.'[63]

Augustine, we will recall, referred to the Pelagians' 'cruel praise' of human nature, and we have also mentioned that in its mistaking the nature of sin Pelagianism denies the Gospel. The 'cruelty' of the Pelagian doctrine ought, by now, to be clear, and so, too, how very much more evangelical is the second anathema of the Barmen declaration – 'we reject the false doctrine that there could be areas of our life in which we belong not to Jesus Christ, but to some other Lord, and in which we do not need justification and sanctification through him'.[64] To deny that our sexual natures are fallen and thus to deny that they stand in need of justification and sanctification through him, far from being a kind and gentle word, is to maintain that here we may and must stand on our own two feet. Our sexual natures do not need justification and sanctification. They are possessed

---

[63] Cited in Brown, *Augustine of Hippo*, 373.
[64] *The Barmen Declaration*, trans. D. S. Bax, *Journal of Theology for Southern Africa*, 47 (1984), reprinted in E. Jüngel, *Christ, Justice and Peace* (Edinburgh, 1992), article II.

of the innocence of Eden. Any bad choices are simply and only bad choices. But against such a judgment – which will be a harsh one for all but the most tranquil celibates – the anathema of Barmen asserts that in this sphere, which for all its potential as a source of fellowship turns out so very often to be a sphere of conflict and exploitation and utter loneliness, we find not this harshness, but rather the judgment of Christ which is always a judgment concealed within the liberating word of reconciliation.

To argue, as we have been in effect, that the logic of Augustine's treatment of sexuality as good but fallen is right, is not, however, to agree with the substance of his account of the precise way in which it is fallen – a point made by Paul Ramsey in his careful and cogent exegesis of Augustine's thought in his article 'Human Sexuality in the History of Redemption'.[65]

On Augustine's behalf, Ramsey argues that, over against the dualism of his past and present opponents, Augustine understood sexuality in such a way as to place it firmly and unequivocally in the history of redemption. That is to say, that for Augustine human sexuality does not transcend the story of creation, reconciliation and redemption which has its centre in Jesus Christ, but can only be understood in the light of this story. Far from splitting soul and body, this understanding thinks of them as together taken up in the reconciliation which presupposes creation and promises redemption – and thus is to be contrasted with all those trivialising modern accounts which treat human sexuality as standing innocently outside this story. If, however, Augustine is right to treat our sexuality as fallen and thus to ask in what respect it is fallen, his precise answer to that question, so Ramsey argues, cannot be accepted as it stands. Why not?

Augustine's analysis of the flaw in human sexuality takes as its starting-point his understanding of the predicament of fallen humanity as consisting in the division of the will against itself, a division most memorably presented in Book viii of the *Confessions* when he recalls the struggle by which he finally resolved,

[65] P. Ramsey, 'Human Sexuality in the History of Redemption', *Journal of Religious Ethics*, 16 (1988), 56–88.

who 'was bound not by an iron imposed by anyone else but by the iron of my own choice', to live a celibate live.[66] This deliverance from 'the chain of sexual desire'[67] could only be a work of God's grace, since of itself, the 'half-wounded' will of 'a son of Adam', to use Augustine's description of his condition, could not will the good whole-heartedly, but instead found itself divided against itself.

As I deliberated about serving my Lord God which I had long been disposed to do, the self which willed to serve was identical with the self which was unwilling. It was I. I was neither wholly willing nor wholly unwilling. So I was in conflict with myself and was dissociated from myself. The dissociation came about against my will.[68]

Now, if Augustine's general analysis of the human predicament lay in this notion of the division of the self against the self, it was specifically his understanding of human sexuality, as set out in, for example, Book xiv of *The City of God*. The dissociation of will and reason in the overwhelming passion of carnal desire (*concupiscentia*) was, according to Augustine the very element of human sexuality which was to be accounted for by the Fall – a fall which had its outward sign in the disorder of the sexual organs themselves, which, whether in a state of arousal or in a state of impotence or frigidity, repeatedly made humans aware of the estrangement of the body from even the reasonable will. And it was this sense of the dissociation of body, reason and will which, said Augustine, was the cause of shame in Adam and Eve at their nakedness (and in their offspring ever since), this most fitting retribution for their own disobedience, namely the disobedience of their members. In its unfallen state, human sexuality would have been different. The members would have quietly and obediently followed the rational will, and hence Adam and Eve would have been joined in accordance with an intent in no way estranged from, or outside the control of, their conscious selves, and thus without that *concupiscentia carnis* which now animates human sexuality.

[66] Augustine, *Confessions*, viii, 5, 10.
[67] Augustine, *Confessions*, viii, 6, 13.
[68] Augustine, *Confessions*, viii, 10, 22.

We note, of course, that contrary to some of his early thoughts and contrary to the thoughts which his modern critics would often foist upon him, the disorder in human sexuality is not a disorder of the body which afflicts the soul, but rather a disorder of the soul which afflicts the body – it is the misdirected will which sets the self against the self and so brings about the malady in the body, not matter in general, nor the body in particular which brings about the malady in the soul. Be that as it may, however, the point which Ramsey makes is that Augustine's conception of unfallen sexuality as a sexuality without passion, though not without pleasure, is, so to speak, a cure too far.[69] For, if it is true that in sexual passion the reason is, so to say, overwhelmed, it is not thereby true that it is overcome or contradicted. In banishing passion from the garden of Eden, Augustine banishes too much, finding shameful not only the contradiction of the reasonable will by sexual desire but the very existence of human action not immediately subject to the will. As Ramsey puts it, what Augustine 'finds shameful is the operation of sexuality without the personal presence of the man and the woman in it'; there is, however, a mistake in

[69] For a typical comment on this matter from Augustine, see *Contra Julianum*, iv, 14, 70: '[T]hat pleasure about which you argue with me so contentiously, does it not engage the whole soul and body, and does not this extremity of pleasure result in a kind of submission of the mind itself, even if it is approached with a good intention, that is, for the purpose of procreating children, since in its very operation it allows no one to think, I do not say of wisdom, but of anything at all? But, when it overcomes even the married, so that they come together, not for propagation, but for carnal delight, which the Apostle says is concession not command, and after that whirlpool the mind emerges and inhales, as it were, the air of thought, it may follow, as someone [i.e., Cicero in *Hortensius*] has truly said, that it regrets its close association with pleasure. What lover of the spiritual good, who has married only for the sake of offspring, would not prefer if he could to propagate children without it or without its very great impulsion? I think, then, we ought to attribute to that life in Paradise, which was a far better life than this, whatever saintly spouses would prefer in this life, unless we can think of something better.' It is worth noting, however, that in certain places Augustine seems, on the face of it, not to be ruling out passion as such, but only passion which is not, in the first instance, directed by the reason. Thus, again in *Contra Julianum* at v, 12, 48, we find him saying that 'The point at issue between us is this: whether before sin the flesh lusted against the spirit in Paradise; or whether this does not now take place in spouses, when conjugal modesty itself must restrain the excess of this same concupiscence, whether this opposing force to which man may not consent, lest it proceed to its excesses, is not an evil.' Note here, the emphasis on the 'excess' of passion.

supposing that the only form of personal presence is 'rational or deliberate presence'.[70] Here, as his references to Cicero in *Contra Julianum* suggest, Augustine is under the influence of late antique and stoic manners. But, however that may be, Augustine's discussion of sexuality in general suffered from the fact that he could not allow, as he should have allowed, that an act could be truly personal and yet not wholly, thoroughly and exclusively at the bidding of the will.

On this point, Aquinas provides a better guide. He notes Jerome's observation that during the sexual act 'the prophet's heart cannot be touched by prophecy', but does not think this decisive.

> The fact that the reason's free attention to spiritual things cannot be simultaneous with the pleasure does not show that there is something contrary to virtue here, any more than when reason suspends its activity according to right reason. Otherwise it would be against virtue to go to sleep.[71]

Hence, if the fact that 'sexual desire and pleasure are not subject to the sway and moderation of reason is part of the penalty of original sin',[72] Aquinas does not understand the penalty in the way Augustine does, with his vision of the cool, calm and collected sexual activity of the garden of Eden. To picture human sexuality before the Fall, does not require the banishment of passion, but just that the passion should, as it may, serve the human good. What is wrong with sexual desire is not that it overwhelms the reason, but that it sometimes – often – contradicts it, and also, of course, that it serves a 'reason' which is corrupt. It is in this that the fallenness of sexuality consists.

This, however, is only to indicate the concerns and questions which will be motivated by our second thesis, rather than to attempt to offer full answers to them. Christian sexual ethics, so we have said, will speak of the falleness of human sexuality and will find that fallenness in the divergence between the good

[70] Ramsey, 'Human Sexuality in the History of Redemption', 60.
[71] Thomas Aquinas, *Summa Theologiae*, 2a2ae, 153, 2, trans. T. Gilby in vol. XLIII of the Blackfriars edition (London, 1968).
[72] Ibid.

which human sexuality should properly serve, and the direction which it actually takes and the purposes it actually serves in human life. But if it is to speak of these things, it will need to have to hand not only a sufficiently rich phenomenology of human sexuality, but also an account developed out of a fully Christian anthropology of the true meaning of sexual life.

IV

If God is known to us as creator and reconciler he is also known to us as our redeemer – as promising to us not simply the restoration of the created order, but its transformation in his good future. The task of Christian sexual ethics at this point then, will be to understand and represent life in this sphere as determined by this eschatological hope. And this task, no less than the others we have mentioned, will be essential to the dogmatic adequacy of sexual ethics. But what is it, we might ask, for us so to understand Christian sexual ethics?

If on the last question we contrasted Augustine and Aquinas to the credit of the latter, on this question, without finding it possible to take Augustine's position simply as it stands, it is to be preferred in its general terms. The difference between the two is starkly revealed in Thomas's treatment of the relationship between virginity and marriage. In answer to the enquiry 'is virginity better than marriage' he maintains that virginity embraced for the sake of the contemplation of truth is more excellent than marriage as directed not to the human good, but to the divine:

It was the error of Jovinian, attacked by Jerome, to deny that virginity should be placed higher than matrimony. He is refuted above all by Christ's example, who also chose a virgin mother, and by the teaching of the Apostle, who counsels virginity as the greater good. He is also refuted by reason. In the first place, because divine good is better than human good, and in the second, because the values of the contemplative life are to be chosen rather than those of the active. Virginity is for the soul's good in the life of contemplation, mindful of the things of God. Marriage is for the body's good, in the life of action namely the growth of the human race. The men and women who embrace matrimony must needs think of the things of this world, to quote

St Paul. And so without doubt virginity is to be esteemed more highly than conjugal continence.[73]

Here there is much that could be found in Augustine, but the significant differences are clearly shown up when Thomas deals with the question 'is virginity lawful?' The thought which lies behind this seemingly odd question is that marriage appears to be a matter of precept – thus in Genesis we read 'Increase and multiply'. Hence the question about the lawfulness of virginity resolves itself at this point into the question which Thomas poses elsewhere, whether matrimony still comes under a precept.[74]

Now, Thomas's answer cannot be a simple 'yes', since a simple 'yes' would require him to say that virginity is, as a matter of fact, unlawful (when, note in the passage above, he thinks its superiority is known even to reason!) But Thomas also declines to give a simple 'no' – 'the precept has not been recalled' he says.[75] In fact, his answer to the question whether matrimony still comes under a precept is a 'yes and no'. 'The command to be fruitful falls on the people as a whole' and 'they are bound not only to multiply in body but to grow in spirit'.[76] But 'the human family is sufficiently provided for if some undertake the responsibility of bodily generation, while others are free in order to devote themselves to the study of divine things, for the health and beauty of our race. An analogy', he continues, 'may be drawn with an army; some soldiers guard the base, others direct the tactics, others do the actual fighting, duties to be discharged by all together, but not by each'.[77] Nor is any difficulty created by the existence of these different duties since:

Human nature has a general inclination to various offices and acts . . . But since it is variously in various subjects, as individualized in this or that one, it inclines one subject more to one of those offices, and another subject more to another, according to the difference of temperament of various individuals. And it is owing to this difference,

[73] Aquinas, *Summa Theologiae*, 2a2ae, 152, 4.
[74] Aquinas, *Summa Theologiae*, *Supplement*, 3a, 41, 2, trans. Fathers of English Dominican Province (reprinted Westminster, MD, 1981).
[75] Ibid.
[76] Aquinas, *Summa Theologiae*, 2a2ae, 152, 2.   [77] Ibid.

as well as to Divine providence which governs all, that one person chooses one office such as husbandry, and another person another. And so it is too that some choose the married life and some the contemplative.[78]

Now, were we to ask Augustine whether marriage still comes under precept, the answer would be a clear and unambiguous 'no'. At first sight, and taking some of his formulations out of context, we may misconstrue this 'no' and attempt to make sense of it as arising from a scorn for marriage. Thus we find him saying that 'even they who wish to contract marriage only to have children are to be admonished that they practice the greater good of continence',[79] and again, that 'Christian doctrine, having diligent question made of it, makes answer, that a first marriage also now at this time is be despised unless incontinence stand in the way.'[80] Indeed, these formulations, read without reference to the wider context, might seem to have come from the pen of Tertullian or Jerome; the latter for example, at least in unguarded moments, seems to suggest that celibacy is good whereas marriage, albeit better than fornication, is barely to be tolerated.[81] Reading him thus, we may find Thomas's view, that marriage and celibacy are related in a division of labour in which the latter is a higher way, altogether preferable to the downright scorn of marriage which might be suspected here.

This reading and comparison overlooks, however, one element in Augustine's account of the relationship between virginity and marriage which is vital to a proper understanding of him and to our learning from him what we can – marriage does not come under precept, not because it is quite simply bad, but only 'now at this time', to note that phrase in the last quotation. For Augustine, marriage was indeed once required

---

[78] Aquinas, *Summa Theologiae, Supplement*, 3a, 41, 2.

[79] Augustine, *De Bono Conjugali (On the Good of Marriage)*, PL 40, 373–96, trans. C. T. Wilcox in *Augustine: Treatises on Marriage and Other Subjects* (New York, 1955), 9.

[80] Augustine, *De Bono Viduitatis (On the Good of Widowhood)*, PL 40, 429–51, trans. C. L. Cornish in *Nicene and Post-Nicene Fathers*, 1st series, vol. III (Edinburgh, 1988), 11.

[81] For Jerome, see *Adversus Jovinianum (Against Jovinianus)*, PL 23, 221–352 and *Letters*, PL 22, 325–1197, xlviii-l, trans. W. H. Freemantle in *Nicene and Post-Nicene Fathers*, 2nd. series, vol. VI (Edinburgh, 1989). For Tertullian, see *Exhortatione Castitatis (Exhortation to Chastity)*, trans. S. Thelwall in *Ante-Nicene Fathers*, vol. IV (Edinburgh, 1994).

of Israel, in order 'to propagate the people of God, through whom the Prince and Saviour of all peoples might be both prophesied and born'.[82] But 'the mysterious difference of times' ('temporum secreta distinctio')[83] has displaced this requirement and now, since the service of God no longer demands procreation, all are to be exhorted to practice continence in which a concern for the things of God is more properly expressed and which will be rewarded by a 'special glory' ('egregia gloria')[84] in the life to come. The point to stress in Augustine's account is that, though celibacy is preferred to marriage, it is not thought of as a recapturing of a pre-fallen past or as the avoidance of sinful or polluting intercourse, but rather as 'an angelic lot, and a foretaste in the corruptible flesh of perpetual incorruption. Let all carnal fecundity and all conjugal chastity bow to this. The former is not within one's own power, the latter is not found in eternity; free choice does not control carnal fecundity, heaven does not contain conjugal chastity.'[85] Thus the practice of continence does not witness against marriage as if it were an evil, but witnesses that, though marriage is good, it is a good which will be surpassed.

There are problems with this account, but what is right is surely this: both marriage and celibacy must have the precise meaning they do have 'now at this time', from the coming eschaton. It is thus one thing to think that Augustine has misdescribed the meaning and significance that they do indeed now have, but quite another to judge him wrong, as against Aquinas, in seeking to understand them in thoroughly historical and eschatological terms.

One element in this misdescription was, in actual fact, to be as significant in the loss of an eschatological perspective in Christian sexual ethics as was the attempt by Aquinas to found the good of marriage in the division of labour, spiritual and worldly, which he posits. Though, for Augustine, the avowed

[82] Augustine, *De Bono Conjugali*, 9.
[83] Augustine, *De Bono Conjugali*, 17.
[84] Augustine, *De Sancta Virginitate* (*On Virginity*) PL 40, 396–428, 14, 14, trans. J. McQuade, in *Augustine: Treatises on Marriage and Other Subjects* (New York, 1955).
[85] Augustine, *De Virginitate*, 13, 12.

sexual abstinence of either sex does, indeed, take its meaning and significance from the eschaton, it takes this meaning in a rather particular way. Thus, in *De Virginitate* he contends that:

Certainly they shall possess something greater than others in that common immortality, who in the flesh already possess something not of the flesh.[86]

It is in that sentence that Augustine gave a particularly unfortunate hostage to fortune, so to say. When the Reformers came to treat of celibacy, their chief concern was twofold: to attack the conversion of what should be a calling into a duty attached to particular offices within the Church, and, in the second place, to deny the supposed superiority of celibacy to marriage.[87] It is significant, however, that though these criticisms did not render celibacy objectionable as such, a point about which Luther was quite explicit,[88] to all intents and purposes, until very recent times, the practice of celibacy ceased almost entirely to play a recognised role in the life of Protestantism after the Reformation. The explanation lies, so one might speculate, in the fact that the link between celibacy and the eschaton in many treatments of it is just the one Augustine has made here with his suggestion that 'they shall possess something greater than others in that common immortality, who in the flesh already possess something not of the flesh' – that is, that celibacy relates to the eschaton as a work to a reward. Thus it is hardly surprising that Luther should connect virginity so closely with his view of monasticism as inherently founded on faith in works; it was, however, unfortunate just because it precluded his developing an understanding of celibacy independent of this particular account of it.

Where the relation of both marriage and celibacy to the good future which God intends is either ignored or misdescribed – either because marriage is understood apart from the fact of

---

[86] Ibid.

[87] For Luther, see especially *On the Estate of Marriage*, trans. W. I. Brandt in vol. XLV of Luther's *Works* (Philadelphia, 1962), which is followed in its main lines by Calvin in *Institutes of the Christian Religion*, iv, 13.

[88] Luther, *On the Estate of Marriage*, 46: 'I do not wish to disparage virginity, or entice anyone away from virginity into marriage. Let each one act as he is able, and as he feels it has been given to him by God.'

this future, or because the relationship of celibacy to the eschaton is misconstrued – a vital theme in Christian sexual ethics is lost. The punishment for this forgetfulness may be said to be the emergence of 'family values' which, as Stanley Hauerwas puts it, is 'how Americans talk about "blood and soil"'.[89] We shall only do better as we maintain the eschatological framework which we discover in Augustine, while handling the relationship between marriage and celibacy somewhat differently. This may be done by treating of marriage and celibacy as two vocations both of which relate, though in different ways, to the coming kingdom of God.

Of celibacy we may say that it is a sign of the fact that 'When they rise from the dead they neither marry nor are given in marriage, but are like angels in heaven'; which is to say, to quote O'Donovan, that 'humanity in the presence of God will know a community in which the fidelity of love which marriage makes possible will be extended beyond the limits of marriage'.[90] Celibacy, in other words, is a form of life not in which the good of human community is denied, but in which expression is given to the hope that the good of community will be realised in a radical non-particularity which transcends the possibilities of purely human community, and the hope, furthermore, that this future may be present not just in a sign, but in the reality of a community, the Church, which reaches beyond the ties of marriage and kinship by which human communities are constituted. But our understanding of marriage and the family must itself transcend any justification of them in terms only of such created goods, even if marriage and the family do serve these goods. Rather, we must find a way of conceiving of the goods of marriage and the family as directed to and perfected in the eschaton, as does John Paul II when he speaks of the family's share in the threefold ministry of the Church, and thus its part in the mission of the people of God whereby 'in ordering creation to the authentic well-being of humanity, in an activity governed by the life of grace, they share in the exercise of the power with which the Risen Christ draws all

[89] S. Hauerwas, *Dispatches From the Front* (Durham, NC, 1994), 158.
[90] O'Donovan, *Resurrection and Moral Order*, 70.

things to himself and subjects them along with himself to the Father, so that God might be everything to everyone'.[91] The same concern is also evident in Barth's treatment of anthropology, since here the notion of the 'natural' is radically transformed with the insistence that the covenant is the basis for creation; that is, that the natural or created good is not only known theologically, but is inherently eschatologically ordered. Thus, it might be said, for Barth the *sacramentum* of sexual relations belongs to them not as an addition, but in their essence, and consists materially not in the indissolubility of marriage alone, but in the incorporation of sexual relations within a being in fellowship, or covenant, which witnesses to its prototype.

v

Rembrandt's *Bathsheba* amply warrants Kenneth Clark's description of the painter as an 'enlightening and . . . profound' interpreter of the Bible,[92] for in his treatment of this subject he effectively displays the location of human sexual life in the threefold history of creation, reconciliation and redemption which, so we have claimed, is the very place from which sexual ethics must begin if it would be Christian.

In the first place, Bathsheba is portrayed with that unblinkered and yet unblinking gaze so characteristic of Rembrandt's work, in which he is, as Clark puts it, 'in rebellion against the classical legacy of Rome'.[93] Bathsheba is a woman, not woman. She is not an idealised type, for such an idealisation would speak of essentially Manichaean fantasies and longings for an existence which is not the existence of this material world which

[91] John Paul II, *Christifideles Laici*, English trans. (London, 1988), para. 14. See also *Familiaris Consortio*, English trans. (London, 1981). It is worth mentioning that these works are complemented by John Paul II's important apostolic exhortation *Vita Consecrata*, English trans. (Vatican City, 1996), which certainly avoids the mistaken emphases in Augustine's handling of celibacy. *Vita Consecrata* represents an endeavour to understand the consecrated life in general, and celibacy in particular, principally as part of the mission of the Church and thus as making a contribution to the renewal of society.

[92] K. Clark, *An Introduction to Rembrandt* (London, 1978), 115.

[93] Clark, *An Introduction to Rembrandt*, 61.

God has created. In her solidity and imperfection she is a woman, and Rembrandt's portrayal accepts this woman and invites us to see one who is desired and desirable, bathed in a warm, golden light from which she has no reason to hide, her nudity as seemingly innocent and unabashed as that of Eden.

And yet, in Bathsheba's expression, Rembrandt depicts a melancholy like Augustine's, to whom, as Brown puts it, 'the fatal flaw of concupiscence would not have seemed so tragic . . . if he had not been ever more deeply convinced that human beings had been created to embrace the material world'.[94] In her melancholy, Bathsheba seems aware of this flaw, which draws her to the embrace of David who himself exists outside the pool of light in which she sits, and thus in the darkness which surrounds her. Her melancoly has something of an air of resignation and hopelessness about it, then, as if what will unfold, as she is drawn into the darkness of the rather seedy transactions which will engulf her, her husband Uriah and David, has a certain irresistable inevitability, even while it does not present itself to her as the irresistable inevitability of the good. Recognition of the good calls forth the unequivocal joy of Adam declared in his great 'now, at last!'; Bathsheba finds no such joy in the summons of David, even while hearing it as a summons she must and will, of herself and yet against herself, obey.

The golden light which falls on Bathsheba illuminates not only this melacholy creature, but also, and as if unnoticed by her, a figure who attends her as she bathes, washing her feet. And what is this but an anticipation of the fact that the history which is about to unfold is one which has the redeemer, Jesus Christ, as its goal? And it has Christ as its goal not only in the sense that the very genealogy of Christ will be traced from 'David the king', 'that begat Solomon of her that had been the wife of Uriah',[95] but also because the story of fallen creation is one which will be completed in the life of the redeemer, who is among us as 'one who serves',[96] and 'even girded himself with a

---

[94] P. Brown, *The Body and Society: Men, Women and Sexual Renunciation in Early Christianity* (London, 1988), 425.
[95] Matthew, 1: 6–7.   [96] Luke, 22: 27.

towel' that he might wash the disciples' feet.[97] Thus the light that falls on Bathsheba is not only the light of Eden, but the light of the 'holy city, the new Jerusalem', which 'has no need of sun or moon to shine upon it, for the glory of the Lord is its light, and its lamp is the Lamb'.[98] Though she does not know what could only be known prophetically, even now her existence is taken up in God's good future. Thus, even now, her melancholy is a token of what, in virtue of that knowledge, would become an eschatological hope which may and must determine her existence.

What Rembrandt paints, this chapter has merely sketched, indicating some of the lines of inquiry which will arise in pursuit of the task of understanding and representing life in this sphere as lived in knowledge of the threefold claim made upon us by the grace of God shown in Jesus Christ. The purpose of this chapter, that is to say, has not been to give an account of the content of Christian sexual ethics as such, but to identify the questions which Christian sexual ethics, as Christian sexual ethics, will ask and seek to answer. This task, however humble, is none the less a necessary one; it contributes to the peacefulness of a church in which (as *The St Andrew's Day Statement* properly understands[99]) the discussion of these issues is all the more vexed just because there is so manifestly a failure to locate the issues within the context of those dogmatic assertions which alone can ensure their proper framing and resolution.

---

[97] John, 13: 4. [98] Revelation, 21: 2 and 23.
[99] *The St Andrew's Day Statement*, now reprinted in *Anglican Life and Witness*, ed. V. Samuel and C. Sugden (London, 1997), 29–33.

Bibliography

Ariès, P., *The Hour of Our Death*, trans. H. Weaver (Harmondsworth, 1983).

Aristotle, *The Politics*, trans. B. Jowett (Oxford, 1905).

Armstrong, A. H., 'Plotinus' in *The Cambridge History of Later Greek and Early Medieval Philosophy*, ed. A. H. Armstrong (Cambridge, 1967), 195–268.

Arrow, K. J., M. L. Cropper, G. C. Eads, R. W. Hahn, L. B. Lave, R. G. Noll, P. R. Portney, M. Russell, R. Schmalensee, V. K. Smith, R. N. Stavins, *Benefit–Cost Analysis in Environmental, Health, and Safety Regulation: A Statement of Principles* (Annapolis, 1996).

Attfield, R., *The Ethics of Environmental Concern* (Aldershot, 1994).

Augustine, *Confessiones* (*The Confessions*) PL 32, 659–868, trans. H. Chadwick (Oxford, 1991).

Contra Julianum (*Against Julian*), PL 44, 641–880, trans. M.A. Schumacher (Washington, 1957).

Contra Mendacium (*Against Lying*), PL 40, 517–48, trans. H. Browne, in *Nicene and Post-Nicene Fathers*, 1st. series, vol. III (Edinburgh, 1988).

De Bono Conjugali (*On the Good of Marriage*), PL 40, 373–96, trans. C. T. Wilcox in *Augustine: Treatises on Marriage and Other Subjects* (New York, 1955).

De Bono Viduitatis (*On the Good of Widowhood*), PL 40, 429–51, trans. C. L. Cornish in *Nicene and Post-Nicene Fathers*, 1st series, vol. III (Edinburgh, 1988).

De Civitate Dei (*City of God*), PL 41, 13–804, trans. H. Bettenson (London, 1972).

De Doctrina Christiana (*On Christian Doctrine*), PL 34, 15–122, trans. J. F. Shaw in *Nicene and Post-Nicene Fathers*, 1st series, vol. II (Edinburgh, 1993).

De Nuptiis et Concupiscentia (*On Marriage and Concupiscence*), PL 44, 413–74, trans. P. Holmes and R. Wallis in *Nicene and Post-Nicene Fathers*, 1st series, vol. V (Edinburgh, 1991).

De Sancta Virginitate (On Virginity), PL 40, 396–428, trans. J. McQuade, in *Augustine: Treatises on Marriage and Other Subjects* (New York, 1955).

Bailey, D. S., *Homosexuality and the Western Christian Tradition* (London, 1955).

Banner, M. C., 'Catholics and Anglicans and Contemporary Bioethics: Divided or United?' in *Isssues for a Catholic Bioethic*, ed. L. Gormally, forthcoming.

'Directions and Misdirections in Christian Sexual Ethics: A Survey of Recent Books', *Epworth Review*, 19 (1992), 95–108.

'Nothing to Declare', *The Church Times*, 16 June 1995.

'Sexualität' in *Theologische Realenzyklopädie*, (Berlin, forthcoming).

'Sexuelle (Ethique)', in *Dictionnaire de Théologie*, ed. Jean-Yves Lacoste (Paris, 1998).

'The Taboos of Bioethics', *Minerva*, 34 (1996), 199–204.

Barmen Declaration, trans. D. S. Bax, *Journal of Theology for Southern Africa*, 47 (1984), reprinted in E. Jüngel, *Christ, Justice and Peace* (Edinburgh, 1992).

Barry, B. and R. Sikora, *Obligations to Future Generations* (Philadelphia, 1978).

Barth, K., *The Christian Life*, trans. G. Bromiley (Edinburgh, 1981).

Church Dogmatics, I: 2, trans. G. Thomson and H. Knight (Edinburgh, 1956).

Church Dogmatics, II: 2, trans. G. Bromiley et al. (Edinburgh, 1957).

Church Dogmatics, III: 1, trans. J. Edwards et al. (Edinburgh, 1958).

Church Dogmatics, III: 2, trans. H. Knight et al. (Edinburgh, 1960).

Church Dogmatics, III: 4, trans. A. T. Mackay et al. (Edinburgh, 1961).

Church Dogmatics, IV: 1, trans. G. Bromiley (Edinburgh, 1956).

Church Dogmatics, IV: 2, trans. G. Bromiley (Edinburgh, 1958).

Ethics, ed. D. Braun, trans. G. Bromiley (Edinburgh, 1981).

The Knowledge of God and the Service of God (London, 1938).

'No!' in Brunner and Barth, *Natural Theology*, 67–128.

Bauckham, R., *The Climax of Prophecy: Studies on the Book of Revelation* (Edinburgh, 1993).

The Theology of the Book of Revelation (Cambridge, 1993).

Beckerman, W. and J. Pasek, 'Plural Values and Environmental Valuation', *Environmental Values*, 6 (1997), 65–86.

Bell, J. M. and S. Mendus, eds., *Philosophy and Medical Welfare* (Cambridge, 1988).

Benedict, *The Rule of St Benedict*, trans. J. McCann (London, 1976).

Bentham, J., 'An Essay on Pederasty', in *Philosophy and Sex*, ed. R. Baker and F. Elliston, revised edn (Buffalo, NY, 1984).

Bernauer, J. W. and M. Mahon, 'The Ethics of Michel Foucault', in *The Cambridge Companion to Foucault*, ed. Gutting, 141–58.

Bethge, E., *Dietrich Bonhoeffer*, trans. and ed. E. Robinson (London, 1970).

Biggar, N., *The Hastening that Waits: Karl Barth's Ethics* (Oxford, 1993).

Board for Social Responsibility of the Church of England, *Homosexual Relationships: A Contribution to Discussion* (London, 1979).

Something to Celebrate (London, 1995).

Bonhoeffer, D., *The Cost of Discipleship*, trans. R. H. Fuller (London, 1959).

Ethics, ed. E. Bethge, trans. N. H. Smith (London, 1955).

Life Together, trans. J. W. Doberstein (London, 1954).

Bonner, G., *St Augustine of Hippo, Life and Controversies*, revised edn (Norwich, 1986).

Boswell, J., *Christianity, Social Tolerance and Homosexuality* (Chicago, 1980).

Brennan, A., ed., *The Ethics of the Environment* (Aldershot, 1995).

'The Moral Standing of Natural Objects', in *The Ethics of the Environment*, ed. Brennan, 35–56.

British Medical Association (BMA), *Our Genetic Future: The Science and Ethics of Genetic Technology* (Oxford, 1992).

Report of the Working Party to Review the British Medical Association's Guidance on Euthanasia (London, 1988).

Brock, D. W., *Life and Death: Philosophical Essays in Biomedical Ethics* (Cambridge, 1993).

Broome, J., 'Goodness, Fairness and QALYs' in *Philosophy and Medical Welfare*, ed. Bell and Mendus, 57–73.

Brown, P., *Augustine of Hippo* (London, 1967).

The Body and Society: Men, Women and Sexual Renunciation in Early Christianity (London, 1989).

Brunner, E., *The Divine Imperative*, trans. O. Wyon (London, 1937).

Man in Revolt: A Christian Anthropology, trans. O. Wyon (London, 1939).

'Nature and Grace' in *Natural Theology*, E. Brunner and K. Barth, trans. P. Fraenkel (London, 1946).

Bulger, R., E. Heitman and S. Reiser, eds., *The Ethical Dimensions of the Biological Sciences* (Cambridge, 1993).

Bultmann, R., *Theology of the New Testament*, vol. I, trans. K. Grobel (London, 1952).

Burnaby, J., *Amor Dei: A Study of the Religion of St. Augustine* (London, 1938).

Busch, E., *Karl Barth: His Life from Letters and Autobiographical Texts*, trans. J. Bowden (London, 1976).

Cahill, L. S., *Between the Sexes: Foundations for a Christian Ethics of Sexuality* (Philadelphia, 1985).

Callicott, J., 'Animal Liberation: A Triangular Affair' in Elliot, ed., *Environmental Ethics*, 29–59.

In Defense of a Land Ethic: Essays in Environmental Philosophy (Albany, 1989).

Camus, A., *The Myth of Sisyphus*, trans. J. O'Brien (Harmondsworth, 1975).

Carradine, K., 'Introduction' to *Nostromo*, J. Conrad (Oxford, 1984).

Catechism of the Catholic Church, English trans. (London, 1994).

Cervantes, M. de, *Don Quixote*, ed. E. C. Riley, trans. C. Jarvis (Oxford, 1992).

Chadwick, O., *John Cassian*, 2nd edn (Cambridge, 1968).

The Making of the Benedictine Ideal, The Thomas Verner Moore Memorial Lecture for 1980, St. Anselm's Abbey (Washington, 1981).

Chiovaro, F., 'Relics' in *New Catholic Encyclopedia* (New York, 1967).

Christiansen, D., 'Ethical Implications in Aging' in *Encyclopedia of Bioethics*, ed. W. T. Reich (New York, 1978).

Clark, K., *An Introduction to Rembrandt* (London, 1978).

Clark, S., *How to Think About the Earth* (London, 1993).

The Moral Status of Animals (Oxford, 1977).

Clement of Alexandria, *Stromata*, trans. W. Wilson, *Ante-Nicene Fathers*, ed. A. Roberts and J. Donaldson, vol. II (Edinburgh, 1977).

Who is the Rich Man That Shall be Saved?, trans. W. Wilson, *Ante-Nicene Fathers*, vol. II.

Conrad, J., *Nostromo*, ed. C. Watts (London, 1995).

Cook, D., 'Abortion' in *New Dictionary of Christian Ethics and Pastoral Theology*, ed. D. J. Atkinson and D. H. Field (Leicester, 1995).

Countryman, L. W., *Dirt, Greed and Sex: Sexual Ethics in the New Testament and their Implications for Today* (London, 1989).

Culyer, A. J., 'Needs, Value and Health Status Management' in Culyer and Wright, eds., *Economic Aspects of Health Services*, 9–31.

Culyer, A. J. and K. G. Wright, eds., *Economic Aspects of Health Services* (London, 1978).

Daniel, N., *Am I My Parents' Keeper: An Essay in Justice Between the Young and the Old* (Oxford, 1988).

Department of the Environment, *Policy Appraisal and the Environment* (London, 1991).

Drummond, M. and G. Mooney, *Essentials of Health Economics* (Aberdeen, 1983).

Elliot, R., ed., *Environmental Ethics* (Oxford, 1995).

Engels, F., *The Condition of the Working Class in England*, trans. of 1886 revised (Harmondsworth, 1987).
Origin of the Family, Private Property and the State, trans. A. West (London, 1972).
Outlines of a Critique of Political Economy, vol. III of Marx and Engels, *Collected Works* (Moscow, 1975).
Field, M. A., *Surrogate Motherhood* (Cambridge, MA, 1988).
Fincham, J. R. S. and J. R. Ravetz, *Genetically Engineered Organisms: Benefits and Risks* (Milton Keynes, 1991).
Finnis, J., *Moral Absolutes: Tradition, Revision, and Truth* (Washington, 1991).
Natural Law and Natural Rights (Oxford, 1980).
Fisher, A., 'Individuogenesis and a Recent Book by Fr. Norman Ford', *Anthropotes*, 8 (1991), 199–244.
' "When did I begin?" Revisited', *Linacre Quarterly*, 58 (1991), 59–68.
Ford, N. M., *When Did I Begin? Conception of the Human Individual in History, Philosophy and Science* (Cambridge, 1988).
Foster, J., ed., *Valuing Nature?* (London, 1997).
Foucault, M., *The History of Sexuality*, trans. R. Hurley: vol. I, *An Introduction* (London, 1978), vol. II, *The Uses of Pleasure* (London, 1986), and vol. III, *The Care of the Self* (London, 1986).
Frend, W. H. C., *Martyrdom and Persecution in the Early Church: A Study of a Conflict from the Maccabees to the Donatists* (Oxford, 1965).
General Assembly of the Presbyterian Church, *Presbyterians and Human Sexuality* (Louisville, 1991).
Goodpaster, K., 'On Being Morally Considerable', *Journal of Philosophy*, 78 (1978), 308–25.
Gormally, L., ed., *Euthanasia, Clinical Practice and the Law* (London, 1994).
'Walton, Davies, Boyd and the Legalization of Euthanasia' in *Euthanasia Examined*, ed. Keown, 113–40.
Gregory of Nyssa, *De Hominis Opificio* (*On the Making of Man*), PG 44, 123–256, trans. W. Moore and H. Wilson, *Nicene and Post-Nicene Fathers*, 2nd series, vol. V (Edinburgh, 1994).
Grisez, G., *Abortion: the Myths, the Realities and the Arguments* (New York, 1970).
The Way of the Lord Jesus: Christian Moral Principles (Chicago, 1983), *Living a Christian Moral Life* (Quincy, IL, 1993), and *Difficult Moral Questions* (Quincy, IL, 1997).
'When Do People Begin' in *Abortion: A New Generation of Catholic Responses*, ed. S. J. Heaney (Braintree, MA, 1992), 3–27.
Grove-White, R. and O. M. T. O'Donovan, 'An Alternative Approach' in *Values, Conflict and the Environment*, ed. R. Attfield and K. Dell (Oxford, 1989), 73–82.

Guroian, V., *Ethics After Christendom: Toward an Ecclesial Christian Ethic* (Grand Rapids, 1994).

Gustafson, J., 'A Response to Critics', *Journal of Religious Ethics*, 13 (1985), 185–209.

'The Sectarian Temptation: Reflections on Theology, Church, and the University', *Proceedings of the Catholic Theological Society*, 40 (1985), 83–94.

Gutting, G., ed., *The Cambridge Companion to Foucault* (Cambridge, 1994).

Halperin, D. M., *One Hundred Years of Homosexuality: and Other Essays on Greek Love* (London, 1990).

Hanke, L., *Aristotle and the American Indians* (Chicago, 1959).

Harris, J., 'EQALYty' in *Health, Rights and Resources: King's College Studies 1987–8*, ed. P. Byrne (London, 1988), 100–27.

'More and Better Justice' in *Philosophy and Medical Welfare*, ed. Bell and Mendus, 75–96.

Hart, J. T., 'The Inverse Care Law', *The Lancet*, 1971, i–i, 405–12.

Hauerwas, S., *Dispatches from the Front: Theological Engagements with the Secular* (Durham, NC, 1994).

'Will the Real Sectarian Stand Up?', *Theology Today*, 44 (1987), 87–94.

Hays, R. B., 'Relations Natural and Unnatural: A Response to John Boswell's Exegesis of Romans 1', *Journal of Religious Ethics*, 14 (1986), 184–215.

Herbert, G., *The Country Parson*, ed. J. Wall (New York, 1981).

Himmelweit, S., 'Reproduction and the Materialist Conception of History' in *The Cambridge Companion to Marx*, ed. T. Carver (Cambridge, 1991), 196–221.

Holdgate, M., *A Perspective of Environmental Pollution* (Cambridge, 1979).

Holland, A., 'The Assumptions of Cost–Benefit Analysis: A Philosopher's View' in *Environmental Valuation*, ed. Willis and Corkindale, 21–38.

Holzherr, G., *The Rule of St Benedict: A Guide to Christian Living*, trans. by monks of Glenstal Abbey (Dublin, 1994).

House of Bishops of the Church of England, *Issues in Human Sexuality: A Statement by the House of Bishops* (London, 1991).

Human Fertilisation and Embryology Authority (HFEA), *Donated Ovarian Tissue in Embryo Research and Assisted Conception: Public Consultation Document* (London, 1994).

Donated Ovarian Tissue in Embryo Research and Assisted Conception: Report (London, 1994).

Hume, D., *An Enquiry Concerning the Principles of Morals* in *Enquiries Concerning Human Understanding and Concerning the Principles of*

Morals, ed. L. A. Selby-Bigge, 3rd. ed., rev. P. H. Nidditch (Oxford, 1975).

Hursthouse, R., *Beginning Lives* (Oxford, 1987).

Ingram, D., 'Foucault and Habermas on the Subject of Reason' in *The Cambridge Companion to Foucault*, ed. Gutting (Cambridge, 1994), 215–61.

Jerome, *Adversus Jovinianum (Against Jovinianus)*, PL 23, 221–352, trans. W. H. Freemantle, *Nicene and Post-Nicene Fathers*, 2nd series, vol. VI, ed. P. Schaff and H. Wace (Edinburgh, 1989).

Letters, PL 22, 325–1197, trans. W. H. Freemantle in *Nicene and Post-Nicene Fathers*, vol. VI.

John Paul II, *Centesimus Annus*, English trans. (London, 1991).

Christifideles Laici, English trans. (London, 1988).

Evangelium Vitae, English trans. (London, 1995).

Familiaris Consortio, English trans. (London, 1981).

Vita Consecrata, English trans. (Vatican City, 1996).

Johnson, L., *A Morally Deep World* (Cambridge, 1991).

Jonas, H., 'Contemporary Problems in Ethics from a Jewish Perspective' in *Philosophical Essays* (Chicago, 1974), 165–82.

Keown, J., ed., *Euthanasia Examined: Ethical, Clinical and Legal Perspectives* (Cambridge, 1995).

'Euthanasia in the Netherlands: Sliding Down the Slippery Slope?' in *Euthanasia Examined*, ed. Keown, 261–96.

'Some Reflections on Euthanasia in the Netherlands' in *Euthanasia, Clinical Practice and the Law*, ed. Gormally, 193–218.

Kierkegaard, S., *Philosophical Fragments*, ed. and trans. H. V. and E. H. Hong (Princeton, 1985).

Las Casas, B. de., *The Defence of the Most Reverend Lord, Don Fray Bartolemé de Las Casas, of the Order of Preachers, Late Bishop of Chiapa, Against the Persecutors and Slanderers of the Peoples of the New World Discovered Across the Seas*, ed. and trans. S. Poole (DeKalb, IL, 1974).

Laslett, R., 'The Assumptions of Cost–Benefit Analysis' in *Environmental Valuation*, ed. Willis and Corkindale, 5–20.

Layard, R. and S. Glaister, *Cost–Benefit Analysis*, 2nd edn (Cambridge, 1994).

Le Grand, J., 'The Distribution of Public Expenditure: The Case of Health Care', *Economica*, 45 (1978), 125–42.

Lenin, V. I., *Collected Works*, vol. XXXV (Moscow, 1966).

Leopold, A., *A Sand Country Almanac* (New York, 1949).

Linacre Centre for Health Care Ethics, 'Submission to the Select Committee of the House of Lords on Medical Ethics', reprinted in *Euthanasia, Clinical Practice and the Law*, ed. Gormally, 111–65.

Lockwood, M., 'Quality of Life and Resource Allocation' in *Philosophy and Medical Welfare*, ed. Bell and Mendus, 33–55.

Lucas, J., *On Justice* (Oxford, 1980).

Luther, M., *On the Estate of Marriage*, trans. W. I. Brand, in *Luther's Works*, vol. xlv (Philadelphia, 1962).

MacIntyre, A., *After Virtue: A Study in Moral Theory*, 2nd edn (London, 1985).

'Moral Relativism, Truth and Justification' in *Moral Truth and Moral Tradition*, ed. L. Gormally (Dublin, 1994), 6–24.

Three Rival Versions of Moral Enquiry (London, 1990).

Whose Justice? Which Rationality? (London, 1988).

Macquarrie, J., *Principles of Christian Theology*, revised edn (London, 1977).

Marx, K. *Capital*, trans. S. Moore and E. Aveling (London, 1878) and the 4th edn, trans. E. and C. Paul (London, 1974).

Marx, K. and F. Engels, *The German Ideology*, vol. v of *Collected Works* (Moscow, 1976).

Manifesto of the Communist Party, in K. Marx, *Later Political Writings*, ed. and trans. T. Carver (Cambridge, 1996).

May, W. F., *The Patient's Ordeal* (Bloomington, IN, 1991).

The Physician's Covenant: Images of the Healer in Medical Ethics (Philadelphia, 1983).

Maynard, A., 'Markets and Health Care' in *Health and Economics*, ed. A. Williams (London, 1987), 187–200.

McCormack, B., *Karl Barth's Critically Realistic Dialectical Theology* (Oxford, 1995).

McCormick, R., *Notes on Moral Theology: 1981 Through 1984* (Lanham, MD, 1984).

McGinn, B., *The Presence of God: A History of Western Christian Mysticism*, vol. i, *The Foundations of Mysticism* (London, 1992).

McNeill, J. J., *The Church and the Homosexual* (London, 1977).

Meilaender, G., 'Corrected Vision for Medical Ethics' in *Theological Voices in Medical Ethics*, ed. A. Verhey and S. Lammers (Grand Rapids, 1993), 106–26.

The Limits of Love: Some Theological Explorations (University Park, PA, 1987).

Methodist Conference, *Report of the Commission on Human Sexuality* (Peterborough, 1990).

Michalson, G. E., 'The Response to Lindbeck', *Modern Theology*, 4 (1988), 107–20.

Midgley, M., 'Duties Concerning Islands' in *Environmental Ethics*, ed. Elliot, 89–103.

Miles, M. R., *Augustine on the Body* (Ann Arbor, MI, 1979).

Naess, A., 'The Deep Ecological Movement: Some Philosophical Aspects', *Philosophical Inquiry*, 8 (1986), 10–31.
'A Defence of the Deep Ecology Movement', *Environmental Ethics*, 6 (1984), 265–70.
'The Shallow and the Deep, Long-Range Ecology Movements', *Inquiry*, 16 (1973), 95–100.
Nagel, T., 'Sexual Perversion', *The Journal of Philosophy*, 66 (1969), 5–17.
Nelson, J., *Body Theology* (Louisville, 1992).
Embodiment: An Approach to Sexuality and Christian Theology (London, 1979).
Nietzsche, F., *The Anti-Christ*, trans. R. J. Hollingdale (Harmondsworth, 1968).
Ecce Homo, trans. R. J. Hollingdale (Harmondsworth, 1992).
Noonan, J. T., 'An Almost Absolute Value in History' in *The Morality of Abortion: Legal and Historical Perspectives*, ed. Noonan (Cambridge, MA, 1970), 1–59.
O'Donovan, O. M. T., *Begotten or Made?* (Oxford, 1984).
The Christian and the Unborn Child, 2nd edn (Bramcote, Notts., 1975).
Resurrection and Moral Order (Leicester, 1986).
'Transsexualism and Christian Marriage', *Journal of Religious Ethics*, 11 (1983), 135–62.
Office of National Statistics, *Britain, 1998: An Official Handbook* (London, 1998).
O'Neill, J., 'The Varieties of Intrinsic Value', *The Monist*, 75 (1992), 119–37.
O'Neill, O., 'Principles, Judgments and Institutions' in *Laws, Values and Social Practices*, ed. J. Tasioulas (Aldershot, 1997), 59–73.
Origen, *Contra Celsum*, trans. H. Chadwick (Cambridge, 1980).
Pagden, A., *The Fall of Natural Man: The American Indian and the Origins of Comparative Ethnology*, 2nd edn (Cambridge, 1986).
Parliamentary Office of Science and Technology, 'Fetal Awareness', POST note 94 (London, 1997).
Partridge, E., ed., *Responsibilities to Future Generations* (New York, 1981).
Passmore, J., 'Attitudes to Nature' in *Nature and Conduct*, ed. R. S. Peters (New York, 1975), 251–64.
Man's Responsibility for Nature: Ecological Problems and the Western Tradition (New York, 1974).
Perkins, W., *Christian Oeconomie: Or a Short Survey of the Right Manner of Erecting and Ordering a Family, According to the Scriptures* (Kingston, 1618).
Pezzey, J., 'Sustainability: An Interdisciplinary Guide', *Environmental Values*, 1 (1992), 321–62.

Sustainable Development Concepts: An Economic Analysis, World Bank Environment Paper No. 2 (Washington, 1992).

Pinckaers, S., *Sources of Christian Ethics*, trans. from 3rd edn, M. Noble (Edinburgh, 1995).

Placher, W. C., 'Revisionist and Postliberal Theologies and the Public Character of Theology', *The Thomist*, 49 (1985), 392–417.

Plato, *Republic*, trans. F. M. Cornford (Oxford, 1941).

Priestman, T. J. and M. Baum, 'Evaluation of Quality of Life in Patients Receiving Treatment for Advanced Breast Cancer', *The Lancet*, April 1976, 899–901.

Prior, A., *Past, Present and Future* (Oxford 1967).

Rachels, J., *Created from Animals: The Moral Implications of Darwinism* (Oxford, 1990).

Ramsey, P., *Basic Christian Ethics* (Chicago, 1950).
'Human Sexuality within the History of Redemption', *Journal of Religious Ethics*, 16 (1988), 56–88.

Ratcliffe, D., ed., *A Nature Conservation Review* (Cambridge, 1977).

Regan, T., *The Case for Animal Rights* (Berkeley, 1983).

Report of the Committee of Inquiry into Human Fertilisation and Embryology, The Warnock Report (London, 1984).

Report of the Committee on the Ethics of Gene Therapy, The Clothier Report (London, 1992).

Report of the Committee to Consider the Ethical Implications of Emerging Technologies in the Breeding of Farm Animals, The Banner Report (London, 1995).

Ridley, J., *Thomas Cranmer* (Oxford, 1962).

Rist, J. M., *Augustine* (Cambridge, 1994).
'Plotinus on Matter and Evil', *Phronesis*, 6 (1961), 154–66.
Plotinus: The Road to Reality (Cambridge, 1967).

Rolston, H., 'Challenges in Environmental Ethics' in *The Environment in Question: Ethics and Global Issues*, ed. D. Cooper and J. Palmer (London, 1992), 135–46.
'Duties to Endangered Species', in *Environmental Ethics*, ed. Elliot, 60–75.
Environmental Ethics: Duties to and Values in the Natural World (Philadelphia, 1988).

Roussel, R., *The Metaphysics of Darkness* (Baltimore, 1971).

Sagoff, M., *The Economy of the Earth* (Cambridge, 1988).

Sanders, E. P., *Paul* (Oxford, 1991).

Schleiermacher, F., *Predigten über den christlichen Hausstand*, trans. as *The Christian Household: A Sermonic Treatise*, D. Seidel and T. N. Tice (Lewiston, NY, 1991).

Schuurman, D., *Creation, Eschaton, and Ethics: The Ethical Significance of the Creation–Eschaton Relation in the Thought of Emil Brunner and Jürgen Moltmann* (New York, 1991).

Scroggs, R., *The New Testament and Homosexuality* (Philadelphia, 1983).

Séjourné, P., 'Reliques', *Dictionnaire de Théologie Catholique*, 13 (Paris, 1936) 2312–76.

Singer, P., *Animal Liberation* (New York, 1975).

St Andrew's Day Statement, reprinted in *Anglican Life and Witness*, ed. V. Samuel and C. Sugden (London, 1997), 29–33.

Stalley, R. F., 'Aristotle's Criticisms of Plato's *Republic*' in *A Companion to Aristotle's Politics*, ed. D. Keyt and F. D. Miller (Oxford, 1991), 182–99.

Taylor, C. C. W. ed., *Ethics and the Environment* (Oxford, 1992).

Taylor, G., *Pride, Shame and Guilt* (Oxford, 1985).

Taylor, P. W., *Respect for Nature: A Theory of Environmental Ethics* (Princeton, 1986).

Tertullian, *Ante-Nicene Fathers*, vols. III and IV, ed. A. Roberts and J. Donaldson (Edinburgh, 1976).

Thiemann, R. F., *Constructing a Public Theology: The Church in a Pluralistic Culture* (Louisville, 1991).

Revelation and Theology: The Gospel as Narrated Promise (Notre Dame, IN, 1985).

Thomas Aquinas, *Summa Theologiae*, 2a2ae, qq 141–54, trans. T. Gilby in vol. XLIII of the Blackfriars edition (London, 1968).

Summa Theologiae, 3a, qq 16–26, trans. C. E. O'Neill in vol. L of the Blackfriars edition (London, 1965).

Supplement to *Summa Theologiae*, 3a, trans. Fathers of English Dominican Province (reprinted Westminster, MD, 1981).

Thomas, K., 'Introduction' to *Ethics and the Environment*, ed. C. C. W. Taylor (Oxford, 1992), 1–11.

Man and the Natural World (New York, 1983).

Tolstoi, L., 'Postface to *The Kreutzer Sonata*' in *The Kreutzer Sonata and Other Stories*, trans. D. McDuff (Harmondsworth, 1985), 267–82.

Tonti-Filippini, N., 'A Critical Note', *Linacre Quarterly*, 56 (1989), 36–50.

Tooley, M., *Abortion and Infanticide* (Oxford, 1983).

Toulmin, S., 'Nature and Nature's God', *Journal of Religious Ethics*, 13 (1985), 37–52.

Townsend, P. and N. Davidson, eds., *Inequalities in Health: The Black Report* (Harmondsworth, 1982).

Tracy, D., *The Analogical Imagination* (New York, 1981).

Treasury, *Appraisal and Evaluation in Central Government* (London, 1997).

Troeltsch, E., *The Social Teaching of the Christian Churches*, vol. II, trans. O. Wyon (London, 1931).

United Nations Conference on the Environment, Stockholm, 1972, *Declaration of Principles*, reprinted in *Reflecting on Nature: Readings in Environmental Philosophy*, ed. L. Gruen and D. Jamieson (Oxford, 1994), 179–82.

United Nations World Commission on Environment and Development, *Our Common Future (The Brundtland Report)*, (Oxford, 1987).

United Reformed Church, *Homosexuality: A Christian View* (London, 1991).

United States Catholic Conference, *Human Sexuality: A Catholic Perspective for Education and Lifelong Learning* (Washington, 1991).

Vitoria, F. de, *De Indis*, in *Political Writings*, ed. and trans. A. Pagden and J. Lawrance (Cambridge, 1991).

Vogüé, A. de, *Community and Abbot in the Rule of St. Benedict*, trans. C. Philippi, 2 vols. (Kalamazoo, 1979 and 88).

La Règle de S. Benoît, Sources Chrétiennes, 181–6 (Paris, 1971–2).

The Rule of St. Benedict: A Doctrinal and Spiritual Commentary, trans. J. B. Hasbrouck (Kalamazoo, 1983).

Webster, J., *Barth's Ethics of Reconciliation* (Cambridge, 1995).

Weir, R., *Selective Nontreatment of the Handicapped Newborn* (New York, 1984).

Wiles, P., *Price, Cost and Output*, 2nd edn (Oxford, 1961).

Williams, A., 'The Budget as a (Mis-)Information System' in *Economic Aspects of Health Services*, ed. Culyer and Wright, 84–91.

'Creating a Health Care Market: Ideology, Efficiency, Ethics and Clinical Freedom', *Occasional Papers of the Department of Economics York* (York, 1989).

'Efficient Management of Resources in the National Health Service' in *Health Service Finance and Resource Management*, ed. H. S. E. Gravelle and A. Williams (London, 1980), 65–78.

'Ethics and Efficiency in the Provision of Health Care' in *Philosophy and Medical Welfare*, ed. Bell and Mendus, 111–26.

Williams, B., 'Must a Concern for the Environment Be Centred on Human Beings?' in *Ethics and the Environment*, ed. Taylor, 60–8.

Willis, K. G., and J. T. Corkindale, eds., *Environmental Valuation: New Perspectives* (Wallingford, 1995).

Wilson, B., *Religious Sects* (London, 1970).

'Sects' in *Dictionary of Ethics, Theology and Society*, ed. P. B. Clarke and A. Linzey (London, 1996).

Social Dimensions of Sectarianism (Oxford, 1990).

Winkler, J. J., *The Constraints of Desire* (London, 1990).

Index